DATE DUE

DEMCO 38-296

Also by Brian Duffy

THE GOOD GUYS
How We Turned 'Round the FBI—
and Finally Broke the Mob
(With Jules Bonavolonta)

TRIUMPH WITHOUT VICTORY
The Untold Story of the Persian Gulf War
(With the Staff of *U.S. News & World Report*)

HEAD COUNT
(A Novel)

THE FALL OF PAN AM 103
Inside the Lockerbie Investigation

Jim McGee and Brian Duffy

MAIN JUSTICE

The Men and Women

Who Enforce the Nation's Criminal Laws

and Guard Its Liberties

SIMON & SCHUSTER

SIMON & SCHUSTER
Rockefeller Center
1230 Avenue of the Americas
New York, NY 10020

Designed by Jeanette Olender
Manufactured in the United States of America

10   9   8   7   6   5   4   3   2   1

Library of Congress Cataloging-in-Publication Data
McGee, Jim.
Main justice : the men and women who enforce the Nation's criminal laws
and guard its liberties / Jim McGee and Brian Duffy.
p.   cm.
Includes index.
1. United States.   Dept. of Justice.   Criminal Division.
2. Criminal justice, Administration of—United States.
3. Law enforcement—United States.
I. Duffy, Brian.   II. Title.
KF5107.M34   1996   363.2'3'0973—dc20   96-20421   CIP
ISBN 0-684-81135-9

CONTENTS

CONTENTS

INTRODUCTION

This book is about the men and women who run the U.S. Department of Justice in Washington, D.C. They work in a headquarters known as Main Justice, a name denoting its command over the huge apparatus of federal law enforcement that reaches into every American city and out beyond American shores. Main Justice is the top of the pyramid, the seat of government for thousands of agents and prosecutors. With its control of the Federal Bureau of Investigation, Main Justice is the most powerful law-enforcement institution in the world.

Two centuries after the founding of the Republic, America has become a dangerous place, set upon by terrorists, ethnic mafias and huge drug cartels. These threats are transcendent and sophisticated, modern evils that only a muscular federal presence can possibly challenge. In the face of such threats, the Justice Department is the nation's best hope that the Rule of Law will prevail.

No federal entity wields more power that can more directly touch an American life than the Justice Department. The Central Intelligence Agency can dispatch spies and the Pentagon can launch cruise missiles, but the Department of Justice can eavesdrop on your phone conversations, search your home with a warrant or threaten you with federal prison. The enforcement of criminal federal law is a primary means by which each administration carries out its domestic political agenda. For that reason, the Justice Department has become one of the biggest prizes of every presidential campaign.

Here is the story of the institution through the work of its most important and powerful component—the Criminal Division. Because the department is so big, so compartmentalized and so densely encased in myth, the work of the Criminal Division is little understood, even by many within the department itself. Few Americans could name the most important career officials in the division, yet their anonymous labors are often the stuff of front-page headlines and congressional hearings.

As reporters, we have covered the Justice Department from several vantage points: from the street level where agents make arrests, from the courtrooms where prosecutors seek verdicts and from the executive suites in Washington where managers implement national policy. Our backdrop is the past fifteen years, a time of explosive growth for the institution. We do not mean to be encyclopedic. Rather, we have chosen four areas where the performance of Main Justice is crucial: drug enforcement, violent crime, professional discipline and counterintelligence. In different ways, these four areas reveal the book's true subject: the awesome power of Main Justice and the consequences of so much power being vested in its hands.

We tell our story in roughly the same way that the Justice Department actually operates, with one foot in Washington, the other in one of the ninety-four districts where local U.S. attorneys prosecute most cases in federal court. When the resources of Main Justice and its U.S. attorneys are used for smart, focused, good faith investigations, the results can be impressive. In the case against the Cali cocaine cartel, the reader will encounter the best of modern federal law enforcement making good use of its most powerful weapons. In a world where crime is a clear and present danger to what the U.S. Constitution calls the "domestic tranquillity," those who do this work give new meaning to the term "patriot."

The price of this power is the book's second theme. An institution strong enough to combat the nation's worst enemies risks becoming huge and impersonal, its personnel desensitized to the impact of draconian legal measures. Because the federal system is run by human beings, it is not immune to excessive zeal, personal ambition or political malice. Unfair or unprofessional prosecutions are the exception, but their number and severity are on the rise.

The nation's founders had vivid memories of life under a tyrannical monarch whose edicts were enforced by his legal representatives. Our ancestors conceived of a separation of powers in which the judicial branch would restrain the power of the central government's executive and legislative branches. While they understood human nature, the framers of the Constitution could not have imagined—or allowed for—an institution as powerful as today's Department of Justice.

Laws passed by Congress and rulings by the Supreme Court have made the federal justice system a harsh and pitiless arena for defendants. Over time they have transformed the federal prosecutor into the most powerful figure in the justice system. The new powers and prerogatives of an assistant U.S. attorney arguably transcend those of federal judges. The rules and laws that once encouraged fair play in federal court have been eroded. Increasingly, the most meaningful safeguard against abusive federal prosecutions is Main Justice itself and the fragile instinct of government lawyers to honor fairness and to insist on professionalism.

The good news is that Main Justice has a strong professional culture and a cadre of career lawyers who generally live up to the promise of the Bill of Rights. The bad news is that their client—a federal government run by politicians—often does not. Therein lies the paradox of Main Justice today. No other institution has the resources to protect Americans from the worst kinds of crime. No other institution presents a more immediate threat to our freedom to live in an open society where individual liberty is protected by law.

PART
ONE

THE FAMILY

B ehind the gleaming hearse, the limousines were drawn up tight in a line, headlights burning under a spring sky. The newspaper obituary had described the deceased simply: "Eugenia M. Keeney, 69, homemaker, former teacher."

Waiting outside the St. Catherine Labouré Church in a leafy suburb several miles from the White House, even the mourners who had never met Eugenia Keeney knew that she was more than that—more than the mother of five accomplished children, more than the patient teacher who had gentled her charges through their jumbled conjugations of impossible Latin verbs.

Janet Reno was among those who had never met Eugenia Keeney. Forty days earlier Reno had been confirmed as the Clinton administration's attorney general. On April 19, 1993—the day Eugenia Keeney died—Reno had watched in horror as flames licked from a matchstick collection of buildings near Waco, Texas. At least eighty people died in the fiery rubble of the compound owned by the religious sect known as the Branch Davidians. The tragedy had shaken the Department of Justice to its core. Despite the public acclaim she had received in the days after the conflagration in Waco, Reno was numbed by the events there. Others among the mourners at St. Catherine—Justice Department lawyers, agents of the FBI—shared responsibility with Reno for the tragedy at Waco.

No organization of 93,000 souls could properly call itself a family. The Department of Justice is a vast, unruly kingdom. It has huge baronies, such as the FBI and, spread across the country, ninety-four autonomous fiefdoms lorded over by local U.S. attorneys. As big as the imposing headquarters building of Main Justice looks from the sidewalk at Tenth Street and Constitution Avenue, it is little more than an anteroom into a far greater complex. The lawyers and agents of the Justice Department are spread throughout seventy buildings in Washington. They specialize in everything from Indian affairs and anti-trust matters to environmental crime and tax law.

Within the Department of Justice, however, one group of lawyers did view themselves as family—the men and women of the department's Criminal Division. They had come to St. Catherine Labouré not only to mourn Eugenia Keeney's passing but also to support, in the only way that seemed possible, the man who, more than any other, had served as the Criminal Division's steadying hand, its institutional conscience.

As a towheaded young Irishman, John C. Keeney had joined the Justice Department on March 19, 1951, just a year after he married the former Eugenia Brislin and six years after he was demobilized from the old U.S. Army Air Corps, in which he had served as a navigator before being shot down over Nazi Germany and taken prisoner in the final months of World War II. Keeney had served in the Department of Justice under ten presidents and more than twice as many attorneys general. He had chased spies during the Eisenhower administration, Mafia hoods during the Kennedy years, and stock swindlers, crooked politicians, drug dealers and terrorists in the years since. When political scandals rolled over the nation's capital like big winter storms, Keeney's counsel on the legal issues had mattered.

Yet Keeney and his colleagues were not creatures of Washington. Although they were no strangers to the corridors of power—

on sensitive matters, they conferred with the attorney general and paid visits to the White House and Capitol Hill—they shunned the Georgetown dinner parties and took care to distance themselves from politics. In a city where politics often appears to be all that matters, Keeney and his colleagues in the Criminal Division were anti-matter—anonymous men and women whose decisions could result in hobbled presidents, jailed congressmen, disgraced judges. The decisions Keeney and his colleagues made often landed on page one of the nation's newspapers. But it was the decisions, not the people who made them, that got the attention. The decision makers—properly, they believed—remained back in the shadows.

A handful of the Criminal Division's best lawyers had come of age professionally together. Three were especially close to Keeney, and he had sought them out to serve as pallbearers for his beloved spouse. David Margolis, Paul Coffey and Gerald McDowell were legends within the Criminal Division, less well known in other divisions within the Justice Department, virtually anonymous outside the thick walls of Main Justice.

Keeney had interviewed Margolis for a job at Main Justice back in 1969. An assistant U.S. attorney in Hartford, Connecticut, Margolis was a character, long-haired, flamboyant, a smart-ass. Keeney had seen through the veneer. In a handwritten memo on a Justice Department "buckslip," a tissue-thin piece of routing paper, the older man had recounted his first impression of the young prosecutor. As custom dictated, he concluded with a recommendation. "While this guy dresses like a mobster and wears his hair like Joe Namath," Keeney wrote, "he is an experienced Assistant United States Attorney who comes highly recommended. . . . It is my recommendation that we hire him." Margolis had been hired. He and Keeney have been fast friends ever since.

Paul Coffey arrived at Main Justice soon after Margolis, and Keeney took him under his wing. Precise, dapper and compulsive about sports (he played basketball in the FBI gym several nights a week), Coffey appeared to be the antithesis of Margolis, for whom a couple of packs of Marlboros and two desserts at lunch were standard daily fare. Like Margolis and Keeney, Coffey was an

"O.C. guy," having made his bones prosecuting organized crime cases against the Italian Mafia. There were distinct fraternities within the specialized disciplines in the Criminal Division. Among them, the prosecutors of organized crime—the men and women who had brought the first big cases against the Italian Mafia—cut the widest swath.

Gerry McDowell was another O.C. guy. He had first worked for Keeney in 1967, when the older man was the deputy head of the Organized Crime and Racketeering Section under Henry Petersen. More than anyone else, Petersen had set the tenor and standards for Criminal Division lawyers. He had begun work as a clerk at the FBI in 1947 before moving over to Main Justice and a prosecutor's job in the Criminal Division.

Over the years Petersen became known as a tough prosecutor, a lawyer who had no problem standing up to the likes of the famed trial lawyer Edward Bennett Williams. In the Petersen ethos, however, "tough" worked both ways. While it was important to prosecute criminals aggressively, it was just as important to stand up to overzealous prosecutors. Petersen had drilled that notion into his subordinates, young lawyers like David Margolis and Jack Keeney. If a defense lawyer wanted to come in and present arguments for leniency, Petersen urged his charges, by all means, let him do so. The Criminal Division had an obligation to listen. It was the right and smart thing to do. Nobody wanted to see a bad case go forward. And sometimes it was their job to tell prosecutors they could not seek an indictment.

More patient and soft-spoken than Petersen, Keeney was just as unyielding, just as tough. Keeney sought to emulate Petersen's ethic of fairness and fidelity to fact and law.

It was in the Petersen-Keeney tradition that Gerry McDowell had grown up as a lawyer in the Justice Department. He had worked as a Strike Force prosecutor in Boston, then moved to Main Justice, first serving as a subordinate in the Organized Crime and Racketeering Section, then assuming control of the Criminal Division's Public Integrity Section for an unprecedented twelve years. Phlegmatic but sometimes garrulous, McDowell had helped put away crooked congressmen, judges and government bureaucrats in record numbers during the 1980s and early 1990s.

Besides these Criminal Division lawyers with whom Keeney was closest, there was Mark Richard, a trusted friend and confidant, who had the office just down the hall from Keeney's on the second floor of Main Justice. Richard reciprocated the affection. "As long as Jack's around," Richard said, laughing, "I can be an asshole because he's the senior guy. He's like a father figure to me." A tall, gentle man, Richard had done more than any other lawyer in the Criminal Division to extend the reach of the Justice Department beyond America's shores in pursuit of foreign spies, drug barons and international terrorists. This was the crime war of the next century. Richard had already entered the lists. He oversaw the Criminal Division's most important international cases.

Richard had nearly died a year earlier. Some of the nation's best surgeons had pronounced his cancer of the esophagus inoperable. Richard didn't believe it and had persuaded a team of doctors at Johns Hopkins in Baltimore to try something—anything. The surgeons had attempted a rare procedure, one that had been used fewer than half a dozen times. Richard had come through splendidly, his diseased esophagus removed in favor of a polymer replacement. His many friends were delighted. The new esophagus had done nothing to modify the distinctive cadences of Richard's native Brooklyn.

Behind Richard outside St. Catherine Labouré, the ranks of Jack Keeney's friends and admirers were dense. As Margolis, Coffey and McDowell helped load Eugenia Keeney's casket into the waiting hearse, Keeney and his children—John Jr., Terence, Eugenia, Joan and Kathleen—climbed into the first car in the long procession. Keeney's closest friends knew how acutely he felt the loss of his wife. He had not allowed it to interfere with his work, though. When Margolis, Richard, Coffey or McDowell volunteered to step in, Keeney declined. He still convened the most important meetings of the Criminal Division's lawyers.

Janet Reno was operating with the barest skeleton of a senior staff. As they had during the months when the Clinton administration fumbled the nominations of Zoë Baird and Kimba Wood,

Keeney and the senior career lawyers at Main Justice were still running the department's day-to-day affairs and managing its biggest crises. Waco had emerged as a potential crisis within the first weeks of the new administration, right on the heels of the bombing of the World Trade Center in New York. Both were classic examples of crises where Main Justice needed to take charge because local police agencies simply could not, and where violations of federal law gave the Justice Department overriding jurisdiction. In New York, there were intelligence concerns that only the federal government could address: Were the bombers agents of a foreign country or terrorist group? In Waco, federal agents had been killed or wounded. There the issues were tactical and tricky: how to get the Branch Davidians to surrender without causing further tragedy.

Keeney, as head of the Criminal Division, and for the eighth time in his career, the acting assistant attorney general, had overall responsibility for both matters at Main Justice. Crime waited for nothing—not for illness or death and certainly not for politics, Keeney knew. Prosecutors needed decisions made. Keeney had been there to make them.

Under the bright sky outside St. Catherine Labouré, the hearse finally moved out. Behind, the limousines bearing mourners fell into line. More than a decade earlier, a prosecutor named Jo Ann Harris had come to Washington to work for Jack Keeney as the head of the Fraud Section in the Criminal Division. Remembering how he had helped her and the other lawyers in the division, Harris called Keeney "the glue that holds the world together." On the day he buried his wife, it was Keeney's well-ordered world that felt as if it was coming apart.

That did not happen, though. Keeney was with people he loved, people who loved him. As the long line of the funeral procession extended across the bursting spring countryside, it was that thought that sustained and comforted those who knew the old man of the Criminal Division best. The glue had been tested. It had not yielded, though. It had not broken.

CHAPTER TWO

TAKING COMMAND

One clue to Janet Reno's vision of her new job was the portrait that hung above the handsome granite fireplace in her office on the fifth floor. It was a large oil painting of Robert F. Kennedy. The artist had captured a young Kennedy walking on the beach at Hyannisport, his shoulders hunched under a dark windbreaker, his hair tossed by the ocean breeze.

In both substance and style Kennedy's tenure, from 1960 to 1963, had left a lasting impression on the Justice Department. He had created the Organized Crime Strike Forces, which sent federal prosecutors into major cities to make legal war against the Italian Mafia. He also turned the Civil Rights Division into an aggressive law-enforcement presence. With his energy and charisma Kennedy had raised the profile of Main Justice and inspired a generation of young lawyers to government service.

Reno would have a chance to leave her own imprint. Like Kennedy, she would stake out an expanded role for federal prosecutors, pushing them deeper into the world of violent crime. Despite a widely held perception that Reno is more social worker than crime fighter, she would oversee and expand the use of the

Justice Department's most powerful weapons against criminals of all sorts. During her stewardship Main Justice would approve a dramatic increase in the use of electronic wiretaps in both criminal investigations and national security surveillance operations. Reno invested her own quirky charisma in shoring up the Justice Department's public image, at the same time using her high position as a bully pulpit to focus attention on the root causes of crime. Unlike Kennedy, however, Reno would not have the unequivocal support of a strong president. Bill Clinton was neither powerful nor particularly close to Reno. Over time, the distance between Main Justice and the White House—and the administration's contentious relationship with Congress—would constrain Reno and narrow the limits of what she attempted. Adding to her burden was the weight of the many problems of the Justice Department she inherited.

The place almost defied management. Under Presidents Ronald Reagan and George Bush, the Justice Department had seen phenomenal growth. In 1981 it had an annual budget of $2.3 billion. On the day Reno moved in, the budget was $9.8 billion. Over that same period the number of Justice Department prosecutors had nearly doubled, to 7,881. Unlike the downsizing going on elsewhere in official Washington, at Main Justice the budget numbers were headed up—inexorably up, it seemed, given Americans' amply documented fears about crime.

The growth had not been without problems. Up and down the corridors of Main Justice, the career people knew that some of these ills were probably not subject to cure. As they did every four years, the career lawyers braced themselves for tumult. A new cast of political appointees could bring new energy and new ideas to the Department of Justice. But the newcomers also tended to grate upon a professional culture, many of whose members believed that a new political administration could work only at the margins of the department's areas of responsibility. An attorney general could set a tone and take up a handful of new initiatives. Otherwise, the bulk of the Justice Department's business was handled by a huge and diffused institution that tended to go its own lumbering way.

Reno had followed the 1992 presidential campaign closely. By and large, she liked what she had heard from Bill Clinton. She was a lifelong Democrat, a state prosecutor who had been re-elected repeatedly in the conservative, crime-ridden metropolis of Miami. Reno and Clinton differed on capital punishment, but on broad, overarching legal issues they generally agreed. Reno could not have been more pleased when Clinton defeated George Bush in November 1992.

What kind of Justice Department did the new president want, though? What did he envision? During the campaign Senator Albert Gore, Clinton's running mate, had been especially vocal in chastising Bush and his administration over the so-called Iraqgate scandal. The case arose from a 1992 prosecution that involved billions of dollars in U.S. government-backed loans to Iraq, some proceeds of which had allegedly been diverted to the government of Saddam Hussein before he invaded Kuwait. The money, according to the allegations, had gone to help arm the Kuwaiti invasion force.

A federal judge in Atlanta had gone public with charges of a cover-up; newspapers and magazines had launched investigations. High-profile columnists like William Safire of *The New York Times* had been relentless. In column after column, Safire called President Bush's attorney general, William P. Barr, "the cover-up general." Congressional Democrats had done their best to trumpet the controversy as a major scandal.

In Iraqgate, Reno detected the sharp smell of trouble, but that wasn't the only source of odor. During the preparations for her confirmation hearings, Reno had heard accusations that Justice Department lawyers had botched an investigation a few years earlier into BCCI, the rogue Bank of Credit and Commerce International. BCCI's collapse stemmed from the largest international bank fraud ever. A London-based financial conglomerate controlled by a handful of Middle Eastern backers, BCCI had allegedly acquired illegal control of a major Washington bank.

There were other allegations. Justice Department lawyers had been accused of mishandling a mysterious case called Inslaw. This involved accusations that had been festering for years, based on claims by a software company that senior officials in the Reagan administration had defrauded the company and stolen their product. A special counsel's investigation had refuted the allegations, but it had not put the controversy to rest.

The cases were cited in an unbound report, four inches thick, titled "Justice/Civil Rights Cluster Briefing Book." For a new attorney general who was also new to Main Justice, it was a page turner. The introduction explained why: "This briefing book is designed to provide the President-elect, the Vice-President-elect, the Attorney General-designate and other senior Justice Department appointees with a concise but comprehensive overview of the Department's missions and functions, and of the issues and problems the Department will confront immediately."

After Clinton nominated Reno for the attorney generalship in February 1993, she had taken a furnished apartment just across Pennsylvania Avenue from Main Justice, in a newly refurbished building overlooking the Navy Memorial. Poring over the briefing book with the intensity friends had long since come to recognize, Reno focused on the two words in the introduction: The first was "problems." The second was "immediately."

The briefing book was the result of an exhaustive review of the Justice Department's many and varied operations. The review was run by two men. One was Bernard Nussbaum, the combative New York securities lawyer President Clinton had named as his White House counsel. The other was Peter Edelman, a highly regarded professor at the Georgetown University Law Center. Edelman had been named chief counsel to Donna Shalala, Clinton's new secretary of the Department of Health and Human Services.

It had been years, the Clinton transition team believed, since an outside team of lawyers had taken a hard look at the Justice Department and its operating divisions. When George Bush succeeded Ronald Reagan as president, he had not bothered to find a new attorney general. He had simply reappointed Richard Thornburgh. Business continued as usual.

Nussbaum and Edelman assembled a team of 120 people to begin studying the Justice Department. The team included academics, law-enforcement officials and former Justice Department prosecutors. It was divided into subteams, each assigned to a different division in the department. With newly issued security clearances, the team members fanned out through the Justice Department, asking questions and looking at documents. Their written reports became chapters in a book-length product, along with executive summaries co-authored by Nussbaum and Edelman.

The end product was an indictment of sorts, one written by Democrats assigned to contemplate the effect of twelve years of Republican rule. Nussbaum and Edelman had not minced words. In the "Tab 1" section, which dealt specifically with the Office of the Attorney General, they excoriated the stewardship of the Reagan and Bush administrations at Main Justice. "The attorney general shapes the image of Justice by communicating the core values and ideas that all Americans expect from the government's lawyers," Nussbaum and Edelman wrote. "The Department now faces a crisis of credibility and integrity. Its performance over the past twelve years has diminished the trust and respect the Department once enjoyed among the Bar, the legal academy and political leaders. . . . [The Department] is perceived as politicized when it speaks on matters of central importance: civil rights, abortion, criminal justice, religion and access to the federal courts. The Department has lost its reputation as an even-handed tribune for those needing judicial and other legal protection."

As a bill of particulars, this was scathing. But were its conclusions valid?

Nussbaum and Edelman had reserved some of their most pointed criticism for the Criminal Division, basing it on a fact-finding report that stressed the decline of the division's influence during the years of Republican rule. "The image and authority of the Division have been badly tarnished in recent years," the report stated, "by a perception that the Division's handling of high-profile cases is politicized."

Even on routine matters where politics presumably did not intrude, the report said, the Criminal Division appeared to be floundering. The Bush administration had made a conscious effort to limit the division's role and even went so far as to bring politically appointed U.S. attorneys from across the country to manage programs at Main Justice. "The Assistant Attorney General of the Criminal Division has lost considerable authority and influence over the . . . United States Attorneys," the Nussbaum-Edelman report said, "making coordination oversight of criminal justice activities far more difficult."

The problems did not end there. The Organized Crime and Racketeering Section of the Criminal Division had been slow to focus on the rise of ethnic mafias, Nussbaum-Edelman said. The Internal Security Section, responsible for prosecution of espionage cases, had rocky relationships with the Central Intelligence Agency and the State Department. Federal drug enforcement was rife with duplication and conflicts. The Drug Enforcement Administration and the FBI acted like competing newspapers chasing the same story.

The Nussbaum-Edelman team described an institution that was disorganized and out of touch. Main Justice seemed to lurch from crisis to crisis, reacting to congressional pressure or evading heat from the news media. No one at Main Justice seemed to be looking out over the horizon at what the future held. "The Division and law enforcement entities [like the FBI and Drug Enforcement Administration] are operating in a context that has evolved rapidly in recent years and it is far from clear that the Department had kept pace with the changes," the report went on. The U.S. intelligence agencies were muscling their way into federal law enforcement. They were actively gathering information on international criminals, which had caused problems in individual cases: "An important long-term issue is the relationship between the Justice Department and the intelligence and foreign relations departments and agencies."

There was also growing concern about the fairness of federal prosecutions. In an era when criminal law had become profoundly pro-government, some observers questioned whether America still had a truly adversarial legal system. Increasingly, the practice of criminal law in the nation's federal courts resembled the more inquisitorial legal systems of Europe.

There were several reasons for this. Besides the Justice Department's phenomenal growth in the 1980s, Congress had given broad new authorities to federal prosecutors. These ranged from asset-forfeiture laws that permit the seizure of homes and businesses to expanding the list of crimes that could be charged under the powerful anti-racketeering statutes. At the same time the Supreme Court had cut back on several time-honored protections for defendants, adopting the "harmless error" rule and restricting the ability of federal judges to sanction prosecutors for abuse of the grand jury process. Congress, clearly, was responding to the public's concern over crime. A conservative Supreme Court appeared to be responding to past rulings by a more liberal court, rulings that some of the newer justices believed had hamstrung prosecutors.

The effect of the three forces—growth that brought more prosecutors, laws that created more powerful legal weapons and rulings that sharply reduced judicial constraints—had significantly enlarged the role of the Justice Department in American life. In the name of countless worthy causes, from ensuring civil rights and protecting the environment to fighting the Mafia and stemming the supply of cocaine, the Justice Department had become the primary means by which the federal government projected its coercive force into American cities and towns.

Where this newly muscular Justice Department might have been expected to have a dramatic impact on crime and the supply of drugs, however, it had not. From 1986 to 1992 the rate of violent crimes committed by strangers had jumped from 16.3 per thousand to 19.3 per thousand. The rate for all categories of violent crime had increased from 28.1 per thousand to 32.1 per thousand. Despite spending $5 billion a year on drug-enforcement programs at the Justice Department, the availability of cocaine had remained essentially unchanged.

Reno knew the numbers, and they troubled her. In Miami, as the top state prosecutor for fifteen years, she had seen firsthand the toll that drugs and violence took on a community. As the nation's chief law enforcement officer now, she was in control of a huge institution that, in theory, could do much about the violence being inflicted on the nation's cities. The question was whether Main Justice, with all its resources, could make a difference in the level of crime. The Bush administration, for example, had poured hundreds of millions of dollars into interdicting cocaine shipments on the high seas to little long-term avail.

Because of the enormity of the place and the difficulty of turning a vast bureaucracy in a new direction, there were only a small number of issues on which an attorney general could exert profound influence. Even a modest agenda could be disrupted overnight, however. If a group of terrorists blew up a skyscraper in New York or the brutality of police officers sparked a riot in Los Angeles, that would drain huge amounts of money and attention from Main Justice, leaving an attorney general bereft of foot soldiers to implement the items on her agenda.

Like most new attorneys general, Janet Reno confronted a series of questions both profound and urgent. What could she do about violent crime? Should she restructure federal drug enforcement? How much of her time and political capital did she owe to the issue of prosecutorial fairness, to the standoff at the Branch Davidian compound in Waco, Texas? Should she wade into the process of dealing with Congress on the budget or defer to the White House? Most immediate of all, who inside Main Justice could she safely turn to for help? The answers to these and other questions would determine the scope and size of Janet Reno's agenda as attorney general. She was committed to doing something to attack violent criminals, and since her arrival in Washington, Donna Shalala and a handful of President Clinton's other cabinet officers had encouraged Reno in that goal. That was one agenda item. The rest would be worked out as time and future emergencies allowed.

The White House gave Janet Reno her chief deputy, Philip B. Heymann. He had worked most recently as a professor of law and government at Harvard University. Besides having an impressive reputation as a scholar, Heymann had served in the Department of Justice in five administrations. Twelve years earlier he was running the Criminal Division for Jimmy Carter's attorney general, Griffin Bell. For Heymann, leaving Cambridge was not easy. But returning to Main Justice was not difficult, either. In a sense it was

legacy of Henry Petersen in mind. Petersen "had a humongous set of balls," Margolis said. "He was very direct, and he would look at issues, and he would say, 'What is the correct decision?' not 'How will it play?'"

Much the same could be said of Margolis. Over the years he had stood down powerful White House advisers and pompous congressmen, instructing one committee, in a moment many career prosecutors recounted gleefully, that he would not tolerate lawmakers "using a proctoscope" in questioning young prosecutors from the Justice Department. Inside Main Justice, prosecutors and federal agents knew Margolis's reputation. Those who sought to bluff him or fob him off with pat answers were quickly shredded. Few tried.

Margolis's counsel was particularly sought in cases where politics intruded, or threatened to. In his new office on the fourth floor, Margolis served as a screen for Philip Heymann, going through his mail in the morning to sort out those letters that dealt with pending criminal cases or seemed to invite some untoward political entanglement. Heymann decided early on that he would let Margolis deal with the White House as well.

Across the hallway from Heymann's suite of offices, Margolis had his dozens of photographs hung on the wall, the ubiquitous pack of Marlboros crouched at his elbow. "There are three kinds of violations of law," Margolis told a visitor to his new quarters. "There are felonies, misdemeanors and infractions. What you are now about to witness," Margolis said, gently closing the door to his outer office and firing up a Marlboro, "is an infraction." As it happened, Main Justice had been designated a smoke-free workplace. As it also happened, David Margolis didn't give a good goddamn.

Because Main Justice had operated for nearly four months without a deputy attorney general, Margolis had a lot of issues to wade through. To outsiders it might have appeared that Margolis's transfer to the fourth floor would have removed him from the sphere of criminal prosecutions. That was not so. While the deputy attorney general is required to handle a broad range of matters from all corners of Main Justice, Heymann wanted Margolis to focus on issues relating to the Criminal Division and to law enforcement generally. This reflected a quirk of the department's professional culture. Every new administration made changes, but they all had to rely on the same core group of senior career deputies. The job titles of those career officials might change, but they often wound up handling similar duties.

Whatever title Margolis held, he tended to get the hot-button issues. There were plenty of those piling up in the spring of 1993. There was, for example, the standoff after the raid on the Branch Davidian compound, the controversy over the FBI shooting in Ruby Ridge, Idaho and the bombing of the World Trade Center. Others were less dramatic, but no less messy or politically charged. There was the effort to merge the Drug Enforcement Administration with the FBI. There was the fate of the embattled FBI director, William Sessions, a grim matter that had been put off too long.

Finally, there was an issue that was invisible to the public but that resonated deeply within the culture of Main Justice—professional discipline—how to handle abusive conduct by federal agents and prosecutors. On Margolis's watch, the issue arose as a question: Should the Justice Department's Office of Professional Responsibility (OPR) be merged with the Office of Inspector General? OPR is the Justice Department's ethics watchdog, an internal affairs unit comprised of investigative attorneys who probe allegations of professional misconduct against Justice Department lawyers and oversee similar units at the FBI and the DEA. The OPR's counsel and lawyer-in-chief was Michael E. Shaheen Jr. To colleagues and casual observers, Shaheen was friendly, easygoing, unflappable. To those whose professional lapses caught his attention, he was a figure of fear, relentless and unstoppable. Raised in Mississippi, Shaheen had come to work at Main Justice two decades earlier. In 1975, Attorney General Edward Levi created the Office of Professional Responsibility, hoping it would serve as the "eyes and ears of the attorney general." He named Shaheen OPR counsel. Shaheen had held the job ever since.

When the OPR's work came to public attention, it usually involved official misconduct by senior appointees, including attorneys general. Shaheen had, for example, conducted the investigation of FBI Director Sessions that had documented numerous ethical lapses and thus clouded his future. Investigative reports by Shaheen and his staff often made big headlines, as they had in the case of Sessions. But Shaheen and his staff of lawyers had a second, less glamorous job that was equally essential to the credibility of Main Justice and the ninety-four U.S. Attorneys' Offices across the country. The OPR investigated allegations of prosecutorial misconduct in criminal cases and issued secret, internal "findings" on whether the department's professional standards of conduct had been violated. A gradual increase in the seriousness of such incidents during the Bush administration had focused new attention on how Shaheen did this job. Some Democrats in Congress had questioned the OPR's diligence in this area. They asked whether the job should be done by the inspector general instead.

The issue was a slippery slope for Janet Reno. The Clinton transition team had singled out the need to restore the department's sense of professionalism as the first priority of the new attorney general. But if Reno got tough on prosecutorial misconduct she would risk alienating the corps of lawyers who did the Justice Department's heavy lifting in the nation's courtrooms. Reno wanted a hard look at the OPR, however. In January 1993, *The Washington Post* had published a series of articles about cases where judicial findings that criticized the prosecutors' conduct had derailed important cases. The Clinton transition team's review had also addressed the problem directly. The new leadership at the Department of Justice "will face the difficult task of setting a new tone of moral leadership," the transition report said, "in handling criminal cases without appearing to undercut and condemn the many hardworking and ethically scrupulous prosecutors." During her meetings with senior officials at Main Justice, Reno asked pointed questions about the OPR. Why were cases of prosecutorial misconduct not resolved more quickly? Why can't we be more forthcoming? Why couldn't information be made public once cases were resolved? Was the OPR doing its job? What should they do about the merger proposal? Reno assigned the issue to Heymann, who assigned it to Margolis as one of his many new tasks.

David Margolis respected Shaheen. Several years earlier, as a supervisor in the Criminal Division, Margolis had been investigated by OPR. He had been exonerated—and had appreciated that such a mechanism existed in the department. Now, as a member of the deputy attorney general's staff, he was responsible for reviewing OPR investigation reports. "What he brings to the job," Margolis said of Shaheen, "is fairness, thoroughness. And what he produces is a product—an independent investigation—that is respected both inside and outside government."

That was Shaheen's reputation—smart and incorruptible. He would also fight like a tiger, Margolis knew, against any attempt to challenge OPR's singular status within Main Justice.

One of the many photographs on the walls of Margolis's office was of himself, taken many years earlier when he was a young prosecutor, a graduate of Harvard Law School who was carrying Justice Department credentials. He was shirtless, young and wiry, his shoulder-length black hair tangled by a stiff breeze. Heymann couldn't believe Margolis had actually hung the photo in public. The deputy attorney general yielded to no one in his respect for Margolis's judgment and abilities, but Heymann thought Janet Reno ought to know just what a peculiar bird she had working for her.

Margolis was at his desk one day in mid-June, the big Fedders window air conditioner fighting a losing battle against the miserable Washington summer. "There was a knock at the door," Margolis said. "And before I could say anything, the attorney general was there, with Phil standing behind her."

"David," Reno said, without pausing, "Mr. Heymann just told me that back in the seventies, you used to come to work in blue jeans and T-shirts. I find that hard to believe."

Reno didn't know the half of it. When he first showed up for work at Main Justice in 1969, after Jack Keeney approved his job application, Margolis sported a pair of pointy cowboy boots, screaming bell-bottoms and a shiny windbreaker with big letters on the back that said "Hank Williams Jr. and the 'Bama Band." It was Margolis's personal testament of affection for Williams, who ranked only just below Elvis Presley in his personal pantheon.

(Another highly prized photo on Margolis's walls was of Elvis standing with President Richard Nixon at the White House.) On the back of his office door soon after he arrived at Main Justice, Margolis had hung a single suit, "in case," he said, "the attorney general wants to see me." The suit was salmon pink.

Gazing at Reno from behind his desk, Margolis did nothing to conceal his burning Marlboro. The photo of the shirtless young lawyer that Heymann had remarked on was a few feet from Reno, on the wall. Margolis ignored it, employing the voice he had used in his best courtroom summations. "Your Mr. Heymann," Margolis told Reno, "he has an overactive imagination. I assume you will find that out very quickly."

Reno and Heymann laughed.

Margolis went back to the stacks of paper on his desk.

CHAPTER THREE

THE DRUG WAR

When Janet Reno came to Washington she brought with her five special assistants. Four were prosecutors who had worked in the Dade County State Attorney's Office. The fifth was a career federal prosecutor, Richard Scruggs. He had joined the Justice Department under the Honor's Program in 1978. He worked for several years in the Internal Security Section in the Criminal Division, then became an assistant U.S. attorney in Miami. There he successfully prosecuted a murderous religious sect led by a fanatic who called himself Yahweh Ben Yahweh. Scruggs had impressed many people in Miami, not the least of them Janet Reno.

One of the more pressing issues Reno inherited after her confirmation as attorney general was the need to do something, finally, about the disorder and dysfunction of the federal drug-enforcement effort. The issue had been emphasized by the Clinton transition team's examination of the Department of Justice. Reno decided to take on the issue as one of her first priorities, having seen for herself in Miami how turf battles were compromising the drug war. From her office on the fifth floor of Main Justice,

Reno summoned Scruggs and asked him to look into the possibility of merging the Drug Enforcement Administration and the FBI. Come up with a plan, she said, but do it quietly.

Scruggs took up the assignment immediately. In short order, the former prosecutor from Miami ordered up a financial analysis by the Justice Management Division, the department's bean counters. The analysis showed that a merger would cost roughly $5 million in the first two years. After that, however, the efficiencies created would result in tens of millions of dollars in savings. Scruggs did not need to be persuaded that a merger should occur; the financial numbers alone made a compelling case. Because he had supervised numerous drug prosecutions in Miami, Scruggs knew firsthand about the bitter rivalry between the FBI and the DEA. It was the same in every major U.S. city. The clearest evidence was the proliferation of separate but virtually identical drug task forces. The FBI had theirs, the DEA had theirs. Sometimes there was a third set, sponsored by the Treasury Department's Bureau of Alcohol, Tobacco and Firearms.

The rivalry between the FBI and DEA was worse than counterproductive. When it came to the vital task of intelligence gathering, for instance, the two agencies acted like hostile clans. The FBI had large regional drug-intelligence squads in major cities, while DEA's intelligence collection was directed from the agency's Washington headquarters. Though they ostensibly pursued the same kind of high-level targets, neither agency had access to the other's intelligence databases.

After studying the financial analysis from the Justice Management Division, Scruggs met quietly with the FBI brass at the J. Edgar Hoover Building. Senior executives there favored a merger with DEA. Combining the two big police agencies would work, the FBI brass told Scruggs, but they were reluctant to lobby openly for a merger. That would cause problems. Scruggs understood the desire to move cautiously. Still, the more he studied the question, the more he became convinced the best course of action was to be bold. Simply issue each of the nation's 3,700 DEA agents new credentials from the FBI. Present DEA with a *fait accompli* and take the heat.

Reno seemed to appreciate Scruggs's logic. Budgets were tight, she knew; a merger would enable her to do more with the resources at hand. Scruggs and Reno went to the White House to discuss the issue with the staff of Vice President Al Gore. President Clinton had ordered a top-to-bottom analysis of government waste and placed Gore in charge of it. Called the National Performance Review, it aimed to identify redundancies and inefficiencies in the federal government, then root them out. The Gore team was looking hard at law enforcement. More than 140 federal agencies enforced 4,100 criminal laws that had been passed over the years by Congress. The overlap in drug-enforcement efforts made no sense, the Gore team believed. At the White House, Scruggs outlined the plan to merge the FBI and the DEA and explained the savings such a move would yield. Reno indicated her support.

The Gore team thanked Scruggs and Reno. As described, merging the FBI and the DEA seemed a sensible move.

Back at Main Justice, Scruggs arranged a meeting to review the mechanics of a merger with Philip Heymann and senior FBI officials. To Scruggs's surprise, Heymann expressed strong reservations about a merger. Around the long conference table in his fourth-floor office, the former Harvard professor focused the discussion not on the potential savings and efficiencies a merger would allow but on the problems it would create. Putting the two big federal police agencies together, Heymann said, simply would not work. He also made it clear that he was not pleased that such an important issue had gotten so far down the track without his input. He had conducted the review of the FBI's operations for the Clinton transition team studying the Department of Justice and knew how the place worked. The FBI, the department's lead investigative agency, is about three times the size of the DEA. The drug agency has principal authority for narcotics-trafficking investigations. But the lines of authority between it and the FBI became jumbled when Ronald Reagan ordered the bureau into the drug war, in the early 1980s, and Congress gave the FBI authority to enforce federal drug laws. Heymann knew how much the FBI and the DEA loathed each other. In the report he had prepared for the Nussbaum-Edelman transition review, Heymann had couched his description of the relationship in diplomatic terms. The FBI and the DEA, he wrote, "have displayed a debilitating rivalry."

The Scruggs recommendation of a merger, Heymann believed, was problematic. He thought the disruption could prove a logistical nightmare and bring chaos to the federal anti-drug effort for several years. Heymann would assume control of the merger issue, he told Scruggs and the FBI brass, and, with his staff, conduct a full-dress review.

The move by Heymann did not stop the Gore staff in its work on the National Performance Review. Gore and his aides were proceeding on the understanding that Reno saw the wisdom of a merger and that officials at Main Justice had a plan to make it work. Like Scruggs, the White House analysts were inclined to address the issue head-on. "Too many cooks spoil the broth," the Gore team wrote in its published recommendations. "Agencies squabble over turf, fail to cooperate and delay matters." Just do it, the Gore team said in its report. It will save money and create a "much more powerful weapon in [the] fight against crime."

Folding the operations of the DEA into those of the FBI might make sense on one level, but it also violated certain sacred, unwritten Washington rules of turf. Soon enough, word of the merger plan leaked out. A merger threatened the DEA's very existence. After learning of the proposal, DEA's managers went on a war footing, mounting a vigorous nationwide lobbying campaign. DEA headquarters took the extraordinary step of sending a memorandum to all field offices encouraging all agents, supervisory personnel and their family members to contact their representatives in Congress and urge them to oppose the merger. Reno was informed of this fact, but did nothing to stop it.

In the weeks that followed, she was deluged with facts about the value that DEA added to the anti-drug effort. That value was considerable. The jewel in the agency's crown was its worldwide network of agents and investigators. Some 343 DEA agents were posted in fifty countries. In most of those places, DEA personnel had forged close relationships with local authorities. Unlike the

FBI, the DEA has never been involved in counterintelligence work, so there was no basis for suspicion that its agents abroad were spies.

The DEA had other selling points. On a per-agent basis, the agency was way ahead on statistics, with five times as many wiretaps, four times as many arrests and six times as many convictions as the FBI. Like the FBI, the DEA had proven itself highly adept at mounting large and technically sophisticated investigations. An adroit undercover sting in California called Operation Green Ice led to more than two hundred arrests in several countries; a big wiretap investigation in New York had eliminated a large cadre of Cali cartel cocaine distributors.

Playing for keeps, DEA executives offered an audacious counterproposal to the merger idea. Instead of moving the DEA into the FBI to eliminate duplication, why not strip the FBI of its authority to make drug arrests and transfer the hundreds of FBI agents working narcotics cases over to the DEA? The gauntlet had been thrown down.

Others soon entered the fray. President Clinton's drug czar, Lee P. Brown, who was in charge of the Office of National Drug Control Policy and a member of the cabinet, was not thrilled by the idea. A merger, he warned, might make it appear as if the Clinton administration was backing away from the drug war. On one level, the decision was merely a matter of bureaucratic reshuffling. On another, however, it was about politics—or at least their appearance. As the months passed Reno declined to commit herself publicly on the question, saying it was being studied by Philip Heymann. In May 1993, at a conference on drug policy, Reno said she was still considering the issue. "The one thing I cannot abide are [sic] turf battles," she said. ". . . one agency going in one direction and the other going in the opposite direction and never talking."

Heymann, too, was concerned about the wrong signal a merger would send. By effectively closing down the DEA, it might make it seem as if the Clinton administration was leaving the field in the drug war. Heymann had other concerns, though, operational ones. The DEA had a strong organizational culture, one very different from that of the FBI. Heymann believed that competition among federal agencies was not all bad. It often fostered creativity and enterprise that might be stifled by the creation of a single, all-powerful drug enforcement bureaucracy. Among other factors, the FBI had hardly distinguished itself in drug enforcement in the decade since President Reagan had ordered it into the drug war. In the three fiscal years from 1990 through 1992, for instance, FBI investigations of narcotics traffickers had resulted in only 1,200 drug convictions.

As the principal reviewer on the issue at Main Justice, Heymann allowed the DEA and the FBI plenty of time to marshal their arguments. By late summer of 1993, executives of both agencies had staked out positions. The FBI brass, now openly favoring a merger, had a detailed proposal for creating a new and greatly enlarged Organized Crime/Drug Division within the FBI. DEA brass, by contrast, were sticking to their guns: If there was going to be a merger, it ought to involve the transfer of all FBI agents working narcotics cases over to the DEA.

By September 1993, Janet Reno's resolve to press ahead with a merger of the two agencies had crumbled. Appearing on her behalf before a House subcommittee looking into the merger issue, Heymann, who had never believed the idea was wise, could not bring himself even to talk about the original idea of transferring DEA agents into the ranks of the FBI. Instead, he outlined four alternatives. Congress could maintain the status quo, an idea he called "unacceptable." It could merge the FBI's narcotics program into DEA, transferring FBI drug agents and the FBI's intelligence files to the smaller agency. A third course would be to merge the FBI and the DEA into "one federal drug enforcement super-agency." A fourth, which Heymann outlined, was the course suggested by the Justice Department review that he had supervised. If followed, he said, that course of action would result in the creation of an executive oversight board composed of the heads of the FBI, the DEA and other Justice police agencies. This body would be a single point of authority on all federal narcotics-enforcement matters. The board would have the authority to establish investigative policy and to force federal police agencies to cooperate with one another. "The Attorney General has come close to reaching—although she has not yet reached—a conclusion on the best resolution of these issues," Heymann said.

In fact, the plan to merge the DEA into the FBI was dead, smothered by Heymann's close analytic scrutiny and Reno's reluctance to wage a pitched battle against the DEA, an institution with an established and powerful political constituency.

The decision not to merge the DEA and the FBI was seen by some inside Main Justice as not just a failure of will on Janet Reno's part but as an unnecessary hindrance to a more effective federal war on drugs. If that was so, it was compensated for, at least in part, by the energy, brains and commitment of the Justice Department's top career prosecutor in the drug war. Mary Lee Warren is a slender, intensely private woman who puts in terribly long hours and expects no less from those who work for her. Friends and colleagues described her as "a force of nature" and "a bulldog."

Several years before Janet Reno's arrival at Main Justice, Warren had been drafted by the Bush administration from the U.S. Attorney's Office in Manhattan to run the Criminal Division's Narcotics and Dangerous Drugs Section at Main Justice. In New York and Washington, it was not unusual for the cleaning staff to find Warren still at her desk after midnight, or for a colleague to come in early and discover that she had not gone home at all, but caught a few hours sleep on her office couch.

From her office at Main Justice, Warren was both quarterback and cheerleader for the many teams of field prosecutors and government agents working on cases across the country. On big, wide-ranging drug prosecutions involving multiple jurisdictions, it is not uncommon for agents and prosecutors to bump into one another. One of Warren's jobs was to minimize the number and the significance of such collisions, and to bang heads when overeager government lawyers refused to cooperate with one another because of concern for turf. Given the normal aversion of prosecutors in the field to supervision from Washington, Warren's role might have earned her nothing but enmity and dark suspicion. In fact, she not only inspired prosecutors in the field by her phenomenal energy, she was also a valuable resource, a prosecutor who had cut a swath in the tough pits of New York's busy federal courts.

A magna cum laude graduate from the Boston College of Law, Warren had clerked for a federal judge in Atlanta before taking a job in 1980 as an assistant U.S. attorney in the Southern District of New York—one of the best prosecution offices in the nation. In Manhattan, Warren had gravitated almost immediately to prosecutions of organized crime cases, taking on a violent crew of the Gambino Mafia family and a murdersome Manhattan gang called the Westies. In 1987 she was named chief of the narcotics unit in the U.S. Attorney's Office and coordinator of the Organized Crime Drug Enforcement Task Force for the New York-New Jersey area. Among the narcotics traffickers Warren sent to federal prison for long periods were a major crack dealer who had set an innocent citizen on fire and a doper who had attempted to murder a DEA agent.

In Washington, Warren's office was on the top floor of the Bond Building, a handsome commercial structure two blocks from the White House. The responsibilities she inherited are among the most burdensome and important at Main Justice, where narcotics enforcement is big business. Beginning in 1981, when President Reagan declared a federal war on drugs, the drug-control budget had rocketed upwards, from a modest $1.5 billion in 1981 to the $12.2 billion the Clinton administration would spend in 1994. By 1994, fully one-fourth of the Criminal Division's $76 million annual budget went for narcotics prosecutions. The ninety-four U.S. attorneys across the nation spent, on average, a full third of their budgets prosecuting drug cases.

When Main Justice announced a new drug indictment, spokesmen never mentioned the price tag. But a routine federal drug case could easily cost tens of thousands of dollars. Expenses in a long-term case that required wiretaps could exceed $1 million. The cost of a truly major prosecution could be breathtaking. The tab for prosecuting Panamanian dictator Manuel Noriega, for example, exceeded $5 million.

In drug enforcement, the federal government spent money as if it really was fighting a war. Little thought was given to cost. But insiders who had calculated the average cost per drug case, knew that the bottom line was sobering. In 1994, U.S. attorneys spent $211 million to prosecute 12,150 drug defendants. That boiled down to $17,376 per defendant. The DEA spent $769 million to make 9,688 drug arrests, at $79,376 per collar. The FBI spent considerably more. Drug funding accounted for approximately one-fourth of the FBI's budget. In 1994 the bureau charged 1,827 individuals with violations of federal narcotics laws. That translated to more than $260,000 per arrested defendant.

The drug war never had a stronger supporter than President George Bush. He showered the nation's drug warriors with money—nearly tripling the overall anti-narcotics budget from $4.3 billion in 1988 to $11.9 billion in 1992. The results were disappointing. After four years there was more cocaine on the streets than ever. Naturally, it was also cheaper than ever. Based on intelligence assessments, in 1988 there were 361 tons of cocaine available in the United States. By 1992, the figure had risen to 376 tons. The homicide rate, often thought to be driven by drug-related violence, also rose. In terms of the overall crime rate, there was no progress at all. The rate was roughly the same in 1992 as it had been in 1989 when Bush took office.

Inside Main Justice, such numbers were depressing. "I don't know what lessons to draw," Jack Keeney said, "because it's a frustrating area. We haven't solved the problem." David Margolis had supervised the Criminal Division's anti-narcotics efforts in the early 1990s. "We could keep on prosecuting big cases," Margolis said. "We could try and stop the flow of drugs at the border. And we could go after the drug financiers. But we've done all that, and we still have a drug problem."

To those outside the law enforcement community, it might have seemed an ironic, even heretical notion, but to many of the career lawyers and prosecutors inside Main Justice it was an article of faith that solving the nation's drug problem could not be accomplished by prosecutions and jail sentences alone. Keeney, Margolis and other Criminal Division lawyers had long since reached a conclusion they thought was self-evident: Education, rehabilitation and improving the grim lot of those most prone to drug addiction ought to become national priorities. "Education and fixing the underlying conditions that lead people to take drugs," Margolis asserted, "that's what's needed. Anyone who thinks that drug enforcement is primarily a law enforcement issue, they're smoking wacky tabacky."

The drug war had had an extraordinary impact on the Department of Justice, particularly on the Criminal Division. Roughly every two years during the Republican era—in 1984, 1986, 1988 and 1990—Congress passed major new anti-crime bills that gave Main Justice more powers and broader jurisdiction. More aggressive use of wiretaps, undercover operatives and confidential informants allowed the federal government to take out larger and more sophisticated drug-trafficking organizations. New laws allowing the federal government to seize financial assets and detain some categories of serious criminals before trial without bond gave prosecutors still more tools with which to work.

It made those years an exciting time to be a young federal prosecutor. Like Mary Lee Warren, a new generation of prosecutors grew up fast fighting the drug war. Younger lawyers took readily to techniques that an earlier generation had viewed warily. By the time Janet Reno took office, this generation was hitting mid-career. Having won big cases in Miami, New York, Los Angeles, Chicago and Houston, many were formidable courtroom advocates. There was a great irony in this phenomenon. The federal government had mastered the craft of prosecuting large drug-trafficking organizations, but that expertise had made almost no difference. As the Justice Department got better at drug enforcement, the drug problem got worse. Not since Vietnam had a national mission failed so miserably. From 1981 through 1993 the federal drug-control budgets added up to more than $80 billion. During that period the availability of cocaine on the nation's streets had changed hardly at all.

While it had not resulted in a defeat for narcotics traffickers, America's war on drugs had changed Main Justice. During the 1980s and early 1990s, largely because of drug enforcement, prosecutors became more heavily involved in directing investigations and operating overseas. Coordinating those efforts was the job of

Main Justice. So big was the job—it involved chasing drug fugitives and negotiating extradition treaties abroad—that the Criminal Division set up a new Office of International Affairs. Main Justice also became more closely involved with the CIA and other espionage agencies that gather information secretly overseas. The Department of Defense, the CIA and the National Security Agency spent hundreds of millions of dollars a year gathering drug intelligence. They did much of this work overseas, where the U.S. Constitution does not apply. Often, their information could not be used in court without jeopardizing sources and methods—some of which could not stand revealing.

Over time, the Narcotics and Dangerous Drugs Section at Main Justice became the handoff point through which drug intelligence from America's spy agencies could pass into the hands of its drug agents and prosecutors. This was one of the most important parts of the job Mary Lee Warren inherited after she arrived in Washington. Despite the negative review that the Clinton transition team gave to the Criminal Division, Warren was tagged as one of the top performers. "She is universally praised for her dedication and leadership," said the transition team's report.

By late 1993, Warren had so impressed Reno that she was promoted to succeed David Margolis in the post of deputy assistant attorney general in the Criminal Division, with responsibility for all aspects of federal drug enforcement. As the narcotics section chief, Warren had already been a fixture at the interagency working groups on narcotics. Now she became a commanding presence. If there was a problem with a DEA office, if an investigation was running off the rails somewhere, Warren didn't hesitate to call a senior official at home late at night. Even with her new clout, however, bending the system to her will was difficult. On many issues, several cabinet agencies—State, Treasury, Defense and Justice—had an interest, along with numerous subagencies like the CIA. Sometimes as many as forty different bureaucracies weighed in on a drug issue. Each had what bureaucrats called "equities" in drug enforcement. It was a nice way of saying they had a dog in the hunt.

Despite her newly enhanced position as the top drug prosecutor at Main Justice, Warren's authority was circumscribed. In domestic drug-enforcement operations, there were two jealous twin brothers. One was the Department of Justice, which has authority over the FBI, the DEA, the U.S. Marshals Service and the Immigration and Naturalization Service. The other was the Department of the Treasury, which is responsible for the Internal Revenue Service, the U.S. Customs Service and the Bureau of Alcohol, Tobacco and Firearms. In the same way that the Navy and the Air Force maintain separate fleets of jet fighters and bombers, these agencies had built up their capacities in drug enforcement, each generally going its own way. Having studied the waste and redundancy created by this deployment of resources, Vice President Al Gore's National Performance Review team recommended that the attorney general be named as a new director of federal law enforcement. In this capacity, the attorney general could make all the assets—those of the Treasury and Justice Departments—march in the same direction. The idea had been around for years. It went nowhere.

Reno sought other means to exert control. Having decided not to merge the FBI and the DEA, she embraced Philip Heymann's idea to create an Office of Investigative Agency Policies. A half step to merger, it would create an oversight board comprised of the head of the Justice Department's different police agencies. FBI Director Louis Freeh was named the executive director of the new office. In a few months, Freeh and Reno had developed a close working relationship. In seeking to bring greater discipline to drug enforcement, Reno's instinct was to consolidate the department's enforcement assets at the operational level and to enhance the oversight role of career prosecutors in the Criminal Division.

The Organized Crime and Drug Enforcement Task Force program was born in the Reagan administration. OCDETF (the jumble of letters is pronounced *oh-si-def*) was primarily a source of money. In 1994 some $382 million was earmarked to pay for federal prosecutors and federal agents to work specifically on major drug cases. The cases were pursued and prosecuted by thirteen regional OCDETF task forces comprised of local, state and federal investigators. The program gave U.S. attorneys in the OCDETF cities greater influence over the big federal police agencies. Still, many prosecutors in the field faulted the program's management at Main Justice. During the Bush administration, OCDETF had been administered by a small staff in Washington that reported to the deputy attorney general.

Reno changed that. She decided to push the OCDETF program out of the deputy's office and into the Criminal Division, where Mary Lee Warren assumed control of it. The move gave Warren a better grasp on the purse strings and a surer means of monitoring the work of the thirteen task forces. Main Justice didn't start dictating how to run the individual cases; Warren knew better than to try that. She had been the OCDETF coordinator in Manhattan, an office that was notoriously independent. But the new funding gave the Criminal Division more control over drug-enforcement strategy.

That was important. The job of the Criminal Division deputy who oversaw narcotics prosecutions was increasingly strategic. The cocaine industry had begun as a disorganized mass of freelancers in the mid-1970s. In the two decades since, control of the cocaine market had been consolidated in the hands of an oligarchy of producers in Colombia. The DEA called them "kingpins" and grouped them into "cartels." In fact, the big cocaine producers were loosely joined, competitive factions that shared the common goal of moving their product to the United States.

When Janet Reno became attorney general the dominant drug cartel was based in the beautiful Colombian city of Cali. The drug distribution process had become so refined and so integrated that by the early 1990s most big federal cocaine prosecutions ultimately led back to the same large Colombian producers and distributors—to the kingpins. Other regions produce cocaine, but none rivaled the hundreds of tons produced annually in the Andes, processed in Colombian labs, then shipped abroad.

Strategy mattered. The Bush administration had emphasized a plan to stop the flow of cocaine in transit by dispatching Navy ships, radar planes, even helium-filled blimps to patrol the Caribbean. A lot of cocaine was seized, but the cartels easily replaced the product lost and devised ingenious ways of evading the high-tech surveillance. As a former local prosecutor, Janet Reno didn't think a big emphasis on interdiction was worth the money, not while American cities were seething with violence. Her professional advisers agreed.

Politically, Reno and the Clinton White House could not appear to be walking away from the drug war. But a reallocation of assets, something modest, was possible. Reno's experience in Miami told her that much violent crime was drug related. It was not a novel insight, but it clashed with a long-standing bureaucratic imperative: that funding for drug enforcement was sacrosanct. This ethic was built into the OCDETF legislation, which said the money could not fund other kinds of investigations. Reno's answer became the equivalent of "Not any more." Along with moving the OCDETF program into the Criminal Division, Reno approved a one-year plan to allow OCDETF-funded drug fighters—prosecutors and agents who were supposed to work exclusively on drug matters—to assume "collateral" duties. That meant targeting street gangs that fomented drug-related violence. Reno's decision was a shock to the traditionalists who viewed the OCDETF program as an inviolable source of drug funding. Reno was determined, however. The drug war was not going to stall, she said; there would still be the big cases against the cocaine cartels. Mary Lee Warren's job was to make sure of that. But henceforth the focus would not be on numbers of arrests or tons of seized cocaine but on criminal organizations. And the big tools would be used, especially electronic wiretaps.

Warren was key. Reno's aides got used to the sight of the narcotics section chief slipping quietly into the attorney general's office at 7:30 A.M. The subject might be something large, like a special operation along the Mexican border, or something sensitive, like a back-channel message from the government of Colombia. Whatever it was, the transaction was swift and subdued.

In Reno's view, drug enforcement was more complicated than simply bringing the big prosecutions Mary Lee Warren oversaw. In December 1993, prosecutors and investigators from the thirteen OCDETF cities gathered in New Orleans for an annual conference. It was as close to a summit for operational drug fighters as occurs in the United States. Reno used the opportunity to explain herself. "People ask about the drug policy of this nation," she said. "I not only want to maintain our efforts at drug enforcement, I want to see those efforts enhanced. I want to go after the kingpins, but I want to do more. . . . We have to make sure that we not only go after the kingpins, who too often can be easily replaced, but that we go after the entire network. And after getting rid of the network in a neighborhood, we come in with positive prevention . . . initiatives that fill the vacuum with positive forces rather than the guy down the street who steps into the vacuum and increases the network."

Like David Margolis and Jack Keeney, Reno understood the importance of prevention efforts in slowing the nation's galloping drug epidemic. Prevention was not a popular idea with politicians, however. As much as those at Main Justice believed in it, their overseers in the White House and Congress emphasized enforcement. Sadly, the one came at the expense of the other.

CHAPTER FOUR

OPERATION CORNERSTONE

D rug enforcement during Janet Reno's stewardship of Main Justice would take American law enforcement to heights seldom reached before. The most significant prosecution would be directed at the Cali cartel, the world's largest exporter of cocaine, one of the biggest criminal enterprises in the world. The efforts undertaken on Reno's watch were based in part on years of investigative spadework dating to the 1980s. By 1994, there were major federal investigations of Cali cartel operations and employees in New York, Houston, Chicago, Los Angeles and San Diego. But the most significant case by far was built in Miami, Reno's hometown, a city that had historically been the primary staging area for the Cali cartel's biggest and most ambitious American operations. The investigation started long before Reno became attorney general, but it would become the transcendent drug case of her tenure. At a critical juncture, it would push Main Justice to the outer limits of its legal authority and have a dramatic impact on events in Colombia.

The case was called Operation Cornerstone. A key moment in its development occurred on a warm morning in June 1993, at a federal prison not far from Miami's downtown. There, a portly man named Harold Ackerman shuffled aboard a waiting bus outside the Metropolitan Correctional Center along with two dozen other inmates. The prison bus followed the same route every day, wending its way from MCC to the smaller lockup adjacent to the federal courthouse downtown.

Ackerman's was not an ordinary journey. Two months earlier he had been convicted of a raft of serious narcotics-trafficking charges by a federal jury in Miami. The convictions were enough to earn Ackerman the equivalent of seven life terms in prison. Because he was getting on in years and his health was not good—he had a bad heart—the convictions were like a death sentence. Ackerman was desperate for a way out.

At trial, an energetic U.S. Customs agent, Edward Kacerosky, had been the star witness against Ackerman. Though he had nineteen years on the job, Kacerosky still had a boyish, earnest manner, and he was blessed with two gifts particularly useful for a criminal investigator. Besides his nearly photographic memory, he was possessed of the confidence man's ability to establish rapport with almost anyone.

For all Kacerosky's skill, it had taken considerable effort to persuade the jury of Harold Ackerman's guilt. Ackerman did not look like a drug dealer, for one thing. To his neighbors in the quiet suburb of North Miami Beach, Ackerman was a good family man who, with his wife, operated a successful garment-making factory. He had a son in medical school at the University of Miami. The family went to synagogue every week. Before work each day Ackerman took a leisurely jog through the shady streets around his home.

For the jurors, the Customs Service agent and the prosecutors who led him through the evidence painted a far different picture. They told jurors about the $500,000 in cash Ackerman kept on hand in his home. There was the small armory of Uzi submachine guns and C-4 plastic explosives that Ackerman's employees maintained for difficult moments. Most important, Kacerosky recounted how, through careful planning and logistics, Ackerman maintained an endless supply of cocaine pouring into communities across the United States. In all, Operation Cornerstone had intercepted 12,250 kilos of cocaine.

Ackerman was the Cali cartel's man in Miami, the point of the spear the cocaine barons had thrust at the United States. He did not need any warning about what would happen to him if word got out that he was cooperating with the team of federal agents and prosecutors pursuing the cartel. Ackerman had worked for the Cali businessmen long enough to know. What Ackerman did need was an honest lawyer, and by grace and good fortune he had one. This was not always true when it came to arrested employees of the cartel. As a rule, the organization provided defense lawyers for its arrested managers, whose assets were generally frozen by the government. Not uncommonly, there were doubts about the loyalties of these attorneys and whether they would seriously negotiate a plea agreement that required their client to become a government witness against the cartel. As it happened, Ackerman's family back in Cali became concerned about his representation. For the trial, they hired Edward Shohat, a topflight Miami litigator who was not part of the cartel's network of American lawyers.

After his conviction Ackerman arranged to talk with Shohat privately. If the lawyer could convey the message discreetly, Ackerman said, he was prepared to provide evidence against the Cali cartel. Shohat had gone to see Assistant U. S. Attorney William Pearson. The son of a distinguished former state appeals court judge, Pearson is dark haired and intense, with the courtroom manner of a counterpuncher. He had been a public defender for years in Miami before switching sides and becoming a prosecutor. After talking with Shohat, Pearson agreed to have a talk with Harold Ackerman. The bus ride from the Metropolitan Correctional Center was the result. It was the latest chapter in what seemed to be developing into an Ackerman opus. No one knew how it would end, but everyone agreed it was far too intriguing to put down.

For more than fifteen years, the Justice Department had pursued the cocaine barons of Colombia. The Cali cartel and the U.S. Drug Enforcement Administration had grown up with each other, their size and sophistication developing along parallel tracks. The two founders of the Cali cartel—Gilberto Rodríguez Orejuela, the cartel's corporate visionary, and José Santacruz Londoño, its chief operations manager—were nearly apprehended at the very beginning of their careers. Even in the early 1980s the federal government had plenty of traps laid. A DEA–New York Police Department Task Force raided a series of stash houses used by Santacruz in Queens, where they found financial records showing $26 million in transactions, along with silencer-equipped machine guns.

The men from Cali were clever entrepreneurs. They were also elusive. Periodically, they were detected doing drug deals inside the United States, but they always managed to slip away. In Los Angeles, DEA agents narrowly missed arresting Gilberto Rodríguez in a 200-kilo deal. In New York, Rodríguez and Santacruz were indicted together in 1985 for running a smuggling enterprise—but not before they had escaped back to Colombia. In Florida, Santacruz was indicted in 1988 for a big cocaine importation. In Louisiana, Gilberto and his younger brother, Miguel, were indicted in 1987 for arranging a 544-kilo shipment of cocaine. Over the years the cases piled up, the quantities grew larger. Coming into his own as a kingpin, Miguel Rodríguez was charged in Tampa with supervising a multi-ton shipment of cocaine concealed inside hollowed-out lumber. Meanwhile, the DEA–New York Police Department Task Force, led by their relentless supervisor William Mockler, never stopped pursuing Santacruz. In 1990, working with authorities in Europe, they helped police agencies unravel a money-laundering scheme that had concealed $65 million in drug profits controlled by Santacruz.

Each of the older federal cases stood on its own, with separate sets of witnesses and evidence. Taken cumulatively, the evidence was becoming a mountain of proof against the three businessmen from Cali. But Colombia refused to extradite its citizens to the United States. As a consequence, the indictments lay idle and impotent in federal courthouses.

The problem of geography—and the barriers of national sovereignty—made the Cali cartel harder to destroy than the Justice

Department's other big targets. The Italian Mafia in the United States sought control of neighborhoods and domestic industries and fostered relationships that defined the term "crime family." The big street gangs treasured their turf in inner-city neighborhoods and tended to have close ethnic ties. They were surrogate families of young gunslingers. Unlike the kingpins from Cali, who rarely visited the United States, relying on intermediaries like Harold Ackerman, members of a Mafia family or a street gang could be targeted more easily by federal investigators. But fifteen hundred miles of ocean separated the Cali cartel kingpins from the nearest federal courtroom. Moreover, the men from Cali cared nothing about fostering relationships, only profit. To their way of thinking, they were running an international shipping business that faced an inconvenient American embargo. They had figured out a franchise system that relied upon independent contractors. This shielded them from arrest and blunted the impact of federal prosecutions.

The men from Cali were also wiser about politics than some of their brethren in the cocaine business. During the early 1980s the cocaine kingpins from the Colombian city of Medellín had conducted their business largely through a campaign of fear and violence. If they didn't actually invent it, kingpins from Medellín carried the practice of narcoterrorism to new levels. Ultimately, it caused their downfall, because it temporarily awakened the wrath of the Colombian Army and national leadership. The kingpins of Medellín were hunted down and either jailed or killed in gun battles. In their air-conditioned mansions in the green hills above Cali, the cartel leaders had drawn the appropriate lesson from Medellín. For Miguel and Gilberto Rodríguez Orejuela and José Santacruz Londoño, violence for its own sake was worse than foolish; it was counterproductive. Naturally, the gentlemen from Cali had a number of accomplished assassins in their employ. But they also had money managers with MBAs—men like Harold Ackerman.

More than anything, Edward Kacerosky believed, the barons from Cali were guilty of a certain hubris. They smiled indulgently over the ways of the old "moustache Petes" of the Italian Mafia. About the strutting macho ethos of their brethren from Medellín, the men from Cali laughed.

They were better—far better—they believed. Over the past one hundred years the upper strata of Cali society had been molded from a long line of immigrants from Europe. These were cultured families—families of wealth and breeding, and of proven business acumen. It was among these people that the cocaine barons of Cali moved. Such was their arrogance that they expected little significant interference from the plodding federal police agencies in America.

Kacerosky had used the arrogance of the Caleños to his advantage. He had broken their codes of communication, then listened as they conducted their business in the very neighborhood where he coached his son's Little League team. The patience had paid off.

In other hands, the government's evidence might have been less persuasive to a jury. How could an outsider make sense of the codes, the obscure Spanish dialect? Kacerosky, certainly, seemed among the least likely to succeed at such a task. A scrappy youngster who grew up on the tough streets of the Bronx not far from Yankee Stadium, he had followed his Polish-American father, a policeman, into a career in law enforcement, signing up first as an agent with the Immigration and Naturalization Service. Not long after, he married a pretty young woman newly arrived in the United States from the Dominican Republic. Out of deference to his new bride, Kacerosky had become fluent in Spanish, husband and wife finishing each other's sentences in rapid-fire bursts of Spanish and English. As a criminal investigator with the immigration service, Kacerosky worked the streets for several years before he was assigned to the DEA-NYPD drug task force. There he teamed with agents of the U.S. Drug Enforcement Administration who had been pursuing the Cali cartel. Kacerosky's fluency in Spanish had helped him get the prestigious slot.

The task force was still being led by William Mockler. Through long hours and late-night stakeouts, he coached Kacerosky on technique and imbued in the young agent a drive to see the big picture in criminal investigations. Take the mopes (low-level dealers) and the drug couriers off the street, Mockler told Kacerosky, and what happens? The organization that hired them will simply replace them with more mopes and couriers, that's what. In the 1970s, DEA was still known for its "buy-bust" approach. An undercover agent arranged a drug purchase, the cocaine was delivered, the courier was arrested. Mockler had a broader vision. He wanted his agents to be detectives, not mere drug agents. He wanted them to assemble bits of information—notes found in trash, fingerprints on a matchbook—into a pattern. It was Mockler and his task force who first named the members of the Cali cartel, José Santacruz and Gilberto Rodríguez. They did it by identifying Santacruz's fingerprint on a soft-drink can found in a drug stash house and bank deposit slips for accounts held by Rodríguez. It was all about persistence and seeing patterns, Mockler instructed Kacerosky. Mockler sat the young agent down and showed him how to divine the workings of a criminal network from a stack of telephone toll records. Stay focused on the people at the top, he counseled. Stay focused. Kacerosky never forgot the lesson.

With Harold Ackerman, Edward Kacerosky and his fellow agents and prosecutors had not gone for the midlevel employees, the distributors. Rather, they had bided their time. The result was that in *U.S. v. Ackerman*, American law enforcement had for the first time placed a senior manager of the Cali cartel before the bar of justice. In trying him in a federal courtroom, prosecutors had also exposed some of the most privileged business communications of the gentlemen from Cali.

The cartel leaders were dangerous adversaries. Like the Italian Mafia years before, the men from Cali had few qualms about attacking the American criminal justice system head-on. The cartel's managers murdered snitches and looked for corrupt cops to bribe. They bought lawyers and used them as intelligence agents to find out about investigations. Where the Colombians differed from the Italians was in the sophistication and sweep of their ambition. The five Italian Mafia families that dominated New York until the late 1980s had run their share of million-dollar operations, raking off money from building-trade unions, from the ports and assorted markets. But they had never attempted anything as brazenly organized as the cocaine barons from Cali.

With José Santacruz, the Rodríguez brothers moved 7,000 to 10,000 kilos of cocaine into the United States on just about a monthly basis. Nothing was left to chance. Before they left Colombia, the 2.2-pound packets of cocaine were wrapped in heat-sealed plastic, then carefully stowed in large cargo containers. The big metal bins were hoisted aboard ships, bearing hundreds of such containers. Upon arriving at a U.S. port, they were off-loaded by cranes, packed onto tractor-trailer trucks and transported to air-conditioned commercial warehouses. There, at a leisurely pace, cartel employees unpacked the cocaine. They divided it into lots and parceled it out to regional distributors, who came from around the nation to pick up their consignments.

By analyzing telephone toll records as Mockler had taught and through the aggressive use of wiretaps, Kacerosky had broken the operation. Ackerman's conversations with the Rodríguez brothers and with other employees of the cartel had been recorded with court permission under Title III of the Omnibus Crime Control and Safe Streets Act, passed in 1968. The Safe Streets Act became the centerpiece of Richard Nixon's War on Crime, but federal police services like the FBI had not begun strategically using Title IIIs, as agents and prosecutors called wiretaps, until the mid-1980s—against the Italian Mafia. One reason was that Title IIIs were expensive. Teams of agents had to monitor the wiretaps, spending hours and hours "on the muffs." Agent overtime meant dollars. Translators and transcripts cost still more money.

But dollars were less of a hindrance than other concerns. Philosophically, J. Edgar Hoover's FBI had had no problem with wiretapping. What it did have a problem with was keeping wires up for any extended length of time. Hoover's FBI was driven by numbers. Indictments, arrests and convictions were the coin of Hoover's realm, and agents and supervisors who had the most got the promotions and pay raises. That meant turning cases around quickly. What it seldom meant was spending months and perhaps years on a single case—even if that one case could put a world-class criminal organization out of business.

Over the years after Hoover's death the strategic approach to criminal investigations gradually won favor among FBI managers. It began with the FBI's efforts against the Italian Mafia in New York, said Stephen Trott, who served as associate attorney general at Main Justice during the Reagan administration. Soon after, the DEA, U.S. Customs Service and other federal police services began following the FBI's lead.

In Miami, Edward Kacerosky and his team of agents and prosecutors had carried the strategic employment of Title IIIs to new lengths. If Ackerman was now truly prepared to cooperate with the government, as he had told Edward Shohat, it would be the biggest break in the Cornerstone case yet.

By including Ackerman in the routine prisoner transfer from the Metropolitan Correctional Center to the temporary lockup downtown, the agents and prosecutors were taking a gamble. They were hoping it would not alert the cartel's many watchers and spies, which was more likely to happen if they met with him at the federal correctional facility. But would the meeting yield results?

Shohat, the defense attorney, and Pearson, the prosecutor, decided to find out. They met in a secluded conference room in the federal courthouse for an encounter that would send Harold Ackerman on a rare journey into danger and redemption.

When the prison bus disgorged its daily freight of federal prisoners, a deputy marshal separated Ackerman from the others. A few minutes later the Colombian businessman was led into the room.

The two lawyers, joined by agents Kacerosky and DEA Special Agent Louis Weiss, rose to greet him. As always, Kacerosky was impressed by the man's self-possession. Even in these humbling circumstances—his freedom gone, his name disgraced, his assets forfeited—Ackerman was a perfect gentleman, polite and dignified, soft-spoken and articulate.

Pearson wasn't interested in appearance, however. He got right to the point. You tell us the whole truth, he said. If you hold anything back or shade the truth in any way, the deal's off. We'll be relying on your testimony. If you can't live with full disclosure, then we shake hands and say goodbye. No hard feelings.

Ackerman didn't hesitate. He was a realist. For the Cali cartel, he had earned tens of millions of dollars; for himself, a life sentence without parole. He was ready to cooperate.

Shohat spoke up and said he'd like to see a written cooperation agreement before they started. His client waved him aside. They could work out the details later. Ackerman was ready to answer Kacerosky's questions.

Kacerosky wanted to test the man. Everywhere he went he carried a carefully organized notebook full of photographs, nearly all of them taken by government surveillance cameras outfitted with long telephoto lenses. Kacerosky did not know who all the men and women in his photographs were. He had ideas, though. Taken from Ackerman's home were coded ledgers that he used to keep track of his employees. In them were repeated references to a Number 24. The reference was clearly to an important person, Kacerosky knew. Sitting across the cramped table from Harold Ackerman, Kacerosky asked him to identify the man.

Ackerman took only a few seconds to flip through the photographs. This one, Ackerman said, pointing to a Latin man. He goes by the name Jesús. His real name is Raúl—Raúl Martí.

Kacerosky felt like grinning but did not. He knew Martí. The thin man had once worked for Ackerman. That was important, Kacerosky thought. Ackerman wasn't bullshitting them. If he would really cooperate all the way, this was a breakthrough. It meant they would be able to escalate the war against the Cali cartel to a whole new level.

Assistant U.S. Attorney Theresa Van Vliet wanted the Cornerstone case—badly. The investigation had been named for one of the Cali cartel's more ingenious smuggling stratagems. Harold Ackerman's colleagues in Cali had stuffed tons of cocaine into hollowed-out concrete posts and cornerstones, then moved the materials by ship to South Florida. It was just such a load that had led Kacerosky to tap Harold Ackerman's telephone.

An alert Customs inspector had discovered the cocaine on a Saturday morning in 1992. To no one's surprise, Van Vliet was working that weekend. When she heard that Customs needed a prosecutor's help in the matter, she perked up. Operation Cornerstone thus became a case that belonged to the High Intensity Drug Trafficking Area task force where Van Vliet worked.

After Ackerman's conviction, control of the investigation slipped away from the HIDTA office and moved into something called the Florida Joint Task Group, Kacerosky's permanent place of assignment. Now that that case was taking on a second life, Van Vliet knew where the Cornerstone case ought to go next: right back onto the HIDTA launching pad.

Van Vliet was a prosecutor's prosecutor. Some colleagues were put off by her charge-ahead style and general disregard for bureaucratic niceties. To her admirers, that was just Theresa, a force of nature that was always drawn to the next big target.

Van Vliet had started work as a federal prosecutor in 1985 and discovered almost immediately that she loved the job. In crime-plagued South Florida, the U.S. Attorney's Office was a place where everyone put in long hours, but no one put in longer hours than Van Vliet. An avid Miami Dolphins fan, she could be found many nights and most weekends in blue jeans, a sweatshirt and running shoes meeting with agents like Kacerosky, pounding out the paperwork for search warrants or preparing cases for trial. To her colleagues, there was no better co-worker. To those who got in her way, there was no more implacable foe. During the investigation of Harold Ackerman, Van Vliet had spent many all-nighters with Kacerosky, preparing applications for permission to wiretap cellular phones used by Ackerman and his employees. Before the case came to trial, the two spent more hours with the two trial prosecutors, Edward Ryan and William Pearson.

After she heard about Kacerosky's conversation with Harold Ackerman, Theresa Van Vliet was more determined than ever to continue Operation Cornerstone from her office. Ackerman's co-operation could move the investigation of the Rodríguez Orejuela organization to a much higher plane. For that to happen, though, the case needed to be handled one way, Van Vliet believed. That's why she had asked Kacerosky to come see her.

The Customs Service agent bounced into a seat in front of Van Vliet's desk with the same nervous energy he brought to every task. With his jeans and casual shirt, the beeper clipped to his belt, a cellular phone jammed in a pocket, Kacerosky could have passed for a foreman on one of South Florida's many booming construction sites. In fact, the beeper and cell phone were the tools of the trade of the federal drug agent in the 1990s.

Kacerosky greeted Van Vliet breezily. "Hey, T."

Van Vliet got down to it. Cornerstone, she explained, should become a HIDTA case. The acronym was yet another brainchild of the Office of National Drug Control Policy in Washington. The High Intensity Drug Trafficking Area concept would have been meaningless or worse but for a simple fact: It came with lots of money attached. Law enforcement is basically a local matter, but in communities like Miami, where big international crime syndicates had set up shop, the local police are outgunned and the federal agencies are turf conscious. The idea behind HIDTA was simple: Use the grant money from Washington to create a high-tech investigative facility that would be so well equipped that it would entice local police and federal agencies to work together on major targets. Operating side by side from the HIDTA platform, the locals and the feds would go after the big drug syndicates together, under the guiding hand of the local U.S. attorney. In theory, it was a terrific idea. Because of turf concerns, however, HIDTA was not an easy sell, especially to the big federal police agencies. During the Bush administration HIDTA was the program no one wanted. People at Main Justice didn't like it because they didn't control the funding. Neither did the FBI nor the DEA. The brass at both agencies didn't like the idea that the HIDTA facility would be managed by the local U.S. attorney.

Van Vliet knew the history. She had moved to HIDTA's offices just west of Miami International Airport in 1991. As the office's chief prosecutor, Van Vliet quickly built a reputation as a savvy strategist who put in the same brutal hours that the big narcotics investigations demanded of agents. It was not uncommon for an agent, bone weary and bleary eyed from a long surveillance, to stop off at HIDTA late at night and find Van Vliet hunched over her computer terminal. She was accessible. If an agent assigned to the HIDTA office had a problem with the U.S. Attorney's Office, he didn't have to stew about it. Agents could walk into Theresa's office and say what was on their minds; Van Vliet would prop her feet up on the desk and hear them out. She might well take up an agent's cause, though it was impossible to be sure. She had been known to tell some agents they were wasting her time. From Van Vliet, her colleagues got straight answers in a squad room vernacular they understood.

Edward Kacerosky had done much of his investigation of Harold Ackerman under Van Vliet's watchful eye at HIDTA. Still, as he settled into his chair, she knew the Customs agent's first loyalty was to his "group," the separate cluster of DEA and Customs agents assigned to the Florida Joint Task Group. The agents worked out of a building across the street from HIDTA's office, though it might just as well have been across town. Kacerosky said as much. He would be a traitor, he told Van Vliet, if he took Cornerstone to HIDTA.

Van Vliet challenged him. Cornerstone was too big for any one person or agency to be proprietary about, she said. The case should be run the way the investigation of Harold Ackerman had been. They should go after the entire Cali organization, not just individual members, one by one. Ackerman was a big case, but it was like a lot of the bigger cases they had done, Van Vliet said. What she had in mind was something larger, more sweeping. There were precedents, she continued. Think back to the Medellín cartel. The big cases against the Medellín kingpins had helped pressure the Colombian government into acting. Or the Commission case against the five Mafia families in New York. There had been lots of individual mob prosecutions that had made no difference, but it was only after FBI agents pulled together years of evidence from those older prosecution files and put it into one big racketeering case that the Justice Department was able to indict and convict the leadership of all five Mafia families. Cornerstone had the potential for just that kind of impact, Van Vliet told Kacerosky—maybe bigger.

Van Vliet had seldom been faulted for lack of ambition. She was overseeing some of the largest drug prosecutions in the nation. But even Kacerosky was taken aback by what she proposed. Use the Ackerman case to take down the cartel? The premise seemed wildly improbable, a stretch that reached far beyond the evidence they had in hand.

They were interrupted by a knock at the door. Van Vliet invited the caller to come in. Before her meeting with Kacerosky, Van Vliet had asked Douglas Hughes to join the conversation with the Customs agent in case she failed to persuade Kacerosky of the rightness of her argument. Doug Hughes was one of the most persuasive men Van Vliet knew. If he couldn't do it, no one could.

Hughes clasped Kacerosky's hand warmly and smiled. A trim man who projected the empathy of a family therapist, Hughes was the HIDTA director in Miami. He also held the rank of commander in the Metro-Dade Police Department. Before coming to HIDTA, Hughes had been a lieutenant on Dade County's extremely busy homicide squad and had run a police substation in the riot-scarred neighborhood of Liberty City.

Ed, Hughes said, leaning toward Kacerosky and picking up Van Vliet's argument, though he had heard none of it, you should continue to work Cornerstone from HIDTA. We have the resources to let you do your best work. The lawyers are here, the wiretapping's here. We have the budget and the equipment to help you see this thing through to the end.

Kacerosky knew HIDTA's capabilities. From the outside, with their well tended gardens and louvered windows, the HIDTA buildings could have passed for an insurance firm or accounting office. Inside, the place was mind-boggling. Instead of file cabinets full of premium notices and balance sheets, there was a comfortable soundproofed booth for wiretapping, undercover phone rooms where agents could talk to informants. There was another room for pen registers, devices that record phone numbers dialed from target telephones. There was an encrypted radio channel so investigators could talk to one another securely, an intelligence center with a direct feed—what Hughes called a "classified pipe"—from the Pentagon, and a technical support center stocked with cellular phones, laptop computers and high-tech video-surveillance cameras. To use all this stuff, HIDTA had more than 250 local police officers, federal agents and prosecutors assigned to a seemingly endless warren of offices. Every investigator had a desk and a computer terminal.

Kacerosky liked Hughes and Van Vliet enormously. Without their help, he could not have gotten as far as he had on the Cornerstone case. Technically, however, Cornerstone still belonged to the joint DEA-Customs task group across the street. They had worked for years against the Cali cartel and had invested thousands of hours into the original Ackerman case. Now that they were finally making headway, Kacerosky told Hughes and Van Vliet, it would be wrong for Customs to move Cornerstone over to HIDTA.

That's where you're wrong, Eddie, Hughes argued. It would still be a Customs-DEA case. You could just come over here and use our facilities—that's what we're here for! You would have a prosecutor working with you on the case. There would be no limits to what you could do.

No, Kacerosky said. It would be disloyal.

Van Vliet shook her head, then looked at Hughes. No one wanted to badger Eddie K. They respected him too much for that. Duplication and rivalry were bred into the bones of the federal criminal justice system. Even the best and most likable agents weren't immune. They would wait for another day.

CHAPTER FIVE

A WEB OF
WIRETAPS

n the weeks after the first meeting between Edward
Kacerosky and Harold Ackerman, in May 1992, the
two men spent many hours together. When Kacerosky
was not debriefing the gentlemanly Colombian trafficker, he and other agents were following the man whom Ackerman had identified as Raúl Martí.

Not long after Ackerman was arrested, Martí had been summoned to Cali. A thin man who used lots of oil to slick back his
jet black hair, Martí checked into a nice room in Cali's Hotel In-
tercontinental. After getting settled he went downstairs and
climbed into a limousine, where he was promptly blindfolded.
Then the car carried Martí to a residence high above the city.

Locals called the place "the Hill." It belonged to Miguel Rodríguez Orejuela. A palatial compound, it served as the Cali cartel's worldwide smuggling operations center.

Inside, Rodríguez greeted Raúl Martí briskly. Rodríguez was still
upset by Ackerman's arrest. It had cost the cartel 6,650 kilos of cocaine. There was always more cocaine, however; the real damage
had been done in exposing one of the cartel's major importation
routes—a route that had taken years to establish. Along with the

smuggling routes, cartel-owned business fronts in Venezuela, Panama, Guatemala, Florida and Texas had also been exposed.

Rodríguez was furious. The question before them, he told Martí, as the two men settled themselves in chairs, was what to do next. The cartel's elaborate production machinery had not stopped churning out new product. The flow of powder from the cartel's clandestine laboratories in Colombia was as robust as ever. What they needed was not product, Rodríguez explained, but a new smuggling route through Miami.

Martí listened, interested. He had worked for Harold Ackerman in Miami and had proven himself reliable.

Rodríguez proposed that Martí set up the new smuggling route. Martí agreed.

Rodríguez gave him instructions to set up a legitimate coffee-importation business in Miami. Martí would be dealing in coffee most of the time. A firm in Panama would be his supplier, Rodríguez said. The company would send large coffee shipments regularly. From time to time cocaine would be concealed inside.

Martí understood. Before, Ackerman had imported frozen vegetables from Guatemala. Rodríguez had controlled a front company in Guatemala City that processed frozen vegetables for shipment to the United States. Periodically, tons of cocaine were layered in beneath the icy blocks of broccoli and okra.

Rodríguez had other instructions for Martí. He was to establish a false identity and use it to set up corporations as front companies. He should learn from Ackerman's mistakes. The cartel had obtained copies of the affidavits that had been filed by Kacerosky and Van Vliet following the arrest of Ackerman. The documents described in detail how the government had intercepted Ackerman's words spoken over cellular phones. Study those documents, Rodríguez instructed Martí. Don't make the same mistakes as Harold. Be careful.

Martí did as he was told. He sat in a room of the Rodríguez compound in Cali and read the affidavits. Written by Edward Kacerosky and Theresa Van Vliet at the HIDTA office, the documents explained in detail how the U.S. government had built its case against Harold Ackerman by wiretapping his cellular phones and analyzing his telephone toll records. As required by law, the affidavits had been disclosed during the Ackerman prosecution. The government was required to turn over detailed affidavits that described the investigation. For Raúl Martí, they offered a primer on modern federal drug enforcement.

Before Martí returned to Miami, Rodríguez explained that in light of the Ackerman case, there were going to be new rules. From then on, no cartel business was to be discussed on cellular phones—ever. Rather, Martí and his people would communicate with Cali via pay telephones selected at random on streets and in shopping malls. The calls could be paid for with coins or prepaid debit cards, Rodríguez said. The cards could be purchased from storefront agencies in Miami.

Lastly, Rodríguez said, he wanted regular reports. Martí was to keep careful records, just as Ackerman had done. All deliveries and payments were to be accounted for—to the penny. The information should be faxed to the cartel's accountant in ledger form on a monthly basis.

After Martí indicated again that he understood the rules, he was driven back to his hotel. He checked out, boarded an airliner and returned to Miami.

In his big house on the hill above Cali, Miguel Rodríguez turned to other business. The Cali cartel had opened a new smuggling route.

At the HIDTA office west of Miami International Airport, Theresa Van Vliet was finding out that having lots of wiretaps was a big problem. Because of HIDTA, the South Florida drug scene was wired for sound. The nondescript facility had become a major electronic listening post. But agents in their nicely appointed offices were having a hard time keeping up with the miles of taped conversations and sorting through all the verbiage for valuable evidence.

In her office in an HIDTA building, Van Vliet leaned across her desk and asked John Burlingame a question. A retired U.S. Army colonel, six feet five, with a massive torso developed through a rigorous regimen of weight lifting, Burlingame didn't look like a computer guy, but that's what he was. He had been recruited by Douglas Hughes, the HIDTA director in Miami, who was impressed that Burlingame had once worked at the U.S. Army Missile Command in Huntsville, Alabama. Hughes liked the burly former Army colonel enormously. He also figured Burlingame was a good bet to straighten out HIDTA's balky computers. If he could help keep all of the Army's thousands of missiles aimed in the right direction, Hughes reasoned, Burlingame would certainly have no trouble unscrambling HIDTA's computer system.

It had not been easy—and that fact formed the premise of Theresa Van Vliet's question to Burlingame. There were several big narcotics investigations gearing up in the HIDTA offices. With the identification of Raúl Martí, the Cornerstone case was gaining new momentum. The volume of intercepted telephone traffic flooding into the agency was becoming unmanageable. Couldn't Burlingame's computer jockeys do more to help the agents sort through the recorded evidence? Van Vliet asked.

The top prosecutor at HIDTA, Theresa Van Vliet was not someone to be trifled with, Burlingame knew. He had been an infantry commander in Vietnam, and he had worked for General John Shalikashvili before he became the chairman of the Joint Chiefs of Staff at the Pentagon. Burlingame knew tough, he figured. In his first week on the job at HIDTA, however, Van Vliet had expanded Burlingame's definition of the term. Their first encounter occurred in a hallway. The lawyer had intercepted Burlingame as he was headed to the restroom.

"Are you the new computer guy?" Van Vliet asked.

"Yes, ma'am."

"Well, good." Van Vliet turned and spun on a polished heel. "Because these computers are all fucked up."

Across the desk from Van Vliet, Burlingame was more impressed than ever with the prosecutor's brains and energy. He knew how the volume of wiretap traffic had increased at HIDTA over the past year. He also knew that Van Vliet was largely responsible for it. In 1990 there had been just two federal wiretaps in all of South Florida. The Title III provision in the Omnibus Crime Control and Safe Streets Act of 1968 had rarely been used in Miami. That was the first and loudest complaint Van Vliet had heard from the FBI and the DEA. She answered the charge by promising that if they developed enough evidence—what the courts called "probable cause"—for a wiretap, she would personally shepherd the application through the process. That meant getting it cleared by the U.S. Attorney's Office in Miami and then approved by the Office of Enforcement Operations at Main Justice. That office reported to Jack Keeney. Lawyers there viewed their role as that of a safeguard, to ensure that federal wiretap authority was used only in appropriate cases. Once Keeney or another of the five deputies in the Criminal Division signed off, Van Vliet then had to take the Title III application to a federal district court judge for final approval. It was a lot of work for everyone. The agents had to assemble almost as much evidence as it would take to make an arrest.

But Van Vliet had made good on her pledge. When the agents brought their Title III applications in, Van Vliet reviewed them promptly, then pushed those that passed muster through the system, one after another. She was not shy about pressing Main Justice to move her paperwork. That part had worked. But the whole process would grind to a halt, she worried, if HIDTA was unable to handle the volume of intercepts.

Burlingame told Van Vliet he would pull his staff together that very afternoon to discuss the computer problems. Van Vliet thanked him.

In the hours that followed, Burlingame pondered his new assignment. What Van Vliet wanted, he knew, would require a powerful software program. It could not be bought off the shelf; it would have to be custom-made. That was all right with Burlingame. He had not exactly been relying on department stores all these years. Burlingame wasn't a programmer, but he knew some damned good ones. Some were on his staff; others could be called upon at the Missile Command. One of Douglas Hughes's smarter moves had been to figure out a way to have the Department of Defense assign military specialists to the HIDTA facility. They served as administrative staff and as technical advisers. For that reason, it had not mattered that the FBI and the DEA were unwilling to share their equipment and technical expertise. The computer jocks from the military were happy to assist HIDTA.

Knowing that, Burlingame was reasonably confident. Between his staff and the Pentagon's computer jocks, he believed, he could come up with a solution to Theresa Van Vliet's problem. Burlingame had been at the HIDTA offices for just a few short months. Already, though, the way he saw it, anything Theresa Van Vliet wanted was Job Number One.

It was time to go see Theresa. Edward Kacerosky had met a lot of prosecutors in his nineteen years on the job. There were only a few he cared to work with. Too many prosecutors, in his opinion, were just getting their tickets punched on the way to far more lucrative work in private practice. Or else they were lifers whose niche in the bureaucracy made them averse to taking risks, or overly religious about going home at 5 P.M. That was definitely not Theresa Van Vliet's problem, Kacerosky knew. He had never met a prosecutor who put in longer hours or ran a tighter ship. And she was obviously bright as hell. Aside from his jump shot on a basketball court, Kacerosky was vain about nothing so much as his memory for detail. Yet Van Vliet caught him out every so often on small errors of fact. That got his attention.

There were other things about Van Vliet that impressed Kacerosky. Rarely had he heard a woman talk as tough, giving back as good as she got. She expected everyone to work as hard as she did, and the few who did not were offered no second chances. When Van Vliet lit into an agent for screwing up, it made everyone wince. At the same time, though, she knew how to work the higher-ups. Kacerosky delighted in listening to her take calls from supervisors. Van Vliet's manner then was the essence of collegiality.

Kacerosky had new business to discuss with Van Vliet. He had gotten to know quite a lot about Raúl Martí and his family. The Martís lived in an upper-middle-class neighborhood in southwest Miami. In their driveway was a white Mercury Sable registered to Taino Coffee and Food Importers, Inc. The car had been an early clue to Martí's dual existence. Kacerosky learned that the Cuban businessman regularly employed an alias—Luís Durán. He also kept an apartment on the other side of town. As Durán, Raúl Martí was registered in official incorporation documents as the president of Taino Coffee. Since the first morning it opened for business, Kacerosky learned, Taino Coffee had received eleven shipments of bulk coffee from Panama. That was interesting because Panama does not produce coffee. The shipping company in Panama with which Martí's Taino Coffee was doing business was owned by a man wanted on narcotics-trafficking charges in Mexico. That was even more interesting.

Kacerosky and other agents had begun following Martí. All day long the president of Taino Coffee stopped at banks of public telephones and made calls. Raúl Martí had an office with a phone, but he rarely used it. Kacerosky suspected that Martí was using the pay phones to oversee his end of the drug shipments. A wiretap would help reveal what Martí was up to. But there was insufficient evidence to tap his home or office phones—and he appeared not to be using those anyway. There was only one other thing to do, Kacerosky thought: tap the pay phones.

At the HIDTA offices west of Miami International Airport, Kacerosky sought out prosecutor Edward Ryan, who, with William Pearson, had won the conviction of Harold Ackerman. "I found a new route," Kacerosky told Ryan, smiling broadly. Hurriedly, the Customs Service investigator rattled off the details of the life and times of Raul Martí. After noting the man's odd telephone habits, Kacerosky explained that there was something called a "roving" wiretap that would allow them to tap dozens of public pay phones.

Ryan looked up, amazed. He had no idea such a thing could be done. After studying the law, the prosecutor started telephoning around the country looking for other assistant U.S. attorneys who had used the technique. Roving wiretaps were not common, but they were doable. In the days that followed, Kacerosky got to work on an affidavit, blending his own detective work with the statements from Ackerman. Ryan took the affidavit and prepared a formal application that would pass muster at Main Justice.

By mid-August, the paperwork was ready. Kacerosky and Ryan

walked the documents into Theresa Van Vliet's office and showed her their handiwork. Ryan thought of Van Vliet as a source of "constant moving energy," but now she sat back in her chair and read slowly. Watching her, Ryan recognized the reaction. "She was getting that smile on her face," he said.

As she read, it took Van Vliet a moment to grasp the implications of Kacerosky's and Ryan's proposal. Then her smile widened. Here was the Customs agent whose work had already culminated in some of the largest cocaine seizures in the hemisphere. He had been the case agent on the most important Cali cartel prosecution ever brought to trial in the United States. Now, it appeared, he wanted to launch another damn-all investigation. Well, Van Vliet wondered, why not?

Once again, Edward Kacerosky and the prosecutors would seek to extend the reach of a wiretap. This time, however, they had to explain why they needed the authority to tap public pay phones in a major American city—phones any law-abiding citizen might drop a quarter into to call home to a spouse or touch base with an employer. After Van Vliet gave her okay, Ryan put the finishing touches on the paperwork for Main Justice.

On August 18, 1993, the application for a roving wiretap on public telephones in South Florida used by Raúl Martí arrived at a tall office building in the District of Columbia. This building, Washington Center, is the place where the Criminal Division administers the federal government's most powerful weapons against organized crime, including electronic surveillance, the witness security program and the racketeering statutes.

The wiretap application was accompanied by Kacerosky's affidavit summarizing his investigation. It was delivered to the Office of Enforcement Operations, the unit that screens proposals to install telephone wiretaps or hidden microphones during federal investigations.

The Martí case was assigned to staff attorney Janet D. Webb. A career prosecutor who joined the Criminal Division after ten years as a county prosecutor in Maryland, Webb had worked in the Fraud and Narcotics and Dangerous Drugs sections before taking a job that involved close study of the federal wiretapping statute. Enforcement Operations is one of those invisible units in the Criminal Division whose role is pivotal to both the war on crime and efforts to preserve constitutional rights. The Title III statute under which wiretaps are installed made the attorney general personally responsible for their authorization. The possibilities for abusing the statute are obvious. It was the attorney general's job to make sure wiretaps were not abused, even in a good cause. That authority was delegated to a deputy assistant attorney general in the Criminal Division, who in turn relied on the recommendation of the Enforcement Operations office.

It was rare for lawyers in the office to reject a proposed wiretap. Out of more than a thousand applications a year—for a new wiretap or to reauthorize an existing tap—the Criminal Division might deny ten. A denial always involved review by senior officials.

Frederick D. Hess, the longtime director of Enforcement Operations, knew exactly how many times a federal court had suppressed wiretap evidence because it thought the surveillance was improperly authorized: only once in twenty-five years. Part of the reason for this impressive record was that the Criminal Division insisted on a level of proof, known as probable cause, that was several notches above what most trial judges would accept. If prosecutors could clear the division's slightly higher hurdle, they were virtually certain to satisfy the courts.

The Title III law requires a federal judge to approve a wiretap application before a recording device could be installed. Most did so routinely. By the time they saw the application, judges knew that it had been screened by a lawyer in the Criminal Division, someone like Janet Webb. "We are in essence exercising the Fourth Amendment here," Hess explained. "And we are not going to seize a person's conversation unless the statute and the Constitution are satisfied. No one, not even the government, should listen to anyone's conversation unless there is probable cause to believe that a crime is being committed under the statute, that it is being committed over the specific phone and that it is being committed by the people we have listed in our affidavit."

When Webb's supervisor, Maureen Killion, gave Webb the application for the roving wiretap from Theresa Van Vliet, Killion said she had some reservations. Once Webb started reading, she could see why. Kacerosky's affidavit had two compelling narrative threads. The first summarized the evidence from the Ackerman case and what it showed about the operations of Miguel Rodríguez Orejuela. The second told the story of the circumstantial evidence Kacerosky had gathered against Raúl Martí.

To Webb, it was perfectly obvious that Raúl Martí deserved to be investigated. At the same time, however, Webb saw what she considered two big holes in the affidavit.

First, there was no evidence that indicated who Martí was talking to when he used the pay telephones and whether such conversations had anything to do with drug smuggling. This omission went to a basic question that the Title III statute wanted answered: Is there proof that the target telephone is currently being used for a criminal purpose? The lawyers in the Enforcement Operations office call this the "dirty call" question. In most cases the answer is provided by hard proof, such as statements the suspect makes to an undercover agent, telephone toll records or incriminating conversations intercepted by other wiretaps.

The second missing element was even more basic. This was a proposed drug case, yet there was no direct proof of the presence of cocaine in Raúl Martí's coffee shipments. Kacerosky could prove that Martí had once worked for Ackerman and that he was using an alias in his coffee business. But there was no evidence that cocaine had been smuggled through his coffee-import company. To the contrary, the affidavit reported that Customs inspectors had looked at some of Martí's coffee and found no cocaine.

Webb could see that the Martí case was important; no one needed to explain to her the urgency of pursuing Miguel Rodríguez Orejuela. Enforcement Operations was a nexus in federal law enforcement, and as such it had a panoramic view. Webb and her colleagues reviewed wiretap affidavits submitted by every federal district. As a rule, these documents laid out all the latest evidence against the largest criminal organizations, be they Mafia families or drug cartels. Nevertheless, Webb's job was to screen each application according to the standards of Main Justice. The review involved a technical and legal analysis of the facts. So far as Janet Webb could see, the Martí proposal did not meet the test.

Once she reached this judgment, Webb began looking for ways to cure the affidavit's ills. Frederick Hess, the director of the office, wanted his reviewers to use common sense and help solve problems as they were discovered. Webb talked with Theresa Van Vliet and suggested that they obtain telephone toll records showing calls by Martí to known cartel phone numbers. It would be even better, Webb said, if Customs could do a discreet "border search" of a Martí coffee shipment and establish that it contained cocaine.

Van Vliet countered that she and Kacerosky had already considered these steps. The phone company could not provide toll records of calls made from public phones. Besides, time was of the essence. A new load of Martí coffee had already arrived. If it contained cocaine, it was likely that Martí would be discussing logistics with his confederates. Kacerosky wanted to intercept these conversations.

In Van Vliet's view, the border search was equally problematic. They had learned during the Ackerman case that cartel operatives watched their shipments at U.S. ports to see if they attracted any special attention from Customs inspectors. Martí's new load had already moved out of the Customs area and into a warehouse. A search at this point would almost certainly tip off the cartel. Besides, Van Vliet insisted, the probable cause outlined in her affidavit was more than sufficient. She was sure a judge in South Florida, looking at the same facts, would approve the application. The Enforcement Operations staff ought to do the same so they could get on with the business of fighting the Cali cartel.

After more review Webb and her supervisor, Maureen Killion, tried to resolve the impasse with a conference call. Maybe by talking out the problems with Van Vliet and Kacerosky they could come up with a solution. Within minutes, however, it became clear there was little common ground. Washington thought Miami was being unreasonable. They were asking for the most intrusive kind of electronic surveillance, an open-ended roving wiretap good for any public telephone Martí happened to use, but they were unwilling to do the necessary homework. Miami thought Washington was nervous about approving a roving wiretap and was looking for reasons to turn down the application.

Standing around the speakerphone at the HIDTA office in Miami, Van Vliet and Kacerosky defended their work. Martí was obviously a player in the drug business, they argued. He had a phony import company and was using a fake name. He had been listed in Harold Ackerman's smuggling records, and Ackerman had confirmed that Martí was setting up a new smuggling route using coffee shipments as a cover. Moreover, Martí was clearly making unusual use of public telephones.

Webb countered sharply. There was no information suggesting the imminent arrival of cocaine, she said. Kacerosky was making an educated guess. As a legal matter, Kacerosky had not established that Martí was using public telephones to arrange drug shipments. In fact, based on all she had seen, Webb said, she did not personally believe there was cocaine in Martí's shipments of coffee.

Kacerosky was incredulous, his tone edging toward belligerence. The proof was deductive, he argued. Martí was importing coffee from Panama, a country that does not produce it. The legitimate shipments of coffee that his company had received were part of the scheme. The cartel assumed the early shipments would be searched. They sent clean loads so Customs inspectors would be lulled into waiving later shipments straight through. To Kacerosky, Webb was being obtuse. It was the difference between the square corners cut in Washington and the blurred edges he had to deal with in Miami. Webb wanted him to draw a straight line from point A to point B, but straight lines didn't begin to address the way things worked on the street.

Van Vliet got more than a little testy. It was as close as she had ever come to yelling at a lawyer from Main Justice. Politely but forcefully, she disagreed with Webb and Killion. The probable cause outlined in the affidavit was more than sufficient, she argued, particularly in light of the indications that Martí was fronting for the Cali cartel. The two sides went back and forth, but the conference call failed to end the dispute.

Webb wrote a memorandum that described the problems with the affidavit. She and Killion had tried to avoid a denial; it was always easier to approve a wiretap. Saying no, as Webb had decided to do, involved contention and the possibility of an appeal by the U.S. Attorney's Office. Almost always, a denial was taken as an affront by the prosecutor in the field. On a more personal level, there was the risk that later events would make the Criminal Division look silly or myopic. In this case they were rejecting an application from one of the country's most experienced drug prosecutors. Theresa Van Vliet had demonstrated repeatedly that she was a canny judge of what the courts in South Florida would approve.

Nevertheless, Webb recommended denial. Soon after, the file was sent to Frederick Hess for review. After reading Webb's evaluation, he concurred with her judgment. The affidavit did not meet their standards. Hess wrote a note to this effect and sent the file on to the next level of review. This involved transferring the paperwork from Washington Center to the Main Justice headquarters building on Constitution Avenue.

Now encrusted with memos from various reviewers, Janet Webb's denial landed on the desk of Jack Keeney. He went over the file again and then made a final decision. Webb was right, he decided. The application lacked sufficient probable cause. Main Justice would not approve a roving wiretap for public telephones in South Florida. Van Vliet and Kacerosky would have to find another way.

In Miami, Van Vliet looked over the affidavit once again. She knew probable cause when she saw it. If Webb wanted to be a purist, that was fine. But Main Justice didn't control everything. She could still, by God, go before a federal magistrate and get a search warrant for Raúl Martí's coffee shipments.

That became Plan B. After the conversation with Webb, Van Vliet sat down at her computer and started to cut and paste. She rewrote the affidavit for a roving wiretap so that it became an application for a search warrant. A new shipment of coffee had arrived for Taino Coffee at the Port of Miami. Some of the product was shipped about thirty miles north, to Port Everglades, just south of downtown Fort Lauderdale. As Van Vliet expected, within days, a magistrate read the new affidavit and authorized searches at both locations.

Just for the hell of it, Van Vliet decided to ride along with the agents to watch the search. As she had extended herself on this case, it would be gratifying to see the follow-through. They went first to Port Everglades in Fort Lauderdale, where it was pouring and hard to see. A big thunderstorm had come in off the ocean. When they found the right loading dock, the investigators brought in a dog. It sniffed around Raúl Martí's load of coffee but did not react positively to cocaine.

That was troubling, but not conclusive. The odor of coffee could mask the smell of cocaine. The agents cut open the containers. They dug through the beans—and they came up with nothing—no cocaine. In the process, Louis Weiss, the DEA agent helping with the case, cut himself. There was blood everywhere. The agents gave up and resealed the coffee containers. A frustrated Van Vliet drove Agent Weiss to a hospital and waited in silence while his hand was stitched. Later, Van Vliet and Weiss met Kacerosky and the other agents at a small roadside bar. It was a sea shanty–type place, one of those rough-hewn South Florida hangouts where cops and construction workers drink cold beer and wolf conch fritters. Around the table the mood was grim. Van Vliet didn't know which was worse, not finding the cocaine or having to admit to Main Justice that her instincts were less than perfect. They had moved heaven and earth, and all they had found was a load of fragrant coffee beans.

The agents and the prosecutor drank a lot of beer, tried out a lot of theories. Martí was moving tonnage, Kacerosky said, there was no doubt about it, just not this time. They would get him next month. The guy's number was definitely up. The Customs agent was still annoyed about Main Justice. He couldn't believe Janet Webb had been so fixated on whether there was cocaine in the coffee. To Kacerosky's mind, the cocaine was secondary. Seizing a single shipment of cocaine was no triumph, not in Miami. What mattered was identifying the organization, the people Raúl Martí was dealing with in Colombia. Those were the targets. It was their voices Kacerosky wanted on tape.

When Kacerosky drove home that night, he was as close to drunk as he had been in twenty years. On the way, he pulled over to the side of the road. Seated in his car, he stared up into the clear night sky. What had he missed? Kacerosky asked himself. What the hell had he overlooked?

The next morning, long before his hangover went away, Kacerosky was headed in to work when a call came in on his mobile phone. It was another agent working the Cornerstone case. He reported that a surveillance team watching the Taino warehouse in Miami had seen some activity. A rental truck had just pulled to the back door. Follow the truck, Kacerosky ordered.

The agents shadowed the rental truck to a house south of Miami. Two days later, after obtaining another search warrant, the agents raided the home. Inside they discovered 5,600 kilograms of cocaine. Raúl Martí had split his shipments, it turned out. He had sent a legitimate load of coffee to Fort Lauderdale; the one with cocaine he had kept in Miami. The raid brought the total amount of cocaine seized in Operation Cornerstone to nearly 30,000 kilos, roughly 33 tons. More important, it opened up new vistas for Kacerosky and his colleagues to explore.

To Kacerosky, the case was instructive. It proved what they were up against. The Cali cartel's network of coca farms and processing labs was an agricultural combine, an assembly line that never stopped churning out processed cocaine. The Cali cartel had absorbed the big hits from Operation Cornerstone with hardly a shudder. The supply of cocaine in the cartel's warehouses in Colombia was undiminished. All they had to do was set up another route, find another middleman. As Raúl Martí had shown, there was always another aspiring entrepreneur willing to take the place of the fallen, the tumbled functionaries like Harold Ackerman.

Not long after the arrest of Raúl Martí, in July 1993, Edward Kacerosky and his bosses in the U.S. Customs Service got religion. Operation Cornerstone was bigger than they had planned for. It was beginning to look like one of the biggest cartel-related cases ever. That made it wise to reconsider the offer of Theresa Van Vliet and Douglas Hughes to move the case to HIDTA.

Kacerosky was spending more time at HIDTA with the two prosecutors who had handled the Ackerman case, Edward Ryan and Bill Pearson. Kacerosky was intensely competitive, especially when it came to the DEA. Throughout much of the Ackerman investigation, he and the prosecutors had kept the most sensitive information to themselves, sharing it with the DEA on a need-to-know basis. But it was hard to maintain that attitude at HIDTA. The whole setup conspired to break down the walls that naturally grew up between the various federal police-agency fiefdoms.

Nearly everyone assigned to the HIDTA facility found it a terrific place to work. The agents and detectives were assigned to groups of about twenty investigators. These squads were a mix of local police detectives and agents from the FBI, DEA, IRS and the Bureau of Alcohol, Tobacco and Firearms. As the facility produced successes like the Ackerman case, word got around. Many of the best drug agents gravitated to HIDTA. It was a place where things got done right. One reason for that was the full complement of federal prosecutors at the facility. They specialized in big narcotics prosecutions and gave HIDTA projects lots of careful attention. Douglas Hughes, the HIDTA director, encouraged collegiality; he shunned supervisors who were turf conscious. Hughes arranged for the agents and cops assigned to HIDTA to have access to a nearby gym operated by the Metro-Dade Police Department. Some even took to calling themselves HIDTA agents. They all had to account to their own agencies, of course, but Hughes let each agency claim HIDTA arrests as its own. That kept the bureaucrats in Washington happy. Hughes had a strict rule about publicity: There would be none. HIDTA never issued press releases. Instead, Hughes let the agency bosses call in reporters and announce the big cases.

After work, the HIDTA investigators often repaired to a discreet little bar just down the street. The place was run by the Patrolmen's Benevolent Association. Over beers at the PBA—and near the punch bowl at the Customs Service Christmas party in 1993—Hughes and Van Vliet had continued to prod Kacerosky about the Cornerstone case. HIDTA had two major investigations going against the cartel in Cali, Van Vliet pointed out. One was an FBI-DEA money-laundering investigation. The other was a DEA smuggling-conspiracy case targeting an upper-class group of businessmen who exported cocaine to Europe and North America. Both cases showed promise, but neither had anywhere near the potential of Cornerstone for reaching the cartel's biggest bosses—Gilberto and Miguel Rodríguez Orejuela and José Santacruz Londoño. The way Van Vliet saw it, attacking the Colombian drug cartels was like solving a geometry equation. Correctly completing a series of individual exercises took you step-by-step to a final solution. The trick was to keep working the equation. Destroying a single drug-smuggling cell, even a large operation like that of the Urdinolas, was the equivalent of solving only part of the equation. It made for great newspaper headlines, but it got you only so far.

What it came down to, finally, was money. Operation Cornerstone was shaping up as a big, labor-intensive investigation. HIDTA was willing to foot the bill. To the U.S. Customs Service, that was more than appealing. Cornerstone would become a HIDTA case, they decided, worked jointly with the DEA. Louis Weiss, the DEA agent, would be a full partner in the investigation.

Hughes cleared out a large suite of offices for the project. From the beginning, HIDTA had been conceived as a launching platform for big drug prosecutions. Its infrastructure of surveillance electronics and its money were intended to help make cases like Cornerstone more than just theoretical possibilities.

After Customs agreed to move Operation Cornerstone to

HIDTA, Van Vliet sat down with the lawyers and agents and plot-
ted strategy. With Harold Ackerman cooperating, they knew it
was possible—just possible—that they could develop a chain of
evidence that would lead directly to the kingpins. By virtue of the
targets in the Cornerstone case, the resulting indictment was certain to receive a careful scrubbing from the Criminal Division of
Main Justice. Big Florida drug prosecutions had a way of blowing
up into even bigger foreign policy issues. The Miami indictment
of Panamanian dictator Manuel Noriega in 1989 had led ultimately to the invasion later that year of the tiny Central American isthmus in the first year of George Bush's presidency. It had
cost many lives to apprehend Noriega and bring him to Miami for
trial. A Tampa-based money-laundering investigation by the U.S.
Customs Service during the same period resulted in the exposure
of the rogue Bank of Credit and Commerce International (BCCI)
and one of history's largest international bank failures. The combination of the size of the target and the national security implications of the case ensured that, before too long, Edward
Kacerosky, Louis Weiss and the Cornerstone prosecutors would be
having to answer some tough questions from Main Justice.

CHAPTER SIX

GUNS AND GANGS

In the administration of Ronald Reagan, the joke used to be that the right hand didn't know what the far-right hand was doing. At Main Justice, while there were any number of ideological struggles, the real problem was one of scale. The place was just so big. When Mary Incontro read about the Clinton administration's anti-violence initiative in the newspaper, she called a friend and mentor. David Margolis listened to her description of the plan that she had put together with Jim Reynolds. He promised to find out what was going on, then put the two Criminal Division lawyers in touch with the right people.

Jim Reynolds is a slim, fair-haired man who had cut his professional teeth as a prosecutor in the Army's Judge Advocate General's Corps. Promoted to take charge of the Terrorism and Violent Crime Section of the Criminal Division in 1991, Reynolds was part of that generation at Main Justice that was a half step behind the likes of David Margolis and Michael Shaheen.

Reynolds had spent a lot of time thinking about what the Justice Department could do to stem the tide of violence sweeping the nation. During the last half of the Bush administration the issue registered deeply with the American public, particularly during the early 1990s, when the number of violent crimes began to soar. In the final two years of the Bush administration lawyers at Main Justice had cast around for ways the Justice Department could make a difference.

On a bitterly cold day in January 1991, Robert Mueller, the assistant attorney general in charge of the Criminal Division, convened a meeting in his second-floor office at Main Justice. Though he was a Bush political appointee, Mueller was also a veteran prosecutor, well regarded by career lawyers in the Criminal Division like Reynolds.

Mueller wanted to create a new Terrorism and Violent Crime Section in the division, he told Reynolds and the other lawyers present. He knew what he wanted to do in the area of terrorism. The FBI was set up to go after that problem. But what about street violence? How should they handle that? It was a difficult question. Indeed, many in the federal government thought it was a question that didn't need to be asked, believing that violent crime was the responsibility of local law enforcement. Reynolds's own concerns were pragmatic. Without a cohesive plan, he worried, a Justice Department effort to counter violent crime could wind up frittering away millions of dollars while accomplishing little or nothing.

Mueller had summoned lawyers from the Justice Department's Office of Policy Planning and Analysis to discuss the problem. Reynolds sat quietly and listened as these lawyers explained their ideas. "It was social service work," Reynolds recalled, "not very specific. It was a little like trying to pick Jell-O up off the floor." There was a place for such ideas, Reynolds believed, but they were no substitute for prosecuting violent criminals and incarcerating them for long periods.

Mueller, finally, turned to Reynolds. What are your thoughts, Jim? What should we focus on?

Reynolds was blunt. "Guns and gangs," he replied.

Mueller asked the prosecutor to elaborate.

The Justice Department had always known, Reynolds explained, that there were ways to play the federal system off against the state courts and thereby enhance the penalties for armed career criminals who were arrested by local police. Defendants in state cases could be charged under federal firearms statutes. All federal agents had to do was harvest these cases from the local courts and have them refiled as federal prosecutions that would then bring stiffer sentences. It was a cheap and easy way to have an impact on the more serious armed offenders.

As to gangs, Reynolds continued, the Justice Department should aim its limited resources at the most notorious street violence without getting bogged down in an endless reaction to random crime. Federal task forces could target the toughest big gangs in each city. They could reach into the inner cities and rip out these weeds by the roots.

Mueller was intrigued.

Reynolds pressed ahead. For a gang initiative to work, he said, there would have to be coordination from Washington to keep the U.S. attorneys focused on the targets. One district could take on a single branch of the Crips, but that would still leave the larger organization untouched. The Justice Department could do better than that. There had already been plenty of big gang prosecutions. The cases proved that, for all their fearsome aspect, the gangs were relatively unsophisticated. Most street gangs took few of the precautions that the Italian Mafia considered standard operating procedure. The gangs were not easy targets, but once identified, they could be hit hard.

Mueller asked Reynolds to put his ideas on paper. It was a Friday afternoon. Reynolds went back to his office, on the Pennsylvania Avenue side of Main Justice. The ideas were fresh in his mind. He decided to confide them to his word processor before leaving for the weekend. The result, Reynolds recalled, was "a very informal memo."

Mueller read the memo and liked it. It was just the kind of plan the Justice Department needed, he decided, because it focused closely on what the federal government could do against gangs that local police could not. "The feds have unique assets," Reynolds explained. "The use of informants, wiretaps, the witness protection program."

In the parlance of the bureaucracy, Reynolds's informal memo would "have legs." In March 1991, two months after the meeting in Bob Mueller's office, Attorney General Dick Thornburgh announced the "guns" portion of Reynolds's "guns and gangs" plan. It was given a dramatic name: Operation Triggerlock. As Reynolds had suggested, it would use heavier federal firearms statutes to put felons who used guns in the commission of local crimes behind bars for longer periods.

Everyone loved Triggerlock. It required almost no additional funding, and it had the potential to run up big, impressive numbers of convictions. The Bush administration was not ready to move on the "gangs" portion of Reynolds's memo, however. That would have a longer start-up time and require a lot more coordination with the federal police agencies. Reynolds continued to refine his proposal. He had all the top security clearances and access to the freshest intelligence data. And he had a staff that kept coming up with new ideas that might work.

From his seat in Main Justice, Reynolds knew more than most people just how the nation's cities had been transformed into embattled enclaves by violent street gangs. In 1990, as part of a full-scale Justice Department review of its strategy for targeting organized crime, every U.S. Attorney's Office in the nation had been asked to submit detailed reports to Main Justice describing the most serious crime problems in their districts. Most of the larger offices had reported that La Cosa Nostra, the Italian Mafia, remained the most dangerous and entrenched criminal organization in their cities, followed closely by the newly emergent Asian crime syndicates. From city to city, the U.S. attorneys reported, a third category of crime group had muscled its way into the big picture. Under the reporting requirements established by Main Justice, these had to be given a name. They were called "Other Criminal Groups."

These were large, institutionalized street gangs that terrorized big housing projects and inner-city street corners. They were violent motorcycle clubs, whose members trafficked in everything from prostitutes to stolen motorcycle parts to narcotic contraband. Some of the "Other Criminal Groups" had been in business for two decades. The most powerful had spread their tentacles across the nation.

The biggest gangs, which had thousands of members, were the Crips and the Bloods, both products of the mean streets of Los Angeles. The Crips and Bloods had strong entrepreneurial instincts. Like rival chains of successful hamburger outlets, they had established franchises—"sets" as the gangs called their affiliate groups—across the nation. They were the McDonald's and Burger King of organized thuggery. The hamburger chain metaphor was not overblown, Reynolds believed. By the early 1990s, the Crips and the Bloods had chapters in fifty-eight cities and thirty-five states. Their main business was drugs. They purchased bulk cocaine in Los Angeles, then undercut the market in places like Denver and Phoenix. The result: more coke on the street, more violent crime.

The success of the Crips and the Bloods had begotten a number of imitators, primarily in Chicago. The three largest crime gangs there were the Gangster Disciples, the Vice Lords and the Latin Kings. They, too, had spread to other states, primarily in the Midwest and Northeast, where they had organized the distribution of crack cocaine.

From these data, the Criminal Division produced maps that showed the location of the big street gangs by state. It was like looking at biopsies of a lethal, fast-moving cancer.

As if the Crips, Bloods and their progeny were not enough, there were the outlaw motorcycle gangs. The FBI had identified more than two hundred such groups. They had operations in thirty-four states. The Hell's Angels alone had somewhere between 600 and 700 full-fledged members and countless associates. The gang was believed to control the distribution of virtually all illegal methamphetamine on the West Coast. The Pagans, another motorcycle gang with some 200 members, dealt heavily in the drug PCP. Others included the Outlaws (430 members), the

Bandidos (350 members), the Vagos (300 members) and the Sons of Silence (160 members).

While casual violence was a way of life with the street gangs and bikers, none exceeded the Jamaican "posses" for sheer wantonness and brutality. Among the violent gangs in the United States, the Jamaican posses had experienced the most rapid growth, their ranks fed by a seemingly endless supply of hungry, hardened youths recruited from the fetid slums of Kingston. Would-be posse members typically entered the United States on agricultural visas, then disappeared. By the early 1990s, Justice Department intelligence reports identified forty separate Jamaican posses operating within the United States and linked them with at least 3,000 murders since 1985. With a total membership estimated at 20,000, the posses were thought to handle 30 percent of all crack cocaine distributed in major American cities. The largest were the Shower Posse (5,400 members) and the Spangler Posse (4,600 members). The two gangs were so named for their practice of "showering" and "spangling" their enemies with bullets. As the department's 1991 *National Organized Crime Strategy* report put it: "The [posses] appear preoccupied with firearms and violence and display a willingness to use torture that is rare even among gangsters."

Reynolds believed the street gangs, the outlaw bikers and the posses were the targets most worthy of attention by Main Justice. They were a nationwide crime problem that federal prosecutors could, and should, address. Anyone who watched television news in the District of Columbia was familiar with the body bags and gun battles. What people didn't realize, though, were the limits on Main Justice. Its resources were spread over a vast landscape of jurisdiction.

That was the conundrum Reynolds and his colleagues faced during their planning for Robert Mueller. What could Main Justice do with its limited resources to make a difference? Reynolds was convinced they had produced a workable plan for targeting big street gangs, but it had lain dormant through the dying days of the Bush administration. And although Reynolds had slipped a copy of the proposal to the lawyers conducting the Clinton transition team's review of the Justice Department, the anti-gangs proposal had continued to languish during the first few months of the Clinton administration. Janet Reno would change that.

On November 19, 1993, Reno beamed proudly as Jo Ann Harris was sworn in as the new assistant attorney general to lead the Criminal Division. Technically, the appointment was a political one. Jo Ann Harris was no politician, however. She had been both a top-notch prosecutor in New York and a section chief at Main Justice. That's why Reno wanted her for the job.

During the Carter administration Philip Heymann had reached out to Harris, who was then working as a white-collar crimes prosecutor in the U.S. Attorney's Office in Manhattan, to offer her a job at Main Justice. The U.S. Attorney's Office in Manhattan is responsible for prosecutions of federal crimes in what is known as the Southern District of New York. Such was its reputation that federal prosecutors in Washington and across the nation refer to the Manhattan office as the "sovereign district" office. Heymann asked Harris to run the Fraud Section in the Criminal Division, then already on its way to becoming one of the most muscular operations within the Justice Department. Harris was unimpressed. "Phil walked me around the Mall," Harris recalled, "and he really had to do a sales job on me."

Heymann's persistence prevailed. Harris came to Washington to work with Jack Keeney, Mark Richard and David Margolis. It was Harris who had called Keeney "the glue that holds the world together." In a few short years in Washington, she had come to appreciate the traditions of the Criminal Division. Had there been an attorney general other than Janet Reno, however, Harris would have declined the Criminal Division job. "I really shared her strong feelings about how you go about solving the problem of crime in this country," Harris said. Though she had lived in Manhattan for years, Harris had roots in Illinois, the heartland. "I just really feel that what Janet is saying is connecting with the people where I come from."

It was not just her midwestern roots that persuaded Harris to come work for Reno. The attorney general's concerns about violent crime particularly impressed Harris. It had taken Reno several months after her confirmation as attorney general to begin exerting her influence in all the areas she wanted. By the time Jo Ann Harris was sworn in, Reno had key members of her team in place, and she had made it known to all of them that she intended to make a major push on violent crime.

Jo Ann Harris endorsed the idea, cautiously. She had not come directly to the law. She had been a magazine journalist in New York until deciding, at age thirty-six, to become a lawyer. Law degree in hand, she had spent several years representing battered women, doing pro bono work. Eventually, she joined the U.S. Attorney's Office in Manhattan, opting to take criminals off the street instead of defending their victims after the fact. It was after she became a prosecutor, returning from the office in Lower Manhattan to her apartment on Upper Broadway one night, that Harris became the victim of a violent attack. "I got into my vestibule, I had my key in the lock, and I got grabbed from behind," Harris recalled. "I had a handbag over my shoulder, and he had a knife, and I whirled around."

From someone else, the reaction might not have frightened the would-be robber. But Harris is six feet tall and in great physical condition. In her early forties, she continued to star as the sharp-elbowed center for the women's basketball team of the U.S. Attorney's Office in an intensely competitive league. Startled, the robber began to flee. "I totally lost it," Harris related. "I attacked the guy . . . then the guy grabbed my wallet, and the next thing I knew, I was outside chasing him." The younger man was too fleet of foot. After Harris regained her breath, the episode left her shaking. "I didn't walk home the same way after that," she said, "for a year."

Not wishing to make more of the incident than it was, Harris had told few friends about it. Still, it taught her how lasting the impact of violence could be. When Reno first told her about the anti-violence initiative she hoped to begin in the Criminal Division, Harris was cautiously enthusiastic. She believed violent crime ought to be dealt with, but she just didn't know if Main Justice could do much about the problem. "For a new administration to come in and say, 'We're going to target violent crime,' " Harris said, "to me, that was just laughable."

Reno's vision inspired Harris to take up the challenge. Very quickly, she became encouraged. The "guns and gangs" plan that had been developed by Jim Reynolds and Mary Incontro during the Bush administration was the reason. "What Jim and Mary proposed," Harris said, "really intersected with what the attorney general wanted to happen. They had visualized an initiative that really leveraged—or if not leveraged, caused—agencies to work with each other, to get into the sandbox, to get them to stop fighting and to play together."

In their original plan, Reynolds and Incontro had deliberately not suggested the creation of another new mini-bureaucracy within Main Justice. The answer, Reynolds believed, was to create a nationwide network of violent-crime task forces that targeted major street gangs and biker groups. "The goal of the [Justice] Department's violent-crime program," Reynolds wrote, "should be to forge a coalition of all pertinent federal, state and local law enforcement entities so that our efforts can be cooperatively channeled in a manner which most effectively targets for prosecution and incarceration the major violators, career criminals and gang members." In other words, the federal agencies needed to work with the locals.

Reynolds did not want to see the creation of anything like the centrally managed Criminal Division Strike Forces that Robert Kennedy had established as attorney general to combat the Italian Mafia. Rather, he believed, U.S. attorneys ought to take the lead in running violent-crime task forces.

But that posed problems. If the violent-crime task forces were supervised by a local assistant U.S. attorney, there was no way to ensure that the FBI or the DEA would cooperate. The special agents–in–charge of FBI and DEA field offices across the nation considered themselves autonomous administrators, and many did not take kindly to direction from prosecutors. They would be inclined to follow the priorities set by their respective headquarters. As vexing as the bureaucratic problems were, the diffused nature of the gangs to be targeted was worse. The nation's biggest institutionalized gangs, the intelligence reports showed, had spread to numerous cities. Significant gang investigations could quite likely involve several federal districts.

These were two areas, Reynolds believed, where the Terrorism and Violent Crime Section could play a role. The section's lawyers could help pick the most sensible strategic targets, then make sure FBI and DEA headquarters signed onto plans to go after them. "The section could work with the headquarters of the pertinent law enforcement agencies to elicit their cooperation and input in the operation of the task forces," Reynolds wrote. "This will relieve the various violent crime task forces of having to separately obtain input and address problems encountered at the headquarters level."

The Criminal Division's narcotics section had taken a similar approach in its dealings with the nationwide system of organized crime–drug-enforcement task forces. Mary Lee Warren had kept everyone focused on the principal drug-trafficking groups to be targeted, but in most cases the local U.S. attorneys decided when to seek indictments. Reynolds was convinced that he could put together a similar constellation of task forces that would focus on the large street gangs that were terrorizing major cities. Such a program did not have to cost a lot of money, Reynolds believed. It could be done from existing resources.

Like Jo Ann Harris, Jim Reynolds brought a healthy skepticism to the question of what the Criminal Division could and could not do. Reynolds was particularly concerned that whatever they came up with not be looked at by local police as another intrusion by the FBI and other federal law-enforcement police agencies. In his first "very informal memo" on the anti-gangs initiative, Reynolds had devoted about a page to an explanation of why Main Justice should not "try to push the Bureau in on the locals." That would doom their plan. Harris and Reynolds had worked together in Washington years before. They had seen new initiatives come and go, money spent and little accomplished.

On the violence issue, Reynolds believed, success was achievable precisely because he understood the constraints under which a new program would have to operate. The Justice Department did not have the resources to patrol city streets, but it could make cases against the organized street gangs. "Gangs do not have to be a permanent part of our culture," Reynolds wrote, concluding his proposal to attack gang crime. "By effectively combining federal, state and local resources into violent crime task forces and coordinating the activities of these task forces, we can forge a nationwide effort that will rid our communities of violent gangs."

Jo Ann Harris believed the Reynolds-Incontro proposal had it just about right.

Like Reno, Harris put in long hours at Main Justice. She had taken up residence right around the corner from Reno, leasing rooms in the handsome Lansburgh apartments, just off Pennsylvania Avenue. Over the course of many meetings—some early in the morning, others late in the day—Harris and the other Criminal Division lawyers hammered out the details of the anti-violence plan. Harris was leery of overstepping her bounds. As a former "sovereign district" prosecutor in Manhattan, she knew how Washington was regarded by Justice Department lawyers in the field. "There was an historic tension between the Criminal Division and the U.S. Attorneys Offices," Harris said. "I really did know both sides of that." Running the Fraud Section of the Criminal Division twelve years earlier, Harris had seen how Philip Heymann, Jack Keeney and others had pushed U.S. attorneys, how they had guided them and helped them bring prosecutions that otherwise might not have been brought. "It is not easy for the Criminal Division to put together something that really *directs* the U.S. attorneys," Harris said, "but it really makes so much sense" on certain kinds of issues.

Violent crime was one of those issues, Harris believed. Making it a priority was Reno's idea. Now all they had to do was come up with a plan to make it happen.

Few projects at Main Justice have a single author. Early in the administration, Merrick Garland received a telephone call from Philip Heymann. Among those who worked with him, Garland was regarded as a "type triple-A personality." A quick, engaging man, yet another product of the Harvard Law School, Garland was gifted with sufficient energy and ability to balance several daunting projects at once. At the moment he was assigned to the Criminal Division.

After Jo Ann Harris had been nominated as the new head of the Criminal Division, Garland had been summoned to shepherd her through the confirmation process in the Senate, a task that had proven easy. Heymann came up with a second assignment for Garland. The attorney general was interested in having a new proposal for dealing with violent crime, Heymann said. If Garland was agreeable, Heymann would like to have him take the issue on as a project. Garland was happy to do it.

Though he had been working in private practice before the November election, Garland knew more than most people about violent crime. Like Mary Incontro, he had spent several years as an assistant U.S. attorney in Washington, D.C. One of his biggest prosecutions there had involved a violent street gang.

Digging into the assignment, Garland soon learned of the Reynolds-Incontro proposal for dealing with gangs. He found the document persuasive because it advocated leveraging federal powers to enhance local law enforcement.

There was nothing terribly new in the idea of leverage. Twelve years earlier, William French Smith, Ronald Reagan's first attorney general, had come to Washington with the idea of aiming the resources of the Criminal Division at violent crime. How to do it, though? Smith commissioned something called the Attorney General's Task Force on Violent Crime. The panel had two chairmen, Griffin Bell, Jimmy Carter's attorney general, and James R. Thompson, the former governor of Illinois who had served as a very successful federal prosecutor. After holding hearings throughout the country, Bell and Thompson had delivered a sweeping plan for federalizing criminal law enforcement. The chief effect of their recommendations—most of which were ultimately adopted or expanded upon—was to enlarge the role of the federal prosecutor in American cities.

As its premise, the Bell-Thompson task force envisioned a more prominent national role for the attorney general. "The attorney general should exercise leadership in informing the

American public about the extent of violent crime," one recommendation said. It also contemplated making the federal courts a place where justice was swifter and more certain. Bell and Thompson recommended changing the bail laws to allow pretrial detention of some violent criminals, criticized the exclusionary rule on evidence as being overly restrictive and called for mandatory minimum sentences for some categories of crimes.

The Bell-Thompson report urged a more robust role for U.S. attorneys. It was no longer enough for the department's top local prosecutors to simply represent the federal government in court. They were urged to take the lead in organizing all law-enforcement agencies in a coordinated attack on violent crime. The attorney general should "mandate" that U.S. attorneys form Law Enforcement Coordinating Committees in each district, the report said. The coordinating committees would be comprised of local, state and federal officials. Together these local and federal law-enforcement agencies were to plot a joint strategy against crime in their cities, blending their powers and their personnel. "U.S. Attorneys should be responsible," the task force report concluded, "for ensuring the proper participation of all federal law enforcement agencies."

The vision embraced by Bell-Thompson was a fundamental, perhaps historic departure from the past. It drew on momentum that had been building within the nation's criminal justice system since at least the Kennedy administration. The last great leap forward in federal police power had come with the 1968 Omnibus Crime Control and Safe Streets Act. That law gives federal police agencies the ability to wiretap phones, compel immunized testimony from witnesses and file racketeering indictments.

Griffin Bell and James Thompson were pragmatists. The new crime legislation had created the potential for the Justice Department's lawyers to become the most powerful federal prosecutors in American history. What remained was to turn the institution to a more systematic exploitation of those new powers. Bell and Thompson offered fifty-eight recommendations that endeavored to do just that, among them cross-designating state attorneys as federal prosecutors and charging felons arrested with guns under federal firearms statutes, not the weaker state laws.

All of this was suggested in the name of fighting violence. The authors of the report commissioned by William French Smith recognized the enormity of what they were proposing and how it would change the role of the U.S. Justice Department. They saw clearly the risk that their approach posed to the balance of powers in the U.S. Constitution, but they explained that they were acting under duress. "A free society presupposes an orderly community," Bell and Thompson wrote. "The Constitution of the United States, in its preamble, announces that among the purposes of the new union was to 'insure domestic tranquillity,' but nowhere in that document is there any provision for the federal government directly to police its citizens. The Founders sought to combine the advantages of a federal union and the virtue of individual liberty in order to achieve justice and the general welfare."

In its oblique elegance, Bell-Thompson framed the dilemma that confronted American society in the latter half of the twentieth century. "If the delicate balance between . . . the general good and personal freedom was to survive," the authors wrote, "the people of this nation would have to display forbearance, show one another mutual respect, and build self-regulating neighborhoods and communities. If order and tranquility could only be achieved by the exercise of government power, then a free society would be impossible."

A small but rapidly growing segment of American society had not shown respect and forbearance for its other members, however. Many neighborhoods and communities no longer were self-regulating. In too many neighborhoods and communities, the social fabric had been torn asunder by thugs and killers. Nevertheless, said Bell and Thompson, "We are mindful of the risk of assuming that the government can solve whatever problem it addresses. The preamble to the Constitution, after all, promises not only domestic tranquility but the blessing of liberty as well, and we must not risk losing the latter in order to achieve the former."

Those words could be taken as the epitaph for the U.S. Department of Justice as it had once been. No longer would the institution focus on a few federal concerns. Rather, it would start down the path toward a new and larger role in American life. The task force established by William French Smith saw violence and drug trafficking as two sides of the same coin. The final report urged bold federal action to combat both.

Paradoxically, despite Bell-Thompson's acute analysis of the problem of violent crime, the early Justice Department initiatives on violence were quickly subsumed by the efforts of the gathering drug war. Smith made a start at following through on the recommendations. His successor, Edwin Meese III, had different priorities. Meese emphasized pornography prosecutions and expanded the Justice Department's focus on international crime. Meese's successor, Richard Thornburgh, made drug enforcement his priority. It was not until the last half of the Bush administration that Attorney General William Barr returned in a substantive way to dealing with violent crime. One of the first anti-violence strategies Barr embraced, Operation Triggerlock, had been recommended by the Smith task force a decade earlier.

By the time Merrick Garland revisited the subject of violent crime in 1993, the old, agonizing issues about the role of the Justice Department had been settled. There was none of the anguished hand-wringing of the Bell-Thompson report. Through their elected representatives in Congress, Americans had demanded solutions. The only viable course Congress had seen was to create by law and by appropriations a big, powerful and proactive federal law-enforcement presence. In the war on crime, it was Washington's turn to lead.

As Garland read the Reynolds-Incontro proposal, he saw that was precisely what the two Criminal Division lawyers were advocating. Drafting his own report for Philip Heymann and Janet Reno, Garland adopted much of the Reynolds-Incontro plan. "The two-pronged effort is a national and regional attack on gang violence," Garland wrote, "and large drug trafficking organizations and a selective attack on street violence through cooperation and assistance to law enforcement."

Substantively, Garland knew, this could be accomplished in

different ways. The Reagan administration had created thirteen Organized Crime and Drug Enforcement Task Forces around the country. The Bush administration's Operation Triggerlock was bringing stiffer prison terms for local criminals who used guns by charging them with violations of federal firearms laws. Those efforts could be grafted onto new violent-crime task forces whose activities would be overseen by Criminal Division lawyers in Washington. The new task forces, Garland wrote, "should be organized by Main Justice and . . . staffed with lead federal law enforcement agencies, which should play a major intelligence and coordination function." The task forces could use wiretaps and grand juries to go after violent gangs as continuing criminal enterprises, a definition that allowed sentencing penalties as tough as those for racketeering. Garland argued Reynolds's core thesis: The Department of Justice should target those gangs with a nationwide presence, the ones local police simply could not deal with. Those gangs would include the Crips and the Bloods, the outlaw motorcycle gangs and the Jamaican posses.

Once it was finished, Garland's report made its way to Reno's desk. The guts of it was the Reynolds-Incontro plan to attack violent gangs.

After several days the attorney general summoned Garland. They had made great progress, she explained. But this was not how she wanted to proceed.

"Close, but not quite," Reno said.

CHAPTER SEVEN

TURNING THE BATTLESHIP

As the top local prosecutor in Miami, Janet Reno had been put upon more times than she could count by federal law-enforcement people telling her how she had to do her job, or explaining what the feds could do differently or better. Now that she was attorney general Reno wanted her Criminal Division lawyers to listen to state and local authorities, find out what they needed, then help them to help their communities. As a local state attorney "I used to be on the receiving end of them-versus-us," Reno told a gathering of federal prosecutors in Washington, D.C., during her first year in office. "I want to do away with that."

Sharing authority with local law enforcement was not a wildly popular notion among U.S. attorneys. The powerful federal prosecutor of the 1990s was a relatively new phenomenon in American history. In 1789, Congress passed the Judiciary Act, creating the position of United States attorney in every one of the federal districts. Under the law, U.S. attorneys represented the federal government in legal disputes, most of them civil. Over time, the balance shifted to criminal prosecutions. But it was not until the first administration of Ronald Reagan that the Justice Depart-

ment routinely referred to the U.S. attorney as the "chief law enforcement official" in each federal district. As their budgets and
legal authority grew, that is precisely what U.S. attorneys became.
By the early 1990s, most had no wish to share their power with
local law-enforcement agencies. More than a few viewed the locals as bumblers, or worse.

Reno knew that, but she was determined to find ways to transfer to local authorities the far greater legal powers of the federal
system, to create a powerful synergy between streetwise local cops
and federal agents and prosecutors. What she did not want to do,
however, was to pursue this goal by laying on more oversight from
Main Justice. She didn't want U.S. attorneys lording it over local
officials; she didn't want Main Justice getting heavy-handed with
the U.S. attorneys in the field.

Reno's concerns about the proposal were reinforced by
Richard Scruggs, the federal prosecutor Reno had brought with
her to Washington from Miami. At Reno's request, Scruggs reviewed the proposed anti-violence plan. The major problem
with it, he told Reno, was structure. Why was it necessary to
have Criminal Division lawyers in Washington overseeing every
one of the proposed violent-crime task forces in the field? As
chief of the Criminal Division of the U.S. Attorney's Office in
Miami, Scruggs had approved two major investigations of violent street gangs. Both grew out of meetings he had with local
police detectives. "Tell me what your two biggest unaddressed
problems are and what resources you need," Scruggs had asked.
The detectives told him about two inner-city gangs known as
the Boulder Boys and the Murphy Gang. Scruggs approved federal prosecutions against each that led to convictions of gang
members.

Scruggs didn't object to the emphasis that Jim Reynolds and
Mary Incontro had placed on violent gangs in their initial proposal. In fact, he thought Reynolds-Incontro was right on the
money. Gangs were a major cause of violence, but giving the
Criminal Division in Washington a commanding role was a mistake, Scruggs told Reno. No Criminal Division lawyer at Main
Justice would routinely do what he had done in Miami: Sit down

with a few cops, decide who the bad guys were and then go take them down. Reno did not disagree.

Scruggs's objections reflected a bias that was shared by many prosecutors in the field. Though he now helped to shape Justice Department policy as one of Reno's special assistants, Scruggs entertained serious doubts about the relevance of Main Justice when it came to delivering effective law enforcement to communities across the nation. From the point of view of the assistant U.S. attorney in the field, he believed, Main Justice was mostly a source of money and of policies that sounded good in the abstract but were problematic in practice. Part of it was the Justice Department's professional culture. Within the institution, Scruggs noted, there were two breeds: the talkers and the doers. On the proposal to target violent gangs, for instance, there was a nice logic to placing command and control of the new task forces in Washington. Many of the violent gangs had spread across the country. They could be attacked by multi-jurisdictional prosecutions that could be coordinated from a headquarters operation. In the abstract, Scruggs agreed, but his own experience argued against that. He had more confidence in what he called the "steely-eyed prosecutors" in the field. They were the ones who should be shaping policy, he told Reno. All that needed to be done was for Main Justice to point its prosecutors at the targets, then get the hell out of the way.

Reno, it seemed, appreciated that view. Scruggs was not surprised. When the new attorney general arrived in Washington there was a great deal she did not know about the federal system of criminal justice. Of the handful of lawyers Reno brought with her from Miami, Scruggs was the only one with federal law-enforcement experience. By default, he became a resource and sounding board for the new attorney general. Scruggs was struck by the dichotomy that was Janet Reno. In public, she used the bully pulpit of her office to focus attention on the root causes of crime, especially the treatment of children. This kind of talk had given her a reputation outside the building as a social worker. In private, however, Scruggs saw a stone-cold law enforcer. She had no problem with long prison terms or aggressive prosecution tactics so long as they comported with the law.

What she did have a problem with was aggressive meddling from Washington. She would not forget her experience in Miami dealing with federal agencies there. As attorney general, she would not inflict the indignities on federal prosecutors that had been inflicted on her as a state prosecutor.

Reno made her decision quickly. She wanted questionnaires sent out from Main Justice to every U.S. Attorney's Office in the nation asking the prosecutors in the field about the causes and remedies of violent crime in their communities. Only after responses were received would Reno and the lawyers at Main Justice propose a solution.

With his colleagues, Merrick Garland went to work on this task. In the months that followed, surveys were sent out to the ninety-four U.S. attorneys asking them what they thought would work in their communities. The responses came back to Jim Reynolds and Mary Incontro on the second floor of Main Justice. In principle, the challenge before the lawyers was a simple one. They were to meld two divergent schools of thought on how to attack violent crime. One espoused a decentralized model, based on the Law Enforcement Coordinating Committee concept proposed by the William French Smith task force more than ten years earlier. The second was a more centrally managed approach, based on the initial anti-gangs proposal Jim Reynolds had drafted back in the Bush administration.

Reynolds did not need to wade through the hundreds of pages of prosecutors' responses to see where they came down on the issue. During a meeting of the powerful Attorney General's Advisory Committee several months earlier, Mary Jo White, the U.S. attorney in Manhattan, had made it very clear, along with a majority of her colleagues, that on violent crime they did not want to see a one-size-fits-all approach mandated from Washington. Reno had dispatched Richard Scruggs as her emissary to the advisory committee meeting. He listened, not at all surprised, as White and the other prosecutors made their concerns known. The causes of violent crime differed from region to region, the U.S. attorneys argued. In Chicago, the problem was big, violent gangs. In rural

North Florida, motorcycle gangs and drug smugglers were the scourge. Scruggs had delivered to Reno a full report on the session.

Shuttling between their offices on the second floor, Merrick Garland, Jim Reynolds and Mary Incontro produced draft after draft of a revised anti-gangs plan. With each revision, the document grew longer. Eventually, it was appended to a still-longer document, a study that described the problem of violent crime nationally and an audit of the resources the Department of Justice could bring to bear on it. Reynolds's first "very informal memo" had matured considerably. Jo Ann Harris, the newly installed assistant attorney general for the Criminal Division, had read that first version and pronounced it "great." Then she asked Reynolds to modify it, to broaden its proposals in some areas, to cut back in others.

Harris was eager for a finished product. On a Tuesday in November 1993, she asked Reynolds if he could have a final draft by the end of the following week.

"Sure," Reynolds replied.

The two prosecutors continued chatting, then Harris asked if Reynolds could deliver the draft a few days earlier, perhaps by the middle of the following week.

"Sure," Reynolds said.

A few more minutes of conversation, and Harris came up with another request. "You know, Jim," she said, "I really would like to have it by Monday. In fact, it would be really helpful if you could bring it over to my apartment about 4 P.M. Sunday, or I could come over there to pick it up."

Reynolds gulped and said he would do his best. In fact, Harris didn't get Reynolds's final draft until 1 P.M. the following Monday. Then she ran it through her own word processor a few more times, working it over like the featured cover story of a national magazine. Harris knew where the land mines were in the proposal she was about to put forth. Making the language as appealing as possible would be crucial to selling the plan successfully. "Jo Ann was concerned about selling it up the line," Reynolds said. "She was one hundred percent behind it. She didn't want to see it not succeed."

For the mugging victim turned assistant attorney general, no issue was more important than developing a strong, workable plan to attack the causes of violent crime. This was why Harris had come to Washington—why she had agreed to give up her comfortable life in New York for the brutalizing hours at Main Justice. Reviewing the final draft prepared by Reynolds, Harris was increasingly convinced of two things. One was that in outlining its plan to attack violent crime nationwide, the Criminal Division of Main Justice should not abdicate the strong coordinating role first advocated by Reynolds.

There was irony in this, Harris acknowledged, coming as it did from a former "sovereign district" prosecutor. She nevertheless believed strongly that Main Justice should take a firm guiding hand in any anti-violence program. Her second conviction also grew out of Reynolds's very first cut at an anti-violence proposal. Any attack on violent crime would be doomed to failure, Harris believed, unless it focused tightly on the problem of gangs. As she revised and expanded the proposal herself, she worked out her ideas. "The growth of violent crime can be tied closely to the development of gangs," Harris wrote. "Although definitive statistics are not available, the assessment of law enforcement professionals is that gang violence is a primary factor—and perhaps the primary factor—in the increase in violent crime during the past decade."

The process of developing the anti-violence plan was a sobering experience. It forced Harris to confront certain immutable realities. There were only 10,000 FBI agents, 3,500 DEA agents and 2,000 federal marshals. All worked for agencies that did many things besides fight violent crime. Nationwide, there were 532,583 state and local police officers. If a half-million police officers were overwhelmed by random street violence, throwing a few thousand extra federal agents at the problem would be a fruitless gesture.

Against these numbers were arrayed a more depressing set of statistics. The rate of violent crime had increased 41 percent in the past ten years, 81 percent in the past twenty years. Major street gangs thrived in seventy-two of the nation's seventy-nine largest cities. Despite the tough-on-crime rhetoric politicians of both parties indulged in so readily, law-enforcement resources devoted to fighting violent crime had declined steadily over the past two decades.

The clearest proof of this was to be found in the state and federal prisons. The rate of reported violent crime had accelerated to horrible levels. Yet a 1993 study by the federal Bureau of Justice Statistics showed that since 1980 the number of state prisoners charged with violent crimes had dropped from about 50 percent of all inmates to less than 30 percent. On a percentage basis, more federal prisoners were serving time for violent crimes in 1970 than in 1990.

The reasons for the drop were not difficult to fathom. During the administration of Jimmy Carter there had been a deliberate reduction in violent-crime enforcement; fraud and other white-collar crimes became a priority. With the brief exception of the first two years of the Reagan administration under Attorney General William French Smith and the final year of the Bush administration under Attorney General William P. Barr, the Republicans had emphasized still other priorities, primarily drug enforcement. That decision had the consequence of filling prisons with drug offenders. While many drug offenders were violent, the shifting priorities at Main Justice over the years had hindered a strong, coordinated attack on the big street gangs responsible for so much inner-city violence.

Now the priorities were about to shift again. Jo Ann Harris and her team in the Criminal Division were confronting a fundamental issue for strategists at Main Justice. How could they make the federal law-enforcement bureaucracy respond in ways that made a difference in the level of violence? Implicit in the question was the same issue that had so troubled the William French Smith task force back in 1981. What kind of Justice Department did America want? The institution was huge and diffused, spread out over fifty states. It was pushed and pulled by different centers of power—by the White House, the Senate Judiciary Committee, the FBI, the U.S. attorneys and the Criminal Division. Its senior management was always in a state of flux, an admixture of political appointees with short tenures and career lawyers with deep stakes in the status quo.

Making fundamental change in the Justice Department's prosecutive priorities, Harris thought, was akin to stopping a huge battleship running at flank speed, then forcing it to reverse direction. The maneuver required lots of ocean and was accomplished one degree at a time.

In her first year at Main Justice, Janet Reno, because of her own late start and the long delays in confirming key personnel, had also come to appreciate the incredible ponderousness of Washington bureaucracy. *The Attorney General's Annual Report* for fiscal year 1993, Reno's first, would take the usual upbeat tone, but anyone working on the issue of violent crime could read between the lines. "Department components continued to search for the most useful ways to use their own unique resources to support community crime-fighting efforts," the report said. It cited Operation Triggerlock and the FBI's Safe Streets task forces that targeted violent fugitives. Both programs had begun during the Bush administration.

Triggerlock and Safe Streets were worthy programs, Jo Ann Harris believed, but more needed to be done. In her proposal to Reno, she was blunt about the Justice Department's failure to take more aggressive action against violent crime earlier. The Reynolds-Incontro anti-gangs proposal should have been implemented, she said. Instead, as they approached the end of 1993, the issue was still being debated. "In spite of the priorities that U.S. Attorneys generally believe should be accorded to violent crime," Harris wrote in a blistering memorandum, "most have not assigned prosecutors to assist gang task force efforts on a full-time basis." The one critical element FBI agents assigned to violent-crime squads said they needed was full-time federal prosecutors.

It was clear from news media accounts throughout the nation that the issue of violence was not going away. One of the first things Reno did each morning was read *The Washington Post*, now her local newspaper. In October 1993 the *Post* published an investigative series by reporter Athelia Knight entitled "The Homicide Files." Based on a systematic analysis of murder cases, it described in precise detail how the District of Columbia's criminal justice system was being overwhelmed by bloodshed and seemed incapable of solving all but the easiest murder cases. The week the articles appeared, Reno attended a dinner party in Georgetown, where she bumped into Bob Woodward, the *Post*'s assistant managing editor for investigations, and lavished praise on the articles. Deputy Assistant Attorney General Philip Heymann was equally struck by Knight's work. He thought it showed a local justice system near total collapse.

Both Reno and Heymann were eager to see some kind of antiviolence initiative quickly. When they traveled outside Washington they were constantly asked about violent crime. Their sense of urgency made itself felt down the chain of command. Jo Ann Harris could not force the U.S. attorneys in the field to act, but as the assistant attorney general in the Criminal Division she had resources she could command. Structural changes at Main Justice could make a start toward addressing the problem, Harris believed. A new violent crime section with regional desks could coordinate intelligence information and give "particular attention" to violent gang activity that crossed state lines. There would be Criminal Division response teams made up of prosecutors specializing in gang crimes who would go out into communities across the nation to help local U.S. attorneys build prosecutions.

Harris was reasonably confident of what she could accomplish at Main Justice. But she knew that for any plan to succeed, the big federal police agencies would have to be on board. They controlled the troops that would have to fight the battles. The cooperation of the FBI, the DEA or the U.S. Marshals Service was not something Main Justice could take for granted.

At Main Justice, Jo Ann Harris put together the equivalent of a fact-finding mission. Merrick Garland and Jim Reynolds were assigned with Kevin DiGregory to pay a series of calls on the leaders of other federal law-enforcement agencies. In Miami, DiGregory had served as Reno's chief assistant for prosecutions of major crimes, which were generally the city's most notorious and bizarre homicides. Slightly younger than Garland, DiGregory had worked as a state court prosecutor his entire career; his first day at

Main Justice was his first direct experience of federal law enforcement. Enthusiastic and well liked, he was a good addition to the team, bringing the perspective of local police and prosecutors. "That was my job," DiGregory explained. "To provide the practical prosecutor's point of view, specifically the local prosecutor's point of view—the real-world take."

At nearly all of the big federal police agencies, the team from Main Justice was given a warm but qualified reception. At the headquarters of the Drug Enforcement Administration, in suburban Virginia just across the Potomac River from Washington, Stephen Greene, the acting administrator, promised that his agency would support the violent-crime initiative. He cautioned the lawyers from Main Justice, though. He did not want to see his agents diverted from their primary mission, high-level drug enforcement. The backbone of DEA's domestic enforcement program consisted of approximately one hundred permanent drug task forces that it had formed with state and local police. DEA would not give those up, Greene said firmly. The agency had six regional task forces devoted to drug-related homicides, however. They would be happy to see those folded into any new violent-crime task forces. And it was fine with DEA if the U.S. attorneys led the charge, so long as they were not directing operations.

At the Treasury Department, Ronald K. Noble, the undersecretary for enforcement, pledged that he, too, would support the violent-crime initiative, but he was concerned about what effect it might have on Treasury's Bureau of Alcohol, Tobacco and Firearms. Would the small, embattled agency be swallowed up by larger FBI-led task forces working on long-term cases? ATF agents were most proficient at quick-hit cases, Noble explained. In a long-term investigation their contributions would go unnoticed, and that could have budgetary consequences with the Congress. Better that ATF agents work in "subtask forces" that were part of the larger group, Noble suggested. And he stressed that appearances were important to morale. The name of the task forces should not be associated with any one federal agency, Noble insisted. That would create tension.

The FBI had already shifted three hunded agents from counterintelligence to working on violent crime. With the collapse of the Soviet Union, that had been a logical step. In most major cities, the FBI had special fugitive squads that were tracking down wanted criminals. With the FBI's Safe Streets program already focused on violent groups, FBI executives said they would fully cooperate with any new violent-crime initiative.

Despite the pleasant words, Merrick Garland, Jim Reynolds and Kevin DiGregory had few illusions about the depths of the problems that lay ahead. They ranged from the petty (the name of the task force) to the philosophical (should DEA agents be diverted from their main mission of fighting drugs?). Within the federal system the various federal law-enforcement agencies were autonomous fiefdoms forever engaged in a game of one-upmanship. If they resisted the proposal, it wouldn't succeed.

Getting control of the agencies was critical to turning the battleship. In that regard Janet Reno enjoyed a unique advantage over other attorneys general. She had had the chance to appoint a new director of the FBI. Louis Freeh had been a respected federal judge in New York, a well regarded federal prosecutor and a decorated special agent of the FBI. With his help, Reno also selected a new administrator for the DEA. Thomas Constantine had been the superintendent of the New York State Police, having risen to the top of the agency over the course of a thirty-year career that began with his making traffic stops as a young trooper riding in an ancient police cruiser. Freeh and Constantine had known and liked each other in New York. They would make a close, cohesive and effective team, Reno hoped, in Washington.

With the contentious proposal to merge the FBI and DEA behind them and the creation of the Office of Investigative Agency Policies under Director Freeh, Reno had people in key places whom she trusted and thought would work well together. In Ronald Noble at Treasury, Reno had another ally who was willing to cooperate. Reno was reasonably sure that on the violent-crime initiative Freeh, Constantine and Noble would support her. Through the Office of Investigative Agency Policies, Freeh could enlist and ultimately enforce the cooperation of other agencies. The machinery was thus in place. They had a cohesive plan of attack, now thoroughly vetted by the Criminal Division. The agencies seemed ready to march in this new direction.

The big question was still the ninety-four U.S. attorneys spread out across the country—the key links in the chain. Each was an autonomous presidential appointee, just like Janet Reno. The question was, would they follow her lead?

On the morning of January 20, 1994, Janet Reno walked into a large conference room at the historic Willard Hotel in downtown Washington to address the annual conference of U.S. attorneys. When she rose to speak Reno was all business. "Clearly," she said, surveying the audience, "violence is the primary, number one crime concern of the American people." Some crimes were automatically considered federal cases—crimes of terrorism or interstate conspiracies. But federal prosecutors had to broaden their focus, Reno said. "We must do everything proper and possible to support, assist and undertake efforts against violence and to assist state and local law enforcement to stem the tide of violence."

Reno ticked off several possible approaches. They could create a violent-crime council, or join existing state or local organizations. Whatever they thought would work was okay with her. "I leave it to you," Reno said, "because you know your area better than I do, and I don't like to dictate."

There was nothing in Reno's speech about the plan Jo Ann Harris had prepared—about a new violent-crime section in the Criminal Division, or about regional desks that would help U.S. attorneys coordinate their investigations. That would come later, during an afternoon panel called "The U.S. Attorney's Role in the Attorney General's Violent Crime Initiative," which unveiled the thinking of Harris and the Criminal Division's top lawyers.

Seated on the dais were Harris; Mary Jo White, the U.S. attorney in New York; Kevin DiGregory, the Reno aide from Miami who helped write the plan; Mary Incontro, the Criminal Division lawyer who had helped Jim Reynolds draft the original gang-fighting proposal, and Thomas Monaghan, the U.S. attorney from Nebraska.

The Harris plan, as it turned out, was still a work-in-progress.

At this conference Reno was trying to get the lay of the land and to build support for an anti-violence plan. It was no accident that Mary Jo White was on the panel with Harris. The chair of the Attorney General's Advisory Committee, White was the most influential U.S. attorney in the nation, a cheerful dynamo who had restored the luster of the U.S. Attorney's Office in Manhattan to the high gleam it had enjoyed under Rudolph Giuliani. White and Harris were old friends. White's presence on the panel sent a clear, unmistakable message to the prosecutors in the audience. The "sovereign district" was on board.

About one principle in the Harris plan, at least, there was no debate. In her written presentation, Harris outlined it briefly and forcefully: "We must make available to local authorities powerful federal crime-fighting tools modified to address local problems." Twelve years after the Bell-Thompson task force on violent crime had broached the subject so tentatively, the concept of extending federal police powers to state and local authorities had become Justice Department policy. Over the past decade more than six thousand local police detectives and state investigators had become de facto federal agents while working on federal task forces. That was the functional equivalent of creating a new federal agency nearly twice the size of the DEA. The Harris plan would take the unofficial merger of the state and federal systems another big step down that road.

The panel discussion of the anti-violence initiative was followed by questions from the floor. The prosecutors' reaction was largely favorable. Still, there was an undercurrent of concern. Washington should take care not to be overly intrusive, several of those present cautioned. Whatever plan Harris ultimately came up with, it should not tell prosecutors in the field how to go after violent criminals in their communities. Prescriptions would vary from place to place; let prosecutors in the field figure them out.

Harris and the other panelists responded to the questions one by one.

On March 21, 1994, Janet Reno employed a state-of-the-art communications hookup to conduct a nationwide teleconference call from the Oval Office to announce the Justice Department's anti–violent-crime initiative. White House technicians connected the offices of the ninety-four U.S. attorneys and the special agents–in–charge of every FBI and DEA field office. Reno was joined in the Oval Office by President Clinton, FBI Director Freeh, DEA Administrator Constantine, Secretary of the Treasury Lloyd Bentsen and Undersecretary Ronald Noble. Reno's message was simple. Everyone, finally, was on board.

The battleship was going to turn.

In the weeks following the U.S. attorney's conference at the Willard Hotel, the Harris plan had undergone several modifications. Virtually all of Jim Reynolds's original ideas for attacking violent gangs had survived intact. Harris's plan to create a violent-crime section with regional desks within the Criminal Division had not. The Criminal Division would retain an important role, however. Jim Reynolds and the lawyers in the Terrorism and Violent Crime Section would have license to prod U.S. attorneys in the field to develop their own operational plans. The division could suggest avenues of attack and mediate problems with the federal police agencies. Prosecutors working in Reynolds's section would also be available to supply guidance and legal expertise on individual prosecutions.

Flexibility was the watchword. In a memorandum to prosecutors following the teleconference call, Reno made this clear. "I am not suggesting that you create a new task force or bureaucracy to address violent crime," Reno wrote, "if you already have mechanisms in place that are working in your district. . . . [The] goal of this initiative is to complement, not supplant, the efforts of state and local prosecutors."

Reno asked that the U.S. attorneys appoint a senior prosecutor as a violent-crime coordinator in each U.S. Attorney's Office and form or support a violent-crime working group with federal, state and local law-enforcement agencies. The U.S. attorneys were asked to describe how they were going to attack their "district's most critical violent crime problems" and then describe the resources that would be devoted to this mission. These local plans were to be sent to Jim Reynolds, who, along with an advisory committee of U.S. attorneys, would analyze them, then suggest prosecutive strategies.

Reno wanted each district to pick a strategy for attacking violent crime, then carry it out. "Possible examples include an attack on violent gangs, or the development of a targeted list of the district's most dangerous violent offenders," Reno wrote in her memo to prosecutors. "The plan should include the use, as appropriate, of federal tools such as wiretapping, pretrial detention, federal statutes aimed at criminal organizations and real-time sentencing under the sentencing guidelines."

Follow-up was swift. The same day Reno announced the anti-violence initiative at the White House, FBI Director Freeh issued a directive in his capacity as director of the Office of Investigative Agency Policies. Freeh was blunt and specific. Every special agent–in–charge in every field office of the FBI, the DEA, the Marshals Service and the Immigration and Naturalization Service was ordered to provide "a current analysis of the violent-crime problem in each federal judicial circuit," the Freeh memorandum instructed. "This violent-crime analysis should include an overview of the individuals and organizations posing the greatest threat to our society, as well as their methods of operation." The special agents–in–charge were further ordered to meet with their local counterparts to discuss the causes of violence in their areas, then "submit a single investigative and prosecutive strategy" for targeting the worst sources of violence.

At the Drug Enforcement Administration, Thomas Constantine had already begun retooling the agency to concentrate more resources on drug-related violence. To encourage agents to focus their efforts more aggressively on violent gangs, he changed DEA evaluation criteria so that cases would not be valued only by the amount of narcotic contraband seized but also by the impact they had on violent drug gangs. Constantine also established special teams of agents who were sent into cities to investigate drug-related homicides.

In the Criminal Division at Main Justice, Jo Ann Harris and the lawyers who had developed the anti-violence initiative were both pleased and anxious. With the new alignment of federal police agencies, Janet Reno had done some substantial re-engineering of the criminal justice system. Every FBI and DEA field office now had explicit marching orders. If federal prosecutors in the field now followed Reno's leadership, Main Justice should soon start seeing results. The operative word, Harris and the other lawyers knew all too well, was "should." Theories were one thing. Results were something else again.

CHAPTER EIGHT

HITTING THE STREETS

B y Washington standards, the anti-violence initiative unveiled by Janet Reno was unusual in two respects. First, many of the people who had to carry out the new program at the local level actually liked it because of its flexibility. In Atlanta, the local FBI office and the Georgia Bureau of Investigation joined forces to create a Mobile Crime Scene Unit that responded to murders, made arrests and gathered evidence. In Sacramento, the city police department took the lead in a multi-agency effort targeting violent career criminals who were fugitives. In New York, joint investigations with police hammered the inner-city gangs, knocking them down one after another like falling dominoes. In Washington, D.C., the FBI began to work side by side with local homicide detectives. In Chicago, a massive joint investigation involving DEA and the FBI working with several local agencies went after the Gangster Disciples.

In Miami, the U.S. Attorney's Office joined local prosecutors in a program that broadened the Triggerlock concept in an effort to increase prison time. Local police built a computer database of 4,600 career criminals, called "signal 100s," who were regarded as the most violent in the community. When a "signal 100" suspect was arrested by local police, the State Attorney's Office faxed the arrest form over to the U.S. attorney. There, one of eighteen federal prosecutors would seek a federal indictment of the suspect, charging the person with violations of federal firearms and other laws.

Second, the anti-violence initiative actually got results. In the months after Reno announced the plan, federal prosecutors across the nation began churning out prosecutions of violent gangs. As requested, prosecutors and investigators in some districts focused on the "sets," or local franchises, of the big national gangs operating in their communities. In Los Angeles, three leaders of the Schoolyard Crips were arrested. In Nevada, twenty-four members of the Southside Village Crips were indicted. In Connecticut, thirty-three members of the Latin Kings were charged in a racketeering case, under the Justice Department's most powerful criminal statute, the Racketeer Influenced and Corrupt Organizations Act. Originally designed to attack the Italian Mafia, the RICO statute was equally well suited to prosecutions of organized street gangs.

At Main Justice, Jim Reynolds and Mary Incontro were pleased. The backbone of the anti-violence initiative was the old plan they had designed. It had been reshaped, refashioned, put through the bureaucratic blender. The fundamentals had remained intact, however. The gangs remained the main target.

The numbers, as they came in, were heartening. In just nine months in 1994, federal prosecutors nationwide filed 5,270 criminal cases against 7,109 violent and repeat offenders. This figure did not include state prosecutions resulting from joint investigations by federal police agencies and local authorities. Clearly, the total included many cases that would have been filed anyway, even if Jim Reynolds and Jo Ann Harris had not come up with a new plan for attacking violent gangs and career criminals. But there were unmistakable signs of impact. By mid-1995 some of the bigger federal districts were reporting marked decreases in violent-crime rates, a trend that was confirmed in the FBI annual report on crime statistics, which stated that the overall crime rate in the nation was declining.

Numbers aside, the political appointees and career officials in Main Justice—acting in concert—had done what so many others in official Washington had not. They had taken a big, slow-moving bureaucracy and forced it to do their bidding.

Two cases reveal the impact of the new federal attack.

In Shreveport, Louisiana, from late 1989 until the summer of 1994, Don R. Wilson and a few of his friends effectively terrorized the residents of the city's poorest neighborhood, Ledbetter Heights, a place of leaning shotgun shacks and weedy lots. For more than a century, locals had referred to the heights as "The Bottoms." No one remembered why. Just west of downtown, a few blocks from the Louisiana Hayride, where Elvis Presley got one of the first big breaks of his career, The Bottoms had been a red-light district, a place of lawlessness, going back to the 1800s. Don Wilson and his friends, who called themselves "The Bottoms Boys," controlled it.

Because The Bottoms was not easy to get to—there were only two narrow roads in and out—it was easy for Wilson and The Bottoms Boys to keep out anyone, including rival street gangs, whose presence offended or challenged them. The Los Angeles–based Crips and Bloods had chapters in Shreveport. Though it is a relatively small city, the FBI ranked Shreveport in the second tier of American cities plagued by gang violence, just below some larger cities, such as Dallas, Houston and Kansas City.

Not only did Don Wilson and his colleagues manage to keep rival gangs out of The Bottoms, they kept the Shreveport police away, too. Police officers responding to emergency 911 calls in The Bottoms had been attacked. Some had been hurt badly. In the words of a sworn deposition filed in federal court in Shreveport, officers "had been stoned and beaten . . . when they attempted to make arrests of [criminal] suspects." For the poor people forced to make their homes in The Bottoms, Don Wilson and The Bottoms Boys were virtually all powerful.

In Shreveport, Will Lueckenhoff ran the local resident agency of the FBI. A resident agency is much smaller than a field office, typically located in more populous cities. In 1992, Lueckenhoff had only eight agents working for him. To him, the FBI was family. His father had been a special agent for twenty-nine years. Lueckenhoff and his twin brother were both building successful FBI careers. Shreveport was the first small city Lueckenhoff had ever worked in. He had been an agent in Chicago and seen the epidemic of gang violence there. Concentrated in a much smaller city, the gang violence in Shreveport was, in many ways, more frightening.

With the money the FBI had allocated through its Safe Streets program, Lueckenhoff's superiors in New Orleans had established a task force targeting violent fugitives. In Shreveport, Lueckenhoff wanted two task forces, one for fugitives, the other for violent gangs. He was told he would have to pick, either gangs or fugitives; there was not enough money to do both. Lueckenhoff made the call easily. In Shreveport, going after gangs would make more of a difference to the people there. Lueckenhoff assigned one of his best agents, Dan McMullen, as the case agent. With the modest sum of Safe Streets money he received from Washington, Lueckenhoff set McMullen up with a budget. Then he leased space for the agent at the top of a commercial building two blocks from the edge of The Bottoms. There, McMullen and a small team of police officers from other agencies went to work. "We went looking for a target," Lueckenhoff said. "It wasn't hard. We were in a target-rich environment."

The Shreveport Police Department had a good database on the city's violent gangs. And Sergeant Steve Floyd, who had made himself the resident expert on the city's gangs, was a key member of the new task force. His information was supplemented by an unusual database established by the Los Angeles Police Department. The system was called GREAT, the Gang Resistance, Education and Training program. It tracked members of the Crips, Bloods and other Los Angeles–based gangs in dozens of cities across the nation. Shreveport, because of its active Crips and Bloods chapters, was a GREAT subscriber.

The way government task forces work, the agency providing the bulk of the money sets the rules. Since that was the FBI in Shreveport, Will Lueckenhoff called the shots. The Shreveport task force would abide by two rules, he said. It would commit itself only to long-term investigations of the city's most violent gangs, and it would work only on one gang or "gang-set" at a time. As far as picking its first target, the task force could go after the local Crips and Bloods chapters, but Lueckenhoff suggested a different set of criteria. He was still getting a feel for Shreveport. Why not target the one gang, Lueckenhoff said, that is doing more than any other to oppress a single neighborhood or group of residents? Steve Floyd, the Shreveport Police Department gang expert, seconded the idea. There was some discussion, but not much. If that was the standard they were going to use, Floyd told Lueckenhoff, only one target made sense: The Bottoms Boys.

By the time Janet Reno announced the anti-violence plan in Washington, Lueckenhoff and Dan McMullen were up and running with an investigation of The Bottoms Boys. The push from Washington only encouraged the Shreveport task force in its efforts. For their lawyer, the task force agents sought out James G. Cowles Jr. He had worked as a local prosecutor in Shreveport several years earlier, then moved to Washington, where he worked as a federal prosecutor alongside Mary Incontro, prosecuting violent criminals in the District of Columbia. Cowles had recently moved back to his native Shreveport to work as a federal prosecutor there. He knew the city cops and the chief of police; he had a good feel for the place. Cowles was enthusiastic. Mary Incontro had told him of the anti-violence initiative she had been working on at Main Justice. Here was an opportunity to put it to the test in his hometown. "We knew Washington was coming out with something," Cowles said. "We were just a little bit ahead of the game."

To get into The Bottoms, Lueckenhoff and his agents came up with a caper. A year earlier Lueckenhoff had supervised a three-city cocaine investigation called Pipewrench: In Miami, Edward Kacerosky and the Cornerstone investigation of the Cali cartel had severely disrupted the flow of cocaine into Miami; in Texas and Louisiana, Lueckenhoff and other federal agents had discovered that Houston was picking up the slack. The Pipewrench investigation identified a direct cocaine connection between Houston and Shreveport. In Houston, the surge in drug trafficking was so great that local FBI agents could hardly identify all the major players. To increase its intelligence base, the FBI created a fictional Hollywood movie-production company called Stardust Productions. Then supervisors sent undercover agents posing as producers into the streets in vans fitted with professional movie-making equipment to shoot street scenes and interview locals for bit parts in a movie. The movie, the Stardust people said, was to be about gangs.

Lueckenhoff had learned of Stardust Productions through Pipewrench. It had proven a useful tool for gathering intelligence on Houston's multiplying drug gangs. In Shreveport, Lueckenhoff requested permission to use the Stardust Productions team again—not to gather intelligence this time, but to gather evidence that could be used in a criminal prosecution.

In New Orleans, Lueckenhoff's superiors approved the request. In Shreveport, Stardust Productions set up shop and announced it was open for business. Two of the undercover agents brought in for the operation were particularly effective. Calvin Shivers and Tina Smith posed as Stardust junior representatives. It was their job to talk up The Bottoms Boys, to put them at ease. After a carefully arranged introduction to several of The Bottoms Boys, Shivers and Smith got them talking. Stardust wanted to make a movie, Shivers and Smith explained, but not another *Boyz N the Hood*. They had come to Shreveport to make a movie about home-grown gangs—gangs like The Bottoms Boys.

The Bottoms Boys listened, pleased. Lueckenhoff had paid to lease a few suites at the local Sheraton. Before long, The Bottoms Boys were dropping by for drinks and meals, meeting with some of the "executives" from Stardust Productions—more FBI agents operating in an undercover capacity.

Tell us about gang life, the Stardust team coaxed. Tell us about life in The Bottoms.

The Bottoms Boys were happy to oblige. Two in particular, Sebastian Richardson and Alfred Brown, had lots of stories to tell. Richardson, who went by the nickname "Bam Bam," was The Bottoms Boys' enforcer. Alfred Brown was "Goat," The Bottoms Boys' narcotics distributor—"the man with the sack." It was

Goat's job to drive his big Cadillac over to Houston, load the trunk with cocaine, then drive the four and a half hours back to The Bottoms and parcel out the drugs to the gang's street sellers. Some were kids just barely out of grade school.

Bam Bam's responsibilities were different. Sprawled across a comfortable couch in the Sheraton, sipping a highball, he described the nature of his work for Shivers, Smith and the Stardust executives. See, Bam Bam Richardson explained, it was Goat who brought in the drugs and helped distribute them, but he wasn't the man in charge; Bam Bam was. Grabbing a pencil and paper, Richardson drew a flowchart of The Bottoms Boys organization. Don Wilson, known to everyone in The Bottoms as "Big Don," was the gang's head man. Below him was Bam Bam. Below Bam Bam was Goat. Bam Bam wasn't just in charge of drug sales, he said. The Bottoms Boys also sold thousands and thousands of guns. Most were stolen, of course. Bam Bam gave the guns to his "sons"—kids, some ten years old and younger—to sell for him on the street. Bam Bam kept the profits.

The Stardust producers nodded appreciatively. This was quite an organization, one said.

Damn right, Bam Bam Richardson replied. "The Bottoms Boys are the best. We're not like the Crips and Bloods. We're home-grown and proud of it."

Shivers, Smith and the other Stardust people nodded again. Embedded in the wall behind them was a miniature video camera. While the tape unspooled, a tiny microphone attached to the furniture captured Bam Bam's voice; the tapes were quickly transcribed.

The movie caper was clever. The only problem was, when Lueckenhoff, Dan McMullen and the other members of the task force went to review the footage and tapes, they got nothing. The videocamera, prosecutor Jim Cowles recalled, "was aimed at a potted plant." As for the "super-duper little mikes," Cowles said, "they didn't work. We got gobbledygook."

The operation wasn't a total washout. Thanks to the boasting of Bam Bam and the other Bottoms Boys during their sessions in the Sheraton, Lueckenhoff, Cowles and the others knew far more than they had just weeks before about the criminal activities of The Bottoms Boys. Bam Bam and the others had talked easily to Shivers, Smith and the Stardust team about drive-by shootings and where they bought their drugs. They had boasted about how the police were unable to touch them.

With the new information, McMullen, Lueckenhoff and Cowles put a new game plan together. "We had people willing to talk, prostitutes, people like that," Cowles said. "Then we reached out to prisoners serving time in state pens around the state. Or we would find people who were on parole, talk to them, see if they were willing to help us."

Many were. In exchange for offers of early parole, clemency or release from prison, former members of The Bottoms Boys testified about the gang's criminal activities before a federal grand jury. Rival gang members did as well, as did some very courageous people who had been victims of The Bottoms Boys.

With the evidence mounting before the grand jury, Cowles decided he wanted to charge The Bottoms Boys with racketeering. In Washington, lawyers in Paul Coffey's Organized Crime and Racketeering Section reviewed the evidence and said no. To charge RICO, Cowles would have to prove two "RICO predicates"—specific felonies committed by every one of The Bottoms Boys defendants. Finding and proving the crimes would be difficult. Linking them to a single criminal enterprise, as required by RICO, would be next to impossible. "The Bottoms Boys," Will Lueckenhoff explained, "were just too shallow an organization."

Instead of RICO, Lueckenhoff and Cowles settled on a different anti-racketeering law, one that had been passed back in 1959. The law, Violent Crimes in Aid of Racketeering, had been enacted to attack the kinds of urban street gangs that began springing up in the 1950s. It had been used in the prosecution of Mafia boss John Gotti in New York in the late 1980s, but aside from that it was employed only rarely.

The beauty of using the Violent Crimes in Aid of Racketeering statute, as Cowles saw it, was that he could cite in a federal indictment a number of state crimes as part of the overall criminal conspiracy of The Bottoms Boys. Cowles and the task-force investigators went through hundreds of old police reports. In the end, in the prosecution memo Cowles sent to the Organized Crime and Racketeering Section in Washington, he cited as part of The Bottoms Boys conspiracy several murders and assaults. In one of the murders, a Bottoms Boys member had been acquitted of all charges in state court. In another, state prosecutors had not even bothered filing criminal charges against a Bottoms Boys member. Cowles decided to have another run at both murder cases.

At the FBI, Will Lueckenhoff wanted to up the ante. By sending his agents into The Bottoms to buy illegal drugs from gang members, he reasoned, they would have another opportunity to get taped evidence of criminal activity that they could show to a judge and jury. Cowles agreed.

The heart of The Bottoms was the 1100 block of Fannin Street. A dilapidated grocery in the middle of the block anchored the street and was the locus of a thriving open-air drug market that functioned round the clock. "The 1100 block," prosecutor Cowles said, "was ground zero for The Bottoms Boys. Sometimes there were traffic jams down there, and all these street sellers would just come running up to the cars."

One after another, Lueckenhoff dispatched teams of agents into the 1100 block of Fannin. The agents were male and female, black and white. The standard procedure police agencies use when making street buys of contraband is to rotate cars frequently so that the drug sellers don't become suspicious. In The Bottoms, Lueckenhoff reversed the procedure. The Bottoms Boys were so unconcerned about police surveillance that they sold drugs openly. Repeat customers got special attention, with senior members of the gang taking over the best repeats as special clients. Lueckenhoff wanted The Bottoms Boys to recognize the cars he was using. Night after night he put the same agents in the same cars. He even enlisted his old Ford Taurus station wagon and threw a bunch of tools in the back. Two of the task force agents drove the Taurus into The Bottoms every few days and tried to buy drugs from as many Bottoms Boys members as they could, but it wasn't easy. A few senior members of The Bottoms Boys wanted the agents in the Taurus as personal clients.

The task force agents used vehicles of all descriptions. The only thing they had in common was a little electronic gizmo affixed to the dash that looked like a radar detector. What it was was a miniature camera. Before Lueckenhoff's operation was over, the miniature cameras had captured close-up videotapes of more than forty Bottoms Boys members and associates selling illegal drugs to undercover FBI agents.

With the videotapes and the grand jury testimony of more than a half-dozen cooperating witnesses, Lueckenhoff, McMullen and the Bottoms Boys prosecution team had more evidence than they needed. In a case of cooperation between state and federal agencies, the district attorney in Shreveport agreed to take the FBI videotape of the drug sales and indict thirty-five Bottoms Boys members and associates for violations of Louisiana drug-trafficking laws. Jim Cowles, meanwhile, won approval from Paul Coffey's office in Washington to bring a sealed racketeering indictment against fourteen of the most powerful Bottoms Boys leaders, including Big Don Wilson, Sebastian "Bam Bam" Richardson and Alfred "Goat" Brown.

The battle was not yet won, however. Because Richardson employed his many "sons" in The Bottoms as flying surveillance squads along the two narrow roads leading into the neighborhood, effecting the arrests of the forty-nine people named in both the state and federal indictments would not be easy; if not done cleverly, it would surely be dangerous.

This is where "the federals," as Cowles called them, played a card that only they could. Lueckenhoff and McMullen put together an arrest team that resembled a military operation. It had helicopters, armor-plated vehicles, more than two hundred heavily armed federal agents and state and local police officers. As a capper, the team had a truck, the operation's Trojan horse. Agents of the Treasury Department's Bureau of Alcohol, Tobacco and

Firearms had supported the investigation of The Bottoms Boys almost from the beginning, assisting with checks of stolen handguns and the like. When it came time to execute the arrest plan, the Treasury Department offered the use of a big oversprung vehicle painted to look like a Budweiser beer delivery truck. The old grocery in the 1100 block of Fannin received deliveries from all sorts of vendors. No one would think twice about seeing a lumbering Budweiser truck snaking its way down into The Bottoms.

Lueckenhoff timed the operation to go down around midday on September 8, 1994. Many of The Bottoms Boys tended to congregate around the grocery during the late-morning hours. In the basement garage of the building the task force was using at the edge of The Bottoms, the Budweiser beer truck was readied. Agents in heavy body armor clutching submachine guns piled into the back; in front the driver and his partner were also armed.

The truck departed for The Bottoms. Once it entered the outermost part of Ledbetter Heights proper, the rest of Lueckenhoff's operations plan clicked into gear. Overhead, agents in helicopters kept watch with binoculars. On the ground, state, local and federal police moved quietly to seal off the two exit roads from The Bottoms.

On the ramshackle front porch of the grocery in the 1100 block of Fannin, Bottoms Boys members hooted and laughed as the big Budweiser truck drew up in front.

"Cocktails," one gang member said.

Not really. In their black body armor that some agents referred to as "ninja" suits, the arrest team swarmed out of the phony Budweiser truck. On the front porch of the grocery store there was cursing and swearing. It did no good. Within an hour, thirty of the forty-nine people charged in the state and federal indictments were under arrest. By the end of the day, officers from the federal, state and local police agencies had every one of the forty-nine defendants in custody.

In police work, as in so many other endeavors, there are circumstances in which it literally is possible to make one's own luck. In the prosecution of The Bottoms Boys, this is what happened. In a Louisiana prison, Bam Bam Richardson's brother, Howard, read about The Bottoms Boys' arrests. Howard Richardson got word to prosecutor Cowles that he didn't want anything in return—no favorable treatment, no reduction in his prison sentence, no consideration—but he would testify in court against his brother and against the other Bottoms Boys.

Why? Cowles asked.

Because, Howard Richardson said, if Bam Bam keeps on this way, he's going to wind up dead. Also, The Bottoms Boys themselves needed to be put out of business.

Again, Cowles asked, why?

Simple, Howard Richardson answered, sobbing. The gang had started out years before as a group of poor young men from The Bottoms. They were into mischief and worse, but their main interest was protecting the community.

And that had changed?

It had, Howard Richardson said. With the emphasis on drugs and guns, The Bottoms Boys had become corrupted. They needed to be taken off the streets. Enough was enough.

At trial, Jim Cowles put Howard Richardson on the witness stand as the prosecution's lead and star witness. "He slammed everyone," Cowles related. "Identified everyone." Then Cowles showed the jury the FBI's videotapes of Bottoms Boys' drug sales in the 1100 block of Fannin. After that, it was pretty much over for The Bottoms Boys. Big Don Wilson, Bam Bam Richardson and the other Bottoms Boys defendants were sentenced to long terms in federal prison. The Bottoms Boys charged in state court received lesser but still lengthy sentences.

As for The Bottoms itself, residents there experienced, if not peace, at least an improvement in the quality of life. In the five months before the arrests in the 1100 block of Fannin, there was one homicide; in the five months after, there was none. The number of other crimes—armed robbery, simple and aggravated battery, use of illegal narcotics and theft—dropped by roughly half after The Bottoms Boys arrests. "I'm proud of what we did in The Bottoms," Will Lueckenhoff said, "because we made a difference for the people who live there." Jim Cowles agreed. "It has been a very quiet neighborhood since the arrests," the prosecutor said. "Kids are playing on the streets."

A few minutes before 4 A.M. on August 31, 1995, a small team of federal agents stepped quietly into a cell deep inside the state prison in Dixon, Illinois. Gently, the agents roused the stocky man sleeping on the pallet-like bed. Less than an hour later Larry Hoover, age forty-four, a man who called himself the "chairman" of the Gangster Disciples Nation, was strapped into a rear seat on a twin-engine government plane, heading for Chicago, his hometown.

After twenty-one years in prison, this was not the kind of homecoming Hoover had dreamed of. A federal indictment waiting for him in Chicago charted with pitiless accuracy a criminal career that spanned a quarter century. For his entire life of crime, which began when he was twelve, Larry Hoover had dealt only with local police and prosecutors in Chicago and Illinois. Now he was about to engage the feds.

At the moment Hoover's plane touched down at Meigs Field on Chicago's shimmering lakefront, 250 federal agents and Chicago police officers were moving in teams through some of the city's grittiest South Side neighborhoods. By midday, twenty-two of the thirty-eight men and women who had been named with Hoover in three related federal indictments were in police custody, awaiting court hearings on the possibility of posting bail bonds; the others not yet in custody would be rounded up over the course of the next few hours. All thirty-nine individuals named in the indictments were members or accomplices of members of the Gangster Disciples Nation.

In Washington, when Jim Reynolds put together his "very informal memo" on how the Department of Justice could begin attacking the nation's most violent street gangs, the Black Gangster Disciples, or BGDs, as they often called themselves, were at the top of the list of targets. It was as much coincidence as anything else that the U.S. Attorney's Office in Chicago teamed with the local Drug Enforcement Administration office and the Chicago Police Department to begin investigating the Gangster Disciples in 1990—while Reynolds was trying to sell his anti-gangs plan to his superiors in the Criminal Division of Main Justice. By the time Jo Ann Harris had finished revising the Reynolds proposal and Janet Reno announced it, the Chicago effort was well underway. The push from Washington encouraged the prosecutors and agents in Chicago. This was precisely where the federal government could make a difference.

The case also showed how violent crime in America had changed so profoundly over the years. Larry Hoover had begun his career in crime like any one of thousands of small-time criminals across the nation. In 1963, at age twelve, he joined a local street gang. By sixteen, he had been shot six times. A few years after that, he was running his own gang comprised of a core group of some twenty-five youths whose base of operations was the corner of Sixty-ninth and Green Streets, on Chicago's South Side. The gang grew quickly. In 1969, on Hoover's nineteenth birthday, November 30, he was in absolute command of a street gang he called the Supreme Disciples numbering five thousand members across Chicago. Larry Hoover had taken to calling himself "King" Hoover.

By the time of his arrest in 1995, Hoover had been incarcerated for murder and confined in the Illinois prison system for twenty-one years. Despite his incarceration Hoover had so skillfully managed a series of gang mergers that the Gangster Disciples Nation had become the largest criminal gang in the Midwest, among a handful of the largest crime organizations in America. In a 1995 report the Chicago Crime Commission placed the membership of the Gangster Disciples at between 18,000 and 25,000. Some Chicago police detectives placed the membership closer to 30,000.

Whatever the true number, the Gangster Disciples had undergone a nearly complete metamorphosis since Hoover's early years as a stick-up artist and drug dealer with a small band of henchmen. According to the indictment of Hoover, "the Gangster Disciples street gang evolved into a highly structured organization. In recent years, the organization was as follows: The Chairman, Board Members, Governors, Regents, Coordinators and Soldiers." These were not just gang members' terms of self-glorification. "Governors, Regents, Coordinators were assigned specific geographic areas of Chicago and surrounding areas," the federal indictment charged. Gang members could sell only "Nation Dope"—cocaine, crack cocaine and other narcotic contraband— "supplied by the ranking members of the Gangster Disciples." Each member was responsible for paying "tax" on the sales, as were nongang members who sold Gangster Disciples drugs or had permission to operate in neighborhoods controlled by the Gangster Disciples. The tax was referred to variously as "the weekly," "the personal" and "the count."

There were the traditional gang penalties for failing to adhere to the rules outlined by Hoover and his chief lieutenants. But the true measure of the Gangster Disciples' sophisticated organization lay in more unusual activities. The gang collected an additional street tax on some drug transactions that was called "political" money, or "the P." Much of that went to fund a Chicago operation called Save the Children, Inc., an organization that sponsored highly popular hip-hop concerts on the South Side. More money still went to an ambitious political operation called 21st Century Vote. It was, according to the federal indictment, "a Gangster Disciples–organized and -controlled political action committee." No fly-by-night operation, it put thousands of dollars behind candidates in several Chicago aldermanic elections and organized several popular demonstrations outside City Hall. (Hoover's wife had opened up a successful clothing business in Chicago's South Side neighborhoods, hawking a fashion line called "Ghetto Prisoner." The most popular merchandise were jackets and T-shirts designed by Larry Hoover from his state prison cell; some of the clothes sported Hoover's prisoner identification number.)

Hoover's success story was all the more remarkable for the fact that he had authored it behind the bars of the Illinois prison system. Hoover had retained his title as chairman of the Gangster Disciples, but he had two boards of directors, one comprised of gang members incarcerated in Illinois prisons, the other made up of gang members still on the outside. The gang inside prison walls was ruthlessly organized. "The Gangster Disciples maintained a strict hierarchical structure within most prisons in Illinois," the federal indictment said. "Gang meetings were held on a regular basis, and violations—that is, financial or physical punishment, including severe beatings, for breaking a Gangster Disciple rule—were administered at these meetings."

The federal effort against the Gangster Disciples was ambitious, involving some ingenuity and much hard work, but it was not terribly complicated. Of Chicago's five largest violent street gangs (the others were the Vice Lords, the Latin Kings, the Maniac Latin Disciples and the Black Peace Stone Nation), the Gangster Disciples Nation was far and away the biggest and the baddest. Operating from an anonymous-looking office building on South Clark Street, the Gangster Disciples investigation was code-named Operation X. It involved agents not just from the Drug Enforcement Administration and officers from the Chicago Police Department but also investigators from the Treasury Department's Bureau of Alcohol, Tobacco and Firearms and the Internal Revenue Service. The prosecution strategy was something Janet Reno could not have been more pleased with. Two assistant U.S. attorneys, Ronald Safer and Matthew Crowl, supervised the investigation, but they shared significant parts of the job with two highly regarded local state-court prosecutors, David Styler and Bernie Murray. At trial, Styler and Murray were designated as special assistant U.S. attorneys.

Operationally, the investigation used the most ambitious federal tools. Constitutionally, there was only so much the Illinois prison authorities could do to constrain Larry Hoover and other Gangster Disciples members behind bars; they could not shut off all communications. Hoover and his underlings had thus used prison phones, the mail system and constitutionally guaranteed meetings with visitors to run their criminal operations. Working closely with Chicago police, DEA agents in Chicago had learned more and more about the patterns of Gangster Disciples drug dealing in the city and surrounding suburbs. In the DEA's offices in the Everett J. Dirksen Federal Office Building in the Loop, agents came up with a novel idea. All visitors to Illinois prisons had to wear a credit card–sized visitor identification card pinned to their clothing where guards could see it. After conferring with prosecutors and agents, federal technicians designed a batch of visitor passes implanted with tiny devices that could record conversations between Hoover and other top Gangster Disciples and visitors discussing instructions about narcotics dealings, enforcement actions and other gang business. This was a variant on the aggressive "roving" wiretap Edward Kacerosky had wanted to use against the Cali cartel in Miami. It was key to making the case against the Gangster Disciples. "The indictments . . . penetrated all the barriers," said James Burns, the U.S. attorney in Chicago. "They even penetrated prison walls."

The federal charges brought against Larry Hoover and the other leaders of the Gangster Disciples were far more punishing than anything local prosecutors would have been able to bring. With the approval of Main Justice, James Burns and his team of prosecutors charged all thirty-nine defendants with violations of the Continuing Criminal Enterprise statute. Like the RICO law, the CCE statute enables prosecutors and federal agents to piece together a pattern of criminal activity going back years and charge defendants with the heaviest federal penalties. This was the very statute Jim Reynolds, in the early versions of the anti-gangs memorandum he produced in Washington, had recommended Justice Department prosecutors use.

Against the Gangster Disciples, the prosecutors outlined a pattern of criminal activity going all the way back to 1970. As a result of the CCE charges filed against Larry Hoover and the other defendants in the Gangster Disciples case, the ultimate penalty upon conviction would be life prison terms in maximum-security federal penitentiaries. For most defendants, there would be no possibility of parole.

Unlike the convictions of The Bottoms Boys in Shreveport, the prosecution of the Gangster Disciples in Chicago did not have an immediate significant impact in reducing crime. The city's other gangs were more than up to the challenge of moving into turf vacated by the Gangster Disciples. The gang Larry Hoover had built from the small crew of street hustlers twenty-five years earlier was not easily displaced. Because the gang had as many as 30,000 members and a strict hierarchical system of leadership, detectives and federal investigators worried that removing Hoover and the top leadership would only clear the way for younger, more violent members of the Gangster Disciples to step to the fore.

CHAPTER NINE

RICO'S NEW USES

W hile Janet Reno and Jo Ann Harris were busy trying to energize prosecutors to redouble their efforts against violent street gangs, the machinery of Main Justice continued to grind along as it always had. The vast majority of federal crime prosecutions were initiated and concluded by Justice Department lawyers outside Washington, with not a jot of input from Jack Keeney and the other deputies in the Criminal Division on the second floor of Main Justice. "Ninety-five percent of the cases— some astronomical number—happen out in the field," Mark Richard said. "And the Criminal Division doesn't even know about them. They are a statistical blip on a chart."

That was true, but it was also true that the most far-reaching federal prosecutions in the United States came through Main Justice, and of those, some of the most significant involved the use of the Racketeer Influenced and Corrupt Organizations Act, the powerful anti-Mafia statute that Congress enacted in 1970 as Title IX of the Organized Crime Control Act. Racketeering prosecutions of the five Italian Mafia families in New York in the

1980s had led to their demise. At Main Justice, David Margolis, then the head of the Organized Crime and Racketeering Section, had vetted the most important indictments along with Paul Coffey, his top assistant for RICO matters. The first of the New York mob cases had targeted the Joseph Bonanno family, a disintegrating but still dangerous gang who trafficked in heroin and other illegal narcotics—heedless of a Mafia pact that supposedly prevented the families from dealing in drugs. Despite the publicity accorded the FBI's investigation of John Gotti years later, the capstone of the Justice Department's use of the RICO statute against the Italian Mafia was the so-called Commission case, in 1986. To build that prosecution, FBI agents had combed through thousands of pages of wiretap transcripts to mine evidence of a historical criminal conspiracy among the leaders of the five New York families. The convictions of the bosses did more than any other prosecution to break the back of the Italian Mafia.

The Commission case involved using RICO precisely as the former Criminal Division lawyer who wrote the law, G. Robert Blakey, intended. Blakey had served in the Organized Crime and Racketeering Section many years earlier before moving to Capitol Hill as the top lawyer counseling the U.S. Senate Subcommittee on Criminal Laws and Procedures. The rarest of Justice Department lawyers, he was both a pragmatic prosecutor and one of the brightest legal minds in federal law enforcement. It was Blakey's vision that the government should not just prosecute members of a criminal organization for their crimes, it should prosecute the criminal organization itself and all of its members. RICO, as Blakey explained it, allows federal agents and prosecutors to use the fact of a criminal act—a murder, the sale of narcotics—as an item of evidence. The idea is simple—connect the dots. Link a murder, a drug deal, an act of money laundering, and all of a sudden you've got a pattern of criminal activity. Link the pattern to a particularly violent street gang or foreign narcotics cartel, and you could prosecute an entire criminal enterprise. Blakey had also authored the 1968 Omnibus Crime Control and Safe Streets Act. Title III—the section of the law that gives government agents authority to wiretap suspects in investigations of violations of federal laws—has done more than anything else to help the Department of Justice escalate the war on crime.

By 1991, Paul Coffey had assumed direction of an Organized Crime and Racketeering Section that had taken RICO to new lengths. He liked and respected Blakey, who has since become a distinguished professor at the University of Notre Dame. Blakey affectionately ribbed Coffey, calling him a practitioner of "old thinking." But Coffey has done more than nearly anyone else in the Criminal Division to extend the use of RICO to targets never contemplated by Blakey. Thanks to the FBI, the Italian Mafia families were no longer significant players in many spheres of criminal activity, although they still maintained a hold over some labor unions. But what the FBI called "emerging groups"—the organized crime syndicates from Latin America, Asia and, more recently, the former Soviet Union—were as dangerous as the Italian Mafia had ever been.

Of the one hundred or so racketeering prosecutions that Coffey signed off on each year, most still targeted traditional organized crime syndicates. But that was less and less the case. Not long after the inauguration of Bill Clinton, Coffey had spent weeks going over a prosecution memo that proposed a massive racketeering indictment of the Laborers' International Union of North America. This was a classic use of the RICO statute. After poring over the proposed indictment and suggesting some changes, Coffey had given the go-ahead to proceed. The result was a massive takeover of the union, with more than two dozen former federal agents and prosecutors installed to run the operation under authority from a U.S. District Court judge.

RICO is a tremendously powerful tool, and Congress has steadily added to the list of crimes it could attack, with five specific amendments between 1978 and 1989. While the number of RICO indictments approved annually by Washington hovered between 100 and 115, more and more were aimed at white-collar criminals. The trend had begun in the mid-1980s in New York. Rudolph Giuliani, then the U.S. attorney in Manhattan, had directed his staff to make prosecutions of Wall Street securities fraud a priority. The results had been impressive. Several big individual traders, people like Dennis Levine and Ivan Boesky, were named in RICO cases. The truly significant cases, however, involved patterns of criminal activity as defined by Bob Blakey. In a flurry of memoranda to Washington, Giuliani's lawyers had proposed charging entire securities firms with racketeering crimes. Two firms in particular stood out. The first was a relatively unknown New Jersey–based brokerage, Princeton-Newport Partners. The second was Drexel Burnham Lambert, a lion of the Wall Street establishment. Through an elaborate scheme of sham transactions involving illegally "parked" securities and phony "buy" and "sell" orders, traders from Drexel Burnham and Princeton-Newport had defrauded thousands of investors of billions of dollars.

In Washington, Paul Coffey, then the deputy for RICO matters in the Organized Crime and Racketeering Section, reviewed the prosecution memos prepared by Giuliani's lawyers. Some refinements in the proposed indictments were needed—they nearly always were. But, clearly, the activities of Princeton-Newport and Drexel met the Blakey standards for both criminal enterprise and the pattern of criminal activity defined as racketeering.

Citing Princeton-Newport, Drexel Burnham and a handful of other successful RICO prosecutions, Justice Department lawyers in the field soon began seeking more creative uses of the statute. The smartest eventually found their way to Paul Coffey's office, on the third floor of an elegant commercial building in downtown Washington, two blocks from Ford's Theatre, where Abraham Lincoln was shot, and four blocks from Main Justice. The petitioners at Coffey's door seldom had an easy time of it.

Coffey and the lawyers in the Organized Crime and Racketeering Section were generally well regarded by assistant U.S. attorneys. But those prosecutors in the field didn't want to be obliged to go to Washington on bended knee for Coffey's permission every time they wanted to use the big gun of RICO. This sentiment pointed to a fundamental question that could be asked about other weapons that Main Justice kept under tight rein.

The Criminal Division had been given the authority to approve RICO indictments on the theory that it could provide an objective review in Washington and thereby protect the statute from legal challenge and abuse. Given RICO's devastating impact on defendants, federal courts were alert to any abuses. Powers granted to the Justice Department could be taken away. Under Coffey's stewardship, the department's handling of RICO had withstood close scrutiny by appeals courts. The attorney general's advisory committee had urged Janet Reno to end Main Justice oversight of RICO prosecutions. After considerable thought Reno had rebuffed the advisory committee. As a result, federal prosecutors seeking to file a RICO indictment anywhere in the nation still had to get Coffey's blessing first.

By the end of the first year of the Clinton administration, the RICO prosecutions approved by Coffey and his staff were more varied than ever. In the pipeline in Coffey's office were proposed racketeering indictments of twenty-two senior executives of the America Honda Motor Company; the attorney general of the state of Pennsylvania; and the founder of the National Hockey League Players Association, a shameless self-promoter named R. Alan Eagleson, who liked to call himself "Mr. Hockey." According to the sixty-five-page RICO indictment approved by Paul Coffey, Mr. Hockey had greatly abused his position as the NHL players' representative in order to loot the pension of former Boston Bruins great Bobby Orr while illegally laying hands on a variety of players' property—everything from free car-wash coupons to gratis air tickets to India.

As varied as those prosecutions were, all relied on the same tried and tested formula Bob Blakey had developed two decades earlier. In each case, the crimes alleged were important, but they were cited as instances in larger patterns of criminal activity that constituted racketeering.

Of all the proposed RICO prosecutions submitted for Coffey's review during the early 1990s, none showed how far the law's reach had extended over the years than the indictment of C. R. Bard, Inc., a highly regarded manufacturer of various medical products. A Fortune 500 firm, Bard produced and sold everything from tongue depressors to heart catheters. In 1992 it recorded annual sales of about $1 billion.

In the late 1980s the market for heart catheters, devices that remove obstructions in arteries near the heart, was very competitive. The devices worked simply, in theory. A wire with a tiny deflated balloon affixed to the end was inserted into an artery in a leg or arm, then maneuvered closer to the heart. A cardiologist positioned the balloon close to the lesion or plaque sediment that caused the blockage. The balloon was then inflated in an effort to break down and dislodge the blockage.

Because of the sensitivity of the operation and the potential danger to patients, the federal Food and Drug Administration was required by law to approve all heart catheters designed for use in humans before they could be sold in the United States. In July 1987, Bard requested FDA approval for a heart catheter the company called Probe A. The FDA gave its approval. Within months, however, a company engineer identified a "critical failure mode" in the catheter: The core wire on the device tended to break off. Bard executives scrambled. The company began running "disaster trials." Then, without securing permission from or notifying the FDA—as required by law—Bard redesigned the Probe A catheter and began selling it. The product was highly profitable. In August and September 1988, Bard earned more than $8 million from sales of its catheters. Then, in late September, tragedy struck. During a routine catheterization the tiny balloon at the end of a redesigned Bard catheter failed to deflate. The way catheters work, the balloons are designed to be inflated for no more than a minute, then deflated to allow the resumption of blood flow through the artery. If the balloon fails to deflate, total arterial blockage can occur. That, in turn, can cause heart failure.

That's what happened in September 1988. A woman undergoing a routine catheterization in Michigan died suddenly when a modified Probe A catheter failed. News of the patient's death circulated quickly within the cardiology community. Sales of Bard's catheters plummeted. Panicked, the company began turning out still newer versions of its catheter. Company officials made another deliberate decision not to seek approval from the FDA for the successor catheters to Probe A. The FDA approval process took too long, the catheter market was too red-hot to wait.

In December 1988 disaster struck again. Three days after Christmas, Eunice Beavers checked into the Oak Hill Hospital in Joplin, Missouri. Her cardiologist had scheduled Beavers for a routine balloon angioplasty catheterization. Beavers was seventy-six, but her overall health was good. Her husband of fifty-two years, her three daughters, and her eleven grandchildren and eleven great-grandchildren were told there was nothing to worry about. The odds against trouble, the doctor said, were "a thousand to one." But Beavers died when the balloon at the end of the Bard catheter failed to deflate. That very day at Bard headquarters in New Jersey, company executives voted to continue selling the company's catheters—even though physicians had begun reporting yet another problem: The tips of some Bard catheters were breaking off during routine procedures. Doctors in some cases had been forced to leave the plastic tips inside their patients.

The "tip problem" soon grew worse, and Bard executives established a "probe crisis team." By March 1989, the team recorded the following: "Three complaints per day for the last few days. Product no longer available for sale. . . . We have reached the limit of our threshold—now is the time to withdraw."

But Bard did not withdraw from the market. Instead, the company's top executives ordered the crisis team and the engineering staff to move more quickly with still more catheter redesigns. Instructions were issued to keep the company's catheters flooding into the marketplace. On April 28, 1989, the probe crisis team noted this injunction from executives: "Don't take your foot off the pedal."

By mid-1989, Bard finally contacted the FDA to inform the agency that it had changed the coating on some catheters. The FDA was not happy. Inspectors suspected that the new coating contained carcinogens. Bard responded with alacrity—and with biocompatibility test data on guinea pigs, dogs, mice and New Zealand white rabbits. The company provided no information at all on how the coating might affect humans. The FDA didn't back down. The coating, the agency said, was "not approvable."

In Boston, Assistant U.S. Attorney Michael K. Loucks was assigned to look at the allegations against Bard. Eunice Beavers had died in Missouri, and Bard's corporate offices were in New Jersey. But for five months in 1988 a Bard subsidiary had shipped more then twenty thousand catheters from an unlicensed manufacturing facility in Haverhill, Massachusetts, claiming that the devices had come from an FDA-approved plant in another city. Bard had earned approximately $6 million from the sale of the illegally manufactured catheters.

The investigation proved slow going at first. Eventually, it moved into high gear. Investigators from the FDA did some of the original spadework. Then criminal investigators from the FBI were brought in. The evidence against Bard piled up rapidly. Confidential sources began coming forward with information; more was obtained through government subpoenas. The head of the Bard division that manufactured the catheters in Massachusetts had established a "breakfast club" of middle managers who met twice a month to discuss problems. Minutes were kept. Soon, the minutes began finding their way to government investigators. The notes were damning, some indicating plainly that Bard was selling new Probe catheters without FDA permission. Notes from the "probe crisis team" meetings also found their way into the hands of investigators. They were more damning still.

The portrait of Bard that began to emerge was frightening. During a carpool ride to work one morning, one of the company's top engineers confided his frustrations to his fellow passengers. "We never give our people enough time to accomplish their jobs but rather rush the program to the next step before it is ready," the man said. ". . . We now find ourselves in the most uncomfortable position of trying to decide what to sell without adequate tests in place. . . . Were we so with the program that we failed to anticipate that something could go wrong? Does asking tough questions or making waves put one in the political shithouse?" Notes of the engineer's comments were typed up. They, too, were passed on to government investigators, who passed them on to prosecutor Loucks. He filed them, obscurely, under the title "notes from a passenger to the driver and other passengers." In his office in Boston, Loucks's investigative file on Bard was getting thicker and thicker.

Clearly, the most significant issue with Bard, Loucks believed, was the pattern of corporate criminal conduct. In addition to the tragedy of Eunice Beavers's death, scores of people across the country had suffered grievously because of Bard's arrogance and greed. As a result of catheterizations where the Bard product had failed or malfunctioned, many people had had to undergo painful emergency surgery.

After discussing the case at length with his superiors in Boston, Loucks began presenting evidence against Bard to a grand jury. Under federal guidelines, outlined in a 240-page "manual for federal prosecutors" on RICO, Loucks was prohibited from threatening to charge Bard or its corporate officers with a racketeering indictment. The most he could say was that a RICO charge was being contemplated, among others; no such charge would or could be brought, however, unless it was approved by Main Justice in Washington. Bard, despite the careful wording, was put on notice.

From Boston, Loucks called Paul Coffey in Washington to discuss the case. Coffey asked some questions. When a prosecutor started talking about bringing a RICO indictment against a publicly held corporation and not a Mafia family or drug gang, Coffey's antennae went up. The interests of shareholders, employees and company vendors had to be contemplated.

As Loucks outlined the evidence, Coffey was impressed. If the facts of the case were exactly as Loucks said, they clearly supported a racketeering indictment. Would Coffey allow him to file against Bard corporately? Loucks asked.

I don't know, Coffey replied. But be prepared for a "no." The bar was very high for charging corporate entities.

A few weeks later, as promised, Loucks sent Coffey the prosecution memo against Bard and five of its most senior executives. Reviewing the memo, Coffey had few illusions that the case would be a simple one. *Fortune* 500 firms never went quietly on cases like this. Already, Bard had retained a trio of talented lawyers from the Washington firm of Williams & Connolly. The firm, founded by the legendary Edward Bennett Williams, had a well-earned track record of recruiting and cultivating top-notch legal talent. Brendan Sullivan, who had defended Lieutenant Colonel Oliver North during the Iran-contra affair, was the firm's best-known partner. But all its lawyers were able adversaries. Coffey had no expectation that they would take the criminal charges lying down. From his corner office on the third floor, Coffey could see Williams & Connolly's offices just across the street. He had a feeling he would be spending a fair amount of time with the lawyers there.

That was all right with him. Coffey was impressed by the detail and specificity of Loucks's prosecution memo. The evidence his investigators had amassed was such that the proposed criminal charges divided neatly into categories. Against the company and its top executives there was compelling evidence of criminal conspiracy, mail fraud, racketeering, false statements to government investigators, the sale of adulterated products in violation of the federal Food, Drug and Cosmetic Act, and, finally, aiding and abetting the criminal conspiracy.

The way Loucks broke it down, the company alone could be charged with 391 criminal charges, a phenomenal number, all the more so because each charge carried a maximum statutory penalty of $500,000. That meant Bard's exposure in the case would be nearly $200 million, a devastating sum for a company with about $1 billion in sales.

Coffey asked Loucks to come to Washington. During a meeting there Coffey worked through the charges with the prosecutor one by one. The evidence was damning as hell.

It was time to take the next step. The way the RICO process works at Main Justice, defense counsel for any individual or corporate entity that is the subject of a racketeering investigation has the right to confer with Coffey and the prosecutors working the case before charges are filed. This is another measure of the care the Criminal Division takes in controlling the use of its heaviest artillery.

The meeting took place in a conference room just down the hall from Coffey's office on the third floor, in early fall 1993. The Williams & Connolly lawyers were there, along with others representing the company and its executives.

Coffey opened the meeting by saying that no racketeering indictment had been approved yet. That's why they were getting together. He would give a detailed description of the evidence without identifying witnesses who might be cooperating with the investigation. Then the defense lawyers would be free not just to challenge the accuracy of the facts as they had been stated, but to argue, as a matter of policy—not law—why a racketeering indictment was not appropriate in the case.

Many of the lawyers in the room had been through the RICO drill before with Coffey. The standards for charging a corporation with racketeering are simple. Basically, they boil down to three. To merit a RICO indictment, a corporation's conduct has to be egregiously and intentionally corrupt. Its misconduct has to be either the direct handiwork of high-level corporate officials or carried out with the knowledge of those officials. And the corporation has to have benefited substantially from the pattern of misconduct. In Bard's case, the three standards for filing the RICO charges had more than been met. The company's conduct had been egregious—people had died as a result of it. The top officers had been directly involved. The evidence cited in Loucks's prosecution memo left no doubt of that. And the company had profited handsomely from its crimes. Its own records showed the flawed catheters had earned Bard millions.

RICO conferences involving the easiest cases last an hour or two. The Bard conference involved two separate meetings on different days. The attorneys representing Bard corporately spent a great deal of time trying to persuade Coffey not to charge the company. This was standard procedure. Before the indictment of Drexel Burnham Lambert, the company's lawyers put on all kinds of evidence about the effect of a RICO indictment on the firm's employees and investors. They had even argued about the impact on the economy of New York City. The Bard lawyers made arguments that were quite similar.

Coffey called the arguments made by lawyers for companies like Bard "the Lizzie Borden argument." As Coffey explained, it was "where you kill both your parents, then throw yourself on the mercy of the court because you are an orphan." Corporate defense counsel, Coffey believed, could not blame every alleged crime on the company's executives and expect the company not to be charged. That just wasn't going to happen.

After the conference Coffey and Loucks agreed that Bard should be charged corporately, separate and apart from its executives. Loucks and his investigators ran the numbers for the company. Its gross sales of the defective catheters were approximately $61 million. The government could seek the maximum penalty against Bard and go for a much higher fine. That was unwarranted, though. If the company signed the plea agreement Loucks and Coffey worked up, it would pay the $61 million, then be quit of both its civil and criminal liabilities. The fates of the company's executives would be decided later.

Eventually, Bard did agree. On December 15, 1993, in Courtroom Number 4 of the old Boston Post Office and Courthouse, an attorney for C. R. Bard, Inc., informed the Honorable Mark L. Wolf that the company waived its right to a grand jury indictment and trial. Instead, Bard would plead guilty to all 391 charges outlined in Criminal Information 93-10279-WF. The company would also pay civil fines in the amount of $30.5 million and criminal fines in the amount of $30.5 million. In addition, as specified in the plea agreement, Bard would hire a new vice president for scientific affairs and an independent outside consultant acceptable to the Food and Drug Administration, and implement a corporate compliance code to ensure that the types of abuses that had occurred during the manufacture and marketing of its heart catheters never occurred again.

The $61 million settlement was the largest ever levied against a corporation in a health-care criminal case; officers of the corporation would be convicted at a later criminal trial. In the statement of facts filed with Judge Wolf in conjunction with the plea agreement, Loucks stated why he believed the case and its resolution were significant: "It is the goal of the United States through the acceptance of this plea, coupled with the pending prosecution of the corporate officers involved, that a clear and harsh message be sent to corporate officers across the United States about the consequences of such illegal conduct: Not only do you risk, through your illicit decisions, betting the company; but you risk significant personal punishment as well. Corporate criminal conduct is among the most deterrable of all criminal behavior. The plea agreement herein proffered to the court for approval is a most significant step in procuring such deterrence." A related Justice Department sentencing memorandum stated the matter more broadly: The prosecution and the fines levied against Bard "will be remembered in corporate boardrooms across the country."

The RICO Act authored by G. Robert Blakey had been drafted to target the Italian Mafia. More than two decades after the law's passage, it was being used to prosecute willful corporate criminals.

CHAPTER TEN

A GENTLEMAN
FROM COLOMBIA

Harold Ackerman, the gentlemanly Colombian businessman who had administered the Cali cartel's operations in Miami, was talking. In small, secret, well-guarded rooms, he answered hundreds of questions from agents and prosecutors. In the fifteen years that the Justice Department had been pursuing the Cali cartel, Ackerman was the most important witness ever to cooperate with the government. He was intelligent, precise, businesslike. Best of all, he had kept careful records of his many dealings with Cali kingpin Miguel Rodríguez Orejuela.

Because of Ackerman's cooperation, Operation Cornerstone had developed into one of the most important narcotics investigations in the country. No expense was spared to exploit its potential. To forestall the threat of retaliation, arrangements had been made to have Ackerman's closest relatives spirited out of Colombia and relocated. Ackerman's family was accepted into the federal witness security program, which was, like wiretapping authorizations, administered by the Office of Enforcement Operations at Main Justice.

From their base of operations at the High Intensity Drug Traf-

ficking Area facility in Miami, the Cornerstone agents were tracking witnesses and evidence throughout the hemisphere. Prosecutors Edward Ryan and William Pearson began to present the
pieces of the Cornerstone case to a grand jury that met once a
week in the federal courthouse in downtown Miami. It was less
than a year since Theresa Van Vliet, the chief prosecutor at
HIDTA, had explained her ambitious vision of what Edward
Kacerosky and Louis Weiss might be able to achieve with Cornerstone. Now it was taking shape.

On a bell-clear Miami day at the end of 1993, the agents and
prosecutors working on Operation Cornerstone pushed the investigation of the Cali cartel one big step closer to the "whole new
level" that Van Vliet had urged upon Kacerosky. Stepping into
the gloomy confines of the old federal courthouse in Miami, the
prosecutors, Ryan and Pearson, and the two federal agents,
Kacerosky and Weiss, made their way down to a windowless group
of rooms known as "the igloo" to talk to Raúl Martí. After several
minutes a federal marshal escorted the disconsolate drug smuggler
into the chamber. The slender Cuban had his black hair greased
back flat against his skull. Even in the crepuscular gloom of the
igloo, Martí's head gleamed with brilliantine.

Three months earlier Kacerosky had led a small group of heavily armed federal agents onto the grounds of a large residential
property in Homestead, where the long Florida peninsula ends
and the Keys begin. The agents had followed four large steel cargo
containers that had arrived from Panama in the Port of Miami.
The containers had been off-loaded and delivered to a warehouse
leased by Taino Coffee and Food Importers. From there, the containers had been moved again, this time in a big Hertz-Penske
rental truck. In unmarked cars, agents had followed the truck west
and then south as it headed toward Homestead. There the truck
had pulled up to a four-car garage where boxes that had been
stacked on wooden pallets within the containers were unloaded.

Kacerosky had seen enough. He compiled this information in a
new affidavit. The judge who reviewed it then granted his permission to execute search warrants at the Homestead residence. During the raid Kacerosky found that the boxes labeled Taino Coffee

contained not coffee beans but cocaine—5,600 kilograms of high-grade coke, to be exact. Below a concrete floor in the garage, agents discovered a stainless steel vault with a familiar design. It was identical to the secret vaults that had been found in warehouses used by Ackerman's employees and in their homes. The vaults had been built by a Cali cartel specialist known as "the engineer," whose job was to go around the country building them for the cartel's cocaine and money.

The most important of the four men Kacerosky arrested after the raid in Homestead was Raúl Martí. The Customs agent strongly suspected that Martí had replaced Ackerman as the Cali cartel's man in Miami. If that was true, it would stand to reason that Martí had dealt directly with Miguel Rodríguez Orejuela.

Kacerosky was dead right. The slightly built Cuban had done just as he had been instructed by Rodríguez Orejuela many months before. Martí had forsworn the use of cellular telephones, purchasing instead a batch of prepaid debit calling cards that he and the cartel's other employees had used at random pay phones in South Florida to communicate with the Rodríguez brothers in Cali. Martí's laziness had helped give the system away. Some days he was simply too overcome by lethargy to travel very far in the Florida heat to place his phone calls. Instead, he had walked down the street from his office and used his debit card at the corner phone booth.

After the Office of Enforcement Operations at Main Justice rejected the application Kacerosky had prepared with Theresa Van Vliet for a roving tap on the pay phones, the Cornerstone team had gone back to basics. They followed Martí, and they watched his warehouses. Taino Coffee was receiving shipments of cocaine, thousands of kilos at a time. Of that Kacerosky was certain. As a U.S. Customs Service agent, Kacerosky could open any shipping container at will in what was called a "border search." But the cocaine was not what mattered; it was the organization they were after. Martí was only one piece on the chessboard. It had been enormously frustrating not to be able to listen in on Martí's telephone.

Now in the igloo with prosecutors Pearson and Ryan, DEA agent

Weiss and Kacerosky, the enterprising Cuban was hinting that he, like Harold Ackerman, might be interested in striking a deal. The prosecutors and agents were ready to take the next step. At first, Martí hung tough and declined to cooperate. But in the days that followed the prosecutors and agents applied more leverage. Martí's attorney had informed his client that Kacerosky had begun to investigate the smuggler's spouse. Martí exploded. It was he who had handled the smuggling operations for Miguel Rodríguez, Martí protested. What did the government want with his wife?

Martí's attorney explained that the evidence was such that the government might charge her with obstruction of justice—a felony. She, too, might be sent to prison. Martí couldn't believe it. He would not permit that to happen to his wife.

In the igloo, after Martí took his seat, the two prosecutors got straight to the point. We have the goods on your wife, they told Martí. She's in big trouble, looking at serious prison time.

Martí was grim. If it would help his wife's cause, he said, he was prepared to cooperate.

Good, Pearson told Martí. Any cooperation on Martí's part could go a long way toward helping his wife.

Kacerosky was delighted. If Raúl Martí proved to be as cooperative as Harold Ackerman—if he could provide them with chapter and verse on the cartel's smuggling operations—they would have two major witnesses with direct knowledge of the Cali kingpins' criminal actions. Kacerosky got down to business quickly, asking Martí about several trips he had made to Venezuela.

Martí gave detailed answers, describing how he was initiated into the ranks of cartel managers and how he operated in Miami. Many of his answers confirmed what Kacerosky knew.

What about communications with Miguel Rodríguez? Kacerosky demanded. How did he reach the drug baron in Cali?

Simple, Martí explained. He called Miguel from public telephones. Rodríguez had insisted on that means of communication. Martí elaborated: Cellular phones had been banned because of the wiretaps in the earlier prosecution of Ackerman. Martí related the story of his visit to Cali and his introduction to the cartel procedure. He told the story of being instructed to study the court affidavits from the Ackerman case. He dealt almost always, he said, with Miguel Rodríguez; Miguel could not leave things alone. He was constantly calling subordinates to check on details. Sometimes, Martí explained, Miguel's older brother, Gilberto, came on the line, too. Or they had a conference call with José Santacruz Londoño, known as Chepe, the co-founder of the Cali cartel. Taking turns, the kingpins would grill Martí about the details of his latest shipment, his preparations, security. Martí had the impression, he told his interrogators, that the big losses caused by the Ackerman case had shaken the Cali cartel's confidence in Miguel Rodríguez. It had lost hundreds of millions of dollars worth of product. Gilberto and Chepe were nervous. They wanted to make sure the new operator in Miami—Raúl Martí—was getting good guidance.

Kacerosky groaned inwardly. He felt ill. All the while he and Theresa Van Vliet had been trying to persuade Main Justice to approve a roving wiretap on the pay phones, Raúl Martí had been talking directly with Miguel Rodríguez and the two founders of the Cali cartel. Had the government intercepted those conversations, Kacerosky fumed, they would have had the purest kind of legal dynamite, some of the strongest direct evidence ever obtained against the Cali cartel: the kingpins talking logistics with a distributor.

Martí had more to tell. He provided Kacerosky, Weiss and the prosecutors with the telephone numbers he had called. They were some of the same home numbers used by the organization in Cali. Martí's demeanor was encouraging, Kacerosky thought. He wanted to do the right thing, to protect his wife from prosecution. A man in that situation does not lie. Kacerosky asked a few more questions, but already he was convinced: Raúl Martí had crossed over.

Three months after the interview with Raúl Martí in the igloo, Edward Kacerosky and Lou Weiss were in Caracas, Venezuela, watching a prosperous-looking man eating breakfast. It had taken a long time to get to Harold Ackerman, a while longer to snare Raúl Martí. Now, because of their cooperation, the Cornerstone juggernaut had acquired a breathtaking new momentum. In Ackerman and Martí, the Cornerstone team had two of the Cali cartel's top business managers in South Florida.

As he gazed across the shimmering swimming pool of Caracas's elegant Hotel Tamanaco, Kacerosky had his eye on a third important Cali employee. Over the course of eight years, Pedro S. Isern had shepherded twenty-two separate multi-ton loads of cocaine into South Florida, concealing the drugs beneath tons of frozen broccoli that came from Guatemala. Isern and his subordinates imported them through a series of legitimate Miami produce companies. The shipments totaled an astonishing 60,000 kilos, worth an even more astonishing $900 million—and that was just the wholesale street value.

By any measure, Pedro Isern had had a remarkable run for the cartel. But smuggling was a stressful life, and in 1990 he had given it up and made way for Harold Ackerman. Isern had fled the United States on the day Ackerman was arrested. Unfortunately, he had not left quite soon enough. Ackerman had consulted Isern as a kind of senior adviser on cartel affairs. A wiretap placed on Ackerman's cellular telephones had picked up those conversations. Miguel Rodríguez's American lawyers had informed Isern that he had been identified: The wiretap evidence had been disclosed in the Ackerman case. Rodríguez had taken care to warn Isern to stay out of the United States or be arrested.

Isern had done as instructed. What he did not know, as he plowed through his breakfast at the Hotel Tamanaco, was that Venezuela is only slightly less safe than the United States for fugitives from U.S. law-enforcement agencies. Unlike Colombia, Venezuela has an extradition treaty with the United States. That meant Isern was fair game for federal agents. Watching the courtly Cuban chatting with his companions, Kacerosky smiled. In his breast pocket he had an arrest warrant for Isern.

After the former Cali business manager finished his meal, he rose from the table and strolled through the Tamanaco's elegant lobby and out the front door. Detectives from the Venezuelan police arrested him seconds later.

Within hours of being put on a plane to Miami, Isern was sitting in an interrogation room at the HIDTA offices, feeling boxed in. He had been hustled off the plane, walked through Miami International Airport and bundled into a government car with darkened windows. The federal agents owned Isern, and he knew it. He knew from the warning he had received from Miguel Rodríguez, and from the court documents in the American case that he had been shown in Cali, that the evidence against him was great. Sitting across from Edward Kacerosky, Isern conceded as much. He was inclined to cooperate, but he was worried. He knew how Miguel Rodríguez operated; he knew the system. If he agreed to cooperate in exchange for lenient treatment by the prosecutors, Isern said, Rodríguez would learn about it from his American lawyers. The men from Cali had no use for snitches.

Kacerosky said he understood. There was a way to work around that, though. Isern should have his wife call Cali immediately, Kacerosky advised, and tell Miguel or one of his associates that her husband was "doing the right thing but that he needed help."

Okay, Isern replied. He placed the phone call to his wife and instructed her on what to say to Rodríguez.

Two days later Isern was sitting in his cell at the Metropolitan Correctional Center in Miami when a guard informed him that he had a visitor. Isern was surprised because he wasn't expecting anyone. The identity of the visitor surprised him even more. Isern was escorted into one of the interview rooms set aside for inmate meetings with lawyers. The tall, well-dressed stranger waiting for him there introduced himself as Donald Ferguson. Isern had never even heard of him.

Ferguson was a former assistant U.S. attorney. After leaving the Department of Justice he had built a reputation in Florida as a solid trial lawyer specializing in criminal defense work. A year earlier Ferguson had been co-counsel on a civil case in Brooklyn, New York. The other lawyers were Francisco Laguna and Michael

Abbell, partners in a small boutique firm in Washington, D.C., specializing in criminal defense work for foreign clients. Abbell was particularly adept in the field. Like Ferguson, he had once worked for the Justice Department, but at a much higher level. He was a contemporary of David Margolis, whom he had known at Harvard Law School, and had also become a career lawyer at Main Justice. A decade earlier Abbell had run the Office of International Affairs in the Criminal Division of Main Justice. In the case in Brooklyn, Abbell, Laguna and Ferguson had sought release of funds in Federal court, claiming at trial that they were representing the heirs of Santacruz's father-in-law. In the civil side of a criminal money-laundering case against the cartel, the Justice Department had seized nearly $30 million of the cartel's cash in a proceeding known as an asset forfeiture. Santacruz had been shuttling more than $60 million around bank accounts in Europe, many of them held in the name of his wife or her family. Authorities in Europe, working with the DEA, had figured out the scam. Federal prosecutors in New York were able to intercept wire transfers going through New York bank accounts. Abbell, Laguna and Ferguson had been hired for the case after they traveled to Cali and had a meeting with Miguel Rodríguez and José Santacruz, the government would later allege in court records.

Now, Donald Ferguson was introducing himself to Isern. In the interview room at MCC, he described his previous work with Abbell and Laguna in the Brooklyn case. Isern did not know Ferguson and had not sought his help. The cartel had gotten the message, via the telephone call from Isern's wife. She had said Isern was "doing the right thing."

That's correct, Isern answered. Please assure Miguel and the others that he was not cooperating with the authorities.

Good, Ferguson nodded. He told Isern to expect a visit soon from another lawyer, Francisco Laguna, who stayed in close touch with Cali. Isern could send Miguel Rodríguez a message directly through Laguna.

Okay, replied Isern. But the evidence against him was overwhelming. Wasn't there some way he could cooperate with the government on a limited basis, tell them things that would not hurt Miguel and the others in Cali?

Forget it, Ferguson said sharply. The government would never be satisfied with limited cooperation. They would want Isern to talk about Miguel and the other cartel bosses. Miguel Rodríguez considered cooperation of any kind unacceptable. It was treachery—no less.

After Ferguson departed Edward Kacerosky paid a visit to MCC. With Pedro Isern's agreement, Kacerosky had arranged to tape-record any conversations between him and whichever of the cartel's lawyers showed up in response to his wife's phone call. Listening to the tape Kacerosky was astonished. Ferguson was a former Justice Department lawyer. Lots of former prosecutors represented sleazeball defendants. That was how the system worked. Even the most guilty criminal defendants were entitled to adequate representation in court. But most former prosecutors were ethical lawyers. They didn't cross the line in representing their clients. They didn't cut corners. Ferguson had crossed the line big time, Kacerosky believed. His words to Isern were veiled, but to the agents and prosecutors there was no question about their meaning. Cooperation of any kind was "unacceptable," Ferguson had told Isern. The lawyer had not said what the penalties were for unacceptable behavior. Clearly, Pedro Isern already knew.

CHAPTER ELEVEN

COUNSEL TO THE CALI CARTEL

For as long as Theresa Van Vliet had been the chief prosecutor at the big High Intensity Drug Trafficking Area facility—indeed, for as long as there had been a HIDTA office in Miami—her main contact at Main Justice in Washington had been Mary Lee Warren. Since Van Vliet and her staff of prosecutors handled so many complex cases involving so many wide-ranging issues, she dealt often with Warren.

Because Van Vliet had emphasized wiretap cases, the eavesdroppers at HIDTA were intercepting calls going to and from branches of the Cali cartel all over the country. In Houston, New York and Los Angeles, other prosecutors had their own Title IIIs in place and were pursuing local branches of the cartel. The nature of the target was a loosely connected group of "cells" held together by the glue of the cartel's control over the supply. Overlapping federal investigations became the rule rather than the exception. Conflicts were routine, which meant that national coordination from Main Justice was vital. U.S. attorneys in different districts were all working on the same target. Somebody had to be the referee.

That was Mary Lee Warren. The countless phone calls and frequent visits by Theresa Van Vliet to Washington had led to a friendship. Warren was impressed by the energy and tenacity of the younger Van Vliet. She was getting results down in Miami. Van Vliet, for her part, could not have asked for a more savvy or supportive superior than Warren. She knew just what a line prosecutor needed to function out in the field.

In a phone call to Van Vliet in early April 1994, Warren broke what she thought would be received as good news. She was being promoted. Jo Ann Harris, the head of the Criminal Division, had just named her as one of her five deputies, bringing her to "the front office," filling the job David Margolis had vacated when he went to work for Philip Heymann.

"How wonderful for you," Van Vliet said. She was pleased for and proud of her friend, but she feigned annoyance. "I can't believe you are dumping me like this."

Warren laughed. "That's what I wanted to talk to you about." Someone would have to take her job running the narcotics section. She told Van Vliet to apply for the job.

Van Vliet was dubious. Washington made her edgy. South Florida was home. She had grown up in Fort Lauderdale, a forty-minute drive up the interstate from Miami. Alternately combative and self-deprecatory, Van Vliet had attended Catholic high school in Fort Lauderdale, majored in English in college, then went to law school. Upon graduation, she won a clerkship for a federal judge who insisted that all his young lawyers-to-be sit with him through the drama and tedium of real trials. It was in court that Van Vliet had her epiphany. She identified most, she told friends, with the lawyers who entered the courtroom with the United States of America as their client.

In 1985, Theresa Van Vliet realized her dream of becoming a federal prosecutor. Ronald Reagan had named Stanley Marcus, an Organized Crime Strike Force lawyer from Detroit who had once worked for David Margolis, as the new U.S. attorney in Miami. The veteran prosecutor moved from Michigan to a city under siege. Miami led the nation in murders. It had just experienced one of the worst urban race riots in history. As if that were not enough, the world's largest drug-trafficking organizations had set up shop in the city, employing its banks, bars and hotels as a series of convenience stops for cash drop-offs, drug deliveries and late-night execution parlors.

The federal prosecutor's office that Marcus inherited was a backwater. His mandate from Main Justice was to shape it up, to energize the place. Marcus set about doing just that. He was given money to hire the best and brightest young lawyers he could find. Theresa Van Vliet had been one of Marcus's new hires. Like every new young prosecutor, she had been thrown into the pit of the Major Crimes Section of the U.S. Attorney's Office, handling whatever criminal cases the federal agents happened to drag in. Washington had flooded South Florida with an army of new federal agents to battle the crime problem. At all hours of the day and night, the agents showed up in Marcus's office, transforming the place from a sleepy government law office to a round-the-clock battlefield command post. It had the feel of a MASH unit just behind the front lines.

Van Vliet loved it. After a year she transferred up to the federal prosecutor's office in Fort Lauderdale. The cases there were every bit as big as in Miami. One of Van Vliet's biggest was a prosecution of the Outlaws motorcycle gang. The Outlaws did a thriving trade in methamphetamine and cocaine throughout South Florida. They also supplied prostitutes who worked as dancers in the topless bars that studded the Gold Coast from Miami north to Palm Beach. FBI agents working the Outlaws case developed evidence of murder, torture and extortion. With a fellow prosecutor, Van Vliet sent a prosecution memo to Washington proposing a sweeping racketeering indictment of the Outlaws. At Main Justice, Paul Coffey in the Organized Crime and Racketeering Section had approved the indictment. Some of the government's best witnesses were young women who had ridden with the Outlaws bikers. They had both endured and been present during some of the gang's worst violence. Part of Van Vliet's role was to shepherd these still-terrified victims through grueling months of trial. Hearing the jury foreman announce mostly guilty verdicts had confirmed Van Vliet's sense of mission. She and her colleagues had used the federal law to confront an authentic evil, a ruthless criminal organization that had flouted state authorities and preyed on society.

That was the kind of work Van Vliet would give up if she moved to Washington, she knew. Building prosecutions and taking them to trial was her joy. She relished the combat of a courtroom; she enjoyed the camaraderie with the agents. Federal prosecutors could make things happen. They controlled the machinery of search warrants and wiretaps. They ran grand juries and drafted indictments. At Main Justice, Van Vliet feared, people mostly went to meetings. There, lawyers were cut off from the action and consumed by office politics. Some of them wouldn't deign to talk with a street agent. If she took a job in Washington, Van Vliet worried, she could no longer do the one thing that she loved the most—going into a federal courtroom on a big criminal case and putting bad guys away. Was Washington really worth it?

Mary Lee Warren urged her to think about it. With her feel for the work, Van Vliet could move easily into the job of coordinating the nation's drug war.

As Van Vliet was considering it, she received some unsolicited advice. Douglas Hughes, her chief collaborator in the running of the HIDTA facility, sat her down and told her she should do it. You can take what you've been doing down here, he said, and spread it around. This was a big step for Hughes. He had no illusions about the importance of Van Vliet. She was HIDTA's main engine. The facility had become a freestanding, $10-million-a-year enterprise with 250 investigators, seven prosecutors and a large support staff. But it still was not wildly popular with the DEA, the FBI or even Main Justice. Van Vliet's iron will and big cases had helped them endure and succeed.

Van Vliet weighed her decision for weeks, then took the plunge. On the morning of May 13, 1994, she rode an elevator to the eleventh floor of a handsome building two blocks from the White House. During the 1980s the Justice Department had outgrown its Art Deco headquarters building between Constitution and Pennsylvania Avenues. All those new prosecutors, investigators and support staff the Congress had authorized over the past decade had to be housed somewhere, so Justice Department administrators had begun leasing and buying office space all over town. The building Van Vliet moved into was just one of many outriders of Main Justice. It was the home of the Narcotics and Dangerous Drug Section of the Criminal Division.

In bringing Theresa Van Vliet up from Miami, Mary Lee Warren and Jo Ann Harris had picked one of the hardest chargers in the field, the prosecutor who had administered some of the biggest cocaine prosecutions in the country. The conviction of Harold Ackerman was the best known of her successes, but there were others. More than her enthusiasm for electronic intercepts on big drug prosecutions, however, what Van Vliet brought to the job was attitude, a conviction that the chaotic process known as federal drug enforcement could actually be made to work.

What made a difference, Van Vliet believed, was keeping the pressure on, especially in the big cities where the cartels focused their importation efforts and had their infrastructure. In those places, Van Vliet contended, big loads of drugs could be seized, trusted managers clapped into jail. The busiest of the Cali cartel's importation cells, as the DEA called them, were in New York, Miami, Houston and Los Angeles. These supplied similarly large distribution cells in Chicago, Atlanta and other major cities. It was a cascading process. Importers like Ackerman brought in multi-ton loads. They divvied up these shipments among regional distributors, usually several hundred kilos of cocaine to each. The importation cells in the gateway cities were the targets with the highest value. If law enforcement also knocked off the distribution cells in the inner cities, Van Vliet believed, they would keep pressure on the entire cartel system and get more and more evidence against the kingpins in Colombia.

As the new narcotics section chief at Main Justice, Van Vliet set out to do on a national scale what she had done in Miami on a regional level. She wanted to be the gnat buzzing constantly in the Cali cartel's ear. To other prosecutors, Van Vliet preached the use of wiretaps as if it were holy writ. The idea was not hers alone, but she was a strong proponent. Years of emphasis at the Justice Department on electronic surveillance were bearing fruit all over the country. More and more federal prosecutors were learning how to do Title III wiretaps. Janet Reno's Justice Department encouraged the trend. During 1993 the number of authorized federal wiretaps in criminal investigations increased 32 percent over the year earlier. In 1994 the number of wiretaps in criminal inquiries increased again, by 23 percent over 1993. Most of the electronic surveillance was aimed at narcotics groups.

Van Vliet was into "disruption." Unable to apprehend the kingpins in Colombia, she wanted to use wiretaps and all the other powerful tools Main Justice had at its disposal to disrupt the Cali cartel: intercepting their biggest shipments, seizing their profits, infiltrating their distribution networks and raiding their stash houses. In Miami, Van Vliet had seen firsthand that good cases forced the cartel to make changes. When the cartel was under pressure, it made mistakes. Traffickers had to go into unfamiliar territory. They had to take in new and less experienced people, replacing a Harold Ackerman with a Raúl Martí. Those people made still more mistakes. Up and down the chain of command people got nervous. Feuds broke out. Discipline collapsed.

Theresa Van Vliet had an all-consuming goal: Someday, somehow, she vowed, Miguel Rodríguez Orejuela was going to be hers. She referred to the Cali kingpin as MRO. Van Vliet loved the fact that Miguel Rodríguez Orejuela flew into blind rages whenever the government seized one of his loads. Miguel was a micromanager, always on the phone to the States, checking on his business and working out logistics. Van Vliet liked that. Keep talking, MRO. Just keep dialing those calls to the States.

In each of the Cali cartel's big hub cities—New York, Miami, Houston and Los Angeles—major prosecutions were moving through the federal courts. After the big cases launched from the HIDTA facility in Miami had gotten the cartel's attention, it had shifted operations to Texas and farther west along the Mexican border. Cities like San Diego began seeing the kinds of cases that were routine in Miami. The Justice Department rushed in resources to meet the new threat. By 1995, several hundred DEA and FBI agents were working on joint investigations along the Mexican border.

At Main Justice, Theresa Van Vliet, who was quarterbacking the operation, dispatched prosecutors from the narcotics section to try cases. But the bigger the case, the bigger the problems it presented. Van Vliet spent a lot of time on the road working to sort them out, trying to prevent problems from cropping up in the first place. One week it was a conference of prosecutors in New Jersey, where she lectured on wiretaps. Another, it was planning a new investigative project in Houston. On the long flights back and forth across the nation, Van Vliet took along reading material— long affidavits about as-yet-unarrested smuggling groups. While her fellow passengers pored over novels by Tom Clancy and John le Carré, Van Vliet devoured fact-filled narratives from the FBI, the DEA and the U.S. Customs Service.

In Washington, there were lots of experts on the so-called drug war. Each seemed to argue for a pet theory, one special approach that would tip the scales. What Van Vliet wanted was flexibility. In Miami, the drug business had been fluid and fast paced. No single approach would work. She and her colleagues had had to improvise. In Washington, Van Vliet encouraged people to do the same. Ideally, she believed, the Criminal Division needed to encourage a mix of proactive investigations—using wiretaps and undercover agents—with historical conspiracy investigations that pieced together years of incriminating evidence. Van Vliet's job was to keep things moving. Was there a problem with DEA in Houston? She'd bring it up at the next interagency meeting. Did a wiretap case in Chicago need more resources? She would check with the FBI. Were two different federal districts at each other's throat over control of an informant? Van Vliet mediated a compromise. Do what's right for the case, she said. This was Van Vliet's mantra. Let's fight the bad guys, she urged, not each other. Van Vliet had three simple rules: Cooperate, cooperate, cooperate.

That instinct, what she called getting all the agencies to "play nice in the sandbox," lay at the heart of a 1995 project called Operation Foxhunt. It began as two investigations. A state prosecutor in New York had identified a large narcotics distributor in Queens. Unbeknownst to the New York officials, the U.S. Attorney's Office in Los Angeles had an FBI case that had identified two major Colombians who were importing large loads supplied by a branch of the Cali cartel. One of them went by the name Zorro, the Spanish word for "fox." The longer the Los Angeles investigation went on, the more it became clear the importers were supplying the distributor in Queens. Couriers drove the cocaine cross-country in cars fitted with secret compartments accessed by ingenious trapdoors. Hundreds of kilos were moved on each trip. Once the cocaine reached the Queens distributor, it was parceled out in smaller batches of several dozen kilos to other local distributors along the eastern seaboard. They, in turn, negotiated one- or two-kilo sales with local dealers who handled street distribution.

DEA agents came up with an ambitious plan. They wanted to use the two cases, in Queens and L.A., to pull down the entire drug distribution network. One of the strongest advocates of the plan was the DEA's William Mockler, who had transferred to DEA headquarters in Washington, where he was placed in charge of major investigations. Mockler was the DEA's ranking expert on the Cali cartel and also one of the driving forces behind Operation Foxhunt.

Theresa Van Vliet loved the plan to tie the New York and Los Angeles investigations together. Wasting no time, she arranged a meeting for the two prosecution teams in Houston, inviting officials from the many local jurisdictions that received some of the smuggling group's product. Prosecutors and agents from several states, some sixty people in all, attended. Van Vliet worked the room like a politician. They were going to take down the New York and Los Angeles operations, she said. That was a given. But they were also going to follow the product down through the system—to track the retailers when they made their pickups and follow the smaller shipments of cocaine back to Missouri or Louisiana or Maryland. Van Vliet had each of the local and federal agencies describe their targets and explain the state of the evidence in each jurisdiction.

Like other bureaucracies, the federal agencies engaged in drug enforcement were often inefficient and hobbled by parochialism. There were rare moments, however, when the gears really meshed. Operation Foxhunt was one such instance. After the meeting in Houston, DEA agents began working more closely with local police. Turf was generally ignored. Prosecutors won court permissions to string more wiretaps. Federal agents followed the drug couriers coast to coast from Southern California to New York. Police detectives bird-dogged local drug dealers in places like St. Paul, Minnesota, and Prince Georges County, Maryland. Over many months, prosecutions piled up. More than 160 people were arrested as a result of the Foxhunt inquiry. Before it was over, the operation resulted in the dismantling of the entire drug distribution network that began in Los Angeles and ended on the streets of Middle America.

This was how things should work, Van Vliet believed. Everyone had to stay sharp. It was fine to have aerial reconnaissance to track a drug plane from an airstrip in Guatemala to a dirt road in Mexico. But then the Mexican Army had to be ready to move. If it got to the scene too late, then DEA or Customs had to pick up the trail. If that didn't work and the drugs got through, then it was important to come back later and build a conspiracy case against the players. Drug trafficking was a fast game—maybe the fastest in the world.

Less than a month after Theresa Van Vliet's arrival in Washington, Edward Kacerosky was once again banging on the front door of the Criminal Division of Main Justice. Encouraged by the decisions of Raúl Martí and Pedro Isern to cooperate with the Cornerstone investigation, Kacerosky wanted another wiretap. Theresa Van Vliet was not at all surprised.

The Customs Service investigator and prosecutors Edward Ryan and Bill Pearson were once again pushing the envelope. With the cooperation of Raúl Martí and Pedro Isern, there was plenty of new evidence to bolster another try for a wiretap. This time, however, Kacerosky was not focused on drug traffickers. He and the prosecutors had been stunned at the casual way that Donald Ferguson, the former federal prosecutor, had shown up in Pedro Isern's jail cell on behalf of the Cali cartel. They had decided to look hard at the defense lawyers, some of whom appeared to have made themselves part of the cartel's ongoing corporate enterprise.

Raúl Martí had helped Kacerosky figure out his next move in Cornerstone. The Cuban had told him about the injunction he had received from Miguel Rodríguez to junk Harold Ackerman's cellular phones and use debit cards instead to make his pay-phone calls back to Cali. Kacerosky had met with officials from the debit-card company to understand better how the system worked. Cards were purchased for fixed amounts, from a few dollars to a few thousand dollars. Charges for calls were deducted from the debit card's purchase price. There had to be a way to tap into that system. The agent consulted with some of John Burlingame's computer jockeys at HIDTA, and they had come up with a plan.

In its application to Main Justice, the Cornerstone team was proposing a slight variation on the concept of a roving wiretap, which could be used on any phone. It was simple in theory, complicated in practice. By doing some research, Kacerosky had learned the debit-card numbers of his targets. The debit cards were issued by a small firm in Miami. In order to bill callers accurately, the company's computers got a signal every time a prepaid call was dialed. If approved by Main Justice and by a federal District Court judge, Kacerosky's plan would require the debit-card company to program its computers to alert a computer at the HIDTA center each time one of the target debit cards was used to make a call. With a timely signal, HIDTA eavesdroppers could plug into any pay telephone and record the conversation. The cartel had come up with a new security measure. Kacerosky had found a way to beat it.

A central figure in the Kacerosky affidavit was Michael Abbell. To many of his former colleagues in the Criminal Division, Abbell's representation of the Cali cartel was troubling. During the early 1980s, he had risen through the ranks of the Criminal Division to head the Office of International Affairs just as its responsibilities were being expanded by William French Smith, Ronald Reagan's first attorney general. Smith believed that the Justice Department needed to be more aggressive in pursuing international criminal organizations. This meant closer coordination with foreign police and prosecutors. Smith and his successor, Edwin Meese, had been successful in signing mutual legal assistance treaties with many foreign governments. There are different kinds of M-LATs, as the treaties are known; not all countries would agree to the same levels of cooperation on criminal prosecutions.

One provision Smith and Meese had worked hard to include in all the M-LATs was extradition. This is an unusual transaction between sovereign nations in which one government would oblige itself by treaty to arrest one of its own citizens when he or she was wanted by another nation for criminal offenses. Even if the person in question was a model citizen with no record of having committed any crime in his or her country, an extradition treaty obliged the signatory government to make an arrest and turn the individual or individuals over to law-enforcement authorities in the requesting country. If convicted, those extradited would serve their sentences in the country where they were tried.

Under Michael Abbell, the Office of International Affairs had worked especially hard on extraditing international narcotics traffickers. By dint of study and long experience, Abbell had made himself one of the nation's leading experts on extradition law. There were few better or more knowledgeable.

The extradition process between Colombia and the United States had worked reasonably well during the late 1980s, most notably in the arrest and prosecution of Carlos Lehder, one of the top leaders of the cocaine cartel from the Colombian city of Medellín. The treaty had given Colombian authorities strong leverage in criminal cases; they could always threaten extradition. And it had freed Colombian prosecutors and magistrates of the difficult—and dangerous—job of holding criminal trials in their country. As a rule, major drug traffickers did not fear Colombian courts, which were lenient and often corrupt. They did fear trial in the United States, however—a great deal.

In Colombia, influential drug traffickers, including the principals of the Cali cartel, undertook a campaign to scotch the extradition treaty with the United States. Its most vocal opponents described the treaty as an affront to Colombian nationalism. They poured money into political campaigns. More usefully, they paid generous bribes to key legislators.

The effort got results. In 1990 a constitutional assembly in Bogotá voted to outlaw extradition of Colombian citizens. Members of the constitutional assembly had been threatened by representatives of the cocaine cartels in Medellín and Cali. One was videotaped by police being handed a considerable payment for his vote. The defeat deprived both the United States and Colombia of a major weapon against the cocaine cartels. The Bush administration offered little public criticism; it laid on no sanctions. There was something more it needed from the Colombians. When the extradition vote occurred the United States was engaged in confronting Saddam Hussein, whose government had recently invaded the oil-rich Persian Gulf emirate of Kuwait. Colombia had a seat on the United Nations Security Council, and Washington had had to negotiate for the Colombian vote supporting the UN resolution authorizing the allied invasion. Bogotá supported the United States in the Security Council; the Bush administration made little noise when the extradition treaty succumbed to the pressures of threat and bribes in Bogotá.

The loss of the extradition remedy was a big setback to police and prosecutors in the United States and Colombia. After the vote in Bogotá representatives of the two nations tried to pick up the pieces. As much damage as cocaine was doing to the United States, it was doing more in Colombia, contaminating the fabric of society with high levels of drug addiction and terrible crimes of violence. For both nations, finding a way forward was imperative. By 1993, the lawyers in the Criminal Division of Main Justice had worked out an agreement with their counterparts in Bogotá. It was simple. If a citizen of Colombia was indicted on criminal charges in the United States, prosecutors in Colombia would bring the same criminal charges against the person in their own courts. They would proceed on the same indictment, with the same evidence. This required Justice Department lawyers to share their evidence with Colombian prosecutors, who worked under a significantly different system of justice. It was an imperfect arrangement, at best. But sharing evidence offered the best hope of successfully attacking the big cocaine cartels that were doing so much to harm the citizens of Colombia and the United States.

By the time the new arrangement was worked out between Washington and Bogotá, Michael Abbell had long since left the Criminal Division. He had not lost his interest in the subject of extradition law, however, or in the ways his old colleagues in the Criminal Division cooperated with their counterparts in Colombia to prosecute that country's citizens. Since leaving Main Justice, Abbell had written several learned opinions analyzing the effect of the law passed by the Colombian constitutional assembly that outlawed extradition. He had co-authored the definitive legal text on international criminal law. He had been busy, too, on cases, traveling to Spain to appear as an expert witness for the defense of Gilberto Rodríguez Orejuela in an extradition proceeding there. The Colombian kingpin had been arrested in Madrid, leading the Justice Department to seek his transfer to the United States to face the criminal charges awaiting him in California, Louisiana and New York.

Gilberto Rodríguez was one of Michael Abbell's clients. He and his brother Miguel had been indicted by a federal grand jury in New Orleans. In 1982 an FBI wiretap had picked up the brothers discussing the importation to the United States of 550 kilos of cocaine. Evidence elicited during the investigation of others involved in the conspiracy had tied the Rodríguez brothers into it more deeply.

Under the evidence-sharing agreement between Washington and Bogotá, the New Orleans evidence had been turned over to the Colombian prosecutors. The Clinton administration was pressing the Colombians to proceed on the cases. In Cali, prosecutors had moved forward on the facts alleged in the New Orleans case and issued arrest warrants for the Rodríguez brothers.

To defend himself, Miguel Rodríguez instructed his American lawyers to obtain affidavits from the American witnesses saying they had never heard of him and had never known him to be involved in cocaine trafficking. If the American witnesses did not implicate Rodríguez, the case would likely fail.

In Washington, this made Michael Abbell a very busy man. There were two witnesses against Miguel Rodríguez living in New Orleans, Thomas P. Gray and Claude Griffin. Both men had been convicted in the original New Orleans case, done their time and gotten out of prison. In August 1993 a government wiretap recorded a telephone call between Gray in New Orleans and Abbell in Washington. During the conversation Abbell explained that he was dispatching his law partner, Francisco Laguna, to Louisiana with some money. Laguna would have $25,000 for Gray, Abbell said, and another $25,000 for his partner, Griffin.

A veteran drug pilot, Griffin had been convicted in 1985 of ferrying shipments of Cali cartel cocaine into the United States. The government's evidence showed that Griffin had been dealing with Miguel and Gilberto Rodríguez. The Justice Department was "sharing" with the Colombians the testimony of Gray and Griffin. The two men were asked to go to Colombia for questioning. The $50,000 Laguna would deliver to Gray and Griffin, Abbell explained, was for "their trip."

Two weeks after the call from Abbell, Gray and Griffin arrived in Cali with Laguna. The two smugglers provided sworn statements to the Colombian prosecutors that they did not know and had never worked for Miguel and Gilberto Rodríguez. They had no idea who the Rodríguez brothers were.

In Washington and New Orleans, Justice Department lawyers knew the statements were false. But in July 1994 a Colombian court relied on the affidavits of the two smugglers to annul the arrest warrants that the prosecutors in Cali had issued for Miguel and Gilberto Rodríguez. The evidence-sharing agreement had worked exactly as planned, but the testimony of Thomas Gray and Claude Griffin had torpedoed the efforts of Colombian and American law enforcement to bring a criminal case.

In retrospect there was only one positive development in the whole sorry episode, Theresa Van Vliet and other American prosecutors believed, but it was an important one. It provided a reasonably clear path of facts that led back to Michael Abbell.

CHAPTER TWELVE

OUT TO THE EDGE

At 8 A.M. on a bright Saturday in July 1994, Edward Kacerosky and DEA Special Agent Louis Weiss were admitted to a small holding cell at Miami's Metropolitan Correctional Center. A wizened little man rose from his hard seat and greeted the Customs Service investigator briskly. "Ed, I know exactly who you are," the old man said. "You've got me. I don't have much time, but I want to save whatever I have left."

The last person in the world Edward Kacerosky had ever expected to see locked up at MCC was George Lopez. It was not because Lopez was a saint. Far from it, Lopez was a virtual legend in the cocaine business. In the early 1980s he had been the Cali cartel's top operations man in Los Angeles. Lopez had moved on to Miami after that. There he had directed the cartel's business affairs in South Florida, before first Pedro Isern and then Harold Ackerman had arrived on the scene. The reason Kacerosky had never expected to see Lopez behind bars was because he had detected a rather heavy surveillance by federal agents and made a clean escape from Miami approximately thirteen months earlier.

Like the Cali cartel's other business managers, George Lopez was not a stupid man. He knew he was in trouble. He had known that if he returned to the United States he would, almost certainly, be arrested on a federal warrant. And yet Lopez had come back. U.S. marshals had arrested him near Miami Beach the evening before. The old man had simply gotten lonely. His family was in Miami. He also had some lady friends there. The family and the lady friends had lured Lopez back. His arrest was a stroke of luck the Cornerstone team had never dreamed of.

Infirm and sixty-eight years old, Lopez had every incentive to talk, to cut a deal. In the holding cell at MCC, the agents decided to reinforce the incentive. We've got you on tape, they told Lopez. We've got you recorded talking about shipments to Harold Ackerman. We've got you.

I know, Lopez replied. What do I need to do to cooperate with you, to help myself?

This was a welcome development, Kacerosky thought. But we have a problem, the Customs Service agent told Lopez. "The lawyers are going to come in big time for you."

Lopez frowned. He knew about the cartel's lawyers.

Not to worry, Kacerosky said. They would work something out. He would be in touch shortly.

Lopez nodded and thanked Kacerosky and Weiss.

As the two agents were driving out of MCC, the beeper on Weiss's belt chirped. The DEA agent checked the number. It was a prison guard station. He had asked the guards at MCC to alert him if George Lopez had any unexpected callers. He used his cellular phone to call the guards. Who was interrupting his quiet Saturday morning to pay a call on the elderly doper?

It's a lawyer, an MCC guard told Weiss. His name is William Moran. He says he's representing Mr. Lopez.

Kacerosky and Weiss shook their heads.

Bill Moran was in his early fifties, a dapper man, a former state prosecutor who had gone on to become one of Miami's most prominent criminal defense lawyers. He specialized in defending drug cases and had paid the price. His law office had been firebombed a decade earlier, presumably by a client unhappy with his representation. A few years after that, Moran's partner had been gunned down in the front door of the office, presumably by another unhappy client. Kacerosky and Weiss didn't need to go back to MCC to find out what William Moran wanted with George Lopez. That they already knew.

The notion of pursuing the cartel's defense attorneys had begun to harden into a moral imperative for the Cornerstone team. The attempt would carry the Justice Department to the outer limits of its powers. It would guarantee that, henceforth, the case would get microscopic review by the most senior lawyers at Main Justice. Historically, the attorney-client privilege has surrounded the private offices of defense counsel with a kind of legal force field, an invisible barrier through which federal agents could not pass. Without this barrier, the right to counsel would be meaningless.

To the determined criminal investigator, the private law office is sometimes less a legal sanctuary than it is a taunt and a challenge. Often, law offices are repositories of the most revealing criminal truths, secrets about clients that, if disclosed, would immediately become evidence.

After prosecutors Edward Ryan and William Pearson settled on their pursuit of Michael Abbell and the other lawyers identified in the Cornerstone investigation, they quickly decided to seek search warrants for their professional offices.

Once again, it fell to Edward Kacerosky to justify this intrusive investigative measure. Sitting down with a yellow legal pad, the Customs Service agent poured out a new narrative in his tight, spidery scrawl. When the affidavit for a search warrant was finally typed on a word processor, it ran to ninety-one pages. In it, Kacerosky laid out chapter and verse on the high crimes he thought had been committed by a handful of criminal defense attorneys on behalf of the Cali cartel. He summarized the statements of Harold Ackerman, Raúl Martí, Pedro Isern, George Lopez and other witnesses. He and the prosecutors wanted to search six law offices in South Florida and Washington, D.C., including those used by Michael Abbell, Francisco Laguna, Robert Moore, Donald Ferguson, William Moran and Joel Rosenthal.

Legally, the Miami U.S. Attorney's Office was under no obligation to obtain approval from the Criminal Division to seek search warrants. But Operation Cornerstone had become one of the most important drug cases of the Clinton administration. Soon after it arrived at Main Justice, Kacerosky's affidavit was routed to the desks of Mary Lee Warren and David Margolis. Invading the premises of a private law office and poring over confidential legal files are extreme actions. Such warrants have the potential to impinge on the right to counsel, a right guaranteed by the Sixth Amendment of the Constitution.

On its face, the Kacerosky affidavit was a devastating document. The Customs Service agent distilled the evidence gathered during the three years of successful Cornerstone cases. He had won the cooperation of four senior managers of the Cali cartel who had been responsible for the great river of Cali cocaine that flowed through Miami in the 1980s and early 1990s. He had other witnesses who had had direct dealings with Miguel and Gilberto Rodríguez in Cali. Much of what the witnesses told Kacerosky had been corroborated by documents or by the ubiquitous HIDTA wiretaps. Some of the most telling evidence against the lawyers named in Kacerosky's affidavit had come from lawyers who were not part of the Cali cartel's secret network. This was the result of the Cornerstone team's sustained focus on the Miguel Rodríguez Orejuela faction of the cartel that Theresa Van Vliet had proposed and Douglas Hughes had agreed to support.

It was also, of course, the result of the furious enterprise of Edward Kacerosky, who had never stopped opening new doors into the cartel's operations. The two factors had overwhelmed the organization's small network of lawyers. So many arrests came so fast that they had needed help. Outside lawyers, who were not part of the cartel system, had had to be brought in. Faced with a choice, reputable defense lawyers like Edward Shohat, who had been hired from one of Miami's most estimable firms to represent Harold Ackerman at trial, refused to betray their clients to protect the cartel. Instead, they were alert to the possibility of negotiating a more lenient sentence in exchange for cooperation.

This was tricky business. Once his client, Harold Ackerman, started to cooperate with the Justice Department, Shohat knew he had to be absolutely candid with the prosecutors. Shohat, too, had evidence to provide. He told prosecutors he had stopped Michael Abbell from trying to persuade Ackerman to sign a false affidavit exculpating Miguel Rodríguez. He said he warned Abbell that he was obstructing justice. Shohat eventually made a decision that was agonizing for a defense lawyer; he agreed to testify about his conversations with Abbell.

The way Kacerosky described the behavior of the cartel's corrupt lawyers in his affidavit was chilling. Essentially, Kacerosky said, the lawyers served as agents of a hostile intelligence agency in America's war on drugs. As officers of the court, they had special access to the pretrial discovery material that essentially revealed the government's methods. They were privy to the inner workings of the criminal justice system and often found out who was cooperating, who was being sought, where investigations were headed. In effect, Kacerosky alleged, the lawyers served as the eyes and ears of the Cali cartel, double agents cloaked in their license to practice law.

Kacerosky's affidavit summarized the testimony of the cooperating witnesses and his own research. The four Cali business managers knew better than anyone else how the cartel employed its legal talent. "All stated that Miguel Rodríguez Orejuela utilizes selected organization attorneys to enter [cases] as defense counsel," Kacerosky wrote, "or simply to conduct jail visits, to reinforce the accessibility of their organization through their attorneys to members of the organization arrested. The goal of this tactic, according to statements made by Miguel Rodríguez . . . is to rekindle the fear that everyone in the group has concerning the power that the 'organization heads' located in Cali possess all over the world and thereby indicate their ability to carry out any previously made threats."

It continued in this vein. Miguel Rodríguez paid for lawyers to represent cartel employees who had been arrested "because he believes this affords him the guarantee of non-cooperation because the arrested member knows of his attorney's role in the organization." There was also the added benefit, Kacerosky had written, that cartel-paid lawyers would "gain access to the government's evidence and the identity of any prospective government witnesses or confidential informants." This, Kacerosky explained, allowed Rodríguez and the other top leaders of the cartel to "keep abreast of government investigations in order to obstruct those investigations and learn of new tactics employed by the government, which would necessitate changes in the organization, to avoid detection."

The documentary evidence cited in the affidavit was damning. There were five lawyers in all. One of them, Joel Rosenthal, was a former federal prosecutor who was well regarded in the Miami U.S. Attorney's Office. The financial ledgers seized from Harold Ackerman's home showed numerous payments to Rosenthal. In fact, so damning was the evidence that Rosenthal, assuming that Ackerman's records were in government hands, decided to cooperate with the Cornerstone investigation. Even though he was under investigation, Rosenthal had provided still more documents implicating Michael Abbell in the Cali cartel's criminal activity.

The picture Kacerosky painted was unrelievedly grim. The charges against all of the lawyers in his affidavit were serious—suborning perjury, conveying threats of harm from cartel managers to their own clients, laundering money by disguising it as legal fees. As fundamental as the specific criminal acts they had committed, he alleged, the lawyers had compromised the legal interests of their clients, thrown them away in exchange for the very generous payments they received from Cali.

His reasons for wishing to search the offices of the Cali cartel's lawyers were clear. Behavior of the type described by Kacerosky could not go unpunished. It was criminal conduct for anyone—lawyer, truck driver or nursery school teacher. At Main Justice, Mary Lee Warren and David Margolis agreed. The application to search the lawyers' offices should be approved, they decided. Now it was time to take the application to court.

On September 1, 1994, a Miami magistrate read and signed the Kacerosky affidavit. A magistrate in Washington, D.C., did the same. A few days later government agents and evidence technicians swarmed through the law offices, shooing secretaries, unplugging computers and packing files.

Operation Cornerstone had finally pushed the Criminal Division of Main Justice to the outer limits of its prosecutorial power. It was a big step to send federal agents into the offices of a defense attorney. The right to counsel and the attorney-client privilege were honored in the United States precisely because they restrain the government. Now, however, because of credible evidence that a group of lawyers had violated their professional trust, the Justice Department was deliberately breaching that barrier. It was one of the government's most intrusive uses of power. Arrayed against the heedless reach of the Cali cartel and its bottomless supply of cash, that power might just prove enough.

CHAPTER THIRTEEN

PUT TO THE TEST

On the bitterly cold morning of March 30, 1995, four men rode an escalator up from the underground cavern of Washington's Metro system. On the street, the men made their way up Pennsylvania Avenue, stepping carefully around the puddles of winter slush. Assistant U.S. Attorneys Edward Ryan and William Pearson had come to Washington to defend their plan to proceed with the next step of Operation Cornerstone. Accompanying the prosecutors were the two agents who had worked on the investigation, Edward Kacerosky and Louis Weiss. For all four, Miami was home, but a summons from Main Justice had brought them hurrying to Washington. The weather was raw—slate-gray and cold. The men from Miami couldn't wait to get back home. First, though, they had to make it through an unusual review process.

After several minutes the four men arrived at the front door of Main Justice. The building occupies a full square block of Washington real estate. Between the Internal Revenue Service building at Ninth Street to the east and the National Archives building at Tenth Street to the west, the Justice Department is an enormous rectangle, the longer sides fronting Constitution Av-

enue to the south and Pennsylvania Avenue to the north. Inside
the rectangle is a handsome cobbled courtyard. In the spring, an
elegant fountain splashes amid stands of well-fed shrubs. On this
day the fountain was dry. A bitter wind whipped the dead stalks of
the past year's bright buds.

There are half a dozen nice hotels within walking distance of
Main Justice, but room rates at each exceed the allowable government per diem. As a result, the prosecutors and agents had spent
the previous night across the Potomac River in suburban Crystal
City, Virginia.

The prosecutors and agents passed quickly through the tall Art
Deco doors that give onto Pennsylvania Avenue, presented their
government identifications to the armed guards inside, then made
their way to the building's second floor. There, Theresa Van Vliet
and the senior person in the group, Mary Lee Warren, greeted
them warmly. Warren ushered the visitors into a conference room
with a worn carpet, but the chairs around the big oak table were
comfortable—deep, leather, government issue.

The Constitution guarantees that federal criminal charges will
be presented to a grand jury to decide on before any prosecution
can take place. This process is considered a vital safeguard against
abusive government behavior. But the words of the Constitution
had been penned in a simpler time. When it came to the most severe federal criminal laws, such as the Racketeer Influenced and
Corrupt Organizations Act, Main Justice had become the most
important check on prosecutors in the field. Before any RICO indictment could be presented, the Criminal Division's senior managers had to sign off. This brought to bear a far more exacting
review of the evidence and the law than a grand jury could provide. In most cases, in a process called RICO review, the Criminal
Division took the unusual step of allowing defense lawyers to
make presentations to the department before a RICO indictment
was approved. Essentially, it made Main Justice a court of appeals
for defendants facing some of the government's most serious criminal charges.

Edward Ryan, William Pearson, Edward Kacerosky and Louis
Weiss had been summoned to Washington for just such a session.

The defense lawyers who represented the targets of Operation Cornerstone had asked for the RICO review. The process would take two days. The sessions began with a general meeting in a conference room on the second floor of Main Justice. As the defense lawyers, prosecutors and Criminal Division lawyers filed into the room, a pecking order soon made itself manifest. At the head of the table, on the government side, sat Mary Lee Warren and Paul Coffey. Then there were Theresa Van Vliet and another lawyer from the Criminal Division, Barbara Kittay. Farther down the table sat the two prosecutors from Miami, Ryan and Pearson. On the other side of the table, the defense lawyers were led by Earl Silbert and Albert Krieger. Silbert had been the U.S. attorney for the District of Columbia who had prosecuted the Watergate burglars. Krieger had represented a host of notorious criminal defendants, including Mafia boss John Gotti. There was also a large contingent of defense lawyers from Miami, including Jay Hogan, a burly man with the manner of a police desk sergeant.

The signal to begin came when David Margolis entered the room. Margolis did not sit at the conference table, but slouched in a seat against the wall. In a room full of big, bursting egos, he seemed almost an afterthought, a minor functionary who had somehow wandered into the meeting by mistake. In fact, his presence underscored the importance of the case at Main Justice. Margolis was the highest-ranking career official in the Deputy Attorney General's Office. On the RICO review of the Cornerstone case, he was standing in for Jack Keeney. Ordinarily, Keeney would have been the senior person in the room. The old man of the Criminal Division had supervisory authority over the Organized Crime and Racketeering Section. Paul Coffey, who ran the section, reported to Keeney. In this case, however, Keeney had decided it would be improper for him to preside. Both Margolis and Keeney had worked closely with Michael Abbell during his years at Main Justice. After Abbell left to go into private practice, he had sought a legal opinion from the department on whether he could ethically represent Gilberto Rodríguez Orejuela. The question was relevant because Abbell had assisted in the pursuit of José Santacruz Londoño, Rodríguez's business partner.

There was nothing untoward in Abbell's request; in fact, it was taken as a measure of his care and prudence. Prosecutors routinely left government to practice as criminal defense lawyers. As long as the lawyer had not substantially participated in a matter during the last year of government service, no legal or ethical taint was attached to switching sides. Keeney had looked into the matter and then written Abbell a letter saying the Justice Department saw no conflict in his representing Gilberto Rodríguez. That action, Keeney now felt, required his recusal from consideration of the proposed Cornerstone indictment of Michael Abbell and his law partner, Francisco Laguna.

The defense lawyers present knew that a prosecution of Abbell, Laguna and three other lawyers on racketeering charges was a possibility, but they had not been told the true scope of the Cornerstone investigation. The lawyers assumed that Harold Ackerman was cooperating with the government, but they had no idea what other witnesses might be providing evidence. The lawyers could not ignore the possibility that the government had employed wiretaps during the course of the investigation, too.

For months, the defense lawyers had been playing a kind of poker with Ryan and Pearson in Miami, trying to flush out information about the evidence and looking for a way to ease the impact on their clients. The defense lawyers had already had a chance to make a presentation on behalf of their clients to supervisors at the U.S. Attorney's Office in Miami, to no avail.

In the second-floor conference room, Paul Coffey made the opening remarks. Despite what anyone in the room might think, he said, the RICO indictment under discussion had not received final approval by Main Justice. Before making that decision, they were happy to hear any arguments about policy or fairness, or about why use of the RICO statute might be inappropriate in the current case.

Albert Krieger, a handsome man with a polished bald dome, rose and began the defense presentation with his trademark baritone rumble. A veteran of many pre-indictment conferences, he knew exactly who his real audience was. "David," Krieger said, addressing Margolis, "we'd like to begin, but we don't know where to start."

Margolis paused a full two beats. "Start at the beginning, Albert," Margolis said dryly.

Margolis had no intention of giving away a single shred of the government's case. The government lawyers were there to listen, not to be drawn into discussions about the evidence. This was not a debate; it was a final appeal before the indictment was presented to a grand jury. If Main Justice reviewed a thousand cases, they might turn down fifty. Almost always this resulted from weaknesses that the defense didn't know about, but that became evident during the review process.

The proposed indictment, Krieger declared, took legitimate attorney-client activities and twisted them into crimes. He told a story about an earlier case that put the issue in sharp relief. During his representation of John Gotti, the Gambino family Mafia boss, Krieger said, it was his intention to win the case, yet he would be false to his core to claim that he did not realize at the time that there was such a thing as a Mafia. If John Gotti was, in fact, the boss of the Gambino family, Krieger continued, then his efforts to win the man's acquittal could be construed as aiding and abetting a criminal enterprise. Such reasoning, he declared, would twist and distort the American legal system. Every defendant, no matter how disreputable, deserved legal representation, and that included the operatives of the Cali cartel. To accuse the lawyers of being part of a criminal organization simply because they provided aggressive legal representation to a client was to assault the constitutionally guaranteed right to counsel. When he represented an unpopular defendant, Krieger concluded, a defense attorney should not be craven or intimidated in any respect.

Krieger and the other defense attorneys in the room were at a disadvantage. They didn't yet know, for example, that three other cartel managers besides Harold Ackerman—Raúl Martí, Pedro Isern and George Lopez—were prepared to testify. Each of the defense attorneys had arguments that were tailored to their client's situation. But their collective goal was to derail the proposed RICO charges and challenge the accusation that the target defense lawyers were part of an ongoing drug-smuggling conspiracy that had imported more than 200,000 kilos of cocaine into the United States. There were several overarching themes: first, that the lawyers' activities fell under the umbrella of legitimate legal representation; second, that the government could file lesser charges that carried sufficiently punishing penalties. If the suspect lawyers had knowingly received drug money as legal fees, then they could be prosecuted for money laundering. Even assuming they had done worse, such as obtain false affidavits or bribe witnesses, that did not mean they were drug dealers. That meant they were corrupt lawyers who had obstructed justice.

Naming the suspect lawyers in the same RICO indictment with the cartel kingpins was bound to smear them as drug traffickers, the defense attorneys insisted. There was no evidence that any of the lawyers were traffickers. They should not be tarred with that brush. Earl Silbert, appearing on behalf of the Ristau & Abbell law firm, was one of the deans of the American legal establishment. He had no real interest or expertise in drug cases. If he had a client who was a drug trafficker, he told the assembled prosecutors, his first instinct would be to negotiate a cooperation agreement with the government. But in his view the public policy questions raised by this case were profound.

Defense counsel had been indicted before on RICO cases, Silbert, Krieger and the other lawyers knew, but never an entire group of attorneys who happened to represent different members of the same alleged criminal enterprise. The import of that went beyond the specifics of the case at hand. Such an indictment would send a chill through the entire defense bar. It put the Department of Justice in the position of appearing to intimidate lawyers who zealously defended their clients in criminal prosecutions. Once the department started down that road, Krieger and Silbert argued, where would it stop? How could any defense lawyer agree to represent a client in a criminal case and be certain that he or she was not assisting a larger criminal organization? Surely there were less draconian ways to proceed.

The other defense lawyers in the room quickly jumped in.

What about fairness? they asked. Even assuming that their clients had obstructed justice or paid bribes to witnesses, that did not mean they were drug dealers. Naming them in the same indictment with the cartel kingpins was bound to smear them as drug traffickers. There was no evidence that any of the lawyers were traffickers. They should not be tarred with that brush.

The government lawyers listened politely. The arguments about guilt by association were unpersuasive. The essence of the RICO theory of prosecution is that all members of a criminal organization—no matter what role they performed—are held responsible. If the attorneys had acted as in-house counsel for the cartel, they had already made the choice to lend their talents to aid the world's largest drug-trafficking enterprise.

The argument about attacking lawyers generally was more fundamental. Former Attorney General Richard Thornburgh had used the defense bar—which he pointedly called the criminal defense bar—as a whipping boy. He had quarreled openly with the American Bar Association and had authored the infamous "Thornburgh Memo" that allowed prosecutors to speak directly with defendants who had already hired or had appointed a defense lawyer. That had been a lot of tough talk; what the Miami prosecutors were proposing was tough action. It was a serious matter to indict a large group of lawyers. It was more than possible that a defense lawyer could represent indicted Cali cartel members, even aggressively, and not break the law.

In his every act Margolis made it clear that the defense lawyers and their arguments were to be treated with respect. Paul Coffey had said that no decision had been made; Margolis made it clear that this was not a platitude. Main Justice was not going to rubber-stamp the decision of the U.S. attorney in Miami. He conveyed this message in several ways, beginning with the amount of time he insisted that the government lawyers give this review. The dialogue would continue until the issues were fully aired, Margolis vowed. Most important, Margolis kept the tone of discourse civil, disciplined and calm. At one point he cut off a younger colleague whose manner had grown strident.

"It was extraordinary," Krieger said. "Absolutely extraordinary.

There was open discussion. There was confrontation. I can't think of any words to use other than ones that would be extremely flattering of the Department of Justice in how it conducted itself. They were patient, they were considerate of the lawyers who were appearing in the conference. They were not in any respect abusive of the lawyers-soon-to-be-defendants. These were intelligent, thoughtful, emotional discussions."

By midmorning, after the meeting broke up, Paul Coffey stepped out of the conference room and spotted Edward Kacerosky. The defense attorneys had asked that the agents not be present. Somebody at Main Justice agreed, so Kacerosky and Weiss had sat and waited. Coffey grimaced and walked over to Kacerosky. "I've never had any RICO conference," he growled, "without the agent."

David Margolis had decided that each defense lawyer would get an individual session to discuss the Cornerstone case as it involved his client. Before that, however, he and Coffey wanted to hear from the Miami agents and prosecutors. The four men were ushered into a small conference room.

To the prosecutors and agents from Florida, Margolis was the oddest of apparitions. He wore no gold cufflinks or stylish suspenders, no silk tie or black cap-toed shoes. In fact, there was no indication that Margolis had given the slightest thought to his appearance. He wore a threadbare tweed jacket that clashed painfully with a faded plaid shirt worn open at the neck. His trousers had almost certainly come off a department store rack many years before. When he took a seat and crossed his legs, it was not possible to ignore the white socks with the yellow and green stripes at the top. The socks had lost their grip on Margolis's shins and bunched in folds around his ankles. When the other Justice Department lawyers addressed Margolis, however, they used a tone of deference. Even the defense counsel called him "David," not the more familiar "Dave."

"Okay," Margolis said, beginning the session with the Miami agents and prosecutors. He directed his gaze at Edward Ryan, whose unlined face and blond hair made him look younger than his thirty-four years. "Make your opening statement right now on these lawyers."

Ryan was taken aback. He and Pearson had sent a 180-page memorandum to Main Justice outlining the Cornerstone evidence. The case was huge. Ryan was not prepared to make an opening statement. In his dark suit and starched shirt, he leaned forward across the table and did his best. This case is about a large drug-trafficking organization, he said. It is not a case about lawyers. We want to indict the Cali cartel kingpins and their employees—the shippers, the importers, the distributors. The organization also happens to employ lawyers, Ryan continued. They are all part of the same operation.

What about Robert Moore? someone asked. Moore had been one of Harold Ackerman's lawyers.

Ryan ticked off the evidence. Moore was a Miami attorney who moved money around for the cartel, Ryan explained.

What about Joel Rosenthal?

Ryan started to describe the evidence against Rosenthal, the former federal prosecutor. Suddenly, as if a signal had been given, everyone seemed to be talking at once.

William Pearson jumped in. He believed deeply in the Cornerstone case. The conduct of the cartel's lawyers particularly appalled him. Joel Rosenthal and Michael Abbell were both former Justice Department lawyers—Abbell, a high-ranking official whose old office was just down the hall from the conference room they were using. Both Abbell and Rosenthal, Pearson argued, had helped the cocaine barons from Cali avoid prosecution by obtaining false affidavits and making sure potential witnesses remained silent.

Facts poured out of the two prosecutors in a jumble. After several minutes it was clear that Margolis was having trouble following their presentation. The intertwining of dozens of illegal acts was confusing. Pearson could see it, too, and he was more than a little annoyed. He and Kacerosky had spent two weeks holed up in Pearson's home drafting the lengthy prosecution memo. Surely, he thought, Margolis didn't expect them to go through all the evidence again now.

Theresa Van Vliet saw what was happening. Ryan and Pearson

were getting too deep into the details of the case. Facing the brass from Main Justice, the prosecutors were being too precise, too lawyerly. She interrupted. Eddie, she said, speaking to Kacerosky, tell us about the lawyers.

All eyes turned to the Customs agent.

Paul Coffey is a rifle shot of a man whose elegant dress is the exact antithesis of Margolis's. Coffey leaned across the table toward Kacerosky and began firing questions. Tell us, he instructed, what each witness said about each lawyer. Most of the witnesses spoke Spanish. Their statements had been summarized by Kacerosky, Pearson and Ryan in the prosecution memo, in English. Coffey wanted nothing to be lost in the translation. Because of his fluent Spanish, Kacerosky had done the interrogation of the witnesses.

Kacerosky began carefully, and in a moment it was just the two of them—Coffey, the Justice Department lawyer, and Kacerosky, the Customs Service investigator who had given the last three years of his life to the Cornerstone case. Coffey's questions were not hostile, but they weren't friendly, either. His questions were fast and precise. He had read every page of the prosecution memo, but that didn't buy the Cornerstone team a pass. On each guy, Coffey told Kacerosky, tell me what evidence is direct, what evidence is circumstantial. "Start with Robert Moore," Coffey ordered, scribbling notes on a yellow legal pad.

Nobody from Miami needed to be told what was at stake. Three years of work hung in the balance. So did the fates of the defendants. Paul Coffey was the Justice Department's reigning expert on racketeering prosecutions. If Pearson and Ryan were going to get anywhere with their proposed indictment of the Cali cartel and its lawyers, they would have to get Coffey's blessing first. On a RICO case, he had the power to say yes or no. That's how the system worked.

Kacerosky started rattling off facts. Robert Moore had contacted Harold Ackerman's family right after the man's arrest and told them to withdraw money from their accounts and bring it to his law office. A witness to a meeting in Cali said that Miguel Rodríguez Orejuela told Moore to pass along a threat to Ackerman should he cooperate with authorities. Ackerman's wife was prepared to testify that Moore passed along the threat.

As Kacerosky answered, Coffey bent to his legal pad, covering the pages with notes, then looking up to fire another question.

Margolis remained silent, his eyes riveted on the Customs Service agent. The former Mafia prosecutor had vetted hundreds of racketeering prosecutions. He, too, had read the lengthy prosecution memo. But he wanted to hear the evidence marshaled in roughly the same way it might be presented to a judge and jury—facts lined up to match the charges alleged in the proposed indictment.

Not for nothing was Margolis regarded as the Criminal Division's toughest advocate. Seemingly inane questions from the old Mafia prosecutor could hold the sting of a viper's bite. He was the most unassuming of men, yet his oldest adversaries knew that you underestimated Margolis at your peril. The same was true of Coffey; only his style was different. Where Margolis sidled up to an issue, probing gently for trouble spots, Coffey was blunt and badgering, punching away until he was satisfied.

The way Coffey and Margolis saw it, the Cali case posed peculiar problems. The cartel was the single largest distributor of cocaine in the world, the largest shipper of the drug to the United States. The evidence amassed against the organization was impressive. The Cornerstone team had seized more than twenty tons of cocaine, finding it concealed in cement posts, buried under frozen broccoli and hidden within containers of coffee. The newer evidence was joined with proof taken from more than a decade of investigations by the U.S. Drug Enforcement Administration and the FBI—investigations that had resulted in indictments, but no trials of the kingpins. Edward Ryan and William Pearson had drafted a 161-page indictment that blended this old evidence with the new. The result was a dense chronicle of globe-spanning criminal activity.

There was an unspoken subtext to the grilling of Kacerosky. Coffey and Margolis were accustomed to reviewing big organized cases brought in by the FBI. On a case this big, the FBI would have a dozen veteran agents involved. Here, however, they had a lone Customs agent who had delivered what seemed to be the ultimate case against the Cali cartel. The DEA had played a supporting role. A lot would be riding on Kacerosky's composure and command of the facts. Margolis and Coffey wanted to be sure he could stand up to the tough cross-examination that would come from the likes of Albert Krieger, Earl Silbert and Jay Hogan.

On the drug charges against the kingpins, Margolis and Coffey had no problem with the evidence. There was detailed information on three huge shipments of cocaine. There was, moreover, the remarkably detailed testimony of Harold Ackerman, the highest-ranking Cali cartel employee who had ever agreed to testify against the cartel. Ackerman's computer records alone would carry much of the case.

Lumping the lawyers in with the cartel members and the evidence of drug trafficking was a more difficult question, however. Was that the fair thing to do? Did the pattern of racketeering activity truly reveal the lawyers to be active co-conspirators? Or were they merely performing services that defense lawyers are traditionally expected—indeed, are obliged—to perform for their clients?

Outside Main Justice, the shadows grew long on the ground as the afternoon gave way to twilight. Inside, Coffey and Margolis took turns hammering at Pearson and Ryan, Kacerosky and Weiss. Why did the lawyers deserve to be indicted on RICO, or even on the drug charges? Why not simply charge them with obstruction of justice? Margolis and Coffey had decades of experience over Pearson and Ryan, but the prosecutors gave no quarter. Michael Abbell, Joel Rosenthal and the other lawyers were part of the criminal organization that was the Cali cartel, Pearson and Ryan argued. They were participants in the racketeering conspiracy. They had been paid well for their work.

Theresa Van Vliet watched the debate go back and forth. During her time in Miami the Justice Department had chewed up millions of dollars producing indictments of Cali cartel members. At best, the earlier cases had merely slowed the cartel down, inflicting flesh wounds on the cartel colossus. Incremental cases weren't the way, Van Vliet believed. They had to go after the entire organization. But there was only so much she could do in her new role as chief of the Narcotics and Dangerous Drugs Section of the Criminal Division. In the end, the agents and prosecutors had to defend their own work.

Margolis and Coffey believed deeply in attacking criminal institutions. That's how the Justice Department had won its biggest victories against the Italian Mafia. They went after the organizations at every level, especially targeting their financial assets. A RICO case was legal warfare at its most extreme, however. The presence of Earl Silbert and Albert Krieger had left no doubt about one thing: Any RICO indictment naming the cartel's lawyers as defendants would be vigorously fought by a blue-chip defense team. You did not go forth into such a battle, Margolis and Coffey knew, unless you were sure that your agent could stand the heat.

By the end of the day, everyone was exhausted. They were not finished, however. Margolis decided to extend the review another day. They would resume the next morning. There was going to be a prosecution of some kind, that was certain. The big question now involved a matter of policy: Would the Department of Justice be pushing things too far by alleging that five criminal defense lawyers had worked for the same drug organization? Was that the right thing to do, as opposed to proceeding on charges of drug trafficking, conspiracy or money laundering?

Now that they had heard from all the defense attorneys and gone through the facts, Margolis wanted a fuller discussion among the government lawyers of the policy questions surrounding the Cornerstone prosecution. Any and all dissenters would be heard. When the Cornerstone case hit, it would hit hard. Margolis wanted no surprises.

Ryan and Pearson had been paying close attention to the ebb and flow of the questions that had been fired around the table. They had watched Paul Coffey. He was noncommittal. Coffey had pushed them hard on the evidence about Michael Abbell and Joel Rosenthal. When he was not firing questions, Coffey was taking detailed notes. He had nearly filled an entire legal pad. The prosecutors saw what he was doing. In the face of a hugely complex indictment, Coffey had adopted a nuts-and-bolts approach. The detail man, he was making lists of facts and outlining the evidence against each lawyer.

As they broke up for the evening, Ryan and Pearson pulled Coffey aside. Suppose we produce something tonight that outlines the evidence the way you want it? Coffey agreed that might help.

The prosecutors promised to have something by the next morning. Mary Lee Warren arranged to get them a laptop computer.

Back at the hotel, the Miami contingent wolfed down a fast dinner. Then Ryan, Pearson and Kacerosky planted themselves at a desk and set to work. For each of the targeted lawyers, they listed which evidence was direct, which circumstantial.

Pearson has a temper. In a courtroom, his competitive edge complements Ryan's earnest aplomb. Pearson had felt unprepared for Coffey's interrogation. He didn't like that. It was embarrassing, and it wasn't going to happen a second time. In the hotel room, they worked at the laptop until 1 A.M.

The next day's session took place in the same conference room they had used to hear the arguments of Earl Silbert, Albert Krieger and the other defense lawyers the previous day. Having learned of the status of the deliberations, Kendall Coffey, the U.S. attorney from Miami, had flown up for this climactic meeting. No relation to Paul Coffey, Kendall Coffey is a tall, personable civil litigator, a political appointee with no prior experience as a prosecutor. He would nevertheless have to sign the Cornerstone indictment and take any heat that might come from the local bar.

"Kendall," said David Margolis, starting the meeting, "what is your take on this whole thing?"

Coffey's answer sounded ambivalent. He thought this was an important case, he told Margolis, a very strong case against the cartel leaders. But he was not sure himself whether he would sign a RICO indictment charging all of the lawyers. In fact, Kendall Coffey was facing one of the hardest decisions he had had to make as a U.S. attorney. During the preceding weeks he had been besieged with heartfelt pleas from family members of the targeted lawyers, along with cogent arguments from their defense counsel. He had already presided over his own pre-indictment conference in Miami. He had read the affidavits and the prosecution memo. It seemed clear to him that the strength of the cases against the defense lawyers varied; the evidence against some was stronger and more direct than others. Yet the RICO charge would hold all defendants equally culpable of fostering a huge cocaine-trafficking enterprise that had shipped more than 200,000 kilos of cocaine into the United States. On the issue of charging the lawyers, Kendall Coffey said it was a question of national significance, which was certainly true. He said he was prepared to defer to Main Justice.

Margolis thanked Kendall Coffey and turned to the others in the room. What did they think about indicting the lawyers on the racketeering charge? he asked. The talk moved briskly around the room, touching on tactics and strategy.

Theresa Van Vliet said little. Every government lawyer in the room knew what she thought about the case. She had mothered the Cornerstone investigation from infancy, pushing, prodding and cajoling Edward Kacerosky to think in larger terms about what might be done to cripple the Cali cartel.

Margolis pressed the others in the room. Why should the lawyers be linked with the drug defendants? Why not simply accuse them of obstruction of justice or witness tampering? Those were heavy enough charges. The Justice Department had no interest in intimidating the defense bar with a RICO case.

Pearson and Ryan had asked and answered this question a dozen times in the last month. In their view, the lawyers—Michael Abbell, Donald Ferguson, Joel Rosenthal, William Moran and especially Francisco Laguna—were all part of a single large criminal organization. The Justice Department had spent more than fifteen years filing cases against the Cali cartel—all to no lasting effect. The Cali cartel would not be deterred by normal cases. A huge corporate enterprise, it had made itself immune to traditional criminal prosecution, and the defense lawyers had helped. They were an integral part of the scheme, aiders and abettors who helped perpetuate the cartel's existence.

Eventually, the meeting drew to a close. Margolis thanked all the participants, and bade farewell to the lawyers and agents from Miami. He was cordial and businesslike. He also revealed nothing at all about his view of the RICO charges. He would let them know, he said.

CHAPTER FOURTEEN

BRINGING
IT HOME

In Miami, the clock was ticking. For months, Edward
Ryan and William Pearson had been methodically presenting the huge volume of evidence that made up
their case against the Cali cartel to a federal grand jury.
Once a week the anonymous citizens who made up this secret
panel interrupted their lives and journeyed to the bone-white federal courthouse that rises like a gleaming shaft out of a gritty
neighborhood in downtown Miami. So much had they heard
about Operation Cornerstone that these jurors had a better understanding of the case than many of the federal agents who had
recently been drafted to help with the countless chores that attend major criminal investigations.

Upon their return from the March 30 meeting in Washington,
Ryan and Pearson knew they had two weeks left to get an indictment from their grand jury. After April 14 the panel's term of office would expire. So far as the prosecutors were concerned, the
pre-indictment work was nearly done. The grand jury understood
the case; the indictment was drafted. All they needed was approval from Main Justice. After that, it would take only a few
hours to present the indictment to the jurors. The prosecutors had

spent a lot of time with this grand jury. They felt confident the indictment would be returned, but if that didn't occur soon they would have to present the evidence to a new grand jury. The thought of that gave the prosecutors headaches.

Ryan and Pearson felt sure they had successfully run the gantlet at Main Justice. They had a strong case. In the days that followed their visit, the news started to trickle back from Main Justice. At first it sounded good. In general, they had passed muster with David Margolis. But they had not won the crucial vote of Paul Coffey on every defendant. Coffey agreed to filing RICO charges against all but two of the lawyers. He was recommending against filing RICO charges naming Michael Abbell and Joel Rosenthal.

The Miami team was aghast. Kacerosky was barely able to contain his outrage. It reminded him again of the cautious Washington mentality, the same mindset that he still blamed for not being able to intercept Raúl Martí's conversations with the Cali cartel kingpins. Main Justice was always finding reasons to say no.

Nonetheless, Coffey's approval of RICO charges on the other lawyers was good news. It meant the Cornerstone team had a new card to play with their targets. Ryan and Pearson were free to indict Francisco Laguna on RICO charges. Against him, the evidence was overwhelming. Coffey's approval was a powerful piece of leverage. The certainty of a RICO indictment would present Laguna with a strong incentive to enter a guilty plea before indictment and cooperate.

If Paul Coffey wanted more direct evidence against Abbell, the Miami prosecutors knew exactly how to get it. For weeks now the Cornerstone agents had been recording the phone conversations of Abbell's young law partner. Every time Laguna used a prepaid debit card to make a long-distance call to Colombia, the tape recorders at the High Intensity Drug Trafficking Area offices began to spin. One of the most damning conversations came after agents had searched Abbell's law offices. In the hours that followed, Laguna had made several frantic calls to Cali, warning his colleagues to stop using their telephones and to change all the numbers.

Pearson called Laguna's attorney, Fred Schwartz, to ask him to come with his client to the U.S. Attorney's Office for a conference. Before they arrived the grand jury voted a RICO indictment againt Laguna. Pearson had the document sealed. Come what may, the smooth-talking Colombian lawyer was going to spend some time in handcuffs.

Laguna and Schwartz accepted Pearson's invitation to meet. Schwartz is a tough, smart lawyer who had once prosecuted Mafia cases for the Justice Department. Laguna was calm and well dressed. They were invited into a conference with the agents and the prosecutors. Kacerosky sat to one side and watched Laguna. He decided they were dealing with a rookie, a lawyer way out of his depth.

Pearson was all business. The grand jury had indicted Laguna on RICO charges, he told Schwartz. They would like Laguna's cooperation against Michael Abbell. Laguna listened, but the words seemed not to register. According to Schwartz, Laguna was prepared to cooperate, but he didn't seem that impressed. During a break Kacerosky pulled Schwartz aside and laid it out for him. Tell your guy, he said, that every time he used his debit card at a pay phone, the call was recorded. Tell him we've got him talking to Miguel Rodríguez Orejuela. Tell him that after the searches of the law offices in Washington and Florida, he called Rodríguez's secretary and warned them to stop using the phones and change all their numbers. Tell him he's got one chance, right now, to save himself, Kacerosky said. Otherwise he goes down with Abbell.

Schwartz conveyed the bad news to his client. Within minutes Laguna cracked like a piece of china. After that, things went smoothly. They worked out the details. If Laguna admitted his guilt, cooperated fully and told the truth, he would be placed in a special prison facility reserved for convicts accepted into the witness security program.

During the next several days Laguna submitted to lengthy interrogations about his work with Abbell. The substance of his statement was later presented in a federal indictment. In 1991, soon after graduating from law school, he said, he joined the Abbell law firm as a salaried employee. He was hired partly because he is Colombian and speaks Spanish, he said. In fact, Laguna explained, he got his job right after a meeting in Colombia attended by Abbell and Donald Ferguson and the two kingpins, Miguel Rodríguez Orejuela and José Santacruz Londoño. At this meeting, Laguna said, according to court records, Abbell and Ferguson were hired to seek the return of nearly $30 million seized in a New York money-laundering case involving Santacruz. They later filed a claim for the release of this money on the grounds that it belonged not to Santacruz, but to his father-in-law and that man's heirs. To bring this claim in federal court in Brooklyn, he said, Santacruz's accountant prepared false financial records as justification. When the first set of forgeries proved unsuitable for filing in court, Laguna continued, Abbell sent him back to Colombia to obtain a better-quality set. Thereafter, Laguna continued, Michael Abbell had used him as an errand boy and translator. Abbell was the senior man, the expert on extradition law.

Laguna couldn't stop talking. Abbell had instructed him, he said, to take the false affidavits exculpating Miguel Rodríguez to federal prisons and get them signed by Harold Ackerman and another cartel employee, Pedro Gomez. Laguna knew the affidavits were false, he said, but he didn't know how they would be used in Colombia. After Raúl Martí was arrested, Laguna explained, Abbell had ordered him to distribute subsistence payments to Martí's wife. When the witnesses in New Orleans, Thomas P. Gray and Claude Griffin, were scheduled to go to Colombia to testify about Miguel Rodríguez, Laguna said, Abbell instructed him to bring them $50,000.

After his lengthy confession Laguna agreed to enter a plea of guilty to obstruction of justice and conspiracy to import drugs. His testimony would greatly bolster the case against Michael Abbell. He could explain to a jury what the prosecutors believed was Abbell's pivotal role in the cartel's affairs.

Once Pearson had the gist of Laguna's statements, he wasted no time. He called Theresa Van Vliet in Washington. Sitting at her desk in the Bond Building, not far from the White House, she made a list of the new admissions. Kacerosky had always maintained that Laguna was the legman for the cartel's lawyers. It sounded now as if Laguna was prepared to admit to this role and testify about what Abbell instructed him to do on behalf of the cartel. Moreover, Laguna was willing to plead guilty to a drug conspiracy charge, thereby bolstering the government's contention that the lawyers were active members of a narcotics-trafficking enterprise.

To Van Vliet, Pearson's report had the solid feel of a door slamming shut. Paul Coffey had wanted more direct evidence of Michael Abbell's culpability. Laguna's statements might just fit the bill. She rifled the news up the chain of command. Main Justice had taken its time; it had weighed the issues. Now, those carefully marshaled defense arguments that had given Paul Coffey pause were about to feel the force of new evidence. Michael Abbell's junior law partner had crossed over.

In Miami, the grand jurors who had been hearing the Cornerstone evidence for the past eighteen months knew their time was running out. There were only two days left in their term. Trying to be helpful, the grand jurors told the prosecutors they were prepared to come in on off days if it would help conclude the Cornerstone investigation. Pearson and Ryan thanked the members of the panel.

But now came more bad news. Despite Margolis's favorable view of the proposed Cornerstone indictment, the decision was not final. There was going to be yet another review at Main Justice. Deputy Attorney General Jamie Gorelick had declared that she intended to personally review and approve the indictment. The decision no longer lay just with Paul Coffey.

Pearson and Ryan looked at the calendar in dismay. When they pointed out to people in Main Justice that the Cornerstone grand jury was to be disbanded, the prosecutors were told that Gorelick was busy with other matters. She would not be able to get to their case immediately. They would just have to present the proposed evidence to a new grand jury. Everything was on hold.

Jamie Gorelick's many admirers consider her an adroit, hands-on manager. She had come to Main Justice from the Department of Defense, where she had been general counsel, the Pentagon's top lawyer. Gorelick's detractors consider her a control freak, someone who is forever vetting major decisions for their political impact. Unlike her predecessor, Philip Heymann, Gorelick had never been a prosecutor, nor had she worked at any important job in Main Justice. An accomplished Washington lawyer, Gorelick brought no special expertise to the review of the proposed Cornerstone indictment. On the other hand, she was second-in-command at Main Justice, and she had made a reputation for herself as a high-level troubleshooter. A big case was not going to spin out of control and catch them by surprise the way the Bush administration had been blindsided by Iraqgate and the investigation of BCCI. The upshot: The Cornerstone indictment was not going to be approved before the Miami grand jury's term expired.

The team of Cornerstone agents and prosecutors took the news badly. Pearson and Ryan had pinned down every last piece of evidence. They had framed the language of the indictment so that it would not raise questions of double jeopardy on old prosecutions of Cali cartel members. In Washington, they had jumped through every hoop the lawyers at Main Justice had held up. And now they were being stymied by a political appointee who had never prosecuted a criminal case. If they had to take the Cornerstone case before a new grand jury, it would mean bringing in all the witnesses for a whole new round of testimony and having them explain the long, complicated story to a new group of citizens. Kacerosky, Pearson and Ryan couldn't believe it. It felt, they said, as if they had been returned to square one.

When it comes to work, Jamie Gorelick is tireless. A breed apart even among Washington's Type-A superachievers, she is a mother of two and a former president of the District of Columbia Bar. Gorelick often took home two briefcases of work at night only to return the next morning, the paperwork digested, a daunting list of "to do" memoranda filed neatly inside.

Gorelick had replaced Philip Heymann, who had returned to Cambridge. The working relationship between him and Reno had simply not worked. Reno and Heymann had blamed "chemistry" for their inability to get along. Even close friends and associates had found it hard to know what to make of that. Reno, they thought, had been overbearing. She had refused to hire a chief of staff, saying she didn't want "a gatekeeper" preventing Justice Department lawyers from coming in to talk with her about problems. The result was that mundane matters that would ordinarily have been routed to secretaries and staff assistants had wound up on Heymann's desk. Reno had been relentless in following up on every one.

But even old friends recognized the truth of the complaints about Heymann. He was dead honest and loved the institution of the Justice Department. He was a thoughtful and deliberative person, a leader who surrounded himself with bright, young analytic minds. When he worked on an issue, Heymann wanted every assumption challenged. Often, his decisions were inspired, but many were a long time aborning, critics said, and Heymann was not the best administrator in the department. His departure saddened lawyers not just within the Criminal Division but throughout Main Justice. To the likes of Jack Keeney, David Margolis and Paul Coffey, Heymann was more friend than professional colleague. To others like Mark Richard, he was a leader and visionary.

Jamie Gorelick brought different skills and talents to Main Justice. One, admirers and critics agreed, was an ability to "make the trains run on the time." Although Gorelick did not have the benefit of Edward Kacerosky's nineteen years investigating crime, she had at hand two resources that he did not.

The first was a deep bench of senior aides, beginning with David Margolis. He worked out of an office just across the hall from hers on the fourth floor. Next was her hand-picked deputy, Merrick Garland, a former assistant U.S. attorney with a piercing intellect and a ferocious appetite for work. Finally, she had, at a moment's notice, the best thinking of the two career deputies who had overall command of the narcotics section, Mary Lee Warren and Theresa Van Vliet. Between these four lawyers there was no meaningful question about the Cornerstone case that could not be answered.

The second resource was less tangible, but no less empowering. This was a field of vision that was available only at the upper reaches of Main Justice. On the margins, the function of the deputy attorney general changes from one administration to the next, but at its core it is always a job of synthesis and command. An attorney general could define a policy or launch an initiative, but it was "the deputy" who made the vast bureaucracy respond. To be successful, the attorney general's number two had to be lawyer and manager, tactician and bureaucrat, politician and police chief.

Issues on each day's agenda bubbled up from the depths of the bureaucracy: from the ninety-four autonomous U.S. attorneys, from the police agencies such as the FBI and from the divisions within the Justice Department itself. Outside the ring of these internal components were the external forces that come to bear on Main Justice: the Congress, the federal judiciary, the news media and the other departments of the federal government.

It was through her special lens that Jamie Gorelick focused on the Cornerstone case. The central tenet that shaped the thinking of Clinton's political appointees at Main Justice was to avoid a debacle. They had seen George Bush lose an election less than two years after posting some of the highest approval ratings any president had ever enjoyed. Rightly or wrongly, they attributed this decline, at least in part, to the haze of scandal that had descended over Main Justice. It did not change the lesson for these Clinton appointees to discover that most of what had been alleged about the stewardship of Bush's attorney general, William P. Barr, was wrong or grossly distorted. The realization merely underscored the importance of looking out over the horizon for the next case that might blow up into a scandal.

Gorelick had made it her primary mission at Main Justice not to be blindsided. She had taken note of a loud warning shot that had been fired at Main Justice just as David Margolis was beginning to focus on the Cornerstone case. This was a RICO and drug conspiracy indictment called *U.S. v. Hallinan*. Like the proposed indictment in Cornerstone, the Hallinan case involved a massive drug-smuggling conspiracy in which a defense lawyer was charged as a member of a criminal enterprise. Like Cornerstone, Hallinan had been carefully vetted by Paul Coffey and the Criminal Division.

The case raised vexing issues. Patrick S. Hallinan, a name partner in a prominent San Francisco law firm, at age sixty had been charged with fifteen counts of racketeering, obstruction of justice, money laundering and abetting a drug-trafficking organization. The government's chief witness against him was a longtime client, a convicted drug dealer. During the trial Hallinan's defense attorneys argued that his indictment was brought by prosecutors determined to intimidate an aggressive and effective defense lawyer. The prosecution hotly disputed that. The assistant U.S. attorney trying the case told the jury at trial that Hallinan helped the smuggling enterprise "manage its way through the dangerous reefs and shoals of the American legal system."

Up until that point the parallels to the Miami case were merely interesting. In early March, however, the Hallinan case produced a shock. The trial judge dismissed the racketeering and drug-conspiracy charges for lack of evidence. Soon after, the jury acquitted Hallinan on all the remaining counts in the indictment. After many weeks of trial, jurors took only four hours to decide that the government's evidence was not credible. The impression of prosecutorial overreaching was heightened when U.S. Attorney Kathryn Landreth announced, just one day after the verdict, that there would be no appeal of the judge's dismissals. "I think that one of the lessons we learned has to relate to the credibility of the witness," Landreth told the *San Francisco Examiner*.

It had taken awhile for the shock and outrage of the Hallinan case to ripple through the legal community, but over time its waves began to be felt inside Main Justice. It became Exhibit A for those who would make the case that the Justice Department was bent on intimidating aggressive defense lawyers.

That was one concern for Jamie Gorelick as she began reviewing the proposed Cornerstone indictment. A second was quite different. The Clinton administration's relations with the government of Colombia were delicate. Mary Lee Warren, occasionally assisted by the attorney general, had worked hard to persuade the Colombian government to mount a serious campaign against the Cali cartel. Central to these efforts was the Justice Department's evidence-sharing program. The Cornerstone indictment, as proposed, could be expected to have a profound impact in Colombia.

It described, for example, how the cartel's American lawyers had arranged false affidavits to be filed in Colombian courts so that charges would be dropped against Miguel Rodríguez Orejuela. The cartel kingpins worked at public relations in their country and tried to foster a benign image as captains of industry who wanted only peace and prosperity.

The Cornerstone indictment would detail numerous instances of major cocaine seizures, an international network of front companies and a series of murders, threats and bribes. Its deep level of detail would refute any suggestion that the cartel's leaders were benign. It would also make crystal clear that there was now a wealth of direct evidence that could be used in Colombia against Miguel Rodríguez Orejuela. Either factor was the sort of issue that Gorelick would have noted. Coming together, they made the Miami case a matter that she wanted to review herself. "I wanted to be certain," Gorelick explained, "that the case was there."

The nature of the deputy attorney general's job is such that events often intrude on the best-planned schedule. On April 19, 1995, a truck bomb exploded in front of the federal courthouse in Oklahoma City. Suddenly all the issues that Gorelick had planned to consider in the Cornerstone case were swept aside. She took day-to-day command. Merrick Garland was dispatched to Oklahoma to set up a command post of prosecutors.

There are times when the powers of Main Justice can be diffuse and scattered. This was not one of those times. During the bombing investigation the full force and expertise of Main Justice and the Criminal Division were focused like a laser on Oklahoma City. The shaken city had a relatively small U.S. Attorney's Office. Soon enough, Garland had arranged for some of the Justice Department's best lawyers to be thrown into the investigation.

Meanwhile in Miami, prosecutors Ryan and Pearson had started bringing a new grand jury up to speed on the huge case against the lawyers and the Cali cartel. Agents Kacerosky and Weiss were hustling old witnesses into the grand jury. To save time, the prosecutors had clerks from the U.S. Attorney's Office appear in the grand jury, sit in the witness box and read aloud from transcripts of earlier testimony.

Finally, in early June, Gorelick returned her attention to the issue of Operation Cornerstone. Her review was swift. After summoning Theresa Van Vliet and Mary Lee Warren to her fourth-floor office, Gorelick asked Van Vliet to outline the direct evidence against each of the lawyers. It was time to make a decision.

It had been three years since that Saturday morning when Van Vliet had happened to hear about the surprise seizure of cocaine at the Port of Miami concealed inside cement posts and corner-stones. She, and the case, had come a long way. In her hand, Van Vliet had a memorandum that described the evidence against each lawyer, but it was hardly necessary. Precise and lawyerly, she gave the closing argument for the Main Justice review. Soon after, Gorelick made her decision. If Warren and Van Vliet were satisfied that the case was ready for indictment, then so was Gorelick. In Miami, prosecutors Ryan and Pearson were informed that they could proceed with the Cornerstone indictment.

On Friday, June 2, the grand jury returned the 161-page indictment with attachments outlining various properties, vehicles and bank accounts the government of the United States wished to seize from the named defendants. By Friday evening, arrest teams were scouring South Florida. Three of the six defense lawyers named in the indictment had either pleaded guilty to criminal charges or indicated, through attorneys, their willingness to do so.

The Cornerstone indictment was made public on Monday, June 5. A national news media long since bored by big drug prosecutions gave the story front-page treatment. Both *The Washington Post* and *The New York Times* carried lengthy stories, focusing on the role of the former prosecutors. Four days after the indictment was publicly unsealed and its wealth of detail was widely circulated in Colombia, authorities in that country acted. On the evening of Friday, June 9, Colombian police, proceeding on evidence provided by informants for the Central Intelligence Agency and the U.S. Drug Enforcement Administration, entered an anonymous apartment in a quiet neighborhood of Cali. On the second floor, in a small but comfortable chamber cleverly concealed behind dummy walls, the police discovered Gilberto Rodríguez Orejuela. So as not to call attention to the residence he shared several days a week with a girlfriend, Rodríguez had stationed his heavily armed security detail about a mile away. When police discovered him, Rodríguez was frantically trying to reach his security men; it was too late.

The other arrests followed swiftly. On the Fourth of July, an undercover Colombian police detective spotted José Santacruz Londoño having dinner in a comfortable Bogotá steakhouse. "Chepe" Santacruz suffered from an irritating skin disease and so rarely wore socks. After confirming the identity of the sockless steak eater, the detective alerted General Rosso Serrano, the respected director of Colombian police. Fearing the cartel's many spies would recognize his car before he could get to the steakhouse, General Serrano phoned his wife's security detail. The four armed men entered the restaurant minutes later. Believing the place was surrounded, Santacruz, the most violent of the Cali cartel's leaders, surrendered quietly. The arrest of Miguel Rodríguez—the much-pursued cartel micromanager whom Theresa Van Vliet called MRO—followed soon after that of Chepe Santacruz.

The massive Cornerstone indictment had presented the Colombian government with an encyclopedic index of the evidence against the three Cali kingpins—Gilberto and Miguel Rodríguez Orejuela and José Santacruz Londoño—traffickers who had allegedly been moving tons of cocaine to the United States since the mid-1970s. It was clear that the American police agencies had done a prodigious amount of evidence gathering. In fact, the case put on public display the Justice Department's most powerful weapons. There were the RICO charges, for example, which allowed the use of years of evidence about the organization against each defendant. There was the maze of electronic wiretaps that had captured so many incriminating conversations. There were the searches of the lawyers' offices. There was the sheer, mountainous weight of the detective work that had been done by dozens of federal investigators who had pursued the Cali cartel for more than fifteen years. Finally, there was the carrot and the stick of draconian drug sentences and the federal witness security program. Facing a lifetime in federal prison, cartel employees Harold Ackerman, Pedro Isern, George Lopez, Raúl Martí and Francisco Laguna had done the unthinkable. They had agreed to testify against the Cali cartel, a dangerous step that meant their families would live forever in fear.

Whatever trade-offs had been made in the Cornerstone case, it was clear that a strategy of penetrating American investigations, coupled with persistent pressure on the Colombian government, had paid at least short-term dividends. Things had gone just about the way Theresa Van Vliet had thought possible when she had urged Edward Kacerosky three years earlier to move the Cornerstone case to her office at the High Intensity Drug Trafficking Area (HIDTA) facility and take his investigation to a higher level.

All week after the arrest of Gilberto Rodríguez in Cali, friends called Van Vliet at her office in downtown Washington with their congratulations. When she answered the phone, her voice bore the tone of triumph. This was right up there with the Miami Dolphins winning a Super Bowl.

"How 'bout those Colombians," she cheered.

In Washington, in the middle of the roundup of the Cali cartel, David Margolis died. And then he came back to life.

On a brutally hot afternoon in his office on the fourth floor of Main Justice, Margolis was already immersed in another big project. He had had a lot of responsibility for the Cornerstone case, but only at one critical juncture. Then it had moved on into the hands of others, and Margolis had turned his attention to the next big criminal matter.

Behind his desk Margolis started feeling woozy and disoriented. He called for his secretary in the outer office, but there was no answer. Perspiring, he stumbled across the room and lay down on the comfortable leather couch. There his heart stopped.

What happened next was unusual, but not as rare as it might seem. When a human heart stops beating, it sometimes causes the body to convulse, briefly and violently. That's what happened to Margolis, and the spasm pitched him from the couch onto the carpeted floor. The jolt from the fall restarted Margolis's heart, or so his doctors concluded. His secretary found him a minute or two later. Less than ten minutes after that, a team of paramedics was whisking an inert Margolis across town to the Ronald Reagan Trauma Center at George Washington University Hospital. Doctors at the emergency facility had treated President Reagan there after he was shot by John Hinckley, Jr. Fortunately for Margolis, a team of heart surgeons was on hand to treat him almost immediately. The physicians performed a quadruple bypass on the former Mafia prosecutor who had gotten by for so long with two desserts at lunch and a nearly unbroken chain of Marlboros from dawn to dusk. Amazingly, Margolis suffered no heart damage. All he had done was scare his many friends and admirers at Main Justice half to death.

When news reached the big building at Tenth and Constitution that Margolis would be okay, there was a palpable feeling of relief, particularly in the Criminal Division, Margolis's professional home for so long. Like just a very few others—Jack Keeney, Mark Richard, Paul Coffey, Gerry McDowell—it was hard to imagine the place without Margolis's cool head and quirky wit. The lawyers who had come of age together in the Criminal Division over the past two decades were getting on in years. Keeney had lost his wife of more than four decades. Richard would have lost his life had it not been for some courageous doctors and a rare cancer treatment. Margolis—well, Margolis had died and then come back to life, seemingly none the worse for wear for the experience.

What was true of all three men was that the pain, the loss and the personal emergencies intensified, not diminished, their devotion to the Department of Justice. They wielded a power that was transitory but real. A case would come into their hands from Miami or Phoenix, Seattle or Kansas City, and for a few minutes or a few weeks their decision was all that mattered. They would look at the facts and the law and then decide someone's fate. Most Americans, even most people in official Washington, had never heard the names of the veteran Criminal Division lawyers. Yet the impact of their judgments was often billboarded on the front pages of the nation's newspapers. In a society where fewer and fewer individuals could make a difference in the quality of life, they had. And they had done so with the law. Not a few of their friends, who made much more money in private law practice, envied the freedom Margolis, Keeney and Richard had to make decisions "for the good of the case" and for no other reason.

The veterans of the Criminal Division treasured and guarded that freedom. It was, they believed, the very thing that guaranteed the Justice Department's integrity when so many other factors conspired to undermine it. "I never intended to make a career of this," Mark Richard said. "But I fell in love with the department. It rises above the political bullshit. You look at the amount of influence the political process has, and it's minimal. There are traditions here. Really, it's a beautiful department. It's a terrible love affair you have with the department. And in many ways, she can be a most jealous mistress."

Where those outside Main Justice saw politics or worse, those inside saw tradition. It was a kind of dissonance not peculiar to Washington; everywhere governments operate, perceptions of the governed are at variance with those who wield power. Still, because of the importance of the issues the Department of Justice deals with, especially issues relating to integrity, crime and violence, the confidence of the governed is critical; minimizing dissonance is vital.

There are many ways of doing that. Janet Reno had tried, by talking and leading. Jo Ann Harris had as well, by throwing her all into developing the program to attack violent criminals. For all the results the political leaders of the Justice Department achieved—and the records varied considerably from one administration to the next—the most significant measurement of Justice Department performance is the quality of the cases it brings to court, and the number of cases it refuses to bring because of evidentiary and other problems. No matter who sits in the White House or in the Attorney General's Office on the fifth floor of Main Justice, that measurement—the quality of cases brought and not brought—is determined by the career lawyers of the Department of Justice. And because the public perception of the department rises or falls largely in consequence of the calls made on criminal prosecutions, the career lawyers of the Criminal Division have profound influence on how the Justice Department's performance is measured.

PART
TWO

CHAPTER FIFTEEN

THE PRICE
OF POWER

The investigative tactics and legal authorities that enabled the Department of Justice to cripple international cocaine cartels were impressive. They also were relatively new. The full array of federal crime-fighting weaponry had created a force in the United States that was never contemplated by the framers of the U.S. Constitution. That defining document gives the federal government virtually no role in domestic law enforcement. By the final decade of the twentieth century, however, the federalization of criminal law had a huge momentum, and its chief effect was to turn the nation's seven thousand federal prosecutors into the most powerful civilian officials in the country.

The weapons that assistant U.S. attorneys or Department of Justice lawyers wield are those most commonly associated with totalitarian regimes. With the full authority of U.S. law, federal prosecutors can arrange for telephones to be tapped and bedrooms to be bugged with listening devices. They can summon people for secret grand jury interrogation or allow agents to raid a family's home in the middle of the night. They can use the testimony of a witness who is coerced with the promise of a reduced prison sen-

tence. With the stroke of a pen, a prosecutor can draft an indictment so that the penalty under the mandatory sentencing guidelines will be a virtual life sentence.

Federal prosecutors are vested with this power for the best
of reasons—to enforce the Rule of Law and get at the truth
about federal crimes. But in giving so much discretion to government lawyers, the United States assumes a risk that its leaders in Congress and the White House barely acknowledge. The
country has decided to trust the judgment of lawyers who are under intense pressure to get results in the War on Crime, even as
they serve an ever-changing group of ambitious political appointees.

One measure of the risk could be made in the growing inci-
dence of prosecutorial misconduct, improper actions that give the
government an unfair advantage in a criminal trial. A second
measure could be seen in the nature of prosecution campaigns driven by politics. Whether Democrat or Republican, new administrations seeking to remedy a social ill or win favor with voters
could and did commandeer the Justice Department's authority in
ways that put constitutional rights in jeopardy. Both forms of
excess—by well-intentioned individual prosecutors or heedless
political managers—were exceptions to the rule. But neither was
unprecedented in the federal justice system. By 1995, their number and seriousness was increasing.

At Main Justice the lawyer responsible for rooting out and punishing instances of prosecutorial misconduct is Michael E. Shaheen Jr. In December 1995, Shaheen marked his twentieth
anniversary as chief counsel in the Office of Professional Responsibility (OPR), the Justice Department's ethics watchdog. For
better and for worse, no other department lawyer had had more
impact on how the institution viewed its ethical and professional
obligations. With the possible exception of David Margolis, no
senior career official played a more pivotal role in the controver-
sies that rolled over Main Justice during the tenure of Janet
Reno.

Like his colleagues at Main Justice, Shaheen's influence is situational. Cases are referred to him from all corners of the Justice Department. Once they enter the opaque glass doors of the Office of Professional Responsibility on the fourth floor, they belong to Shaheen. It is only after he and his staff make a finding of fact that cases move out the door and into the hands of someone else, usually the deputy attorney general.

Over the years Shaheen and his staff had acquired a reputation as dragon slayers. The reputation was not unwarranted. Shaheen's lawyers built the case that led to the removal of FBI Director William Sessions. It was Shaheen again who exposed flaws in the FBI's investigation of several top managers in the tragic shooting at Ruby Ridge, Idaho. Shaheen has investigated several attorneys general, including Benjamin Civiletti during the Carter administration and William French Smith and Edwin Meese during the Reagan years. His findings in those cases were unsparing and added to his reputation as the in-house guarantor of the Justice Department's integrity.

As important as such high-profile cases were, the less heralded job of policing the Justice Department's corps of line prosecutors had more relevance to the way ordinary Americans were treated in federal court. On this score Shaheen's legacy was ambiguous and more difficult to calculate. "We believe," Shaheen said, "that we are the only component in the department that is the ultimate check on behalf of the attorney general against prosecutors and misconduct by them . . . and abusing the machinery that they have at their disposal, which is awesome."

The very existence of the Office of Professional Responsibility at Main Justice made a promise to the nation and the criminal justice system. On behalf of the attorney general, Shaheen and his investigators would root out integrity problems at the top of the institution and serve as a deterrent to unprofessional conduct by rank-and-file federal prosecutors. Integrity and misconduct were the two sides of OPR's promise.

A private man, Shaheen was regarded by many inside Main Justice as an ominous figure. He had retained his job at Main Justice over the course of two decades in part because of a cadre of powerful patrons on Capitol Hill. Senator Joseph Biden, the Democratic former chairman of the Senate Judiciary Committee, counted himself a Shaheen ally, as did his Republican successor, Utah Republican Orrin Hatch.

Attorney General Edward Levi created the Office of Professional Responsibility in 1975, one of several Watergate-era reforms at the Justice Department. Levi was faced with an FBI reeling from a series of scandals, an FBI that could not be trusted. Not long after he assumed the attorney generalship, Levi found that he had no regular means of sorting out complex allegations of corruption or misconduct. He wanted a permanent in-house staff of lawyers who would be the "eyes and ears" of the attorney general. When things happened that were out of the ordinary, Levi wanted these lawyers and investigators to step forward and find out why.

Shaheen assumed the leadership of the Office of Professional Responsibility after Levi created it. Raised in the small but prosperous town of Como, Mississippi, the son of its wealthiest family, Shaheen won admission to Yale University and thereafter earned a law degree at Vanderbilt. He returned to Como and ran for mayor. With his family's backing, and that of Como's black community, Shaheen was elected on a promise to desegregate the all-white police force. In late 1972, Mayor Shaheen was nearing the end of his first term when a friend talked to him about moving to Washington and taking a job at the Department of Justice. It had been a decade since Robert F. Kennedy pushed the Justice Department to become the protector of civil rights and the scourge of the Mafia. Soon enough, Main Justice would be coming to grips with the twisted legacy of J. Edgar Hoover. The one-term mayor of Como was intrigued by the possibilities of Washington. He decided he would not seek a second term.

At Main Justice, Shaheen thrived, becoming a supervisor in the Civil Rights Division. Mature for his age, he had an ability other young strivers admired—he won the confidence of superiors easily. When one of his bosses was appointed special counsel on intelligence matters, he asked Shaheen to become his deputy. Together, the two lawyers spent the next few months processing classified material for release to the Senate Select Committee on Intelligence headed by Senator Frank Church.

As Shaheen was completing his task, Edward Levi summoned him to his fifth-floor office. The attorney general was a trim, bookish man, almost elfin in appearance. Standing behind his desk, a wry smile on his face, Levi slid a document across to Shaheen. "I want you to look at that," he said. It was an order creating a new unit that Levi was calling the Office of Professional Responsibility. "I want you to do it," Levi told Shaheen. "Think about it overnight, and get back to me."

Shaheen read the document and was disheartened. The title and the description of the job made it sound as if the chief lawyer in the new Office of Professional Responsibility would be the Justice Department's nanny, an ethics monitor who would go around counseling other lawyers about their obligations. That's not what he had in mind when he left Como for Washington. Shaheen said as much to Levi the next day.

Levi listened patiently, then waved the young lawyer's objections aside. He wanted Shaheen to take the job.

"Why?" Shaheen asked.

"Because you know where all the bodies are buried," Levi explained. "And that's an important capacity to have in a start-up operation for an office like this."

Levi wanted the Office of Professional Responsibility to be much more than an ethics cop. In his view the Justice Department needed to undergo a painful catharsis, one that would clear the air of allegations that were false while uprooting certain dark truths, no matter how much they hurt.

Reluctantly, Shaheen took the job. Levi thanked the young lawyer, then he gave him his first big assignment. The attorney general wanted an examination of the FBI's investigation of the assassination of Martin Luther King Jr. The FBI had been spying on members of the civil rights movement in an effort to discredit Dr. King and destroy the movement, government files showed. There had been burglaries and illegal wiretapping on a grand scale. Hoover's minions had obtained recordings of King in embarrassing conversation. Agents had assembled the most graphic of these recordings on a single tape that was circulated to senior government officials and newspaper editors. In subsequent congressional testimony, William Sullivan, Hoover's intelligence chief, explained that the ground rules for the FBI's efforts against Dr. King were simple: "No holds were barred."

After Dr. King's assassination, conspiracy theories abounded. Hoover had tried to kill Dr. King's career as a civil rights leader, they reasoned; perhaps the late FBI director had finally opted for more direct action. Levi asked Shaheen to follow the evidence wherever it led, to determine whether the FBI's investigation of King's murder was "thorough and honest" and "whether there was any evidence that the FBI was involved in the assassination."

A task force of lawyers overseen by Shaheen went to work. Ultimately, they concluded that despite Hoover's animus toward King the murder investigation was "thoroughly, honestly and successfully conducted." The FBI inquiry had led to the capture and conviction of King's assassin, James Earl Ray. Shaheen and his team drew a second conclusion, however. "The Bureau files reflect a significant degree of disdain," they wrote in a concluding report, "for the supervisory responsibilities of the attorney general and the operating divisions of the [Justice] Department."

The evidence was impossible to ignore. The FBI didn't like the U.S. attorney in Memphis, where the crime had occurred. Unbeknownst to Main Justice, FBI lawyers had drafted a criminal complaint against Ray and then had it filed in Birmingham, Alabama, thus shifting jurisdiction to a U. S. attorney they preferred. When Main Justice complained it was being "kept in the dark" about the King investigation, the FBI simply ignored demands for information. "The task force views this lack of coordination and cooperation as highly improper," said the OPR report.

The fear of alienating Hoover had made the Criminal Division at Main Justice a bystander in the King investigation and an accomplice to years of illegal domestic surveillance. "The attorney general and the division charged with responsibility for internal security matters failed badly in what should have been firm supervision of the FBI's internal security activities," said the report.

With the King report, Shaheen laid down several important parameters. The Criminal Division was responsible for overseeing the FBI, not serving as its convenient mouthpiece. The first and most important recommendation in Shaheen's final report was a demand that the Criminal Division start doing its job. "The progress of such sensitive cases as the King murder investigation . . . [is] properly the ultimate responsibility of the Division or the Department," said the report. Shaheen argued that Main Justice was the parent, not the sibling, of the FBI. "The attorney general and his assistants are the officers most accountable to the electorate and they, not the police agency, must maintain effective supervision."

The Shaheen task force said, further, that FBI agents were duty bound to come forward as whistle-blowers and report abuses to the Justice Department or to Congress. Both "should be expressly designated . . . to be a place to which Bureau subordinates may complain, confidentially and with impunity, of orders which they believe to threaten a violation of the civil rights and liberties of citizens and inhabitants of the United States."

For Main Justice, the import of these statements was profound. They would echo down through the years, in cases as diverse as the Abscam undercover operation of crooked members of Congress and the illegal surveillance of American citizens who supported leftist groups in El Salvador. Perhaps the most important marker of all was the message the King report conveyed about this new unit called the Office of Professional Responsibility: It was going to tell the Department of Justice the hard truths.

After twenty years Michael Shaheen betrays little of the weight he bears as the chief enforcer of the code of professional discipline at Main Justice. A trim man in his early fifties, his soft Mississippi accent deepens when he tells stories about past encounters with an attorney general or some self-important curmudgeon on Capitol Hill. Innately cautious, he is a tough bureaucratic infighter who has survived more than one challenge to his long tenure.

By most accounts, Shaheen is a brilliant supervisor of investigations and a tough interrogator. In nearly two decades of service at Main Justice, however, he has never tried a criminal case. What he knows about the realities of criminal prosecution he learns secondhand from reading transcripts or consulting with lawyers who have tried cases. In the very early years of the Office of Professional Responsibility, Shaheen and his staff tended to handle complaints by mail. They would ask the prosecutor to submit a written explanation of his conduct. When there was a clear case of an abusive prosecutor, Shaheen pursued it, hunting down the facts and confronting the lawyer involved. As often as not, wayward prosecutors would be apprised that Shaheen and his staff were coming up with strong evidence of misconduct. They were given time to return to private practice with their professional reputations intact. "It's an easy solution for us," Shaheen said. From 1985 through 1991 twenty-two Justice Department lawyers resigned during OPR investigations, roughly three or four a year.

Shaheen saw risks in overly aggressive inquiries by his office. If he initiated an investigation during the middle of a pending prosecution, for example, he could ruin a good case. If he authorized full-blown investigations too easily, that could have a chilling effect on government lawyers who were working in an adversarial arena. If federal prosecutors were going to take on the nation's worst criminals, they needed to be aggressive. It was their job to stand up to well-paid defense teams and wage legal combat. In the United States, the legal process is supposed to be adversarial. Shaheen dreaded the advent of what he considered the worst-case scenario: a savvy defense lawyer using the prospect of an OPR complaint to intimidate a federal prosecutor.

Main Justice held out Shaheen's office as the only proper place for resolving complaints about the professionalism of federal prosecutors. If a judge condemned an assistant U.S. attorney in a published opinion, it was sent to Shaheen. If a prison inmate wrote a letter to the Senate Judiciary Committee saying he was wrongly convicted, it was routed to Shaheen or his staff. The same was true if a defense attorney claimed to have witnessed unethical conduct; he or she was instructed to talk to the OPR. The inquiries Shaheen conducted were covered by the federal Privacy Act; they were personnel matters involving employees. This meant that most prosecutorial misconduct inquiries were conducted in strict secrecy. Only in the most controversial cases would the Justice Department release a summary of OPR's findings. On occasion the department released annual reports, usually several years after the fact, that contained statistical information about OPR's caseload, along with brief summary anecdotes about selected cases, sanitized of any names, dates or locations.

Over the years the secrecy of OPR's work infuriated many people who filed complaints. It meant that their pleas were most often met with silence or a brief, noncommittal letter from Shaheen. The few prosecutors who committed egregious ethical violations walked away from the job, unscathed and untarnished. Within the department, OPR acquired the aura of a place where inquiries were lengthy, deliberative and cautious. It was a tone set in an era when the Justice Department was a much smaller place, when a wayward prosecutor could be reined in by a judge's scowl.

Few people outside the legal profession have any idea what constitutes "prosecutorial misconduct." Historically, Americans were taught that judges stood between the individual defendant and the all-powerful sovereign and enforced rules of fairness. There was a time not too long ago when federal judges did serve that function and had quite a lot of power to ensure the fairness of criminal trials. But for a variety of reasons they have lost much of that authority. This sea change in federal jurisprudence has shifted more of the burden of ensuring fairness onto the shoulders of Main Justice and OPR.

As counsel to the attorney general, Shaheen looks at the facts of a prosecutor's conduct through a lens that is different from the one used by a federal judge. Unless the case involves outright corruption, the OPR evaluates a prosecutor's performance as an employee who has a unique set of ethical obligations. Since many of the best-documented cases of prosecutorial misconduct are described in judicial rulings, this inevitably puts the OPR in the position of second-guessing federal judges.

Shaheen does not hesitate to do so. He is one of the most autonomous career officials at Main Justice. Generally speaking, he has greater access to evidence than most federal courts. Trial judges rule on the testimony and statements put before them in a court record. The OPR has a broader field of vision. Shaheen's lawyers can review all the evidence not presented in court, including grand jury testimony. They can question the prosecutor at length and talk to his colleagues and supervisors. "Whatever is in the realm of the relevant we can get," Shaheen said. David Margolis calls Shaheen's function "quasi-judicial." His findings bear the imprimatur of the Department of Justice; he is an agent of the executive branch of government and is not required to defer to the judiciary. Shaheen, in other words, is the de facto arbiter of what constitutes intentional prosecutorial misconduct in federal court.

The federal government's War on Crime is generally dated to the Nixon administration, but the expansion of federal crime-fighting authority has been bipartisan. The Carter administration prosecuted the Abscam defendants and emphasized pursuit of white-collar crime. The two Reagan administrations poured billions into fighting organized crime and drug trafficking and sent the Justice Department on a hiring spree for federal prosecutors. The Bush administration did the same and fought to expand the autonomy of federal prosecutors. Congress happily funded all this growth.

By the early 1990s, there were warning signs that this rapid expansion in size and power had brought with it some unintended consequences. The most explicit warning signal was a series of major federal prosecutions that were crippled or killed by judicial findings of prosecutorial misconduct. Even under the relatively lenient federal rules of criminal procedure, the courts found, Justice Department prosecutors had gone too far. In several cases, judges focused not only on the failings of individual prosecutors, but also on the oversight of senior managers. The cases involved important and expensive prosecutions, several of which had been vetted by the Criminal Division.

In Chicago, years before the indictment of the Black Gangster Disciples, the U.S. Attorney's Office had brought one of the biggest gang cases in history, a RICO prosecution against members of a murderous street gang known as the El Rukns. The government had pushed the racketeering statute to its outer limits, charging thirty-five defendants with 175 counts of criminal activity. When it was released, the indictment was the size of a big-city telephone book, weighed nearly four pounds and covered a period of twenty-three years of crime, stretching back to when some of the defendants were children. The indictment was so big a judge insisted it be broken into three separate charging documents. Three trials resulted in convictions and long prison sentences for the defendants.

Only after the trials did the judges learn that the prosecutor had not disclosed exculpatory evidence that undermined the credibility of the government witnesses. So damaging were the problems this created that the judges overturned the criminal convictions.

Marvin Aspen, the chief U.S. District Court judge in Chicago, said it was "the most painful" decision he had ever made. "It is a tragedy that the convictions of some of the most hardened and anti-social criminals in the history of this community must be overturned," Aspen stated. "It is tragic that the United States of America has squandered millions of taxpayer dollars and years of difficult labor by the courts, prosecutors and law enforcement officers in the investigation and trial of these botched prosecutions."

He suggested the case was ruined by misguided zeal. "It is a personal tragedy for the El Rukns prosecutor who, in seeking to attain the laudable goal of ridding society of an organization of predatory career criminals, was willing to abandon fundamental notions of due process of law and deviate from acceptable standards of prosecutorial conduct. The others who followed his lead or failed to supervise him properly, of course, share in this disgrace."

In Miami, another big RICO case crashed and burned. In 1991, U.S. District Court Judge Jose Gonzalez concluded, in both sadness and anger, that he was forced to release one of the city's most notorious criminal suspects, Alberto San Pedro, because federal prosecutors had "set up" the defendant in an unusual grand jury proceeding. "The foundation of the Republic will not crack if the

United States fails to put Alberto San Pedro in a federal prison," Judge Gonzalez said. "It will shatter, however, if the American people come to believe that their government is not to be trusted."

Many of the judges were reacting to their own sense of fairness and the devastating effect that a federal prosecution could have on defendants. In the District of Columbia in 1989 a judge stopped a trial involving a large fraud conspiracy case. He had listened to the government's case for six weeks and decided it had no proof to support the charges. "Much of what the government characterizes as incriminatory evidence is not persuasive of guilt when viewed in its full context," U.S. District Court Judge George Revercomb said. "In fact, some of the government's evidence is exculpatory and points toward innocent conduct." The judge granted an acquittal.

Some of the problems arose from the new demands that international crime was making on the U.S. legal system. In Los Angeles, an important international heroin case was destroyed after it was revealed that the federal prosecutor in the case was using a witness brought from the Republic of China who had been coerced into cooperating by officials in that country. When the witness admitted he was lying, U.S. District Court Judge William Orrick concluded that the prosecutor had "lied to the court" about the matter and engaged in "deliberate concealment" of exculpatory evidence. The prosecutor had "buried in his files" memos from Hong Kong prosecutors that alluded to the coercion of the witness, according to Orrick. "The facts show such a clear, flagrant and shameful violation of the [witness's] rights under the Constitution that they shock the conscience of the court," the judge concluded in a written opinion.

The Clinton transition team's report on the Justice Department suggested strongly that judges like Aspen, Gonzalez, and Revercomb were on to something. "Our consultations with a broad cross-section of the leaders of the American Bar convince us that the Department of Justice has lost sight of its mission and its sense of justice," the transition team report said. "The [Justice] Department over the past twelve years has diminished the trust and respect it once enjoyed among its natural constituents: the Bar, the legal academy and political leaders."

Publicly, the Justice Department denied there was a problem, but behind this brave exterior lay a different truth. The internal files at the Office of Professional Responsibility established that both the federal judges and the Clinton transition team were right to be concerned. Between late 1992 and 1993 there was an unprecedented, albeit secret, surge in the number of complaints against federal prosecutors—an increase of 78 percent. Moreover, prosecutors who faced OPR inquiries were resigning at six times the normal rate. In fiscal 1993 there were twenty such departures, compared with the usual rate of three or four a year.

It was hard to know why, exactly. The Justice Department had hired large numbers of new prosecutors during the Reagan and Bush administrations. Moreover, there was no doubt that in recent years attorneys general had set a no-nonsense tone that encouraged toughness. President Reagan's second attorney general, Edwin Meese, talked about prosecution as nothing less than a historic crusade. "The Rule of Law has managed to maintain a precarious edge over the forces of chaos ever since the revival of Western civilization," Meese said. "In a sense we are facing up to another barbarian-type invasion." His successor, Richard Thornburgh, championed the aggressive prosecutor. "You are putting bad guys in jail," he said during a 1991 interview on CNN. "You're trying to get every edge you can on those people."

Throughout the twelve years of Republican administrations, the Congress and the U.S. Supreme Court had gone along with efforts to empower federal prosecutors and extend their autonomy. Both official bodies had occasion to address complaints from people who believed themselves victims of prosecutorial misconduct. Periodically, both the High Court and the Judiciary Committees in Congress had made it clear that they were inclined to let the Justice Department police the conduct of federal prosecutors.

As a consequence, on the day that Janet Reno took office as attorney general, the nation's three branches of government were essentially relying on one man, Michael Shaheen, to keep the system honest and fair.

CHAPTER SIXTEEN

A JUDGE'S ANGER

Of all the federal judges who thought they had witnessed prosecutorial misconduct in their courtrooms, it fell to Judge James M. Ideman to lay the issue squarely at Janet Reno's front door. In doing so, he revealed a disturbing aspect about a little-known policy in the Office of Professional Responsibility. He set in motion a process that drew a line in the sand for two powerful groups. The outcome of the case cited by Ideman signaled to federal prosecutors that the Justice Department's professional discipline process would no longer be a leisurely or entirely secret affair. It also put federal judges on notice that they risked public censure if they sanctioned a prosecutor for misconduct.

Appointed to the federal bench in Los Angeles by President Reagan, Ideman is a burly man with an engaging manner. A respected former state prosecutor, he is a model of the kind of law-and-order trial judge Ronald Reagan tended to put on the federal bench. It was therefore a shock in 1989 when Ideman dismissed a major racketeering indictment against Joseph Isgro. In the months that followed, Ideman would criticize the Department of Justice in language seldom heard before from a Reagan judge and present the Clinton administration with a challenge. "I think there is a real problem in this country," Ideman declared. "I think that Ms. Reno and others in the Department of Justice ought to take a very serious look at what's going on."

Joseph Isgro was a wealthy independent music promoter charged with money laundering related to payola, the practice of bribing disc jockeys to play certain records. The prosecution had begun as an investigation by the Organized Crime Strike Force Office in Los Angeles back when David Margolis was still running this program from the Criminal Division. Margolis had assigned the case to a close friend and respected colleague, William S. Lynch. "I wanted a hot-plate lawyer to put the case together," Margolis explained, "to indict it and try it."

One of the best trial lawyers in the Criminal Division, Lynch had thirty years of unblemished government service, during which time he helped run the organized crime section. Unlike some of his peers at Main Justice, Lynch loved the rigors and rewards of trial work. In midcareer he had decided to return to the courtroom, taking on a series of high-profile prosecutions of the Mafia. By 1989 he had earned the title senior litigation counsel in the Criminal Division.

The payola case against Joseph Isgro was just one more challenge. Lynch assembled a state-of-the-art prosecution to go after him, starting with a cluster of payola charges, which were misdemeanors. Lynch then obtained Isgro's bank records, which showed unusual transactions that were characteristic of money laundering. Next he tracked down a bunch of disc jockeys who were prepared to swear that they had received money or cocaine in exchange for playing records promoted by Isgro.

Lynch took all this evidence and crafted a fifty-seven-count racketeering indictment. Central to the case was the testimony of Isgro's accountant, a defrocked former Internal Revenue Service agent named Dennis DiRicco.

During pretrial hearings Isgro's lawyers filed motions for discovery of any exculpatory evidence prosecutors had found during their investigation. The government is required to produce such evidence under the Brady rule, which refers to evidence that might exonerate a defendant. Two weeks before trial Lynch assured Judge Ideman that he had turned over all Brady material. He said he also had turned over a second kind of evidence, called Jencks material, which is evidence that might impeach the government's witnesses.

After the trial began Isgro's lawyers announced that they had just received six volumes of testimony by DiRicco, the accountant, during an earlier trial in San Francisco. In that testimony, the defense lawyers said, DiRicco exonerated Isgro and denied laundering money. When asked about the testimony, Lynch told Ideman that the newly discovered testimony by DiRicco "does not contradict" the testimony he was expected to give against Isgro. This point was significant. If there was no contradiction, then there was no problem.

On the other hand, if the accountant's earlier testimony contradicted his more recent grand jury testimony against Isgro, then there was a problem. It would mean that the government's star witness in the RICO case might well be a perjurer. The older testimony would arguably qualify as both Brady material and Jencks material. It might exonerate the defendant or impeach the government's witness.

When Ideman appeared to take the matter seriously as a potential Brady violation, Lynch said he had "held nothing back deliberately." Besides, he argued, no real harm had been done to the defendant. DiRicco had not yet testified. Isgro's lawyers had the transcript in time to use it during the trial.

"Nope, that's not the point," Ideman said. "The point is, it was the obligation of the government to voluntarily give it up."

Things soon got worse for Lynch. The defense cited seventy-four statements from DiRicco's earlier testimony that it said contradicted the grand jury testimony used to indict Isgro. This included an unequivocal denial from the accountant that he had helped Isgro launder money. Moreover, the judge noted that Lynch had not told the grand jurors that his chief witness had changed his story under oath. That information might have affected their decision on whether to approve the indictment.

Lynch argued that he was under no obligation to turn over the transcript of the earlier trial because it was already a public record in San Francisco, freely available to any diligent defense lawyer. Pained by the challenge to his integrity, Lynch swore out an affidavit. "At no time," he stated, "did I intentionally or consciously attempt to hide evidence from the defense. I may have been wrong in viewing the trial testimony of DiRicco as not being impeaching, but that was due to inadvertence."

Ideman faced a dilemma. The Isgro case was a major federal prosecution, and the trial was already under way. The charges in the indictment, if true, meant that Isgro clearly deserved to be prosecuted. The exculpatory evidence had been disclosed, and the government had apologized. Under the judicial philosophy of "harmless error," any violation of the Brady rule could be cured by giving the defense time to analyze the testimony and use it to cross-examine DiRicco.

But Lynch's seemingly contradictory statements had riveted the judge's attention on the issue of governmental misconduct. Ideman decided to read the two sets of testimony himself. When he compared the 1988 trial testimony and the 1989 grand jury testimony Ideman found they were diametrically opposed. Looking at it as a former prosecutor, the judge could see no excuse for withholding the DiRicco trial transcript. Worse, this was not the testimony of just any witness. So far as Ideman could tell, without the accountant's testimony there was no RICO case against Isgro. He was the one witness who enabled Lynch to allege that Isgro was running a racketeering enterprise.

Ideman decided he had no option and he dismissed the case against Isgro with prejudice. That meant the Department of Justice could not refile the indictment. In a memorandum, the judge detailed a series of events that had shaken his confidence in the prosecutor and the fairness of the proceedings. "It was the government's intent not to ever provide the material to the defense for the same reason it was withheld from the grand jury," Ideman wrote. "The prosecution feared the effect it would have upon DiRicco's credibility and thus their case." The judge said the case was an example of "outrageous government misconduct."

Angered about the issue, Ideman had done some research in recent legal opinions on prosecutorial misconduct. "From Idaho to Chicago to San Francisco, these cases are popping up all over the country," he said, in dismissing the indictment against Joseph Isgro. "And the thinking of some of us on the bench is, perhaps this is a symptom of a Justice Department that is simply out of control, that they are badly in need of some adult supervision, and they are not getting it."

Main Justice viewed the Isgro case as an important prosecution and decided to fight the dismissal. In a brief filed before the Ninth Circuit Court of Appeals, an appeals specialist from the Criminal Division conceded that Lynch had erred, but not so grievously as to justify termination of the RICO prosecution of Joseph Isgro. "It was a terrible mistake that Mr. Lynch made," lawyer Frank Marine said during oral argument, but not one that entitled Isgro to escape justice.

Behind the conciliatory language in the government's appeals brief was an unmistakable claim of prosecutorial autonomy. "The court has no authority to fashion rules for conduct" for the prosecutors, Marine declared. Even assuming that Lynch abused the grand jury process and violated the Brady rule, the sanction of dismissal with prejudice—with the prohibition against refiling a criminal case against Joseph Isgro—was too severe.

The Supreme Court had ruled that trial judges could not dismiss cases because of concerns about prosecutorial misconduct. Upon reflection, the panel of judges on the Ninth Circuit agreed. "In this case," the court ruled, "the prosecution's misconduct clearly rose to an intolerable level, particularly the misconduct of Mr. Lynch. But dismissing the indictment is simply an unwarranted 'windfall' to the defendants." Rather, said the appeals court, "The Attorney General should examine the conduct of Mr. Lynch" and "consider . . . departmental discipline."

Isgro's lawyer seized upon the Ninth Circuit ruling and filed a petition with the Supreme Court. If the decision was upheld, Isgro's lawyers argued, "the ultimate result is that the government is free to withhold evidence, lie to the court and counsel, and make every effort to illegally and unfairly obtain an advantage over a criminal defendant."

In 1993, the Supreme Court declined to hear the case and sent it back to Ideman's courtroom, almost three years after he had stopped the trial and thrown out the case. Before going forward with a new trial in December 1993, Ideman asked for a report on what the Justice Department had done about Bill Lynch. He was told that Main Justice had yet to initiate disciplinary proceedings. The judge was incredulous. From his vantage point in California it sounded as if Lynch's colleagues at Main Justice were taking a casual view of his transgression. "Your Department has apparently decided to do nothing in the matter," Ideman stated angrily. ". . . Tell them that I think their handling of this case is helping to trash the reputation of the Department of Justice. Tell them I said that."

For his part, Bill Lynch was no longer handling *U.S.* v. *Isgro*. He had moved on to his next case, a Mafia prosecution in Pennsylvania.

For Janet Reno, Judge Ideman's words were painful. She could think of no good reason for the three-year delay in investigating the allegations of misconduct against William Lynch. She summoned Deputy Attorney General Philip Heymann and demanded answers. "She was quite stung by it," Heymann said. He quickly learned that the source of the problem was a policy inside the Office of Professional Responsibility that he had known nothing about.

It came as a surprise to a lot of people. With the approval of past attorneys general, the OPR had adhered to a practice that tended to limit its usefulness as a deterrent to abusive prosecutions. It would not investigate a claim of prosecutorial misconduct in a criminal case until the litigation was ended, including all appeals.

As a consequence, Heymann discovered, Michael Shaheen's office was sitting on a backlog of several hundred uninvestigated cases involving prosecutors and agents.

Many were of little consequence. But each year several dozen cases arrived at the OPR with a solid thud. Typically, these were misconduct allegations cited by judges in published opinions or in legal briefs written by defense lawyers. Often, they were supported by testimony and documents. The OPR policy ensured that some of the best-documented allegations of prosecutorial misconduct got shoved onto a back burner. The prosecutors could move on to other cases. Because appeals in the federal system took years to run their course, many of Shaheen's inquiries were not conducted until long after memories had dimmed and defendants had suffered the consequences of flawed prosecutions.

To Heymann, the effect of this practice seemed untenable. It gave the public the impression that Main Justice was not interested in rooting out rogue prosecutors and enforcing standards of professionalism. That did not serve the department at all, certainly not the Justice Department Phil Heymann wanted to lead. Moreover, it was undoubtedly true that many of the prosecutors who were caught up in OPR matters had been wrongly accused of professional misconduct. The OPR's practice left those lawyers hanging. There seemed no justification for internal investigations to take so long.

Heymann had known Shaheen for years, having served as assistant attorney general of the Criminal Division during the Carter administration. Yet he was surprised to learn how things worked at OPR. It was true that Shaheen's office had a reputation for conducting long, tedious investigations, but few officials attributed this to deliberate delay. Shaheen's admirers noted his legendary thoroughness in major cases. The OPR staff was small, just five lawyers. It had not grown since the early 1980s, even though the number of federal prosecutors had nearly doubled during that period.

Heymann had come to the job of deputy attorney general with reservations about Shaheen. He didn't doubt the OPR counsel's personal honesty or integrity, which were above reproach. Everyone admired Shaheen's determination when it came to investigating senior officials. Heymann just thought Shaheen had been in the same job too long and had said as much to reporters for the *Legal Times* and *The Washington Post* before taking the job of deputy attorney general. Since returning to Main Justice, Heymann had been asked by Reno to look at the proposal to merge the OPR staff with the Office of Inspector General. Related to this issue was her desire to respond to a request from *The Washington Post* that the department begin disclosing the findings of OPR investigations. With other senior officials, Heymann had discussed replacing Shaheen, on the theory that the OPR counsel ought to have the one thing Shaheen lacked—extensive courtroom experience trying criminal cases.

Heymann saw these issues as related and had spent many months hashing out the details. But Judge Ideman's bitter comments in December 1993 suddenly accelerated the pace of change. A three-year delay in conducting investigations had been okay with previous attorneys general, but not with Janet Reno. After reviewing Judge Ideman's remarks and getting a full report from Heymann, she issued several orders. She demanded that the backlog be cleared up. Heymann assigned thirty-six lawyers from the Criminal Division to help Shaheen's staff. She declared that, henceforth, whenever a federal judge criticized a prosecutor, the OPR investigation was to begin immediately, regardless of the status of the case. "Delays in evaluating the allegations of professional misconduct, such as the delay described by Judge Ideman, are not acceptable," she stated. Moreover, the absolute secrecy in which OPR inquiries were shrouded was going to be lifted, at least for serious matters. In the future, Reno said, the department would release a public summary of OPR findings in cases where there was a finding of intentional misconduct or public criticism by a federal judge.

On the more immediate problem of Bill Lynch, Shaheen dispatched lawyers to Los Angeles to begin interviewing witnesses about the allegations in the Isgro case. One of Judge Ideman's charges was quickly determined to be moot. The judge had concluded that Lynch had misled the grand jury by not telling them that the accountant, Dennis DiRicco, had changed his story and had previously committed perjury. At one time Shaheen and his staff paid a lot of attention to complaints of abuse of the grand jury process, but the issue had been rendered nearly irrelevant by a number of Supreme Court rulings. In a line of cases culminating with *U.S. v. Williams* in 1992, the High Court declared that prosecutors had no obligation to tell grand juries about exculpatory evidence.

Instead, the inquiry focused on the allegation that Lynch had deliberately concealed Dennis DiRicco's exculpatory testimony because he feared it would destroy the credibility of his key witness. As they dug into the case, Shaheen's lawyers concluded that there was no way that Lynch's action was inadvertent. The undisclosed transcript of DiRicco's earlier grand jury testimony was eight hundred pages long. Lynch had read it carefully in preparation for DiRicco's grand jury appearance. When the requests for Brady evidence were made, Lynch had not forgotten about the testimony. His co-counsel, a young prosecutor named Drew Pitt, had raised the issue with Lynch, but the senior lawyer said no—they were not obliged to give the defense a public record.

Once Shaheen's lawyers had completed their fact-finding in Los Angeles, the OPR's "quasi-judicial" role came into play. It might be true that a federal judge and appeals court had declared that Lynch had violated the Brady rule. But as far as Main Justice was concerned, this was an open question until Shaheen reached his own independent judgment. In making this decision, he followed a practice that he had trusted for years. He convened an informal, but prolonged, debate among the lawyers on his staff. The OPR counsel took pride in what he considered a collegial environment in his office, and he encouraged his lawyers to argue with him about the merits of the case. In the end, Shaheen concluded that it was unclear whether public testimony was, in fact, Brady material. Lynch might be right on that score. Shaheen ruled that the prosecutor had not "intentionally" concealed exculpatory evidence. It was Lynch's sincere belief, Shaheen concluded, that he did not have to turn over the transcript under Brady.

Several months passed. In the meantime Phil Heymann left the department after it became clear that he and Reno did not work well together. One of the stumbling blocks in their relationship had been the issue of the OPR. Heymann had continued to work toward a merger, having gained the impression that Reno supported this effort. But if she had given Heymann such a signal, Reno had changed her mind. She wanted a process that was effective. For his part, Shaheen played a tough game. He made it clear that he would resign from the Justice Department if the OPR was going to be merged with Office of the Inspector General. In blunt, back-channel communications Senators Joseph Biden and Orrin Hatch let Reno know they would not tolerate Shaheen's removal. When Jamie Gorelick replaced Heymann as deputy attorney general she swiftly put all thoughts of a merger to rest and decided there would be no change in the leadership of the OPR.

That still left the issue of Bill Lynch. On March 22, 1994, Assistant Attorney General Jo Ann Harris, Lynch's supervisor, sat down at a conference table across from him. It had fallen to Harris to resolve the matter of disciplining Lynch. Harris had read the report by the OPR, and she had seen a detailed response from Lynch. It had been three months since Janet Reno had announced her new disclosure policy, yet so far no OPR case had been the subject of public release. Reno was adamant about following through. Given the prominence of the Isgro case and Judge Ideman's pointed criticism of the Justice Department, the case would be a likely candidate for disclosure under the new policy.

The Isgro case was being watched closely. Defense attorneys would applaud if it was made clear that rigorous new standards of professional discipline were being enforced; the thousands of assistant U.S. attorneys in the field would take a different view of such an outcome. Every day these lawyers made decisions that could be second-guessed. Many would wonder if the new policy meant that Janet Reno would hand them up every time they made a mistake. If it could happen to an icon like Bill Lynch, it could happen to anyone.

Then there was the human side. It was certainly possible that Lynch had simply made a mistake. He had filed an affidavit to that effect, and there was good reason to take him at his word. Jo Ann Harris had been told, and she had seen for herself, that Lynch was not making excuses; he accepted full responsibility for the mistakes in Isgro. Clearly, Lynch was mortified by the single blemish on an outstanding career. There was no arrogance in his manner, only honest remorse. Moreover, Lynch had announced his intention to retire from government service. Under every previous attorney general, this step would have been enough to bring a quiet and painless end to the affair. It had been an easy way to resolve messy cases before. It would not work now.

Two days after her meeting with Lynch, Jo Ann Harris signed a letter of reprimand, declaring that the veteran prosecutor had failed to adequately prepare the Isgro case. "The basis of my finding is that in the summer of 1990, when you understood the facts of the case, you did not re-review and recognize the significance of the prior testimony of a crucial witness," Harris wrote. "As a consequence, you failed to produce a document you should have produced for the defense, and exposed the United States Department of Justice to damaging allegations of professional misconduct."

Under the new disclosure policy, the reprimand was made public, paining Lynch's many friends and admirers, not least of them Jo Ann Harris. But to Janet Reno, the step was an important one. "The more you can be open, the better," she said. Opening up a process as delicate as enforcement of professional discipline was a delicate matter, however. Reno had made the commitment; the reprimand of William Lynch was her down payment. Now all she had to do was follow through on it.

For his part in the Isgro case, Judge Ideman also paid a price. When the case was sent back for trial, the Ninth Circuit directed Ideman to choose a lesser sanction than dismissal. The judge decided to suppress the testimony of Dennis DiRicco, the accountant who worked for Isgro. This ruling effectively gutted the RICO case.

Once again the Justice Department appealed. This time the case was heard by a different panel of judges on the Ninth Circuit. Overturning Ideman's ruling, they said it was "sufficient sanction" that the prosecutor had been chastised in a published opinion and subjected to an OPR investigation. To underscore its view, the panel summarily removed Ideman from the case. When Isgro's lawyer asked for a rehearing, a majority of the Ninth Circuit judges declined to hear the case.

This brought a strong protest from four dissenting circuit judges, whose memorandum offers vivid commentary on the state of judicial power in the mid-1990s. The Ninth Circuit ruling "sends the wrong message about the level of conduct expected of counsel for the United States," the judges in the minority said, because a "first year law student" would recognize Dennis DiRicco's testimony as Brady material. The dissenters praised Judge Ideman for being "persistent enough to find out the facts and bold enough to take action."

To emphasize the importance they attached to the case, these judges reached back to a 1935 Supreme Court decision that explained the role and the responsibilities of a federal prosecutor:

The United States Attorney is the representative not of an ordinary party to a controversy, but of a sovereignty whose obligation to govern impartially is as compelling as its obligation to govern at all; and whose interest, therefore, in a criminal prosecution is not that it shall win a case, but that justice shall be done. As such, he is in a peculiar and very definite sense the servant of the law, the two-fold aim of which is that the guilty shall not escape or the innocent suffer. He may prosecute with earnestness and vigor—indeed, he should do so. But, while he may strike hard blows, he is not at liberty to strike foul ones. It is as much his duty to refrain from improper methods calculated to produce a wrongful conviction as it is to use every legitimate means to bring about a just one.

CHAPTER SEVENTEEN

THREE STRIKES

For senior officials in the Criminal Division it was galling to see an important case like *U.S.* v. *Isgro* derailed by an episode of prosecutorial misconduct. Mistakes in the heat of courtroom combat were costly, but another kind of failure was worse: the few cases where good judges became convinced that defendants were innocent of the charges filed against them. The worst of these cases were those where judges concluded that a prosecutor was using unfair tactics. When such elements arose in cases that had been screened by the Criminal Division, the disappointment was especially acute. It implied to some judges that Main Justice had betrayed its trust, or at the very least, that it had been inattentive to abuse of its great powers.

Such cases were rare. One of the most unfortunate occurred on Janet Reno's watch. As often happens, the litigation was born out of a determined prosecutor's vision of what justice required.

The case had a long history, having begun in Miami in the mid-1980s. The defendant, a young lawyer named Kenneth Treadwell, was accused of conspiring in a fraudulent loan scheme at a savings and loan institution that ultimately collapsed.

The tragic outcome of *U.S. v. Treadwell* was significant because the Criminal Division had been fully briefed on the case's problems long before it found its way into court. Senior Criminal Division lawyers, including David Margolis, had given the matter special attention. They had been warned that the evidence against Kenneth Treadwell was flimsy and that the prosecutor was taking a hard line. They were informed of a legal issue in the case that virtually invited a court to take a hard look at the issue of fairness.

Nonetheless, after a pre-indictment review at Main Justice, Jack Keeney, the Criminal Division's most senior career attorney, allowed an indictment of Treadwell to go forward, as did senior officials in the U.S. Attorney's Office in Miami. In the months that followed as the prosecution lurched toward disaster no one at the Department of Justice was willing to step forward and intervene.

Ultimately, however, one man, William B. Hoeveler, did step forward. A tall, silver-haired former marine and a graduate of Harvard Law School, he is one of the most respected federal trial judges in the nation. Hoeveler was named to the federal bench after a brilliant career as a trial lawyer. Although he is known for a legal philosophy that tends to favor the government, Hoeveler's many admirers nevertheless consider him the perfect judge to preside over complex and contentious criminal prosecutions. His oversight of the case against former Panamanian dictator Manuel Noriega, for instance, was praised as a model of judicial administration. Hoeveler's written opinions betray a piercing intellect. As a rule, they are viewed with respect by courts of appeal.

Hoeveler's intervention in *U.S. v. Treadwell* was unusual. For years, the Supreme Court has instructed federal trial judges to defer to the judgment of prosecutors. Trial judges who fail to do this can anticipate short shrift from the appeals courts. Judge Ideman learned that in *U.S. v. Isgro.* There, the appeals court answered Ideman's concerns about prosecutorial misconduct by ordering his removal from the case. An equally vivid example involved U.S. District Court Judge Terrence Hatter. Twice Hatter dismissed a case in which the FBI used a prostitute to encourage a man in his sixties to purchase drugs. An appeals court reinstated the indictment, ruling that even "sleazy tactics" by the government did not justify dismissal of an indictment. Federal trial judges, the appeals court said, should "supervise their own affairs and not those of other branches."

Such rulings have imbued the job of the federal judge with considerable moral ambiguity. As federal penalties have become draconian—up to and including the death penalty—weak cases present the judiciary with much harder choices. A court's doubts about prosecutorial fairness immediately raise doubts about judicial authority. Should judges trust their own perception of the evidence? Do they have the power to stop a lawful prosecution that might also be the result of abusive prosecution tactics? Was it even a judge's business to worry about fairness? The prosecution of Kenneth Treadwell placed all of those questions squarely before Judge William Hoeveler.

The investigation that swept up Kenneth Treadwell began in 1985. That year a thrift institution, the Sunrise Savings and Loan Association of Florida, went belly-up, but not before its executives tried to stave off disaster with a series of fraudulent loan transactions. Sunrise had been formed as a business venture by senior members of a Pennsylvania law firm, Blank, Rome, Comisky and McCauley. Treadwell was a partner in the firm. Just as Sunrise was spiraling toward ruin, Treadwell left Blank, Rome and took a job as general counsel at Sunrise. Before he arrived, Sunrise executives had negotiated several bogus transactions with a few big delinquent borrowers. The goal was to clean the books of bad debts and thereby fool state bank regulators into thinking Sunrise was solvent.

Two of the largest fraudulent transactions were negotiated just before Treadwell assumed his new duties at Sunrise. One was a series of loans made on August 30, 1984. The other was the purchase of a real estate asset called Seawalk. The purchase prices were wildly inflated. Treadwell had nothing to do with setting these prices; that was done by senior Sunrise executives. But as a new member of the Sunrise management team he was aware that the transactions were underway and attended meetings before actually going on the payroll. At one point he walked out of a heated discussion about the August 30 loans, after urging one of the borrowers to get a lawyer. On the Seawalk purchase, Treadwell participated in the final closing.

When Sunrise folded in 1985, state bank regulators and the FBI launched a joint investigation. Treadwell was called in for questioning and decided to cooperate with the government. He met with Lothar Genge, a veteran Mafia prosecutor assigned to the Justice Department's Organized Crime Strike Force Office in Miami. Faced with a daunting fraud investigation, Genge cut a deal with Treadwell in July 1985. In exchange for his cooperation in the investigation, Treadwell would receive immunity from prosecution. He was provided with a written cooperation agreement signed by the prosecutor.

Thereafter, Treadwell was interrogated at length. He told bank regulators and FBI agents which transactions to look at and what documents to seize. After these sessions subpoenas were issued based partly on Treadwell's information. Witnesses were sought out and interrogated. Genge used the evidence to assemble a criminal fraud case against three senior Sunrise executives and two delinquent borrowers. He focused on several deals. One was the purchase by Sunrise of the Seawalk property from a delinquent borrower.

As he proceeded with his investigation, Genge developed strong suspicions about the Blank, Rome law firm. Sunrise had been founded by senior partners of the firm as an investment. Genge discovered documents that suggested the firm viewed the thrift as both a business venture and a source of easy money. Blank, Rome earned several million a year in legal fees from handling the legal work on Sunrise transactions. Given this close relationship, Genge suspected that senior lawyers at the firm also knew about the fraudulent transactions and had conspired with Sunrise to bring them about. He began to contemplate the possibility of indicting the law firm. As an investigative theory, it was perfectly plausible.

Genge soon faced an obstacle, however. He had strong evidence that the Sunrise executives had cooked up the fraudulent transactions. There was no direct proof, however, that senior partners at Blank, Rome knew what was happening. Genge had a solid fraud case against Sunrise executives, but he did not yet have a prosecutable case against the law firm.

What Genge did have was Kenneth Treadwell. Because Treadwell had been a Blank, Rome partner and a Sunrise employee, it was reasonable to suspect that he would know whether his old colleagues at Blank, Rome were aware of the fraudulent transactions. Testimony to that effect from Treadwell might become a bridge that would take the prosecution into the law firm. If Treadwell would testify that Blank, Rome partners knew about and authorized the fraudulent deals, then Genge could consider seeking charges against the firm's senior partners.

But there was a problem to achieving his goal. From the beginning Treadwell maintained that he did not know the Sunrise transactions were fraudulent. As a consequence, he told Genge, he could not honestly say that any of his former colleagues at Blank, Rome had known of or authorized any fraud in the August 30 loans or the terms of the Seawalk purchase.

Genge decided to get tough. He declared that Treadwell's status had changed from immunized witness to a target of the investigation. At a meeting with Treadwell in March 1986, Genge had an FBI agent read Treadwell his Miranda rights. At that meeting, Genge accused Treadwell of holding out. Treadwell's cooperation agreement with the government, and the guarantee of immunity from prosecution that it conveyed, was a two-way street. The agreement required Treadwell to tell all that he knew, especially anything about crimes he himself might have committed. Treadwell's refusal to admit that he was part of the fraud that had been committed at Sunrise constituted a breach of the cooperation agreement, Genge maintained. As a consequence, the government was going to revoke the agreement and take away Treadwell's immunity from federal prosecution.

Treadwell couldn't believe it. Neither could his attorney. But Genge was serious. He made it clear what he expected Treadwell to do. "Look," he told Treadwell's lawyer. "The only thing that we are going to tell you is that we think that he [Treadwell] can implicate other people . . . you bring us Marvin Comisky [a senior partner in the law firm] and then we will be able to talk." The lawyer conveyed the message to his client. Treadwell repeated his earlier statement: He didn't know the loans were fraudulent and was unable to say what his former partners at Blank, Rome might have known about them.

Genge wasted no time. No longer was the lawyer a cooperating witness helping the government build its case. Now he was the target of a federal investigation. The possible charges included criminal conspiracy and bank fraud.

Treadwell needed help—desperately. Irvin B. Nathan agreed to represent him. A Washington-based partner in the law firm of Arnold & Porter, Nathan had worked as a deputy assistant attorney general in the Criminal Division during the Carter administration. He specialized in white-collar crime, representing corporations and wealthy businessmen accused of fraud. Because Lothar Genge was assigned to the Organized Crime Strike Force, Nathan knew just where to turn. Unlike other federal prosecutors, Strike Force prosecutors reported to career lawyers in the Criminal Division in Washington. In order to bring an indictment, Genge had to get approval from Main Justice. Nathan knew that, upon request, a defense lawyer could obtain a pre-indictment conference with the Organized Crime and Racketeering Section and present arguments why an indictment should not be approved. At the time David Margolis was in charge of the Organized Crime and Racketeering Section. Strike Force indictments were rarely rejected, Nathan knew, but lawyers in the section were generally willing to listen to counterarguments from defense counsel.

Thus, in 1987, a meeting attended by Nathan, Genge and a handful of other prosecutors and defense lawyers was held at the Criminal Division, convened by one of Margolis's deputies. Genge had already submitted a detailed prosecution memo that described the evidence against Treadwell and the fraud and conspiracy charges he proposed to bring against him. Nathan's rebuttal focused on the unfairness of revoking a cooperation agreement against a lawyer who every witness agreed had had no involvement in negotiating the fraudulent Sunrise transactions. He also questioned whether there was any credible evidence against Treadwell. Several weeks later Nathan was informed that the division had done the unlikely: It had declined to approve the indictment of Ken Treadwell.

Lothar Genge was undeterred. He returned to Miami and proceeded with the case against the Sunrise executives, obtaining an indictment in February 1987 against Sunrise executive Robert Jacoby and others. At a trial in 1989 before Judge Hoeveler, these executives claimed to have acted on advice from their lawyers. During his closing argument Genge offered a rebuttal that seemed to vindicate Treadwell and his former law partners. "Blank, Rome had nothing to do with that [the purchase of Seawalk], with fixing the price or anything like that . . . no evidence, no papers, no nothing," Genge told the jury. Jacoby was convicted. To Nathan, the outcome seemed to signal that the threat to Treadwell was past. The prosecutor had argued in court what Treadwell had been saying all along: The lawyers had not known about the frauds.

In fact, Genge still considered that an open question and suspected strongly that there was more to the Sunrise case than just the executives in Florida. The relationship between the law firm and the S&L was unusual. With his initial convictions in hand, Genge decided to revisit the idea of pursuing Blank, Rome. This took him back to Kenneth Treadwell, whom the prosecutor still viewed as a potential witness against the law firm. Genge maintained that Treadwell had lost his immunity because he had not told the whole truth. Treadwell's story had not changed, however. He insisted that he was unaware of the frauds and could not implicate the law firm. For a second time, Treadwell faced the possibility of a federal indictment.

Once again Irv Nathan appealed to the Criminal Division. This time David Margolis presided over the pre-indictment conference. It was a marathon, five-hour session held in a high-ceilinged conference room. Margolis encouraged a freewheeling debate that fell somewhere between court hearing and barroom argument. Nathan and other defense lawyers presented their protests; Genge responded with a defense of a case he believed in. When lunchtime came the lawyers were not even close to being finished. Margolis had a couple of foil-wrapped hot dogs brought up from the basement cafeteria. He unwrapped the first one and signaled the lawyers to keep talking.

Nathan argued three points. First, that Treadwell had kept his part of the cooperation agreement. With Treadwell's help, he said, Genge had won his first convictions. It would be wrong to now change the rules and revoke that immunity. Second, he outlined Genge's argument during the trial of the Sunrise executives that they had ignored the "common sense" advice of their lawyers, who were not involved in negotiating the Seawalk purchase. Having done so, Nathan said, it was now wildly inconsistent to turn around and prosecute one of those lawyers on the Seawalk deal. Third, Nathan stressed that Treadwell's version of events had never changed. The defense lawyer offered to have his client take a polygraph test.

Genge countered with a blistering rebuttal. During the original interrogations, he charged, Treadwell had minimized his own role in the bogus Sunrise transactions. He had withheld information he knew the investigators wanted. Treadwell was trained in the law, the prosecutor stressed. He had helped to work out the details of the transactions. There is a concept in law called "conscious avoidance," or deliberately ignoring what is obvious to everyone in the room. Treadwell had to have known what was happening at Sunrise.

During the conference Margolis and his deputies asked lots of questions. What had the government promised in the immunity agreement? What had Treadwell been asked during the interrogations? What, exactly, had he said? How significant was his role in the transactions? As the hours passed, the session grew tense. The table was pounded, voices rose.

As a lawyer, Genge put up a good fight. By this point, however, he had lost an important ally. The FBI office in Miami had distanced itself from the second phase of the Sunrise case. The FBI agent who had led the initial investigation, Anthony Yanketis, objected to revoking Treadwell's immunity from prosecution. The agent had thought Genge was too quick to grant the immunity, without learning all that Treadwell could contribute. Once the deal was done, however, Yanketis thought it unfair to go back and prosecute Treadwell. An assistant special agent in the Miami FBI office looked into the matter, then wrote a letter to the Strike Force saying the FBI was unwilling to invest any more time in the Sunrise investigation.

Several weeks after the pre-indictment conference, David Margolis decided that the Criminal Division would not approve the proposed indictment against Kenneth Treadwell or the case against Blank, Rome. This meant that Treadwell could get on with his life. Nathan could box up his files and send them to storage. Soon, the five-year statute of limitations on the Sunrise transactions would expire. Until then, Genge would have to look for some other way to prove his suspicions about Blank, Rome.

An odd twist of fate kept the case alive. In response to the public's outrage over the collapse of hundreds of savings and loans because of fraudulent practices, Congress had passed legislation that extended the statute of limitations to ten years on certain kinds of financial institution fraud. The actions in the Sunrise case fell under the new law's umbrella. All of a sudden, Lothar Genge had another five years to make his case against Blank, Rome. In the meantime, the two convicted Sunrise executives, Robert Jacoby and Thomas Skubal, had lost their appeals. Facing considerable prison time, the two decided to cooperate with Genge in exchange for reduced sentences.

Treadwell was still in jeopardy. On November 18, 1992, Lothar Genge wrote Irv Nathan a letter announcing that he had discovered "new evidence that was not previously available to the Department of Justice at the time it rejected the two prior prosecution recommendations by our office." The case against Treadwell had come back to life.

By this time, Nathan had strong feelings about Lothar Genge. He respected the prosecutor's skills as an advocate, and anyone could see he was the soul of perseverance. But Nathan had begun to question Genge's fairness and sense of perspective. For his part, Genge viewed Nathan as a well-connected Washington defense lawyer who had exploited his relationships at Main Justice to stop a legitimate indictment. What counted, Nathan knew, was not personal feelings but the evidence. If Genge was telling the truth—if there were indeed new witnesses who would implicate Treadwell—then Nathan's client was unlikely to avoid indictment a third time. Even if the new evidence was not particularly strong, it would be difficult to stop Genge again.

A change had come to the Criminal Division that complicated Nathan's challenge. Genge no longer worked for Margolis. Attorney General Dick Thornburgh, a former U.S. attorney from Pennsylvania, had disliked the Organized Crime Strike Forces and killed off the units. Strike Force attorneys like Genge now reported directly to the local U.S. Attorney's Office. No longer did Genge need to get his indictments approved by the Criminal Division in Washington. He had now joined the ranks of assistant U.S. attorneys, who work for political appointees in the ninety-four federal districts. The local U.S. attorney can approve most indictments.

Nathan thought he knew how Genge would pitch the new case against Treadwell. His supervisors in Miami would want to know why the case had been turned down twice by Main Justice. The answer—or at least someone's answer—had been telegraphed in newspaper stories in Florida based on anonymous official sources. One story, in the *Miami Review*, bore the headline "PRESSURE RISES TO PROSECUTE S&L LAW FIRM." The story carried Genge's picture and portrayed him as a persevering prosecutor whose efforts had so far been stymied by politics. "Genge mounted a second effort to indict the firm," the article said, ". . . but was stopped after representatives from Blank, Rome met with high-level representatives of then-U.S. Attorney General Richard Thornburgh, a former Pennsylvania governor."

There were other news leaks. To Nathan, they were an attempt to do precisely what the *Miami Review* headline suggested: Put "pressure" on the Miami U.S. attorney to approve the indictment of Ken Treadwell.

Of course, Nathan fumed, the anonymous "sources" for these articles in South Florida were only telling the local reporters half the story. Yes, Main Justice had declined two earlier indictments of Treadwell, but not because of intercession by political appointees. The indictments had been turned down by career prosecutors after lengthy debates. The obstacle hadn't been politics, but a combination of factors: Genge's decision to revoke a written immunity agreement, the limited amount of direct evidence against Treadwell, Genge's seemingly contradictory statements during the 1989 trial and the novelty of indicting an entire law firm.

To Nathan, the newspaper stories were an example of how government leaks to the news media were used to keep a weak case alive. It was a phenomenon that David Margolis and others in the Criminal Division had seen before; their decisions had often been the subject of leaks.

Margolis was in the business of fostering significant prosecutions. He hired, trained and promoted tough field prosecutors. He and his colleagues in the Criminal Division took pride in cases where a lone federal prosecutor—usually a young lawyer putting in long hours—prevailed over a large, well-funded defense team. But Margolis and his contemporaries in the Criminal Division had come up through the ranks under the tutelage of Henry Petersen. They remembered the old man as a tough guy who nevertheless insisted that it was important to be fair—and to appear to be fair. That was not always easy, but it was the purpose behind pre-indictment conferences.

In recent years, however, the Criminal Division's pre-indictment review process had become increasingly contentious. The post-Watergate climate of distrust in Washington had infused the exercise with new tension. By its very nature, the review had the Criminal Division sitting as a court of last resort on a proposed indictment. In effect, Main Justice was second-guessing a field prosecutor and possibly preempting a grand jury. At times, the review resulted in career lawyers from the Criminal Division questioning the judgment of a politically appointed U.S. attorney. Among Criminal Division lawyers who did these reviews, nothing was so well understood as their vulnerability to the claim that an indictment had been quashed for improper reasons.

When indictments were rejected it was not uncommon for the Criminal Division to find itself accused of bending to political pressure or doing favors for former colleagues at Washington law firms. To build a major case, a field prosecutor had to invest a lot of time, energy and heart. Having it rejected by Main Justice could be painful and frustrating. Not uncommonly, the local newspapers would know that a major investigation was under way and keep track of the outcome. When an indictment was turned down, reporters would hear a second- or thirdhand version of what had occurred at Main Justice along with the insinuation that the case had been "killed" for political reasons. Part of the legacy of Watergate was that it seemed plausible to journalists that criminal cases could, in fact, be fixed at Main Justice.

In this environment, the easiest course for Main Justice was to approve the case. Even if there were doubts about a case, lawyers in the Criminal Division could rest on the rationale that the court and the jury would sort out the truth.

During the Sunrise case there was little doubt that Lothar Genge and David Batlle, the state banking investigator, were disappointed by Margolis's decision to reject the second proposed indictment of Kenneth Treadwell. According to Batlle, they suspected the decision was not made solely on the merits of the case. "I think it was both the view of myself and Mr. Genge that, not so much political connections, but really the old boy network" had caused the proposed indictment to be rejected, Batlle would later testify.

When it came to Lothar Genge's third attempt to indict Kenneth Treadwell, however, Margolis and the organized crime section were out of the picture. After the Strike Forces were shut down, Margolis had moved to another job. Irv Nathan could still appeal to the Criminal Division, but there was no requirement that he get a third hearing. Main Justice would intervene only in the most egregious circumstances.

Nathan decided to try anyway. He felt strongly about the Treadwell case. Nathan made his living representing defendants in white-collar crime cases. Few of his clients had hands that were entirely clean. During six years as Treadwell's attorney, however,

Nathan had come to the conclusion that Treadwell was the rarest of clients for a defense lawyer—one who seemed truly innocent of the allegation he faced. Nathan was impressed by the fabric of Treadwell's life. By every measure, he seemed a decent man. Treadwell was well regarded by his peers, had a stable marriage and three children. He served as a deacon in his church and volunteered his time as a Boy Scout troop leader. Ken Treadwell, Nathan believed, was someone worth fighting for.

Still, it was not the best of times to be seeking extraordinary relief from the Department of Justice. The Clinton administration had only just taken office. There were no senior political appointees in place in the Criminal Division. The decision on the proposed Treadwell indictment would therefore be left to Jack Keeney, the acting head of the division. Nathan knew Keeney to be one of the most honorable people in the building, a distinguished lawyer whose integrity had not been challenged in four decades of legal practice. Yet Keeney was equally well known for adhering to established procedures. In other words, he tended to back the troops.

Keeney would undoubtedly admire Genge's determination and persistence. Not every prosecutor would stay with a bank fraud case for so long. The Justice Department had been criticized in Congress for not being more aggressive about savings and loan fraud. That could certainly not be said of Lothar Genge. Moreover, Keeney and the Criminal Division had just concluded four years in which the Bush administration had hammered into them the limits of the Criminal Division's role. The Republicans had deliberately constrained the division's prerogatives and decentralized power out to the field. The Bush years had left the Criminal Division lawyers uncertain of their authority; it had made them leery of seeming to "micromanage" criminal cases in the field. Nevertheless, if Keeney was generally inclined to back his subordinates, he still took seriously questions of fairness and the tradition of pre-indictment conferences. If a reputable defense lawyer like Irv Nathan requested a meeting Keeney would give him the time.

On the morning of January 27, 1993, a group of defense lawyers from Washington and prosecutors from Miami assembled in Keeney's spacious office on the second floor with two supervising prosecutors from Miami. Nathan began by recounting the history of the case, including relevant testimony from the 1989 trial of the Sunrise executives. There, he stressed, Genge had won his case by telling the jury that these corrupt businessmen had ignored honest legal advice. Now, he said, because the target was the law firm of Blank, Rome, the government proposed to reverse its logic and claim that Treadwell was part of the conspiracy. There was no evidence that this was so, Nathan argued. Genge's true purpose, according to Nathan, was to get Treadwell's testimony against senior partners at Blank, Rome. For that to happen, Nathan told Keeney, Kenneth Treadwell would have to lie.

Turning to the legal barriers to prosecution, Nathan continued, the only way the indictment could be brought at all was for the government to renege on its cooperation agreement with Treadwell. That was a valid contract, he said, and it should be honored. Treadwell had kept his end of the deal by cooperating. The government should do the same. A judge would look at the sequence of events, he told Keeney, and throw out the case. That would give the Justice Department a black eye.

For more than an hour Keeney listened. A patient and thoughtful man, he possessed a dry, grandfatherly wit. On his walls were photographs signed by former presidents and attorneys general spanning more than a quarter of a century. In a prominent spot was a treasured photograph of Henry Petersen, Keeney's mentor, the tough customer he had replaced so long ago.

When Nathan was finished, Keeney chose not to keep him in suspense. After complimenting the defense lawyer on his presentation, Kenney announced his decision. Speaking softly, Keeney told Nathan that the Criminal Division would not intervene. They would defer to the U.S. attorney. The case against Kenneth Treadwell would go forward.

CHAPTER EIGHTEEN

A FRONTAL ASSAULT

I rv Nathan walked out of the tall Art Deco doors of
Main Justice and raised his right hand. A battered taxi
lurched from the flow of traffic and rattled to a halt.
During the ride back to his law office Nathan boiled
with frustration. Main Justice would not stop Lothar Genge.
Keeney's decision was not a complete surprise. Nathan knew it
had been a long shot. Still, he had hoped that the earlier denial by
David Margolis would have given Keeney pause.

Now, despite the passage of eight years since the collapse of the
Sunrise Savings and Loan and a written grant of immunity from
prosecution, Treadwell would be indicted. It was a mistake,
Nathan believed, a miscarriage of justice. A judge would look at
the cooperation agreement and see that it should not be brushed
aside. If the case went to trial, Nathan knew, it would call for a
frontal assault on the Department of Justice. That was not something Nathan relished. It would mean attacking the motives of a
career federal prosecutor and publicly challenging the judgment
of the Criminal Division. That was a big step for a Washington
defense lawyer who would need to ask for pre-indictment reviews
on other cases.

What Nathan looked forward to even less than the looming battle was the telephone call he now had to make to his client. For nearly a decade Kenneth Treadwell had been on an emotional roller coaster. The ordeal had stunted the growth of Treadwell's promising legal career. It had exhausted his financial resources. Like most American citizens, Treadwell could ill afford a full-blown trial in federal court. In this case, the proceedings were bound to last several months. If Nathan stayed on the case, he would have to live in Florida for the duration, a prospect he was not sure his law firm, Arnold & Porter, would tolerate.

In the months to come, the pressure on Treadwell to cooperate would become immense, Nathan knew. To end his nightmare, all Treadwell had to do was say that he knew the Sunrise deals were fraudulent and that certain senior partners at the Blank, Rome law firm had authorized the transactions known as Seawalk and the August 30 loans. An hour or so of incriminating statements from a witness stand—giving testimony he had insisted would be false—would put Treadwell back in the government's good graces.

It was a seductive option, but there was one other. Genge had approval to seek Kenneth Treadwell's indictment. Well, fine, Nathan thought. He would beat the prosecutor to the punch.

Nathan was sure that a neutral trier-of-fact, such as a judge or magistrate, would see what Nathan thought was so obvious—that it was legally wrong for Genge to rescind the cooperation agreement just because Treadwell would not implicate his former law partners. Genge was acting as if Treadwell could not possibly be telling the truth. In Nathan's view, Genge's approach was coercion pure and simple, a legal means of intimidating a cooperative witness into giving false testimony. Surely a judge would see through the charade.

When he got back to the office, Nathan called together several young lawyers, and they spent the next few hours preparing a civil suit. The complaint sought a temporary restraining order against indicting Treadwell until a judge could rule on the validity of the plea agreement.

For the umpteenth time, Nathan went over the facts: After the Sunrise investigation began Treadwell signed a cooperation agreement that guaranteed him immunity from prosecution in exchange for his truthful cooperation. Treadwell had met several times with investigators and explained how things worked at Sunrise. He told them whom to interview, what documents to look for. Immediately after these debriefing sessions, subpoenas went out for those documents. Treadwell's information contributed to Genge's successful prosecution of the two Sunrise executives.

Nathan booked a seat on the next flight to Miami, then hastened to Washington's National Airport. During his trip south a lawyer at Arnold & Porter, seeking an emergency hearing, placed a call to the chambers of U.S. District Court Judge William Hoeveler. He had presided over the 1989 trial of the convicted Sunrise executives and thus was familiar with the case. Hoeveler's clerk asked to see a copy of the legal complaint Nathan's team of lawyers had drawn up. At Arnold & Porter, the papers were fed into a facsimile machine and transmitted to the judge's chambers. By the end of the day, a law clerk announced that Hoeveler would consider the matter.

On the morning of January 28, 1993, Nathan walked up the steps of the federal courthouse in Miami. In his briefcase was the complaint seeking the restraining order against the indictment of Kenneth Treadwell.

In his empty courtroom Judge Hoeveler instructed the lawyers to make their arguments. The Justice Department was represented by a new prosecutor; Genge couldn't attend. He was in another part of the courthouse, presenting the case against Kenneth Treadwell to a grand jury.

Nathan kept his presentation brief. Treadwell's immunity agreement was still valid and needed to be enforced by court order, he told Hoeveler. It was illegal for the government to breach its agreement after it had enjoyed the fruits of Treadwell's earlier cooperation. A deal was a deal.

Assistant U.S. Attorney Stephen Chaykin disagreed. The court had no authority to prevent an indictment, the prosecutor argued. The proper time for challenging the government was after an indictment was filed.

Hoeveler listened impassively. He would review briefs from both sides, he said. A second hearing would be required.

At the second hearing, several weeks later, Genge was present. The prosecutor assured Hoeveler that Treadwell had violated the immunity agreement by withholding information about his involvement in the fraudulent loan transactions. The government had new witnesses, Genge said, who could implicate Treadwell in wrongdoing. It would become clear that Treadwell had been less than candid about his own role in the scandal at Sunrise.

Hoeveler was torn. He didn't like the sound of this case. It was highly unusual for the government to rescind an immunity agreement. He saw several vexing questions. How, specifically, had Treadwell breached the immunity agreement? That was unclear and would depend on how Treadwell was questioned by government investigators. What effect would breaking the cooperation agreement have on Treadwell's Fifth Amendment rights against self-incrimination? Was it even possible for the government to separate out the information Treadwell had volunteered as a cooperating witness from the evidence it now intended to use against him? And what was the legal effect of bringing charges eight years after the alleged crimes? Could witnesses reasonably be expected to remember details of complex bank transactions so long after the fact? Congress may have changed the statute of limitations, but it could not legislate away the effect that time had on memory.

These were all interesting questions. However, there was a more fundamental issue that Hoeveler had to resolve. Did he, as a federal judge, have any business standing in the way of an indictment? The power to seek indictments rests with the executive branch, subject only to approval by a grand jury. Except in very unusual circumstances, where basic rights are at stake, judges have no role before criminal charges are filed. Upon reflection, Hoeveler decided that he would not block the indictment. Instead, he settled on a compromise. The grand jury could hand up an indictment of Kenneth Treadwell, but before a trial there would be a pretrial hearing on the question of the cooperation agreement and whether Treadwell's immunity could be revoked. "The Court reaches this decision with hesitation," Hoeveler said, "noting the serious allegations against the government."

The government could proceed. In arriving at his decision Hoeveler relied, in part, on the insight of former Supreme Court Justice Felix Frankfurter. "Bearing the discomfiture and cost of a prosecution for crime, even by an innocent person," Frankfurter wrote, "is one of the painful obligations of citizenship."

Kenneth Treadwell was about to learn this lesson.

Treadwell got his pretrial hearing on the validity of the immunity agreement. It took seventeen days and became a searching examination of the government's investigation. During this proceeding Lothar Genge attempted to answer all the old questions once and for all. When Treadwell was first interrogated, Genge argued, he had minimized his role in the fraudulent loan transactions and avoided implicating his former law partners at Blank, Rome. Treadwell had claimed little knowledge of how the price was set for purchase of the Seawalk property. That transaction had been singled out by federal regulators examining the causes of the collapse of Sunrise Savings and Loan Association. Treadwell had claimed to be unaware of any frauds and had the impression the transactions were legitimate. The proof that Treadwell had been involved, Genge said, lay in the new evidence showing that Treadwell helped arrange the loans. The anticipated testimony of the new witnesses, said the prosecutor, would prove that Treadwell had been less than candid about his knowledge of the shady dealings at Sunrise.

The proceeding was called a Kastigar hearing. It was conducted very much like a trial, but without a jury. Nathan filed a standard discovery request for disclosure of Brady material, evidence that tends to exonerate a defendant. Hoeveler issued an order requiring the government to turn over all exculpatory evidence. The prosecutors said they had done so. They had not, although Genge says he was not responsible for the failure to do so.

In his files, Genge had the grand jury testimony of two witnesses. One was Robert Jacoby, the Sunrise executive who had decided the price on the questionable Seawalk purchase. He had said Treadwell was "less involved." The other was Charles Powell, the only Sunrise borrower who had spoken to Treadwell about the loans made on August 30, 1984. He said the transaction was legitimate. The prosecutor did not provide this testimony to the defense. Months earlier Genge had written Irv Nathan a letter stating he had "two additional witnesses, not previously available to the government, who will testify that your client, Kenneth Treadwell, promoted, advised, planned, counseled and otherwise joined with them in the commission of multiple acts of bank fraud." This had been the essence of the argument that Genge had used to win approval of Treadwell's indictment. Nathan assumed that Jacoby and other convicted Sunrise executives would be the government's chief witnesses and point the finger at Treadwell.

After the hearing Hoeveler took the case under advisement for more than a year. During this time the Treadwell case lay dormant. In the meantime Nathan left the case to take a senior post at Main Justice, where he became an assistant to Philip Heymann, the Clinton administration's new deputy attorney general. When Heymann decided to return to the Harvard Law School, Nathan returned to his law firm. The Treadwell case was still waiting.

On July 13, 1994, eighteen months after Jack Keeney had decided to let the courts resolve the fate of Kenneth Treadwell, Judge Hoeveler gave Lothar Genge the benefit of the doubt. He decided to allow the government to revoke the immunity agreement that had been made with Treadwell in exchange for his cooperation. The prosecution of Kenneth Treadwell could go forward. Like Jack Keeney, Hoeveler decided to defer to the U.S. Attorney's Office.

Even as he permitted Genge to pursue his case against Treadwell, however, Hoeveler remained troubled by the facts. "I have labored long and hard over this file," the judge said in a written opinion, "and only after difficult deliberation have [I] come to the conclusion that the Government has met the relatively modest burden of proving its position by the 'preponderance of the evidence.' "

The Treadwell indictment raised troubling questions, Hoeveler continued, about the government's conduct during the ten years it had been investigating Sunrise Savings and Loan Association. On the central issue before him, however—whether the government had properly revoked its immunity agreement with Treadwell—Hoeveler ruled that the government's position was "reasonable." Still, the judge was far from comfortable. "Whether or not this subject will require re-addressing," he cautioned, "depends upon the future course of this litigation." It seemed clear that much would depend on whether the prosecutor could deliver on his promise of new testimony from Jacoby and others that incriminated Treadwell.

Once again Kenneth Treadwell's choices had narrowed. He could go to trial, which would mean trusting that a jury would find sympathy for a lawyer caught up in a savings and loan scandal, or he could admit that he had known about the fraudulent loans and offer testimony against his old law firm.

The trial began. On October 24, 1994, Irv Nathan completed his opening statement to the jury on behalf of Ken Treadwell. Believing that Robert Jacoby was the government's principal witness against his client, Nathan did his best to undermine the executive's credibility. He tried to reinforce Genge's characterization of Jacoby during the earlier trial in 1989. Then Genge had called Jacoby a "brazen perjurer."

A few days later Genge approached Nathan in the courtroom and handed him transcripts of Jacoby's grand jury testimony. Hurriedly, Nathan began to read. By the end of the transcript, he was astonished. Jacoby had not implicated Treadwell directly. In fact, Jacoby's testimony could be read to exonerate Treadwell of involvement in the fraudulent transactions. For example, when Genge had asked Jacoby about Treadwell's role in the August 30 loans, Jacoby had answered that "Ken Treadwell was less involved." When the August 30 transactions were negotiated, Jacoby testified, Treadwell had been in Germany working on other matters. "He wasn't really around." As to the purchase of the Seawalk property, Jacoby told the grand jury that Treadwell had not participated in the negotiations.

This was incredible, Nathan thought. The charges against

Treadwell were based on the August 30 loans and the Seawalk purchase. They were the two pillars of Genge's case. Yet Jacoby, the principal co-conspirator and Genge's best witness, had testified that Treadwell was not really involved in negotiating either of the suspect transactions.

Nathan kept reading. Genge had summoned Jacoby back for a second appearance before the grand jury and probed for more testimony about the lawyers. Once again Jacoby was unable to implicate Treadwell or offer support for Genge's theory about Blank, Rome. "I don't recall if Ken would have been involved," Jacoby testified. "But I don't remember people, then, who were specifically at the law firm involved in that."

There was more. One of the grand jurors had asked Jacoby if he had "anything to gain" by implicating the Blank, Rome lawyers. Jacoby gave a rambling answer during which he said, "I don't have anything to gain, I have no lawsuits."

"So you have no other motivation other than that, right?" a grand juror asked.

"No, sir," Jacoby said.

In fact, upon losing the appeal of his conviction, Jacoby had begun cooperating with Genge's investigation. He was looking forward to receiving Genge's formal recommendation for a reduction in his prison sentence. By appearing before the grand jury, Jacoby had also avoided possible prosecution on perjury charges.

Standing nearby, Genge had allowed Jacoby's testimony to go unchallenged. As far as Nathan could tell from the grand jury transcript, Genge had done nothing to correct the impression that Jacoby left that he was a disinterested witness with no reason to shade the truth.

There was a time, back in the early 1980s, when such conduct might have raised the issue of prosecutorial misconduct. If the omission was egregious it might have been grounds for dismissal of the criminal charges. But a series of Supreme Court rulings had rejected "grand jury abuse" as grounds for dismissal. Grand jury sessions are not trials; they are presentations of evidence by the government. The High Court had specifically freed federal prosecutors from any legal obligation to present exculpatory evidence to a grand jury. Many prosecutors do provide grand juries with balanced presentations and point out to jurors the weaknesses in their case. Under existing law, however, they are not required to raise such matters.

The proudest day of Stephen Chaykin's professional life was the first time he stood up in federal court and announced that he was appearing on behalf of the United States of America.

Of the two hundred or so trial prosecutors in the U.S. Attorney's Office in the Southern District of Florida, there were perhaps a dozen who could be trusted to quarterback the biggest cases. Chaykin was on that short list, and it was fair to say that he had had an extraordinary year. A specialist in white-collar crime cases, he had spent most of 1992 as co-counsel in one of the longest public corruption trials in Miami's history.

Upon winning a conviction, Chaykin and his partner were nominated for the Attorney General's Distinguished Service Award. Soon after this happy moment, however, Chaykin became convinced that the U.S. attorney was improperly meddling in one of his cases. He stood up to the political appointee and suffered the consequences. He was summarily demoted and had to endure a nerve-wracking OPR investigation. Michael Shaheen himself came to Miami to do some of the interrogations. When the dust settled, the U.S. attorney had resigned and Chaykin was promoted to managing assistant of the Fort Lauderdale office.

This made him Lothar Genge's supervisor. In Chaykin's view, Genge was a smart and tenacious litigator who would sink his teeth into a challenging case and never let go. But Chaykin had also formed the impression that Genge could be difficult. His comments to a reporter during this period were a good example. This incident had been especially galling to Chaykin because he had gone out of his way to help Genge get his case into court.

When Genge had sought a third time to get approval to indict Kenneth Treadwell, Chaykin and William Keefer, the second-in-command of the Miami U.S. Attorney's Office, had gone with Genge to Main Justice to argue in favor of the indictment. While it was technically true that the Miami office could proceed on its own, Genge's proposal to indict the Blank, Rome law firm meant that the Criminal Division would want to be involved.

Chaykin hadn't mastered all the facts gathered in the investigation, but he had seen enough to be convinced it was, in his words, a "righteous case." In traveling to Washington, Chaykin and Keefer were showing the flag. They wanted to signal to the Criminal Division that this case was not the misguided obsession of a single prosecutor, but a case that senior lawyers in the Miami office thought should be brought.

With Irv Nathan and other defense lawyers they met first with Gerald McDowell, one of Keeney's most trusted deputies. He listened to presentations of the facts and the law, hearing from both sides. He also heard from lawyers representing the Blank, Rome firm, who argued that it would be unfair to indict the whole firm for the acts of a handful of lawyers.

At the end of this review, McDowell said he planned to recommend that the case against Treadwell and two Blank, Rome lawyers be allowed to go forward. He thought the law firm itself should not be indicted.

After this informal session McDowell and the prosecutors walked down the hall and into Jack Keeney's office, where they were joined by Irv Nathan and several other defense lawyers. Chaykin took a seat on the sofa by the fireplace. He had attended other pre-indictment reviews convened with Keeney, and he always had the same slightly awed feeling. "It is very intimidating to go into Jack Keeney's office," Chaykin said in an interview, "because he is a legend and institution."

Yet Chaykin also knew that Keeney rarely rejected the recommendation of a senior deputy, especially if it took a conservative middle course that allowed a significant prosecution to proceed. During the session the prosecutors listened to Nathan's presentation, much of which they had already heard during an earlier review in Miami.

As the meeting came to an end, Chaykin watched the elder statesman of the Criminal Division look Irv Nathan in the eye and deliver the bad news about Kenneth Treadwell.

The Miami prosecutors had come home with a split decision.

Given the two earlier denials and the age and quality of the evidence, Chaykin thought, it was not a bad result.

As a consequence, he had been astonished when he read a newspaper story soon after in which Lothar Genge suggested that the decision not to indict Blank, Rome had been made as the result of political influence at Main Justice. For a federal prosecutor to publicly insinuate that Jack Keeney had done somebody a favor was not merely silly, Chaykin believed, it was offensive. Keeney had given both sides a fair hearing and then made a decision that was more than reasonable.

Enraged, Chaykin summoned Genge into his office and blasted him with both barrels. Didn't Genge have enough sense to see that his public comments would undermine their efforts to get the prosecution underway? Chaykin railed. Didn't he realize he was giving Irv Nathan more ammunition?

In Chaykin's view, this was typical of Genge. He was an honest prosecutor with a legitimate case, but he seemed to always want to lead with his chin. That was a dangerous way to fight, especially against an opponent like Irv Nathan. Not for nothing was Nathan the head of white-collar litigation at Arnold & Porter. His style was to come sprinting out of his corner and throw fast punches from every angle.

Nathan's pre-emptive civil suit seeking a temporary injunction against the indictment was a good example. Before the grand jury could even vote Nathan was standing in front of Judge Hoeveler and claiming that the prosecution was unfair.

Once Hoelever agreed to hold a pretrial Kastigar hearing on the issue of the immunity agreement, there could be no doubt that the government faced a pitched battle. Blank, Rome had deep pockets. The Miami prosecutors suspected the firm was financing a scorched-earth legal defense. At the very least, it seemed clear that Genge was headed into a firestorm.

A white-collar crime case of this magnitude was the highest form of the prosecutor's art, a test of stamina, intellect and will. Keefer decided that Chaykin should serve as co-counsel with Genge, at least until after the Kastigar hearing, and this proved wise. From the outset Nathan showered Genge with legal motions on every arguable issue and did his best to plant reasonable doubt in the court record.

Nathan's signal accomplishment, Chaykin realized, was to turn the case into a referendum on the methods and motives of Lothar Genge. Unfortunately, Chaykin saw, there were pieces of the case that could be spun against the prosecutor. One of those was Genge's statements about the lawyers during the first Sunrise prosecution in 1989.

In that earlier trial the Sunrise executives, Robert Jacoby and Thomas Skubal, had defended themselves by blaming the advice they got from their lawyers. When the defense asked if there was any evidence in government files that the lawyers were implicated in the crime, Genge said he had nothing "to suggest that the attorneys had anything to do with establishing the purchase price of Seawalk."

In one sense this was true: There was no admissible evidence in that case implicating the lawyers. But it had always been Genge's theory that the lawyers were part of the scheme to defraud Sunrise. He had said as much in his court pleadings: He had told Hoeveler that he believed "the attorneys went along with it; that the attorneys were co-conspirators."

The seeming contradiction was just the sort of issue that Nathan emphasized with Hoeveler. The judge, of course, was the other part of the equation. He was known to be generally receptive to the government's views in criminal cases. But every prosecutor in South Florida knew that Hoeveler paid attention to basic fairness. He was no pro-government patsy.

Another judge might have sloughed off the fact that Genge had seemed to have withheld grand jury testimony of Jacoby and Powell that was arguably exculpatory. Hoeveler took it seriously, however. Genge had chosen the narrowest possible view of his obligation under the Brady rule, and his response to criticism had not helped. He had said, in effect, that while the statements might be exculpatory, he didn't believe the testimony was credible so he had decided not to turn it over. That wasn't a prosecutor's prerogative, Chaykin knew, and so did Hoeveler.

During the Kastigar hearing the critical issue was Genge's decision to revoke Treadwell's immunity from prosecution. More than any other event it raised questions about the prosecutor's good faith. For Chaykin, the grimmest point in the proceedings came when Genge was called to the witness stand and asked to testify about his decision to tear up Treadwell's cooperation agreement. No longer was Genge a lawyer appearing in court on behalf of the United States of America. Now he was just another witness in a criminal case whose testimony was being picked apart for inconsistencies. Nathan's cross-examination was brutal.

Rescinding a promise of immunity is always a sensitive issue. A cooperation agreement is a valid contract. The witness waives his Fifth Amendment right against self-incrimination and agrees to answer the government's questions; the prosecutors agree not to charge him with any crimes based on his admissions. Revoking such a promise of immunity after interrogating the witness is an extreme measure. To make matters worse, Chaykin could see there was no way to separate the evidence that Treadwell had volunteered from the evidence the government had obtained on its own. He decided to admit this to the court and make it clear that if the immunity agreement was reinstated the government would drop the case.

Genge's decision to withdraw Treadwell's immunity had not been unreasonable, Chaykin believed. In his time, Chaykin had had to get tough with a few cooperating witnesses. Sometimes they forgot that the point of the exercise was to tell the truth about their own actions. The agents working on the Sunrise case believed that they had caught Treadwell in at least one lie. Moreover, they said that Treadwell had told them little or nothing about his own culpability in the August 30 transaction or the Seawalk purchase. Genge was emphatic on this point. "There is no doubt in my mind that Mr. Treadwell knew these were structured sham transactions and he should have told us about those and assisted us," Genge would testify.

For Chaykin, the problem was that the whole episode was so poorly documented. The interview notes and FBI reports of the interviews were inconsistent and unclear. In fact, in some places the raw notes of FBI agent Tony Yanketis could be read as support for Treadwell's version of events. It was hard to establish how carefully Treadwell had been questioned, which meant it was not easy to prove he had held back information.

Nevertheless, at the end of the seventeen-day hearing, Hoeveler, despite his reservations, ruled for the government. The immunity could be revoked; the case could go forward. Chaykin thought the outcome was reasonable. The more he had learned about the Sunrise investigation, the more he was convinced that the prosecution of Treadwell was worth pursuing. Was it a hard case to prove? Sure. The events were old and confusing; the evidence was circumstantial and contradictory; some of the government witnesses had credibility problems.

But for all these obstacles, Chaykin thought Genge had it about right. The evidence he saw suggested that Sunrise was a creation of Blank, Rome, a captive client. Genge had obtained an internal memo in which one of the lawyers described their role as a "benevolent dictatorship." To Chaykin's practiced eye, the loans cited in the indictment had all the earmarks of fraudulent transactions that were meant to deceive state bank regulators and keep Sunrise afloat.

Treadwell's role was suspicious, Chaykin believed. An expert in loan "work outs," Treadwell sat in on loan committee meetings at Sunrise and knew the savings and loan was operating on the edge. Moreover, by Treadwell's own admission, he had raised questions about the August 30 loans and gotten into a shouting match with a bank official. Before the fraudulent loans were rushed through, one witness said, Treadwell had asked for a list of delinquent loans on the largest borrower and what it would take to bring the loans current.

To Chaykin, the purchase of the Seawalk property by Sunrise had stunk to high heaven. Nine months before the deal, a big Sunrise debtor had purchased it for $8.5 million. When he fell behind on his payments, Sunrise executives came up with the plan to buy it back for $13.5 million, a 59 percent increase in value in less than a year. The transaction was done in forty-eight hours without the benefit of an appraisal. Most of the proceeds were applied to the delinquent loans balance. Treadwell may not have negotiated the price, Chaykin thought, but he had to have known there was no legal reason for doing the deal. Sunrise was just a few weeks away from being able to foreclose on Seawalk and acquire it for nothing.

The Treadwell case was not a slam dunk. At times it looked like a quagmire. But Chaykin had never thought it was a federal prosecutor's job to take only the easy cases. The Sunrise case was just the sort of murky and complex financial fraud that the federal government had the resources to unravel. In Chaykin's judgment, there was sufficient evidence for a jury to find Treadwell guilty beyond a reasonable doubt of being part of the conspiracy to defraud Sunrise. That was the standard a prosecutor was supposed to follow.

Nathan made a lot of the fact that the Criminal Division had twice turned down Genge's proposal to indict Treadwell. He had characterized this as an example of more perceptive senior officials reining in an overzealous prosecutor.

But Chaykin thought that history could be read another way. It could stand for the proposition that Main Justice had proceeded with great caution on a complex case after giving the defense attorneys ample time to make their arguments.

Genge was a hard-nosed litigator, Chaykin thought, but so what? He was a federal prosecutor who was duty-bound to pursue justice. Sometimes that meant putting nice guys like Kenneth Treadwell in jail.

CHAPTER NINETEEN

TURNING
THE TABLES

The trial of Kenneth Treadwell lasted three months. Every day that his wife, Cynthia, could get off from work she drove to the federal courthouse in downtown Miami. Often she was joined by members of the family's church. Cynthia Treadwell thought of herself as a religious person. Sitting in the courtroom, she would struggle with the anger she felt toward the man who was prosecuting her spouse.

To Cynthia Treadwell, Lothar Genge's pursuit of the Sunrise case had stolen eight years of life's joy from her family. Her marriage and their family life bore the scars of a prosecution that she believed was unprincipled and unfair. The Treadwells' nine-year-old daughter, Kimberly, had hardly known a day when her father was not in trouble with the federal government. The Treadwells' two boys, Andrew, fourteen, and Raymond, twelve, knew the Sunrise investigation as a constant in the family's life, the rude houseguest who never moved on.

At the beginning of the investigation very few people knew that Treadwell had been granted immunity from prosecution in exchange for cooperating with the government. But word had

gotten around. During the worst period there had been threatening phone calls late at night. When she answered the phone Cynthia Treadwell was warned that evil things would happen to her
children if her husband remained a snitch.

The threats were one thing, money was another. Legal fees had
devoured the Treadwells' savings, along with the equity in their
home and their life insurance policies. Relatives had chipped in
with tens of thousands of dollars in loans. The Blank, Rome law
firm had contributed to the defense, too, but it would be years before the Treadwells could pay Irv Nathan what he was owed for his
time. To help defray the family's living expenses, Cynthia Treadwell had gone back to work as a nurse.

Before the trial Nathan had told the Treadwells he wanted to
raise the issue of undue prosecutorial delay. Nathan had asked
Cynthia Treadwell to write an affidavit in her own words about
the impact of the Sunrise investigation on her family. He wanted
to show Judge Hoeveler that this case involved real people who
were feeling real pain.

Cynthia Treadwell had sat down at her kitchen table and ordered her thoughts, then began writing. "Describing what it has
been like to live under the threat of government prosecution for
the last eight years," she began, "is difficult at best because it has
become such a way of life. It is hard to imagine what it would be
like to live with the freedom to do as you wish and plan for the future without waiting for the next blow to come." For years, she
continued, she had walled off her emotions. She loved and trusted
her husband, but they were only human. Their relationship had
suffered. Ken's problem with the government was always bigger
than anything else in their lives, Cynthia said. That meant she
had to take care of the daily stuff of life. There were times when
she felt like a single parent.

The impact on Kenneth Treadwell was painful for his wife. "He
was such an idealist when we got married," Cynthia Treadwell
wrote. "Ken's honesty and integrity were part of his charm. He was
one of the 'good guys' that everyone wanted to be around. Some
of his college fraternity brothers are still among his best friends.

I've watched this young lawyer (because that is what he was when all this started) be beaten down by the system."

The defense lawyers had always said that her husband's agony would end the moment he provided the testimony the government wanted to hear. If Treadwell would implicate the partners at Blank, Rome in the fraud that had been perpetrated at Sunrise Savings and Loan, they said, the case would go away and with it the pain that the Treadwell family had had to bear. Concluding her affidavit for Judge Hoeveler, Cynthia Treadwell stressed that she nonetheless took a bitter pride in knowing that her husband had refused to lie.

Still, the price was steep. "I am haunted," Cynthia Treadwell wrote, "by the thought that this long ordeal will somehow continue to the next century and Ken's innocence will be established once and for all after all three of our children—including Kimberly, who was in diapers when her father was first threatened with indictment—have left home for college with no memory of having lived in a house free of threats, press leaks, innuendo and prosecutorial harassment. Has the situation finally beaten me down? I hope not. But the agonizing torment of the last eight years has been almost more than I could bear and more than anyone should have to bear in a just society."

The trial pitted a determined prosecutor against a combative defense attorney. The eighteen criminal charges against Kenneth Treadwell were all linked in one way or another to two transactions—a series of loans on August 30, 1984, and the purchase by Sunrise of the property known as Seawalk.

Among other things, Genge had to overcome his closing argument in the 1989 trial of the Sunrise executives. Then he had said the lawyers were not involved in setting the price on the Seawalk transaction. Irv Nathan made the prosecutor's job as difficult as possible. During a pretrial hearing, for example, Nathan had questioned Genge about the immunity agreement, wringing from the prosecutor the statement that he thought Treadwell had withheld information about his involvement in the Seawalk transaction.

"And is that what you are claiming as part of the breach of the immunity agreement because he didn't tell you that he played an integral part in fixing the price at Seawalk?" Nathan asked. "Yes or no?"

"He did not," Genge said.

"Is that what you claim as the breach?"

"Yes, sir."

For the moment Hoeveler had accepted Genge's rationale for taking away Treadwell's immunity. That's why the judge had allowed the case to proceed to trial. Now that it was time for Genge to prove his claim, however, the prosecutor was having trouble. When his star witness, Robert Jacoby, took the stand, he was not even prepared to admit that he had known the Seawalk purchase was fraudulent, never mind what the lawyers knew about it. At the end of Jacoby's initial testimony, Hoeveler mentioned that he had not heard Jacoby implicate Treadwell in his testimony.

Several days later Jacoby returned to the witness stand. This time his testimony was more precise—and more incriminating. Treadwell, Jacoby said, "was involved in the transactions, yes, some of them. . . . He was involved to some extent in the August 30th [loans]. To a greater extent in Seawalk." That testimony was the linchpin of Genge's case against Treadwell.

After the government rested its case Nathan again asked for a dismissal, hammering away at the tenuous nature of Jacoby's testimony. Hoeveler dismissed five of the criminal counts relating to the August 30 loans, citing lack of evidence. That left thirteen counts, including those that related to the Seawalk purchase. Hoeveler again allowed the case to proceed, but cautioned Genge about the dearth of evidence linking Treadwell to the Seawalk purchase. "I have some deep reservations about whether or not there is sufficient evidence to go to the jury on Seawalk," the judge said. ". . . I suspect that depending on the jury result, I will be taking some further action on these cases."

During his closing argument Genge sought to erase any impression of weakness in the case against Treadwell. He stressed the importance of Jacoby's testimony. The government's case was strong, the prosecutor told the jury. It was true that during the earlier trial of the two Sunrise executives he had said the lawyers were not involved, but now he had more evidence. If he had erred during the trial in 1989, Genge concluded, that was no reason to disregard the new evidence in 1995. "That is what this case is all about, the defense is all about," Genge argued. "And I respectfully submit that Mr. Nathan's strategy is obvious. Attack the prosecutors, the regulators. And hopefully one or more jurors will agree with you."

On January 18, 1995, the jury returned to Judge Hoeveler's courtroom with a verdict. It had heard from forty witnesses and been bombarded with confusing testimony about complex transactions. The jury rejected all the evidence on the August 30 loans and most of the evidence on the Seawalk purchase, acquitting Treadwell on eleven counts. They found Treadwell guilty on two counts, a conspiracy charge and a single count involving the Seawalk purchase. Cynthia Treadwell was now married to a convicted felon.

After the trial Nathan filed motions to set aside the verdicts, based on lack of evidence. He also asked Hoeveler to reinstate the immunity agreement. To justify revoking the cooperation agreement, Genge had claimed that Treadwell held back information on his involvement in setting the price on the Seawalk purchase. Nathan argued that it was now apparent that the prosecutor could not prove that Treadwell had any involvement in setting the price on Seawalk. How could Treadwell have held back information that he did not possess?

On May 18, 1995, Hoeveler held a hearing on Nathan's posttrial motions to set aside the guilty verdicts. It was four years since David Margolis had refused to authorize the second proposed indictment of Treadwell; it was two years since Jack Keeney had deferred to the U.S. attorney in Miami and thus allowed the third proposed indictment of Treadwell to go forward.

Genge fought hard to save the conviction. He had lived with the case nearly as long as Kenneth Treadwell. The prosecutor had persevered in what he considered a righteous cause. The jury's decision was his vindication. "There were twelve jurors," Genge told

Hoeveler. "They listened to all of the evidence over a three-month period, and Mr. Nathan was not able to pull the wool over their eyes. . . . They saw through it."

Disturbing a jury's verdict went against all of Hoeveler's instincts. There would be no verdict, however, if he had not allowed Treadwell's immunity to be revoked. The judge had made that ruling based on Genge's assurance that he could prove that Treadwell had known about the Seawalk transaction. But as far as Hoeveler could see, Genge had not produced credible evidence of that claim. To his mind, he had allowed a weak case to go to the jury despite his own strong reservations about the evidence.

Not in eighteen years as a federal judge had Hoeveler ever overturned a guilty verdict. He was loath to do so in this case, but he was sorely troubled by the turn of events. He intended to give the matter a lot of thought.

While the judge was considering his options, a new development that involved another allegation of prosecutorial misconduct impinged on the case. After so many complaints against Genge it hardly seemed possible that another could take shape. Yet it had, and it was the most serious of all.

Long after Robert Jacoby had finished providing the testimony that had implicated Treadwell, he had had drinks in a pool hall with some of his former Sunrise colleagues. They had told war stories about the federal investigation and joked about enduring the "wrath of Genge." Jacoby related a tale that none of the others could top. After his initial testimony, in which he had failed to admit his frauds and implicate Treadwell, Jacoby said, he and Genge had had a conversation in a hotel lobby during which the prosecutor threatened to have him taken back to jail if he failed to "come through" with more damaging testimony during another appearance on the witness stand.

This story was too good to stay inside a pool room. It had legs. When it got back to Irv Nathan, his law firm, Arnold & Porter, filed a complaint against Genge with the Justice Department's Office of Professional Responsibility. On receiving it, Michael Shaheen referred the matter to the Public Integrity Section of the Criminal Division. Shaheen's decision was based on his judgment that threatening a witness in the middle of a trial might well constitute the crime of obstructing justice.

Eventually, lawyers in the Public Integrity Section wrote a letter that they were "declining" to prosecute Genge for obstruction of justice. While claiming to have conducted an investigation, they had not interviewed Robert Jacoby, the witness who was allegedly threatened.

If the Criminal Division thought such a response would satisfy Judge Hoeveler it was badly mistaken. He had tolerated quite a lot in the Treadwell case that might have provoked another judge. There had been what Hoeveler considered a serious violation of the Brady rule, for example, when Genge withheld the grand jury statements of the witnesses Jacoby and Powell. In the judge's view, Genge had made numerous improper statements to the jury. Hoeveler had sustained more than two hundred objections against Genge for asking questions that were leading or argumentative. Moreover, the judge had presided at the original Sunrise trial in 1989 and thus had heard Genge argue that the lawyers were not involved in the fraud. Hoeveler had always been put off by the turnabout in Genge's logic. Most importantly, the judge had sat through a full presentation of the government's case that seemed to be naked of direct evidence against Kenneth Treadwell. Now, after all of that, there was this new allegation of prosecutorial misconduct. It hardly seemed possible, but there it was. Hoeveler decided to look into the matter.

Assistant U.S. Attorney William Keefer appeared for the government. Keefer had a special responsibility for the case: He had been the acting U.S. attorney who had signed the indictment of Kenneth Treadwell. Keefer argued that Nathan had used his "prestige and connections" at Main Justice to prompt the investigation of Genge. Moreover, he contended that the case was over. Too much time had passed since the verdict to bring up new allegations of prosecutorial misconduct.

Technically, that was true, but Hoeveler was in no mood for

technicalities. "It seems to me that when a charge is made that a witness has been coerced into giving testimony," the judge said, "it is something we ought to look into."

Jacoby was recalled to the witness stand. Under cross-examination the former Sunrise executive essentially confirmed the story he had told in the pool hall. He testified that after his initial testimony he had met with Genge in the lobby of the Sheraton Biscayne Hotel. There, he said, Genge brought up his plan to ask Jacoby again about the fraudulent loans. The prosecutor shook a finger in his face for emphasis, Jacoby said.

"Mr. Genge turns to me and says, 'Now I know you are going to come through for us or for me,'" Jacoby testified. "'I know you are going to come through on that, and if you don't come through on that, [FBI Agent Anthony Yanketis] is going to put the cuffs on you, and you are going to be out of there in forty-five seconds.'"

Jacoby said he took the warning seriously, but insisted that it had not affected his testimony. He offered the opinion that Genge may have intended the comment as a "joke."

After Jacoby stepped down Nathan argued that it was "baloney" to think of the incident as a joke. Jacoby was depending on Genge's goodwill. Nathan argued that the case had turned on Jacoby's follow-up testimony. He had come back and admitted the Seawalk transaction was fraudulent and said Treadwell was involved.

"Oh, I understand," Hoeveler said. "It was very important to the government's case that Jacoby admit that he committed a fraud."

Throughout the hearing Genge sat silently at the prosecution table. He viewed his comment to Jacoby as a harmless joke, perhaps ill-advised. Keefer did his best to remedy the damage, reminding the court that Genge was a federal prosecutor. "This is not a mob boss sitting here on trial who is intimidating witnesses," he asserted. "This is counsel for the government."

On September 12, 1995, ten years after the collapse of Sunrise Savings and Loan Association of Florida, Judge Hoeveler issued a legal opinion that was understated, scholarly and devastating. For its humility and candor, the opinion has few precedents in federal jurisprudence. In effect, a judge who was justly renowned for both his intellect and his skill admitted that he had erred and erred badly to allow the indictment and trial of Kenneth Treadwell to go forward. Based on all that he now knew, he was "impelled" to go back and correct the injustice of letting the government take away Treadwell's immunity from prosecution. He was now convinced, Hoeveler wrote, of two things: the essential honesty of Kenneth Treadwell and the "bad faith" of Lothar Genge.

It was apparent, the judge continued, that Treadwell's cooperation during the initial investigation "was complete and truthful and that he did not withhold any information from the Government." Despite ten years of investigation and three months of trial, "there was no evidence that Treadwell played a role in negotiating and setting the price of $13.5 million for Seawalk."

On the other hand, said the judge, there was "respectable evidence" that Genge decided to revoke Treadwell's immunity because Treadwell would not "implicate partners at Blank, Rome" or say that he was involved in the frauds. "The complete record," Hoeveler said, ". . . presents a disquieting picture of prosecutorial enthusiasm resulting in advantage being taken of a cooperating witness."

The judge was not unmindful that Lothar Genge had accomplished a great deal of good work on an important investigation. "The enthusiasm and aggressiveness with which the prosecution pursued this case was certainly commendable, at least in the early stages," Hoeveler said. "Unfortunately, that aggressiveness ultimately led to excesses" and made "the pure pursuit of justice . . . secondary to the Government's desire to implicate as many members of the Blank, Rome law firm as possible."

Hoeveler described various allegations of prosecutorial misconduct. Withholding the grand jury testimony of the witnesses Robert Jacoby and Charles Powell was an "inexcusable" Brady violation, the judge wrote. All along, Genge had assured the court that his new witnesses would establish that Treadwell had been involved in the Sunrise frauds and therefore support the claim that Treadwell had not been candid during his time as a cooperating witness. Yet, it turned out that the testimony from these witnesses was "marginal" at best, Hoeveler said.

Much had turned on this assurance, perhaps even the long-ago deliberations of Acting Assistant Attorney General Jack Keeney back at Main Justice. A proposed indictment that was "rejected twice before at the highest levels of the Department of Justice" was suddenly "invigorated" by the promised testimony of the new witnesses, Hoeveler said. Yet at Treadwell's trial, "their testimony was presented under circumstances which now suggest that such testimony may be suspect."

Hanging on this analysis was the fate of the jury verdicts, to which Hoeveler had given much thought. He suspected that this verdict was a "compromise" arising from the "dynamics within the jury room" instead of the evidence. There could be no conviction for conspiracy unless Treadwell was also guilty in the Seawalk transaction, however. To Hoeveler's mind, "no reasonable jury could or should have construed that Treadwell knowingly and willfully misapplied Sunrise funds as part of the Seawalk transaction."

He set aside the verdicts. Correcting his earlier ruling, Hoeveler reinstated the immunity that had been granted to Treadwell under the cooperation agreement. "The vigor and enthusiasm which powers the successful prosecution of those guilty of criminal conduct is commendable and should be encouraged," Hoeveler wrote. "We must never, however, sanction the excesses which result from unchecked enthusiasm."

Two days after Judge Hoeveler issued his ruling, OPR counsel Michael E. Shaheen, Jr. sat at his desk on the fourth floor of Main Justice and read the memorandum opinion in *U.S.* v. *Treadwell*. It was just the sort of ruling that in years past would have been filed away until all court appeals were concluded. But those days were gone. Shaheen already had two lawyers laboring over the massive court record in Miami. Reading Hoeveler's opinion only confirmed for Shaheen that this was a case that needed to be handled carefully. It was shaping up as perhaps the most significant allegation of prosecutorial misconduct on Janet Reno's watch.

In reforming the OPR process, Reno had come to terms with a

hard reality at Main Justice: for any systemic change to become permanent, it had to be embraced by the senior career officials in the Justice Department. On a matter as sensitive as professional discipline, their support was essential. The attorney general could issue new policies, but what counted was how the reforms were carried out.

Reforming any bureaucracy is no easy matter, but change came especially hard at Main Justice. Once a year the Justice Department held a national conference of chief assistant U.S. attorneys, the front-line managers in the field who supervised 95 percent of all federal prosecutions. Shaheen was a perennial speaker at the conferences, but in 1994 his appearance was anything but routine. This was the first chief assistants' conference since Janet Reno had adopted her new policies on professional discipline. To the rank-and-file prosecutors, the new rules had come as a shock. At the 1994 conference Shaheen was accompanied by David Margolis, who had been named chairman of a new professional responsibility board. On behalf of Deputy Attorney General Jamie Gorelick, Margolis reviewed the OPR findings and heard appeals for leniency from prosecutors. It was a difficult assignment but one that was important to the institution.

At the 1994 conference, Shaheen and Margolis appeared together on a panel to discuss the new OPR policies, knowing full well that they faced an audience of skeptics. Many prosecutors had difficulty with the new disclosure policy Reno had laid down; it could lead to the public release of unfavorable OPR findings about line attorneys. The very idea that newspapers might get hold of and publish adverse OPR findings was disheartening to many. During a question-and-answer session, a chief assistant stood and asked a question that was on the minds of many prosecutors: "Does the attorney general not trust us," the chief assistant, a woman, demanded, "or does she just not like us?"

"It is neither," Shaheen replied. "It is neither a question of dislike nor of distrust."

It had taken a while for Shaheen to come to terms with the new attorney general and her approach to the job. Because Philip Heymann had seemed determined to remove Shaheen from the Office of Professional Responsibility and to merge that unit's functions into the Inspector General's office, the OPR counsel had not had much access to General Reno. Once Heymann had left Main Justice, however, Shaheen found that Reno simply wanted the OPR to be more effective. If Shaheen could deliver a credible product in a more timely manner, Reno would be happy to have him as OPR counsel.

Not since Edward Levi had Shaheen seen an attorney general take professional discipline so seriously. General Reno seemed to believe to her core that prosecutors had a special role in society and that their performance therefore had to be measured against high standards. To Reno accountability was more than just a buzzword. The Clinton transition team's report had warned straight out that Americans appeared to have lost faith in their Department of Justice. Reno was determined to restore that faith. "She really honestly believes in those things," Shaheen told the chief assistant prosecutors attending the 1994 conference, "and she believes it is the perception of abuse, if not abuse itself, that has raised questions in the minds of so many in this country that Justice is not impartial."

Reno's new policies had Shaheen's full support, he told the chief assistants. As long as he and Margolis were overseeing the professional-discipline process, no prosecutor was going to suffer because he or she made an honest mistake. But deliberate misconduct was another matter. Such instances would be dealt with rigorously, and the worst cases would be aired in public. "That's the way it is," Shaheen told the prosecutors in the audience. "I have worked for a number of attorneys general. I don't have any questions about these [policies]. If I did, I wouldn't be up here."

A combination of forces had brought a sea change to the Office of Professional Responsibility. There had been the punishing criticism from respected judges, pressure from members of Congress and prodding from The Washington Post. Most important, there had been a genuine problem. The Bush administration had kept the Office of Professional Responsibility small and secretive, even as the Justice Department was experiencing a dramatic surge in allegations of prosecutorial misconduct. President Bush's two attorneys general, Richard Thornburgh and William P. Barr, had been slow to address the issue and thus had had to endure a series of humiliating court rulings that derailed important prosecutions.

On the surface, the Reno reforms could be taken as a repudiation of Shaheen's stewardship of the Office of Professional Responsibility, but President Clinton's attorney general had not rejected Shaheen. Instead, she had turned his office into a larger and more muscular presence at Main Justice. By 1995, Shaheen's staff had grown from five lawyers to fourteen. The backlog from the Bush administration had been cleared, and each month Reno received a status report on pending cases. Periodically she called Shaheen into her office for a talk. The OPR counsel was continually amazed at the level of detail Janet Reno absorbed, and at the attention she paid to serious cases. Jamie Gorelick, Reno's deputy, had the same appetite for detail.

There was abundant reason for Reno and Gorelick to pay attention. More allegations of prosecutorial misconduct were being filed each year. There had been a surge of new complaints against prosecutors in 1993, but 1994 was the real shocker. With more OPR lawyers working at a faster pace, the number of confirmed cases of prosecutorial misconduct rose 300 percent, with twenty-two lawyers receiving adverse findings and six choosing to resign. In 1995, the trend continued, with Shaheen's staff opening 196 new cases involving allegations of misconduct against Justice Department attorneys. In the old days, Shaheen's staff divided its time between investigating Justice Department lawyers and federal agents. By 1995, it was spending 98 percent of its time on attorney misconduct. Rapidly the mission of OPR was changing.

During her planning process for the 1997 fiscal year, Janet Reno queried Shaheen closely about his workload. She worried that even with his enlarged staff the sudden riptide in misconduct allegations would swamp the Office of Professional Responsibility. Shaheen needed still more staff, Reno believed. In her budget request, the attorney general asked for fourteen new OPR positions. If approved, they would double the size of the OPR staff.

By 1996 the Office of Professional Responsibility had undergone profound change. At the annual conference for chief assistant U.S. attorneys, Shaheen made his usual appearance, and this time it was a cakewalk. By now Main Justice had been living with the new OPR rules imposed by Reno for two years, and there had been several surprises. There had been no lawsuits. Indeed, several of the publicly issued reports had dealt with cases in which Shaheen's lawyers had investigated claims of misconduct and found them baseless, vindicating the prosecutors.

The involvement of David Margolis in the process had made a world of difference. When the Department of Justice decided that a prosecutor had acted unprofessionally, this was not the decision of a politically-appointed attorney general but that of a veteran Mafia prosecutor well known for defending Justice Department lawyers in public. Any suggestion that Margolis might allow a trial prosecutor to be abused was laughable.

Moreover, fears that public disclosure of OPR reports would lead to sensationalized news accounts had proved unfounded. One irony of Reno's struggle to bring greater openness to the Justice Department was the utter lack of interest of most reporters who covered the institution. "I have some good news and some bad news," Shaheen told the chief assistant U.S. attorneys in 1996. "The bad news, first, is that the attorney general's public-disclosure policy is intact and has been implemented. The good news is the media could not give less of a damn. They are just not picking up on these public releases."

Relieved chuckles rippled through the room.

Shaheen had touched upon an important lesson. No other public institution, not the press, not Congress, not even the federal judiciary, could play a sustained role in deterring prosecutorial misconduct. The press had a short attention span and ignored all but the most egregious cases. The judiciary committees on Capitol Hill were empowered to conduct oversight hearings but did not. Individual judges wrote opinions, yet they dealt only with individual cases. "There is no other department [of government]," Shaheen said, "that is viewed with comparable terror or fear, because there is no other department that by itself can put you in jail or take your life, liberty or property away from you. The [Justice] Department has the FBI and the other agencies. It has become a

Leviathan in the minds of a lot of people because it is so big and imponderable. I think it is correct to say that no outsider is capable of oversight."

This was the bottom line: if any entity was going to ensure the fairness of prosecutions in federal court, it would have to be the Office of Professional Responsibility. What was also true was that the ability of that office to deter prosecutorial misconduct rose and fell in direct proportion to the personal interest an attorney general devoted to the issue. In the aftermath of Watergate, Edward Levi had created the Office of Professional Responsibility as the eyes and ears of the attorney general. Over time it had become something more: a reliable indicator of an attorney general's commitment to ensuring fair and honest prosecutions.

CHAPTER TWENTY

A COSTLY CRUSADE

E ach administration tends to use the powers of Main Justice in new or different ways. At times the effect can be heartening. The first administration of Ronald Reagan made organized crime a priority, and the leadership of the Mafia was decimated. The Clinton administration's violent-crime initiative was an example of how a determined attorney general could turn the Department of Justice to a mission the electorate admired.

But there is a fine line between using fresh political energy to confront crime and allowing excessive zeal to define and drive a prosecution crusade. That line is usually marked by how nearly a new strategy adheres to the Bill of Rights and whether it squares with the best traditions of the Criminal Division.

For all the ballast that good lawyers and legal precedent give Main Justice, it is still vulnerable to politics. The institution's vast powers can be commandeered by political appointees with big titles who are free to ignore a Jack Keeney or David Margolis. With the backing of a president, clever lawyers can neutralize the institution's internal safeguards.

One of the best-documented instances where this allegedly occurred came during the second administration of Ronald Reagan. In this instance, an unusual legal strategy was created to destroy national distributors of sexually explicit films, magazines and books, a cause many Americans applauded. The Justice Department's anti-obscenity crusade produced an impressive number of successful and important prosecutions and left a permanent imprint on the Criminal Division. But it also brought profound embarrassment. In a case called *PHE, Inc.* v. *the United States Department of Justice*, internal Justice Department files were opened to public scrutiny. They revealed just how fragile the institution's safeguards can be when Main Justice is led by aggressive and determined political masters.

On a cool morning in November 1993, U.S. District Court Judge Joyce Hens Green donned the black robe of her office and swept into her courtroom in downtown Washington to convene a final pretrial hearing in the PHE case. PHE was the parent company of a firm called Adam and Eve, one of the nation's largest mail-order distributors of sexually explicit books, magazines and films. The company had sued the Justice Department to stop several planned obscenity indictments, claiming that the motives and the methods of the prosecutors were unconstitutional. After reviewing the company's complaint Judge Green had taken the unusual step of entering an injunction prohibiting indictments against the company or its officers until civil allegations could be resolved. PHE's lawyers had made a reasonably strong case, the judge found, that Justice Department prosecutors were acting in bad faith.

Main Justice disagreed. Both sides promised an airing of the issues in court.

For six years the Justice Department's National Obscenity Enforcement Unit had poured considerable time and money into an effort to prosecute Adam and Eve and its owner, Philip E. Harvey. PHE was the largest target in a prosecution campaign that had been blessed and extolled by President Ronald Reagan. "Your days are numbered," Reagan had warned pornography distributors in

1987. Using an unusual tactic called simultaneous multi-district prosecution, Department of Justice lawyers had put a slew of obscenity distributors out of business. Many gave up without a fight, signing plea bargains and promising to get out of the business, but not Phil Harvey. He had decided to challenge the government's tactics. Since then his lawyers had subpoenaed government files and taken reams of testimony. Viewed through the lens of the First Amendment, the picture this evidence painted was not pretty. Now, the trial was about to begin—or so the lawyers for PHE assumed.

After Judge Green opened the hearing Thomas Millet, a lawyer in the Justice Department's Civil Division, rose in court and offered a speech of concession. Without admitting that the department had done anything wrong, he threw in the towel. The Justice Department, Millet said, "has authorized me to represent that plaintiffs will not be prosecuted for any matters occurring within the last five years, starting from yesterday." Criminal charges pending against PHE in Utah had been dropped. An investigation in Kentucky would be closed forthwith, without indictment. All that remained was a pending investigation in Alabama, which would be resolved with a corporate plea to a minor charge. As it related to PHE, Millet's statement signaled a retreat from the promise made by President Reagan.

The Justice Department's anti-obscenity unit had employed a novel and aggressive legal strategy against companies that sold and distributed sexually explicit materials through the mails. Under the strategy, a single company was charged with identical violations of federal criminal law in different states simultaneously. Now, Millet told Judge Green, the strategy would be abandoned. "The Department has the existing policy on multiple prosecutions for obscenity cases under review," Millet stated, "and it is anticipated that within the near future that policy will be changed and that the policy will no longer encourage multiple prosecutions in obscenity cases." In the modern annals of the Department of Justice, the PHE case had few precedents.

The idea behind the Justice Department strategy was simple: to file so many indictments simultaneously that a company like PHE would be overwhelmed by legal fees and driven out of business before a jury had decided whether its films or magazines were legally obscene—that is, whether the material could have resulted in criminal conduct. The multi-district strategy had been rolled out by the Reagan Justice Department as the big gun in a prosecution campaign to rid the nation of sexually explicit material. The weapon was manned by a handful of political appointees—U.S. attorneys and assistant attorneys general—who met regularly at Main Justice. For all intents and purposes, they had supplanted the career lawyers in the Criminal Division who traditionally oversaw prosecutions of obscenity cases.

After Millet's announcement of retreat Judge Green demanded that the Justice Department provide assurances that it would change the way obscenity cases were prosecuted. The judge delayed permitting a settlement until that promise was conveyed. Millet agreed.

For Main Justice, the larger lesson of the PHE case had nothing to do with obscene movies or even First Amendment rights. It lay in the relative ease with which a group of political activists had been able to usurp the powers and responsibilities of the Criminal Division. Behind this crusade were Attorney General Edwin Meese III and the prosecutors he encouraged to carry out the anti-obscenity mission. It was well understood within Main Justice that obscenity prosecutions struck perilously close to the heart of the First Amendment. Meese was determined to go after distributors of pornographic materials, however, and he had the backing of a popular president.

The crusade, inspired by high ideals, was also about politics. Pretrial discovery in the PHE case had turned up numerous Justice Department memoranda, including minutes from secret planning sessions, that revealed the political motives behind the anti-obscenity prosecution campaign. In one planning session the prosecutors "stressed again that the political stakes in obscenity enforcement are high and that the credibility of the U.S. Attorney's Office is on the line."

The documents were buttressed by equally illuminating testimony. During a pretrial deposition an FBI supervisor described the prosecutors running the anti-obscenity efforts at Main Justice as "religious zealots" who declared their intention of getting soft-core magazines declared legally obscene. One of the obscenity unit's prosecutors gave sworn testimony that he was ordered to shred a legal memorandum that warned that the obscenity unit's prosecution tactics were probably unconstitutional and might result in criminal cases being dismissed by trial court judges. Even inside the obscenity unit, it appeared, some lawyers feared that the crusade was going too far.

Despite the humiliation of the retreat in the PHE case, the larger purposes of the aggressive anti-obscenity efforts were mostly achieved. Edwin Meese, for all his foibles, was a savvy administrator who understood how to get things done in Washington. When Meese arrived at Main Justice obscenity enforcement was targeted at child pornography, extremely hard-core adult material and the infiltration of the industry by organized crime. Meese changed that. First he sponsored the Attorney General's Commission on Pornography in 1986. After spending $500,000 on a series of public hearings around the nation, the panel offered recommendations that came as no surprise. It called upon the attorney general to take a leadership role on the issue and form a special prosecution unit within Main Justice to coordinate obscenity prosecutions. Following the advice of his commission, Meese created the unit, then gave its prosecutors free rein. Eventually, the anti-obscenity unit became a full-fledged section within the Criminal Division, equal in stature to the sections that prosecute narcotics traffickers and organized crime.

By the time Janet Reno became attorney general, the obscenity section in the Criminal Division was untouchable. Neither Congress nor the Clinton administration had any stomach for uprooting what Edwin Meese had planted. In fact, despite the assurances made to Judge Green during the hearing on PHE, the Justice Department's political managers were even reluctant to follow through on the commitment to forswear multi-district prosecution, preferring to put the issue on the back burner. As of December 1995, that tactic remained on the books as official Justice Department policy.

The anti-obscenity section in the Criminal Division traced its roots to the wealthy lawyer and banker Charles H. Keating Jr., who would fall into disgrace during the savings-and-loan scandals of the 1980s. Keating saw in the law a way to stop the rising tide of sexually explicit material that washed over the nation's popular culture during the late 1950s and early 1960s. Many public interest groups and religious organizations had the same impulse, but Keating's special instinct was to focus on prosecutors. In the late 1950s he set up a nonprofit Arizona foundation, Citizens for Decent Literature, then hired former state prosecutors to work on its staff. CDL encouraged prosecution of criminal obscenity cases, both in state and federal courts. The organization lobbied state lawmakers and members of Congress to toughen existing laws against obscenity. Its members also alerted law-enforcement officials to material they thought might be declared legally obscene.

In later years CDL was renamed Citizens for Decency Through Law. It evolved into a think tank on legal strategy and a support mechanism for law enforcement. This encouragement was important. Many state and federal prosecutors were uneasy with obscenity matters. The law books are full of cases that made the federal government look foolish; a classic was a federal prosecution in New York that challenged James Joyce's *Ulysses* as obscene. CDL lawyers worked to raise the comfort level of prosecutors. They wrote a prosecution manual for trying obscenity cases and provided drafts of legal briefs that could be tailored to specific cases. For local police departments, CDL helped draft search warrants.

Federal prosecutors tended to avoid cases involving adult pornographic material. By focusing on child pornography and distributors with ties to organized crime, they encountered fewer legal disputes; in such cases it was easier to show harm to society. The issue of "harm" was a sore point with many anti-obscenity advocates. Large segments of the public appeared to perceive no harm in a *Playboy* centerfold; anti-obscenity activists, on the other hand, favored the theory that sexually explicit images of all types tended to encourage sex crimes and violence.

The theory received little formal support. In 1970 the National Commission on Obscenity and Pornography published the results of a two-year study on the influence of pornographic materials on society. Charles Keating had pushed for the study and had been named as a panel member. To his great disappointment, the commission concluded that there was "no evidence to date that exposure to explicit sexual material plays a significant role in the causation of delinquent behavior among youth or adults" or that it caused "sex crime or sex delinquency." Adding insult to injury, the panel recommended abolishing all laws that restrict distribution of obscene material to consenting adults in favor of statutes that prohibit specific kinds of distribution, such as of child pornography.

Three years after the commission report, in 1973, the Supreme Court issued a landmark decision on obscenity law in a case called *Miller v. California*. The High Court proposed a test that a jury could use in determining if material was legally obscene. A film or book could be found obscene, the Court ruled, if three factors were present. The first factor was that an "average person, applying contemporary community standards, would find that the work, taken as a whole, appealed to the prurient interest" in sex. Second, that the work depicted sex "in a patently offensive way"—meaning that it exposed sexual conduct that was specifically outlawed by state statute, such as bestiality or child sex abuse. Third, that the "work, taken as a whole, lacks serious literary, artistic, political or scientific value." If a film or magazine failed on all three counts, a jury could declare it legally obscene.

By allowing for a "community standard" to be the deciding factor, the *Miller* decision made obscenity prosecutions a local matter. In effect, it recognized that there was no one national standard. Obscenity was one thing in Manhattan, another in Biloxi. It was up to local juries to draw the line. The cases were not easy to make because they invited a paralyzing intellectual analysis. What was obscene? When did sexually explicit material have artistic value? Where was the line between soft- and hard-core material?

In the history of the Department of Justice, few political interest organizations have had as much influence over criminal prosecution as Charles Keating's Citizens for Decency Through Law. The key to CDL's success was finding champions in the Department of Justice to carry its torch.

Brent D. Ward was a natural. Handsome, articulate and smart, he was named the U.S. attorney in Salt Lake City in 1985. No major distributor of sexually explicit material operated from Utah, but adult films, magazines and books came into Utah by mail. Unlike many U.S. attorneys, Ward was enthusiastic about prosecuting obscenity cases. He knew the arguments about the First Amendment and the shelter it allegedly gives to sexually explicit expression. He thought this was hogwash. "Absolute free speech is neither desirable nor required by our Constitution and laws," he told audiences. The founders, he argued, had never contemplated the mass distribution of dirty movies or smutty magazines.

Ward was the chief proponent of the prosecution strategy that targeted distributors of obscene materials with simultaneous indictments in multiple districts. "If thirty-five prosecutors comprise the strike force," Ward wrote Attorney General Meese in 1986, "theoretically, thirty-five different criminal prosecutions could be instigated simultaneously against one or more of the major pornographers."

Ward's plan was elegant and pragmatic. It took the Miller guidelines—which let local juries set community standards under the three-part test—and hitched them to the Justice Department's ability to file cases in different judicial districts. Ward proposed that federal cases be filed in Utah and other Bible Belt states against national distributors of pornographic materials. If enough federal cases were filed against national distributors, they would be driven out of business nationwide. "This strategy," Ward wrote, "would test the limits of a pornographer's endurance."

Brent Ward was just the lawyer Ed Meese needed. With the attorney general's blessing, Ward became the de facto chief executive officer of the Justice Department's anti-obscenity crusade. Commuting regularly to Washington, he soon wielded more influence over obscenity prosecutions than any lawyer in the Criminal Division. As a vehicle, Ward used something called the Attorney General's Advisory Committee of U.S. Attorneys, or AGAC as it is known at Main Justice. He was named chairman of the AGAC subcommittee on obscenity. From that post Ward seized control of obscenity prosecutions nationwide, and then used his power as the U.S. attorney in Utah to give the multi-district strategy the hard edge it needed to succeed.

Ward's efforts were not universally appreciated or admired within federal law enforcement. The FBI's point man on major obscenity cases was Supervisory Special Agent Robert Marinaro. As the obscenity crusade took shape, he met often with Ward and other U.S. attorneys on the AGAC subcommittee. In a sworn deposition, Marinaro described one such meeting, in February 1986, that made a deep impression on him. Ward and the other prosecutors wanted to "stop the flow of both soft-core and hard-core" pornography, Marinaro said. "Their thoughts were on the line of, you know, trying to keep the soft-core magazines out of 7-Elevens, or whatever. I mean, that was the thinking of the Department of Justice at the time."

According to Marinaro, one of the U.S. attorneys at the meeting had brought a collection of soft-core magazines purchased from newsstands in his district. The publishers of the magazines could be prosecuted, the prosecutor declared, and the materials declared legally obscene. The lawyers passed the publications around a large conference table and nodded their heads in agreement. "They were all in lockstep," Marinaro related, "all in agreement."

When the magazines came to the FBI supervisor, however, he was taken aback. To Marinaro's practiced eye, the publications were definitely soft core and offered no legal basis for prosecution. He knew whereof he spoke. The FBI investigated obscenity cases under a law called the Interstate Transportation of Obscene Materials, or ITOM. Under the statute, the FBI had developed its own investigative guidelines that focused on child pornography, organized crime and "hard-core" materials. Unless a film depicted sexual penetration, the FBI guidelines said, it could not be considered hard core. The soft-core adult magazines Brent Ward and the other prosecutors wanted to put out of business contained no photographs showing sexual penetration. They might be distasteful or offensive, but they were clearly permissible under a long line of Supreme Court decisions. "I had very good reasons to believe at that time, and I still do today," Marinaro said, "that . . . much of the material is protected [by the First Amendment]." When it came his turn to speak, that's what he told the U.S. attorneys. The magazines were not legally obscene, he explained, and the FBI was not going to spend time investigating soft-core products. "I made it absolutely clear," Marinaro said, "that the bureau would not entertain getting involved in any investigation of anything that wasn't real hard-core."

But the FBI would cooperate as far as it thought reasonable. Within weeks of the meeting with Ward and the prosecutors, Marinaro sent a Teletype to all FBI field offices. FBI intelligence showed there were "six to eight major adult pornography distributors" shipping obscene materials across state lines, Marinaro wrote. He urged agents to focus on these targets and to pursue material that was "clearly obscene" under the *Miller* standards. He reminded them that the FBI's guidelines require that investigations of adult material be "strictly limited" to nonsimulated sadomasochism, bestiality or coprophilia (sex involving human excrement).

The Marinaro Teletype was the first concrete signal that FBI headquarters was at odds with the U.S. attorneys leading the charge in the anti-obscenity crusade. Brent Ward was hoping the FBI would go after a much wider range of materials. "He was not pleased with the fact that I was heading the Bureau into a more restrictive type of investigation," Marinaro said. ". . . That wasn't broad enough from his perspective, and I think a lot of that had to do with his religious beliefs."

Ward went over Marinaro's head and wrote a letter to William Webster, then the FBI director, urging that the bureau become more actively involved. He reminded Webster that obscenity was one of Edwin Meese's top priorities. "Significant inroads could be made into the operations of the country's major distributors of pornography through a strategy that employs multiple prosecutors [working] simultaneously in several locations around the country." Alluding to the FBI's more restrictive standard, Ward said, the Department of Justice planned to push the envelope in conservative districts by "pursuing cases involving hard-core adult pornography, even if the material involved is not of the most base and repulsive variety. We believe that successful prosecutions can be brought in many districts based on material that is hard-core, although it may lack 'Times Square' quality."

Ward and the handful of U.S. attorneys behind him continued their pressure on the FBI. In time it had an effect. After extensive negotiations Special Agent Marinaro sent out another Teletype that broadened the FBI's investigative guidelines slightly to include some hard-core adult pornography. Otherwise, the FBI held its ground. "I got the support of my bosses . . . up the line right through to the director in terms of the direction we were going," Marinaro said. "And, notwithstanding [Ward's] letter, we were marching to our own beat in terms of how we were going to go about doing this."

Ward didn't give up. He convened a meeting of federal prosecutors in Washington. A memo about the gathering called it a "Meeting Concerning Targeting of Major National or Regional Distributors of Obscenity." The targeting sessions produced a list of six national distributors Ward considered to be the major targets of the obscenity crusade, among them PHE. Virtually all the companies on the list operated openly in what their executives claimed was legitimate business. Most had been doing so for years. The companies advertised and distributed material they asserted was protected by the First Amendment. Under previous administrations, the Justice Department had let these claims go unchallenged. In one sense the companies were the easiest of targets. Investigations consisted of federal agents ordering magazines and films from the companies' catalogues. When the materials were sent to them through the mail, the government had the makings of a case that the postal system had been used to ship obscene material.

The Ward strategy was given flesh and blood when Edwin Meese created the National Obscenity Enforcement Unit within the Criminal Division in 1987. Its first director was H. Robert Showers, a former assistant U.S. attorney who had made a reputation for himself in North Carolina as a prosecutor specializing in obscenity cases. Part of Showers's new job was to proselytize obscenity enforcement among other federal prosecutors. Soon after Showers assumed direction of the new unit he convened a training conference in Washington for federal prosecutors around the country. The meeting featured presentations by Brent Ward and Richard Lambert, a federal prosecutor who specialized in obscenity cases. They "had a collage of the kinds of material that the different companies were distributing," a participant said, "and [they] asked if any of the assistant U.S. attorneys there would be interested in participating."

Above Ward's level, the senior political leadership of the Justice Department embraced his idea of using successive multidistrict prosecutions. But they also discussed a basic obstacle to the Ward strategy: The *U.S. Attorney's Manual* specifically discouraged the use of simultaneous multi-district prosecutions in obscenity cases. The manual allowed successive indictments, but only in certain rare instances, such as where organized crime was involved. The manual cautioned prosecutors that fairness was a paramount issue in deciding to use the tactic. "The successive federal prosecution policy is intended to regulate prosecutorial discretion," the manual said, ". . . to protect persons charged with criminal conduct from the unfairness associated with multiple prosecutions based on the same transaction." The manual cautioned against "unwarranted successive prosecutions" and required that all such indictments have the "prior approval of an assistant attorney general" of the Criminal Division. This sort of language gave a Jack Keeney the authority to oversee the use of sensitive techniques and to prevent their abuse.

To get Ward's anti-obscenity prosecution strategy off to a good start, the Justice Department decided to do away with these internal safeguards and loosen the rules. Ward and Showers drafted language revising the *U.S. Attorney's Manual.* "Although multiple prosecutions are not generally favored with respect to other crimes," the new language instructs, ". . . multiple prosecutions will be encouraged where the producer or distributor is a large-scale organized entity [that] routinely commits obscenity and related crimes in numerous federal districts." The new policy shifted the power to approve multi-district prosecutions and plea bargains from the head of the Criminal Division to the new National Obscenity Enforcement Unit.

Edwin Meese made other changes. In 1987 and 1988 he exhorted U.S. attorneys to take on major distributors of pornographic materials, suggesting a way around the FBI resistance. "The Postal Inspector is the best federal agent," Meese said, "because he's more flexible."

The new obscenity unit had come up with two lists—one of national distributors of pornographic materials, the other of conservative jurisdictions where they could be prosecuted. A memo prepared by a lawyer in the obscenity unit explained that the goal was to "put major mail-order distributors out of business."

During this period the FBI was not ignoring the issue. At a meeting with U.S. attorneys, James Nelson, a senior FBI manager, unveiled a new investigative plan targeting pornography distributors. The plan had been sent to all fifty-nine FBI field offices, he said. Thirteen offices were focused on a major target in Cleveland that was considered one of the largest distributors of obscene materials in the country, a company believed to have ties to organized crime. This was the kind of case the FBI considered worthy of serious effort.

The approach was not nearly satisfactory to Brent Ward and those U.S. attorneys who supported his aggressiveness. The prosecutors grilled Nelson on the details of the FBI strategy. They didn't like his answers, but Nelson held firm. "We will look at the evidence," he said.

CHAPTER TWENTY-ONE

UNHEEDED WARNINGS

U tah was the chokepoint for defendants named in the new multiple-district obscenity prosecutions. Individuals or companies indicted in New York, Mississippi or Virginia were also charged in Utah. Thereafter, their lawyers were usually told to talk to Brent Ward, the U.S. attorney in Salt Lake City, about resolving the criminal charges. This led to negotiations of "global" plea bargains where all the cases could be resolved. Ward held a strong hand: If the national distributors signed plea bargain settlements agreeing to go out of business nationwide, they could avoid facing conservative juries in Utah. In quick succession, in 1987 and 1988, several distributors agreed to do just that.

It was a period of heady success for the Meese crusade. The community standard of Utah on obscenity was well on its way to becoming the community standard for every major city in the United States.

Then alarms began to ring. On June 8, 1988, in the final summer of Ronald Reagan's second term, the owner of a firm targeted with multi-district prosecutions, Avram Freedburg, fought back. A mail-order pornography distributor from Connecticut, Freedburg was facing grand jury investigations in Mississippi, Indiana, Delaware and, of course, Utah. He sought a temporary injunction in the U.S. District Court in the District of Columbia. Through his lawyer, Freedburg claimed that the multi-district prosecution strategy was designed to drive him out of business before there was any court finding that his material was obscene. Until that finding was made, Freedburg argued, he was protected by the First Amendment.

U.S. District Court Judge Thomas Penfield Jackson was assigned the case, and that same month, after examining the pleadings and studying the law, he issued an injunction stopping any further indictments. Jackson's written order was a stinging rebuke of the Justice Department. "Simultaneous criminal prosecutions of the same individual for the same offense in four separate federal judicial districts ... cannot possibly be consistent with due process," the judge wrote. "An accused can only be present at one trial at a time. His witnesses and his counsel are likewise limited. The prospect of simultaneous prosecutions encounters so many other absolute constitutional obstacles that it is hardly possible for defendants to contemplate such a debacle."

Jackson's ruling cast a pall over other multi-district prosecutions then pending. What it did not do was dampen the zeal of those U.S. attorneys who had thrown in their lot with Brent Ward and committed themselves to his prosecution strategy. At the very next meeting of the obscenity subpanel of the Attorney General's Advisory Committee, Ward led a discussion of Jackson's ruling and its implications. The prosecutor was unable to conceal his disdain. "It is evident from the judge's order that the injunction is without any support in facts or law," Ward said, according to minutes, "but was based upon the judge's conclusion that multiple prosecutions are simply 'unfair.' "

The advisory subcommittee voted to ask Judge Jackson to reconsider his order and to have prosecutors charge ahead with other multi-district cases. The stakes were high, some of the prosecutors said. Marvin Collins, the U.S. attorney for the North District of Texas, warned that the Reagan "administration has to be able to point to accomplishment in the obscenity area, because public expectations are high." Attorney General Meese joined the group and expressed his concerns. They had to make sure the obscenity unit became a permanent part of the Justice Department, Meese said. At the moment it was merely a "unit" sponsored by the attorney general. It would be a more lasting presence if it was upgraded to a permanent section in the Criminal Division. Meese urged the U.S. attorneys to contact anti-obscenity public interest groups and explain "the importance of their efforts in perpetuating enforcement initiatives beyond the present administration." He suggested that the Justice Department might want to make the unit's budget a separate line item so it would be harder to cut. "Members of Congress," he explained, "may not wish to be viewed as opponents of obscenity enforcement."

Following the meeting the prosecutors decided to tackle the problem of the FBI head-on. They were still annoyed by what they viewed as the bureau's overly restrictive rules on pornography investigations. As a group, members of the advisory subcommittee walked across Pennsylvania Avenue to the J. Edgar Hoover Building, where they met the new FBI director, William Sessions. During a seventy-minute meeting the prosecutors presented him with a bill of particulars. The FBI was too reactive, the prosecutors complained. It was not doing the kind of long-term investigations that were needed in the area of pornography enforcement. FBI agents who liked working on obscenity cases got no support; the great bulk of such cases were staffed by rookies or agents near retirement. The FBI needed to get serious, the prosecutors said. It would help if FBI field offices were evaluated annually on their performance on obscenity cases.

Sessions listened politely but made no commitments. He urged the prosecutors to talk with their local FBI offices.

The FBI's discomfort with the Justice Department obscenity unit had deepened with time. FBI managers were particularly uncomfortable with what they perceived as the excessive zeal of Brent Ward and Robert Showers, the head of the unit. "My thoughts were then, and they are now, that these individuals, a number of them—and I am not castigating them, I appreciate their religious beliefs—but I think they became zealots about this area of pornography," FBI supervisor Robert Marinaro stated in testimony. "And their religious beliefs far overstepped good judgment in terms of how they should go about looking at this material."

A second alarm bell rang soon after the meeting of the advisory subcommittee. In Buffalo, New York, Assistant U.S. Attorney Martin J. Littlefield was prosecuting a small pornography distributor who had learned that he faced similar criminal charges in Utah and Arkansas. Littlefield was worried, he told his supervisors, by "both constitutional and practical concerns" created by the multi-district approach. As it happened, the judge in the case had similar concerns.

Littlefield had reason to be concerned. Government searches of the pornography distributor's facility had established that "the bulk of materials handled by this business involved soft-core [although offensive] pornographic materials." The company did not produce or stock hard-core material. It had supplied such products on occasion, but only at the request of undercover postal inspectors who posed as buyers. Littlefield's chief concern was the very essence of the multi-district strategy. "As you are aware," Littlefield wrote in a memorandum to the obscenity unit, "the Supreme Court analysis of First Amendment–protected materials essentially prohibits government activity that would put these companies out of business.... Given the extraordinary procedural hurdles which the government must overcome in obscenity prosecutions, it is clear that the Supreme Court does not want the government to be the decision maker on what is or is not obscene."

Like Judge Jackson, prosecutor Littlefield was reacting to an issue of fairness. "Prosecuting a small company in three widely separated federal districts," he wrote, "might well cause the company to go out of business before any jury had found their materials to be obscene." Littlefield warned that his trial judge in Buffalo might order a hearing on "prosecutorial misconduct" over the related indictments. "We could find ourselves being required to produce postal inspectors and/or [Department of Justice] officials," he continued, "to explain" the prosecutions.

Littlefield sent copies of his memo to Robert Showers at the obscenity unit in Washington and to Richard Lambert, Brent Ward's top assistant for obscenity prosecutions in Utah. The Buffalo prosecutor had pinpointed the strategy's constitutional flaw. The multi-district strategy, in the eyes of Edwin Meese and his subordinates, was doing its job. The mission, as FBI supervisor Robert Marinaro put it, was to "test the pocketbooks of the pornographer and . . . try and put them out of business." It might be unfair or unconstitutional, but it was working and nobody at Main Justice was inclined to stop the juggernaut.

The warnings of Judge Jackson and prosecutor Littlefield had no apparent effect on Brent Ward, Robert Showers and the prosecutors on the advisory subcommittee on Justice Department obscenity prosecutions. Indeed, in accordance with the wishes expressed by Attorney General Meese, Edward S. G. Dennis, the new assistant attorney general in the Criminal Division, announced his intention to raise the obscenity unit to the status of a permanent section. Any future administration that tried to eliminate an entire section of the Criminal Division would face a political firestorm.

The third alarm bell, after those sounded by Judge Jackson and prosecutor Littlefield, was the loudest of all. Oddly enough, it came from a former staffer of Charles Keating's Citizens for Decency through Law. Within a year of graduating from law school, Paul McCommon III had become a lawyer at CDL, where he often urged prosecutions of sexually explicit material. Robert Showers had hired McCommon as a lawyer with the obscenity enforcement unit. Like Marinaro, the FBI supervisor, McCommon had sat through Showers's exhortations about the potential of the multi-district strategy to put national distributors of pornographic materials out of business. McCommon didn't agree with Judge Jackson's legal analysis in the Freedburg case. But he took it as a signal that the federal judiciary was restive about multi-district prosecutions that touched upon First Amendment rights and would scrutinize them carefully for any evidence of improper motive. It seemed to McCommon that the intentions of the prosecutors would be a critical issue.

McCommon had good cause to be worried. In the late summer

of 1988 a new group of multi-district prosecutions, collectively code-named Project Postporn, were ready for indictment. Showers asked McCommon to draft a letter for the U.S. attorneys involved, telling them they could proceed with their indictments. This assignment brought McCommon's anxieties to the surface. For months McCommon had expressed reservations privately about Showers. Now, suddenly, they loomed large. The director of the obscenity enforcement unit was so outspoken about his intentions that McCommon was afraid his words could be used as proof of improper motive.

In September 1988, McCommon, a believer in the the cause of combating obscenity, put his concerns on the record in a memorandum to Showers titled "Project Postporn and the Danger of Multiple District Prosecutions Coordinated from Washington, D.C." "Over the past year, I have become increasingly concerned about 'Project Postporn' and the practice of 'simultaneous multiple-district prosecutions' generally," McCommon wrote, "but particularly where such a project is controlled according to [Justice Department] guidelines from Washington. On several occasions, I have advised you of my concerns, but I don't feel you have taken my warnings seriously."

McCommon's concerns arose out of his training as a lawyer. The Freedburg decision by Judge Jackson had underscored the problems with the obscenity unit's multi-district strategy, McCommon wrote Showers. It was one thing for a U.S. attorney in Utah or Kansas to receive a complaint about a distributor and conduct an investigation. It was another entirely to orchestrate from Washington a series of seemingly independent prosecutions with the express purpose of overwhelming a defendant's ability to fight the charges in court. This was the essence of Brent Ward's strategy—and its basic flaw.

McCommon's immediate concern was the fate of the Postporn cases. "In my judgment," he wrote, "these U.S. attorneys are being given the 'green light' to proceed without sufficient guidance from you as to the inherent risks involved in these cases." Part of the problem, McCommon believed, was Showers's exuberance and his inclination to proselytize. "Much of what I state herein relates to your conduct during the previous eighteen months. The reason for this is that it will always be your conduct which will form the factual basis of a lawsuit, motion to transfer, or motion to dismiss."

That, McCommon saw, was the real consequence of the changes that had been written into the U.S. *Attorney's Manual* at the behest of Attorney General Meese. The revised manual required that all indictments of suspected pornographers be "approved" by the National Obscenity Enforcement Unit. The new rules also gave Showers authority to approve plea bargains between the Department of Justice and distributors of pornography. This gave Showers enormous control over the process and made his motives a relevant issue. It did not help, McCommon stated, that Showers spoke often and publicly about his desire to overwhelm the few law firms that specialized in the First Amendment issues raised by so many obscenity cases. "Since at least March 1987, you have given speeches heard by many AUSAs [assistant U.S. attorneys] and others, where you have stated your purpose for multiple-district cases, which is to keep the defense attorneys busy and running around the country. You have also used the 'bat and ball' analogy—that we want them playing in our ballparks with our bat and ball. I think a judge could easily find improper motivation based on your degree of control."

McCommon was right. Showers's control over prosecutions was significant—much the same as the kind of control Paul Coffey, the chief of the Criminal Division's Organized Crime and Racketeering Section, exercised over Mafia prosecutions. The difference was that the FBI came to Coffey with cases based on evidence it had gathered in the field. "The problem here," McCommon wrote, "is not multiple-district prosecution. . . . The issue here is the appearance of an improper prosecutorial motive and the effect such appearance will have on federal judges."

The McCommon memorandum was an insider's candid assessment of the legal issues that Judge Jackson and other lawyers had already identified as problems. But it was also a challenge to a boss. McCommon sent the memo to Showers and gave a copy to another supervisor in the unit.

Reaction was swift. Showers summoned McCommon to his office. As it happened, Brent Ward was also present. Showers was furious. "He said he had the memorandum in his hand, and he said words to the effect that I shouldn't have drafted this memorandum," McCommon testified afterward. "[He said] that if this memorandum ever got out, it could cause tremendous problems for the cases, not to mention problems for him personally. He handed me the memorandum and said: 'Here is the original. I want you to gather up the copies . . . and I want you to shred it.' " McCommon left the office, chastened.

Word soon spread about his confrontation with Showers. The next day the young lawyer was summoned to a meeting on the second floor at Main Justice. Present were Deputy Assistant Attorney General Jack Keeney; Edward Dennis, the assistant attorney general of the Criminal Division; and Ronald Noble, an assistant to Dennis who would later go on to become the top law-enforcement official at the Department of the Treasury during the Clinton administration. The three lawyers questioned McCommon closely about his memo and about the confrontation the day before with Showers.

The next day Showers was put on administrative leave. The order to McCommon to shred his memorandum raised questions about Showers's judgment. More important than the order to shred the memorandum was the light the incident shed on the new obscenity section of the Criminal Division. Showers's reaction to McCommon's memo exposed the concern within Main Justice that the obscenity section was treading on dangerous ground.

Robert Showers's decision to order the shredding of a Justice Department memorandum was more than many of the career lawyers at Main Justice could abide. After Edwin Meese and his cohort of conservative lawyers took up offices in the big building at Tenth and Constitution, they had set in place a number of new policies and priorities. That was as it should be, Jack Keeney, the deputy assistant attorney general of the Criminal Division, believed. Changes in political administrations—and Keeney had been on hand for every one since the administration of Dwight Eisenhower—should result in changed policies. That was what the American political process was all about. It was not all bad. The arrival of a new group of political appointees, freshly empowered with a mandate from the electorate, could have the effect of new batteries slipped into a fading flashlight. The light from Main Justice suddenly burned with greater brightness and intensity.

The tactics of the obscenity unit Meese created were something else again. Despite the popular perception Meese, in many ways, was a fine attorney general. A veteran prosecutor, he knew criminal law and law enforcement. He did much to extend the reach of the Justice Department overseas, enabling prosecutors to pursue Mafia dons and foreign drug barons. On the other side of the ledger, however, was Meese's aggressive political agenda. When it came to obscenity cases, Keeney had watched Meese and his conservative colleagues graft a freestanding prosecution group onto the Criminal Division, and then give it considerable autonomy. Politics and its appeal to the religious right seemed to be a large part of the obscenity unit's reason for existence.

The unit was no ordinary prosecution group. Meese had signed a policy statement allowing lawyers there to approve their own indictments and negotiate plea bargains. It was sometimes hard to tell the difference between the obscenity unit and a lobbying operation. The lawyers there spent a lot of time cultivating support from anti-obscenity groups. They held conferences. They even wrote legislation. Ordering a lawyer to shred a legal memorandum was another matter, however.

Showers was relieved of his supervisory duties, but the matter could not be left there. The Office of Professional Responsibility was asked to look into the incident. Michael Shaheen's lawyers wasted no time. They questioned McCommon, Showers and others. They looked at the McCommon memorandum that Showers had ordered shredded. After a lengthy review Shaheen's lawyers concluded that there had been no professional misconduct. That did not mollify Jack Keeney and Edward Dennis, the political appointee in charge of the Criminal Division, however. Showers was not going back to the obscenity section, they decided.

After returning from leave Showers served for a brief period in the Criminal Division before leaving to join the National Law Center for the Protection of Families and Children, an anti-obscenity lobbying group in Virginia. There had never been any doubt about Showers's motivation. He hated pornography, and he had been urged by the attorney general to use every available tool to destroy the industry.

The resolution of the McCommon-Showers dispute was the sort of pragmatic solution that Michael Shaheen deemed reasonable. In reviewing the matter it was not altogether clear why a deputy like McCommon would confront his supervisor in so blunt a fashion. There was the possibility that McCommon was playing office politics. It was true that the memo might arguably be subject to discovery in pending litigation. Ordering the memo shredded could be taken by critics as an effort to destroy evidence. But that was speculative and the OPR disagreed with that analysis. Dennis and Keeney had decided to remove Showers from his post. His subsequent departure ended the OPR's jurisdiction.

The episode revealed the limits of Shaheen's role when it came to large questions of policy and the fairness of department practices. As an internal-affairs operation, the primary mission of the Office of Professional Responsibility is to conduct inquiries on behalf of the attorney general. Shaheen and his staff could investigate allegations of impropriety, such as the shredding of a document. But the OPR had no mandate to look into, or challenge, broader issues of policy that had been resolved by the Attorney General's Advisory Committee and the department's senior political leadership. McCommon's memo had squarely framed the questions about the fairness and constitutionality of the multidistrict prosecution strategy. Shaheen was not normally asked to consider the fairness of prosecution policies, however, and did not do so in this case. That was not his role.

Much the same could be said for Jack Keeney or the career deputies who sat in on Brent Ward's meetings regarding the multidistrict strategy. If the political managers insisted on pursuing policies of questionable legal fitness, there was only so much the career lawyers in the Criminal Division or the department's in-house watchdog could do.

PART
THREE

CHAPTER TWENTY-TWO

MARY'S LAW

The relationship between the Department of Justice and the nation's intelligence community saw dramatic change in the 1980s and 1990s. During Janet Reno's tenure at Main Justice the scope and pace of that change accelerated, leading to a de facto merger.

The relationship has never been an easy one. Traditionally, the Department of Justice has served as both watchdog over and partner to the nation's intelligence agencies. Main Justice lawyers maintain legal oversight of intelligence-oriented cases that arise in the prosecution of espionage crimes, such as those involving confessed spy Aldrich Ames. Main Justice also oversees investigations of terrorism cases, particularly of people residing in the United States who are suspected of affiliation with hostile foreign governments or terrorist groups. The signal case involved the bombing of the World Trade Center in New York. But there were many others, cases that never resulted in criminal prosecutions—cases that most Americans knew nothing about.

The intelligence issues that arose in the few years before Janet Reno's arrival at Main Justice, and especially during her tenure there, forced her and her top aides to rethink the relationship and to reorder it in ways that many Americans might find surprising, if not shocking. Main Justice would begin to work more closely than ever with the nation's spy establishment, even as Justice Department lawyers supervised a dramatic increase in domestic intelligence gathering by the FBI.

In the modern age of intelligence gathering and federal law enforcement, no one was more important to the management of the most critical legal issues binding the two communities than a Justice Department lawyer named Mary Lawton. Eccentric and incorruptible, Lawton was possessed of one of the most brilliant legal minds of her generation, and she used her intellect to construct the legal framework in which the nation's spies and spy chasers were required to operate. She functioned in near-total secrecy, in a field dominated by men, her work known only within the cloistered world of the nation's intelligence agencies and the marble corridors of the Department of Justice. Lawton's counsel counted most among the investigators who chased spies and terrorists and among the senior managers of the nation's foreign intelligence-gathering agencies, the spymasters who fought and won the Cold War.

On a brisk day in October 1993, two years after the Cold War ended with the collapse of the Soviet Union, Mary Lawton answered the door of her home on a quiet street in Bethesda, Maryland. A diminutive woman of fifty-eight, she had short dark hair and round spectacles that framed equally dark, penetrating eyes. Lawton was moving slowly. Just home from the hospital, she was recovering from back surgery.

At the front door Lawton was handed a bouquet of flowers, accompanied by a get-well card. It had been sent by a powerful official at the Department of Justice, a man who had known Lawton for more than thirty years and who loved her in the unabashed way that old colleagues often do. Lawton took the flowers and closed the door. Though she had never married, it could fairly be said that Lawton was wedded to the Department of Justice. She had worked under thirteen attorneys general and met every president since Harry Truman. Though she had raised no children, she had mothered the careers of countless women and men, many of whom carried credentials from the FBI. The younger special agents called her Mrs. Lawton, but their bosses knew better than to call her anything but Mary.

Within twenty-four hours of receiving the flowers from Deputy Attorney General Philip Heymann, Mary Lawton was dead of a cerebral embolism. The stroke did what nothing else could, defeating the fierce intellect that had driven Lawton to finish first in her class at Georgetown Law Center and propelled her at a young age to the top ranks of the Department of Justice.

When death came Lawton was alone, in bed, with no one to assist her. That knowledge tormented the men and women who had worked for so many years with Lawton, who regarded her not just as a wise colleague but as a devoted friend. Lawton's solitary death had a special pain because she had never left them alone. When there was trouble on an investigation involving espionage or terrorism, Lawton was always there to provide counsel, and she always stayed until the crisis had passed.

There were a thousand such times. To her friends in the FBI one came back with special clarity. It was in the hours immediately after the bombing of the World Trade Center in New York, when America had found itself newly vulnerable. At 3 A.M. the command center inside FBI headquarters seethed with a quiet frenzy, its big video screens ablaze with data. And she was there, a small, matronly figure down in the swirl of federal agents, dressed for work in sweatpants and cowboy boots. She stayed the night on the chance the agents might need legal advice or require a court's approval to string a net of wiretaps over the suspects.

Her obituary in *The Washington Post* was short and vague, and left the impression that Mary C. Lawton was just another government bureaucrat who had made little mark on life in the nation's capital. Because she was such a private person, Lawton doubtless would have appreciated the brevity of it. In her time she had kept the most sensitive secrets of her government, inscrutable as a mandarin. "There are some times," Lawton once explained, "when it is very difficult to define things, and perhaps they are best left undefined."

After her death Lawton's friends and colleagues attended a memorial service in the Great Hall of Main Justice. Some of the most powerful men and women in Washington came that day, joined by some of the finest minds in American law who sat beside some of the most veteran members of the intelligence community. There were federal judges and legal secretaries, law professors and spies, prosecutors and members of Congress. Five former attorneys general paid their respects. During the service many of her colleagues tried to describe Lawton's impact on the Department of Justice. Lawton, they explained, was the chief architect and general contractor of the law and rules that govern the intelligence community and guide the FBI's most important investigative techniques. Lawton was the chief counsel of the Justice Department's Office of Intelligence Policy and Review, dispatching her wisdom from a tiny warren of rooms on the sixth floor of Main Justice. Hundreds of times a year, the FBI, the Central Intelligence Agency, the National Security Agency and the Defense Intelligence Agency would be at the brink of action and decide to "run it by Mary" before proceeding. All knew they would get a fast answer that would settle the vexing legal questions that invariably attended their work. "She was probably the only person in government who interfaced with all these agencies," former Attorney General Griffin Bell explained. "And it turned out she was the one they trusted most."

For all of that, however, Lawton had a larger vision of her role as a government lawyer. In high school she had won a debate about the meaning of the Constitution. To Lawton, the Constitution was a touchstone. She took seriously the two sides of its promise that the government would both protect "domestic tranquillity" and shun "unreasonable" acts against its citizens. It was true that Lawton had coached the nation's spy chasers, but she had also helped write the Freedom of Information Act, a measure that has afforded a level of access to government information unknown elsewhere in the world. "Mary's client," explained Larry

Sims, a friend and colleague, "was the people of the United States of America."

During the memorial service Attorney General Janet Reno announced that she was naming the prestigious Justice Department's Life Achievement Award after Lawton. The honor placed her high in the Justice Department pantheon. The department's Award for Distinguished Service had been named years earlier for Henry Petersen, the legendary head of the Criminal Division who had tutored the likes of Jack Keeney and David Margolis. That Lawton and Petersen were joined in this way was fitting. For a generation of Justice Department lawyers, Petersen and Lawton had been icons, the father and the mother of the professional culture that had sustained Main Justice over the past quarter century.

When his time came to speak, FBI Director Louis Freeh paid Lawton the bureau's ultimate tribute. A lawyer and former judge who was young enough to be her son, Freeh appointed Lawton a special agent of the FBI, an honor that had been bestowed just eighteen times in its history, mostly on retired presidents and attorneys general. Freeh was young but not so young that he did not know how deep an imprint Lawton had left on the FBI. He had seen for himself how his best agents adored and feared her. "She loved to chew us out," Freeh recalled, "always with a twinkle in her eye. Her favorite expression was: 'You owe me big time' and believe me, we do owe her big time."

Mary Lawton's legacy to the Department of Justice could be dated from 1960, when she first came to work there, but its true measure should be taken from 1975 until her death in 1993. Two decades ago the Watergate scandal had made it clear that a part of the FBI had chosen to operate outside the law and betray its oath to protect and defend the Constitution. At this juncture President Gerald Ford made an odd, and as it turned out, inspired choice. He appointed as attorney general Edward Levi, then dean of the University of Chicago Law School. On the day he moved into his fifth-floor office at Main Justice, Levi assumed control of an institution that had been grievously wounded by Watergate. A quiet, careful academic, he also was a determined lawyer who saw his mission clearly and did not shrink from what had to be done.

For many years afterward, Levi told a story about his initial encounter with the FBI. It was the afternoon of his first day on the job, and after a busy morning the new attorney general decided to take a quiet moment to reflect on his surroundings. "Just as I was settling into my chair and observing the handsome wood paneling of the office," Levi recounted, "an FBI agent appeared at my door without announcement. He put before me a piece of paper asking my authorization for the installation of a wiretap without court order. He waited for my approval." As a law professor Levi had instructed students about how and why the Fourth Amendment to the Constitution prohibits "unreasonable searches and seizures." The full weight of American jurisprudence requires that warrants for any searches and seizures be signed by a federal judge. As Levi studied the document that had been thrust into his hands, he was perplexed. It appeared that he was being asked to sign a warrant to install an eavesdropping device. That, he had always known, was something that only a judge can do.

Levi had no idea whether he should sign the piece of paper or show the FBI agent the door. The new attorney general demurred, telling the FBI agent he wanted to consult with other lawyers before taking any action. The agent looked surprised. He was in a hurry. Levi was polite yet firm, and the FBI agent finally went away, but not before the new attorney general realized that he had a problem on his hands.

The problem was not new, but its scope was only just becoming apparent. The Senate Select Committee on Intelligence, chaired by Frank Church, a respected Idaho Democrat, had produced a torrent of disclosures about government misconduct ranging from illegal bugging to what were euphemistically known as black-bag jobs, or burglaries by FBI agents. Day after day the newspapers carried reports of new government abuses. The overriding theme was the use that the Nixon administration had made of the FBI and other intelligence agencies to discredit its political enemies and spy on hundreds of American writers, politicians and civil rights leaders. One of the most abusive FBI programs was code-named COINTELPRO (for Counter-intelligence Program). Agents assigned to COINTELPRO carried out dirty tricks of one kind or another. And it was not just the FBI. The CIA, the Pentagon and the National Security Agency had all turned their intelligence-gathering capabilities on American citizens.

When getting to the bottom of the pit at the FBI became a priority, Main Justice turned to its most trusted criminal lawyer, Henry Petersen. As the assistant attorney general in charge of the Criminal Division, Petersen pulled no punches. One of his saddest conclusions was that the Internal Security Section of the Criminal Division had permitted the FBI to run wild. "They [the internal security prosecutors] were called upon literally only when the Bureau wanted them," Petersen concluded. That was wrong, but the Justice Department wasn't entirely to blame. For years the nation's political leadership—the Congress and a series of presidents—had encouraged the FBI's zeal and been unwilling to support Main Justice in its dealings with J. Edgar Hoover. "No president ever supported any attorney general," Petersen told the Church committee in 1975, "up until two years ago with respect to supervision of the Federal Bureau of Investigation."

The Church committee's final report stands as one of the most important public documents in the history of American intelligence. Balanced in tone but firm in its judgments, the big volumes meticulously document how the nation's intelligence agencies had ignored and violated the Constitution. The Church committee recommended a series of reforms designed to build a wall between federal law enforcement and the nation's intelligence community. "Domestic intelligence activity has threatened and undermined the constitutional rights of Americans to free speech, association and privacy," the Church panel said. "It has done so primarily because the constitutional system for checking abuse of power has not been applied."

The committee blamed excessive power and secrecy in the executive branch and a penchant for lawbreaking by the intelligence agencies. Senator Church and his colleagues called for centralizing authority over domestic intelligence-gathering activities under the attorney general. Church and his colleagues understood that counterintelligence was essential. But with the explosion of new technologies, the information collected by the nation's espionage agencies presented a potential threat to American civil liberties. The answer, they argued, was to allow intelligence gathering within the United States but to do so under the law. "Attorneys General have permitted and even encouraged the FBI to engage in domestic intelligence activities and to use a wide range of intrusive investigative techniques—such as wiretaps, microphones and informants," the Church panel concluded. "But [we] have failed, until recently, to supervise or establish limits on these activities."

Proper supervision was what the Church committee had in mind. The concern was particularly relevant when it came to the FBI. Of all the agencies that make up the American intelligence community, the FBI is unique, charged with both law-enforcement and intelligence-gathering responsibilities. Thus, its agents work as criminal investigators against the Mafia and as counterintelligence agents against foreign spies.

Toward the end of the Church committee's hearings on intelligence matters, Edward Levi was invited to testify, and he took the opportunity to recall a warning from Harlan Fiske Stone, the attorney general who had created the FBI and appointed J. Edgar Hoover its first director in 1924. "There is always the possibility that a secret police may become a menace to free government and free institutions," Stone had said. ". . . It is important that its activities be strictly limited to the performance of those functions for which it was created and that its agents themselves be not above the law or beyond its reach."

Levi was convinced that the FBI should continue to carry out its traditional counterintelligence mission of identifying and arresting spies. But he wanted a new system of rules to prevent a recurrence of past abuses. Levi's answer was to designate one of the brightest lawyers in the Office of Legal Counsel to draft guidelines for the FBI that would cover the bureau's most sensitive investigations—pursuing organized crime groups, conducting un-

dercover operations and carrying out domestic security and counterintelligence investigations.

The lawyer Levi chose for the job was Mary Lawton. It took
more than a year before she prevailed, but the essence of Lawton's
accomplishment was to free the FBI to act in aggressive new ways
under the legal umbrella of the attorney general. Lawton's was a
simple bargain. If the FBI would play by the new rules, the Justice
Department would defend it to the hilt. These rules became
known as the Levi Guidelines and they have shaped the operations of the FBI to this day. "The rules did what they were intended to do," said Jack Fuller, a special assistant to Levi who
would eventually become the top editor of the *Chicago Tribune*.
"And they were just one of the ways that Mary changed federal
justice in an enduring way."

Levi was pleased by the guidelines Lawton had drafted, but he
remained troubled by the memory of his first afternoon on the job.
The idea that an FBI agent could simply shove a piece of paper
under the nose of a new attorney general and expect him to approve an electronic surveillance operation without a court's approval was deeply troubling. Levi and his aides decided that a new
law was needed that would cover such activities. To help write the
new law, Levi again turned to Mary Lawton.

Even as she began to work on drafting the language of the new
statute, another bright young lawyer at Main Justice was thinking
about other concerns. Michael E. Shaheen Jr. would ultimately go
on to head the Office of Professional Responsibility at Main Justice, but in the mid-1970s he was assigned to review FBI files for
disclosure to the Church committee. As a result, he saw how
Main Justice had been manipulated by the FBI. "It became quite
clear to me," Shaheen said, "that . . . one of the big cracks that
various intelligence components, especially the FBI, availed
themselves of, was the ability to forum-shop within the Department for an opinion." In December 1975, Shaheen wrote a memorandum to Levi explaining the problem and proposing a
solution: "Until J. Edgar Hoover's death, no Justice Department
official was in a position to know very much about intelligence
operations." When the FBI wanted to undertake an intelligence

operation, its agents would go for approval to one of six different offices at Main Justice.

Lawton had been assigned to create a new legal framework for FBI operations, but that meant lawyers at Main Justice would have to review those operations first. How would the Justice Department carry out this new responsibility? Shaheen proposed that Levi create one office that would be the Justice Department's sole point of contact with the FBI and the intelligence community. It would be an independent staff, answerable only to the attorney general, that would enforce Lawton's new rules. "The draft FBI guidelines contemplate that the Department of Justice shall review the results of the FBI's full domestic intelligence investigations at least annually and determine if continued investigation is warranted," Shaheen wrote. "[The attorney general] needs someone who works both with the attorneys in the [Criminal] Division and with the FBI officials and agents who supervise intelligence investigations." Moreover, Shaheen continued, there ought to be a permanent staff of experts in the Justice Department who could provide "independent answers" about domestic intelligence operations.

Shaheen proposed creating an Office of Counsel for Intelligence to review all FBI requests to conduct electronic surveillance in foreign counterintelligence cases and serve as a single point of contact at Main Justice for the FBI in domestic intelligence investigations. No longer would a new attorney general have to go it alone when an FBI agent showed up seeking approval for unusual wiretapping procedures. "A vital feature" of the office Shaheen proposed "is a substantial degree of continuity from one attorney general to the next, so that a new attorney general has somewhere to turn when he arrives and must begin discharging his responsibilities." In time, Shaheen's recommendation led to the creation of the Office of Intelligence Policy and Review.

The new law that Mary Lawton drafted for conducting electronic surveillance in national security investigations was called the Foreign Intelligence Surveillance Act (FISA). Edward Levi could not get the proposed law through a Congress that was still leery and distrustful. After the 1976 presidential election, Levi's Democratic successor, Griffin Bell, took up the cause. Bell was determined to start prosecuting spies, but to do so under the law. He recruited Frederick Baron as a special assistant on intelligence issues. Baron had served on the Church committee staff, and as the two men discussed the proposed wiretapping law, Baron kept citing the work of Mary Lawton.

Eventually Bell grew impatient. "Who," he demanded in his gruff Georgia drawl, "is this Mary Lawton you keep quotin' to me? Let's get her in here."

Lawton was duly summoned, and she told Bell how the proposed FISA statute would allow the FBI and other intelligence agencies to obtain national security wiretaps as long as they did so under the guidance of Main Justice.

Bell liked the concept. To the language drafted by Lawton he added one innovation, placing the entire FISA process under judicial review by calling for a special court of sitting federal district judges who would approve FISA wiretaps the same way that judges and magistrates approved Title III wiretaps in criminal cases. The warrants would be approved in secret hearings, but they would still bear the imprimatur of the judiciary.

The proposal was not an easy sell on Capitol Hill. The memories of Watergate had only begun to dim, and much turned on whether the Congress was prepared to believe that the FISA act would be properly administered by Main Justice. Bell responded that it was time to move beyond the legacy of Richard Nixon. "In a democratic society people have to trust the Government," he told the Senate Select Committee on Intelligence. "Otherwise you go under." Justice Department attorneys would police the FISA process. "There are some honest people left," Bell testified. He promised that when lawyers went into the secret FISA court hearings, "we will go there and act as lawyers and do what good lawyers do. We will be fair with the court, candid, and we won't go unless we have reason to."

Based largely on that promise and the careful particulars Lawton had written into the FISA statute, Congress approved the FISA law in 1978. The Carter administration also embraced

Michael Shaheen's recommendation to establish the Office of Intelligence Policy and Review to administer the new domestic eavesdropping law. Finally, the three critical parts were in place, the new guidelines Lawton had written for FBI counterintelligence investigations, the law that would govern electronic surveillance during the course of such investigations and a staff of lawyers at Main Justice who would supervise compliance with both.

In January 1982, William French Smith, Ronald Reagan's first attorney general, appointed Mary Lawton counsel for intelligence policy, in charge of the Office of Intelligence Policy and Review. It surprised none of her friends that an attorney general appointed by Reagan would select a favorite of the Carter administration for such a sensitive post. Smith brought a harder-edged view to the delicate matters Lawton was now responsible for reviewing. He believed the guidelines Lawton had drafted for FBI counterintelligence inquiries several years earlier—particularly as they related to First Amendment protections—were too restrictive, an overreaction to COINTELPRO that made FBI agents too timid. Eventually, Lawton agreed with Smith. "The Bureau took that, in our judgment, too literally," Lawton later explained. "They started assuming that they could never pay attention to what people said about their intentions to commit political violence. One of the reasons for redoing the domestic intelligence guidelines was to put in language to make it absolutely clear to the Bureau that they could listen to what people said about their intentions."

When it came to the FBI, Lawton tended to be protective. Many FBI agents were Irish Catholics like Lawton. Because the agents trooped into her office in pairs she called them "nuns." She could be tough when she felt the need. On one occasion, having tired of going through a seemingly endless series of receptionists at the J. Edgar Hoover Building, she asked the FBI for a copy of its internal telephone directory. The FBI refused, saying it was a confidential document. Lawton promptly filed a Freedom of Information Act request. Soon enough, a sheepish FBI supervisor walked a copy of the directory over to Main Justice. Another time when the FBI was pursuing a suspected spy in the State Department, agents ran into resistance from a CIA station chief consumed with matters of turf. Lawton sat back in her chair, a cigarette poking from her fingers, and listened to the FBI's lament. Finally, she proposed a solution. "If you had any balls," she said, "you'd open an obstruction of justice investigation." That's exactly what the FBI did.

As the new intelligence counsel, Lawton was a creature of routine. Most mornings she was at her desk at 8:25 A.M., scanning *The Washington Post* and the overnight intelligence reports, the ones with the bright red borders and a cover sheet that said "Top Secret." Not long into the morning, she lit her first cigarette, then the secure telephone on her desk would ring. As likely as not it would be a call from the FBI for legal advice or a plea from the CIA for some fast help with a legal matter. Queries also came from the intelligence committees on Capitol Hill and the National Security Council staff. People throughout the government who had a legal question on national security matters fingered their Rolodex and looked for the name Lawton. Surrounded by a deepening haze of smoke, she worked the phone like a police reporter. On a typical day there would be several meetings—meetings at the White House, meetings with the attorney general, meetings in the secure soundproofed rooms. In one way or another, people on the phone and at the meetings eventually got around to questions about Mary's Law.

Mary's Law was many things, but mostly it was the gold standard of legality in the world of counterintelligence. She had written laws and policies that mattered, and had made most of the rulings and decisions that interpreted those provisions. As chief counsel in the Office of Intelligence Policy and Review, she was the chief enforcer of the Foreign Intelligence Surveillance Act. Only with a FISA authorization could any of the agencies—civilian, military or intelligence—install a national security wiretap. For the community of spies and counterspies, the attorney general's guidelines, Lawton's prior rulings and the FISA statute made up the bible. "The questions that reached Mary Lawton wouldn't wait," said John Harmon, former head of the Office of Legal

Counsel, who said he knew of no case in which the FBI appealed one of her rulings. "The folks that Mary dealt with needed an answer. Yes or no. Yes you can do it, no you can't. And Mary would tell them."

She was a brilliant lawyer, but she had the soul of a street cop. She had seen the wiretap intercepts. "We have a lot of enemies out there," she said. If the FBI's plans to investigate a suspected spy or terrorist were reasonable, Lawton signed off. "I don't think we can afford to pass up these cases," she explained.

Her objective was to foster "common sense" and professionalism among FBI agents, not hem them in with lots of rules. That was the surest safeguard against abuse, she believed, but agents who committed transgressions or deliberately abused their position could not look to Lawton for succor. "In 1975 they elected me their mother," she once said. "But I'm not their mother, and I can't protect them from everything."

While Mary's Law was famous among Lawton's peers, she was the first to tell people that many things were better left out of the federal statutes. An executive order prohibited the government from carrying out "assassinations" of foreign officials. On one occasion several members of Congress decided this was not enough. They thought the law should more precisely define "assassination." The members had their lawyers do what lawyers do. They drafted language defining assassination as the "killing of any officer or employee of a foreign government by reason of his performance of his official duties."

In due course, a copy of the proposed law was sent to the Justice Department and submitted for Lawton's review. Soon after she met with the drafters. "You have, of course, ruled out an Entebbe raid," she said, referring to the successful raid by Israeli commandos who freed a group of Jewish hostages from a hijacked airliner that had landed in Uganda.

The lawyers from the Hill were startled. "No, no," they said, "we haven't done that."

"Yes you have," Lawton said.

"No," said the lawyers.

"There are security guards at that airport," Lawton replied.

"They fired at the Israeli commandos. And the Israeli commandos fired back and killed one. Now he was an employee of a foreign government performing his official duties. You've defined that as assassination."

"Oh," the lawyers said. They could see her point.

"We didn't mean that," they said.

"Then don't write it," Lawton said.

Some things, as she often said, were better left undefined.

It was not possible to participate in national security affairs in Washington without getting to know Mary Lawton. She was a presence, a small, cheerful woman surrounded by dour men in dark suits. Lawton was in the room because of her brains and because so many times before she had sat in the same rooms and heard the same issues debated. She could rattle off the history of intelligence decisions taken in past administrations. "What was always remarkable was Mary's ability to recall with precision the positions each of the various government agencies took over the years," said Mark Richard, the senior career lawyer in the Criminal Division specializing in national security affairs. "She seemed to take pleasure in pointing out our inconsistencies and leaps in logic and faith in the various positions we espoused over time." The infuriating thing about Lawton was that she was almost always right. When she told her political masters that something could not be done under the law, that usually settled the matter.

Lawton knew well the first rule of American jurisprudence, that laws had meaning only to the extent they were obeyed and enforced. The FISA statute was administered in secret by a court that heard only from one government. No opposing attorneys were present to dispute her arguments or challenge her facts. But it was not as if Lawton or Allan Kornblum, her deputy for operations, could merely slap a wiretap application together and run it downstairs to the FISA court. "Each and every application is signed by the intelligence agent and by the lawyer who drafted it," Lawton explained. "But it is also certified by the head of the intelligence agency as being for intelligence purposes. What is more, it must be personally signed by the attorney general of the

United States who signs 'I swear under penalty of perjury that this meets the requirements of the statute.' "

All those signatures served a purpose, to assure the federal judge sitting in the FISA court that a national security wiretap was being sought for "intelligence purposes" and for no other reason— not to discredit political enemies of the White House, not to obtain evidence for a criminal case through the back door of a FISA counterintelligence inquiry. It was a special means by which the government could come in the front door and explain to a duly authorized court that it proposed to exercise its special authority in the interest of protecting the nation's security. Such a representation could not be made lightly. "We have to swear to it," Lawton explained.

There is no record of the FISA court ever rejecting an application to conduct an electronic surveillance, but the absence of such a record should not be construed to mean that the court had become a rubber stamp for Mary Lawton. The court employed its own legal adviser, and if that lawyer or a FISA court judge saw a problem with an application, he or she let the government know, and the application was withdrawn and amended. The FBI was often required to conduct further investigation to flesh out and provide additional information before Lawton and her staff would agree to resubmit the paperwork.

It made a difference that Mary Lawton's word was good with the court. Over the years the FISA judges had observed Lawton's performance in crisis after crisis. U.S. District Court Judge Joyce Hens Green had served a seven-year term as a FISA judge. She was endlessly impressed by Lawton. After Lawton died, Green, like so many others, remembered her encounters with the Justice Department's top lawyer on intelligence issues. Like the other members of the secret FISA court, Green was required to be available twenty-four hours a day for emergency hearings. Early one Sunday morning she received a phone call about an emergency matter the FBI was rushing to investigate. The bureau needed a FISA wiretap immediately. Lawton requested an early-morning hearing at Judge Green's home. The judge told her to come right over. Lawton arrived soon after with an FBI agent in tow. Judge

Green met them at the front door. Lawton's hair was disheveled, and her clothes had obviously been chosen in haste. She was puffing on a cigarette as she approached, then finally dropped the butt. Green watched as Lawton stubbed out the cigarette with her foot on the lawn. It was then that the judge noticed that the Justice Department's distinguished counsel for intelligence was still wearing her bedroom slippers. When Green called Lawton's attention to this fact, the veteran Justice Department lawyer looked down at her feet and laughed.

"Well, judge," she said, "like it or not, this is the real Mary Lawton."

CHAPTER TWENTY-THREE

SPYMASTERS AT LAW

In the early-morning hours of October 10, 1993, an unmarked government sedan rolled slowly down an empty, tree-lined street in a suburb just outside Washington. The FBI agents inside parked just up from a handsome two-story home. The agents knew the place well. Three months earlier an FBI team had gone inside to bug the place. That operation had been a quick in and out. This time the agents planned to stay awhile. The owners were out of town on vacation. The house was vacant.

With several hours to go before dawn, the FBI team slipped inside. Each member was a specialist. There was a document man, whose job was to go through the family's bank books and check stubs, and photograph anything of interest. It was meticulous work because every piece of paper had to be put back exactly as it had been found. There was a computer specialist, assigned to get into the family's personal computer and download its files. As soon as he was seated at the keyboard, the agent saw that the computer had a security program. It was nothing he couldn't overcome, but it would take some time.

The agents worked methodically. When there was nothing else

of interest that had not been examined and photographed, the team withdrew, checking to make sure nothing was left out of place—that was critical. The family would not learn of the search unless the FBI decided to let them know.

The Constitution requires that most searches of a person's home be pursuant to a warrant signed by a federal judge or magistrate. The Federal Rules of Criminal Procedure further require that search parties announce their presence, inform residents of a search and provide them with an inventory of all they seize. But those rules did not apply to this house and this search. There was no warrant, no announcement, no inventory.

Less than twenty-four hours earlier, Attorney General Janet Reno had signed a very unusual document. It was attached to a thick affidavit that described the evidence the FBI had gathered in a case code-named Nightmover. Mary Lawton's Office of Intelligence Policy and Review had recommended that Reno authorize the search of the home owned by Aldrich and Rosario Ames without the benefit of a warrant signed by a court. Since her earliest days as attorney general Reno had known that one of her powers was the ability to approve warrantless searches, but she disliked the idea, and she was not alone. Among her predecessors, Edward Levi in the Ford administration and Griffin Bell during the Carter years had felt likewise. Reno didn't doubt for a minute the necessity of the search. She was familiar with the case, having signed off on an earlier application for electronic surveillance of the Ames home under the authority of the Foreign Intelligence Surveillance Act.

Aldrich Ames was a suspected spy. A sallow, hawk-faced alcoholic, Ames was a CIA officer suspected of having betrayed at least ten CIA and FBI sources to the KGB, causing their executions or unexplained disappearances. A joint FBI-CIA team had documented more than $600,000 in cash Ames had deposited in his and his wife's bank accounts since 1985. Not only had the $62,000-a-year CIA man purchased a Jaguar sedan a year earlier, he and his wife had also paid cash for their $540,000 suburban Virginia home. The FBI-CIA team had also uncovered evidence of meetings Ames had had with a man posted to the Russian embassy as a nuclear weapons specialist; in fact, the muscular, jug-eared man captured by the FBI's surveillance cameras was Sergei Chuvaikhin. He was Aldrich Ames's bagman. Meeting after meeting with Chuvaikhin coincided with, or was followed shortly by, cash deposits to one or another of Rick and Rosario Ames's increasingly healthy bank accounts. The money and the meetings added a sinister gloss to one other fact: Ames was one of just a handful of U.S. intelligence officers who had knowledge of the American spy operations that had been compromised. Evaluating the matrix of factors—the knowledge of the blown spy operations, the unexplained contacts with foreign intelligence officers and the suspicious deposits of large amounts of cash—the FBI-CIA team of analysts put Rick Ames at the very top of their A list of suspects.

Citing this and other evidence, Robert "Bear" Bryant, the head of the FBI's Washington Metropolitan Field Office, had opened the investigation of Ames on May 12, 1993. On June 11, twenty-nine days later, the Nightmover squad had received approval from the secret court that passes judgment on applications for electronic surveillance under the FISA statute to place a wiretap on Ames's home telephone. The investigation was a masterpiece of patient detective work and inductive analysis. The Nightmover team had searched the trash placed outside the Ames residence for pickup and found evidence of a planned meeting with a suspected handler in Bogotá, Colombia. If the FBI's suspicions were correct, Ames was operating as an agent of a foreign power from inside the CIA's headquarters, the very heart of the nation's sprawling intelligence community.

A spy as valuable as Ames would be managed only by senior intelligence officers, and it was the job of the Nightmover squad to identify those individuals if they could and to find out how many and what kinds of classified secrets Ames had given them. If the Nightmover agents watched Ames long enough, they believed, he could lead them to his Russian handlers.

The death of Mary Lawton and the search of Aldrich Ames's home both occurred in October 1993. It was a coincidence, one that would precipitate a conflict inside Main Justice and bring about a bitter contest between two groups of career lawyers there. On one side was Mary Lawton's old domain, the Office of Intelligence Policy and Review, the unit established after Watergate to oversee domestic intelligence gathering. On the other was the Internal Security Section of the Criminal Division, a unit that had distinguished itself over the past two decades with a nearly unbroken string of successful espionage investigations and prosecutions. The battle would have consequences beyond the Ames case and would presage a historic shift in the relationship between the Department of Justice and the nation's powerful and secret intelligence agencies.

The war precipitated by the Ames inquiry had its roots in two conflicting visions of the role of Main Justice and could be traced back more than two decades to some of the darkest moments of the Watergate scandal. At the center of President Nixon's personal tragedy was his willingness to abuse the special powers and prerogatives that the Constitution grants to presidents to protect the nation's security. Because these powers are derived from law, they are often exercised through the Department of Justice. The most extreme of these powers is the president's freedom to authorize legal exemptions to the Fourth Amendment right of "the people" to be "secure" in their persons, houses, papers, and effects, against unreasonable searches and seizures. The right was guaranteed by the federal courts; under the Fourth Amendment, it could be breached in a criminal case only if a court found evidence of criminal activity and signed a warrant authorizing a search. For many decades, presidents had claimed exemptions to Fourth Amendment warrant requirements in cases involving national security, and for just as long the FBI had carried out warrantless searches and installed illegal wiretaps.

"We do not obtain authorization for 'black bag jobs' from outside the Bureau," a senior FBI official wrote in a 1966 memorandum. "Such a technique involves trespassing and is clearly illegal; therefore it would be impossible to obtain any sanction for it. Despite this, 'black bag' jobs have been used because they represent an invaluable technique in combating subversive actions of a clandestine nature aimed directly at undermining and destroying our nation."

The technique was used against the embassies of hostile governments, as well as organizations that J. Edgar Hoover deemed subversive. The practice generated little controversy until the Nixon administration. Nixon had harmed the institutions of government in many ways, but in the area of foreign counterintelligence he put at risk one of the FBI's most important tools for protecting the nation against spies and terrorists.

The Nixon administration's "plumbers" had broken into the office of a psychiatrist who was treating Daniel Ellsberg, the Defense Department official who had given *The New York Times* the lengthy classified study of the Vietnam War known as the Pentagon Papers. Eventually, the Watergate special prosecutor brought a criminal case charging Nixon aide John Ehrlichman with federal civil rights violations, and in time the case came to the question of whether a president has the inherent power to authorize covert conduct in the name of national security.

During the Ehrlichman case the Watergate prosecution team argued that the White House–ordered search of the office of Ellsberg's psychiatrist was a violation of the Fourth Amendment. The lawyers cited a 1972 Supreme Court opinion that determined that "physical entry of the home is the chief evil against which the wording of the Fourth Amendment is directed."

At that moment in 1972, Jack Keeney, even then serving as the acting head of the Criminal Division of Main Justice, had sought to contest this claim. In a letter to the High Court, Keeney signaled that the Criminal Division of Main Justice strongly disagreed with the Watergate prosecutors. The warrantless search of Ellsberg's psychiatric records was "plainly illegal," Keeney said, but only because it had not been subject to the control and direction of the attorney general. Had it been properly "controlled," he argued, it would not have been illegal because the executive branch has the "inherent authority" to exempt itself from the warrant requirements of the Fourth Amendment in instances where the nation's security is threatened.

Underlying this claim was the Criminal Division's fear that the abuses of the Nixon administration would cause the FBI to lose its ability to use secret wiretaps in counterintelligence investigations. If the government lost this tool, Keeney knew, it would have to resort to normal wiretaps and search warrants, which are ultimately made public. As Keeney explained it, in counterintelligence investigations electronic surveillance and physical searches of property were one and the same. "The [Justice] Department does not believe there is a Constitutional difference between searches conducted for wiretapping and those involving physical entries into private premises," Keeney wrote. "One form of search is no less serious than another."

Despite the Nixon abuses the Supreme Court did not end the Fourth Amendment warrant-requirement exemptions in national security investigations, and in the ensuing years lower courts came to establish something approaching a set of rules on the matter. In 1978 the Fourth Circuit Court of Appeals ruled that warrantless electronic surveillance had to be for the "primary purpose" of collecting foreign intelligence, otherwise the evidence would be suppressed. If the purpose shifted so that the focus of the surveillance was to gather evidence for a criminal prosecution, the court ruled, then the government had to obtain a warrant signed by a judge under the Title III criminal statute.

Because spies also commit crimes—espionage is, after all, a crime—this was a hard line to draw. Between May 1977 and January 1978, for instance, FBI agents conducted what an appeals court later called a "massive [electronic] surveillance" of an agent of the government of Vietnam named David Truong, who was obtaining classified documents from the United States and shipping them to the Vietnamese during the 1977 Paris peace negotiations between Washington and Hanoi. Truong had obtained the documents from Ronald Humphrey, an employee of the U.S. Information Agency. Without a court-authorized warrant, the FBI searched the contents of a package Truong used to conceal the classified American documents. Both the electronic and physical searches were approved by President Jimmy Carter and his attorney general, Griffin Bell. After their conviction at trial, Truong and Humphrey appealed, contending that some of the evidence obtained against them from the physical search and the electronic surveillance had been gathered illegally.

The Fourth Circuit Court of Appeals heard the matter and decided that FBI investigators "could proceed without a warrant only so long as the investigation was *primarily* a foreign intelligence investigation." At a certain point, the court found, "the FBI investigation [of Truong and Humphrey] had become primarily a criminal investigation," and the evidence gathered through the electronic surveillance beyond that point could not be used against the two men. Both the trial judge and the appeals court agreed to suppress some of the evidence because FBI counterintelligence agents had met with lawyers of the Internal Security Section of the Criminal Division during the surveillance. While the intelligence gathering continued, the Internal Security Section began assembling a criminal case against Truong and Humphrey.

The Fourth Circuit stated the "primary purpose" test—government agents could use the information gathered during warrantless physical searches and electronic surveillances only if their first intention was to identify threats to the nation's security. If this logic sounded like a particularly fine distinction, there was a reason. Judges were reluctant to prohibit foreign intelligence wiretaps, but neither did they want to let the government obtain a wiretap without court review if the information obtained from the tap would be used to make a criminal case. Intelligence gathering, as one court put it, could not be an "end run" around the Fourth Amendment.

In part because of the issues raised by Truong-Humphrey, the Congress passed the Foreign Intelligence Surveillance Act in 1978. While the law did not enshrine the actual language of "primary purpose," it stated that there has to be a legitimate, continuing intelligence purpose to a FISA investigation while the option of a criminal prosecution was maintained. Congress understood that criminal evidence might turn up in any national security investigation of suspected spies or terrorists, but the FISA law specified that the focus of such an investigation had to be intelligence gathering. "Contrary to the premises which underlie the provision of Title III of the Omnibus Crime Control Act of 1968," members of the Senate Select Committee on Intelligence said in a report in 1978, "it is contemplated that few electronic surveillances conducted pursuant to [FISA] will result in criminal prosecution." Only electronic surveillance was regulated under the new FISA law; physical searches of property in national security investigations still had to be authorized either by the president or the attorney general, with no requirement that a court authorize a warrant. Called to testify about the issue in 1990, Mary Lawton explained that the warrantless searches were used "sparingly," saying that each case received "extremely close scrutiny within the FBI and the [Justice] Department to ensure that the rights and the interests of U.S. persons are fully protected." That was a reference to the oversight role of the Office of Intelligence Policy and Review. In the years to come, it was Lawton and her chief deputy, Allan Kornblum, who most often took the walk downstairs to the attorney general's office to request approval to search the home or property of some unsuspecting citizen.

On the day after Thanksgiving in 1993, not quite a month after Mary Lawton died, Richard Scruggs decided it was time to go through her office on the sixth floor of Main Justice. Since coming to Washington as one of Janet Reno's special assistants in April, Scruggs had been asked to handle a number of sensitive matters for the new attorney general. From the outset, part of his brief involved intelligence issues when they needed the attention of the Attorney General's Office.

Lawton's death came at a time of great turmoil at Main Justice. The fallout from the FBI's ill-fated raid on the Branch Davidian compound in Waco, Texas, was considerable. The Clinton administration was slow in filling key appointments, and Reno's relationship with Philip Heymann, the deputy attorney general, was deteriorating rapidly. In this climate, Reno was reluctant to choose a permanent replacement to head the Office of Intelligence Policy and Review.

Like Lawton, Scruggs had first come to Main Justice under the Justice Department Honors Program, and spent the next four years working on espionage cases in the Internal Security Section.

Like Lawton, Scruggs was also a career government lawyer with experience in intelligence law. Unlike Lawton, Scruggs had extensive experience as a trial prosecutor, having worked as an assistant U.S. attorney in Miami.

Scruggs walked up the single flight of stairs from the attorney general's suite of offices to Lawton's lair on the sixth floor. The place had the feel of a squad room in an inner-city police precinct. Elsewhere in Main Justice, the offices of senior officials had wood-burning fireplaces and fine-brushed murals. Inside the intelligence policy office, the carpet was threadbare, the walls in need of paint. There was a conference room, but its walls were lined with Mosler safes that stood shoulder to shoulder like sentries. That's the way Lawton had liked it—functional and bare-bones. Year after year she had refused to buy new carpets or drapes, preferring instead to turn back unspent funds in her budget.

Lawton's office was eerie—it looked as if she had left only to run a quick errand and might be back at any moment. Nothing had been moved from her last day of work. After Lawton's death, her secretary had simply closed the office door, leaving everything inside just as it was. Scruggs began a methodical examination of the office and its contents. The volume of FISA cases moving through the office was startling, Scruggs thought. The total number of FISA wiretap authorizations had increased steadily over the years. Very quietly, the federal government had been installing more national security wiretaps than criminal wiretaps—an astonishing fact.

The FBI's structure mirrored this trend. With the help of the National Security Agency, the globe-spanning eavesdropping bureaucracy, the FBI operated a network of super-secret eavesdropping facilities that conducted FISA surveillance operations. Government budget documents painted a more complete picture. In 1995 nearly three thousand FBI special agents were assigned to foreign counterintelligence and counter-terrorism investigations, and support, salaries and other costs exceeded $500 million annually. Those numbers were headed up. In 1996 Attorney General Reno and FBI Director Louis Freeh would seek funding to add a thousand persons to their counterintelligence and counterterrorism effort. Reno and Freeh cited the bombing of the Oklahoma City federal building as an example of the need for more vigorous domestic surveillance of anti-government protesters and violent militias. They also cited what they called "significant increases" in the incidence of economic and industrial espionage by agents of hostile and even friendly governments. Between 1994 and 1995 the number of FBI investigations of such instances had doubled, to more than eight hundred active cases. With the new funding and new legislation empowering the FBI to pursue international terrorism, the FBI's counterintelligence capabilities were increased to a level higher than at any time during the Cold War.

In theory, the Office of Intelligence Policy and Review at Main Justice was to impose the legal checks and balances over this vast surveillance apparatus. Yet the deeper Scruggs got into the FISA files after Mary Lawton's death, the more uneasy he grew. His first impression was that Lawton's operation was a horse and buggy cantering down an expressway. Scruggs had supervised the Criminal Division in the U.S. Attorney's Office in Miami, the largest in the country. As a manager he was a little taken aback. Lawton had been a brilliant lawyer, but she had been frugal with her budget and disinclined to expand. It showed. The number of FISA applications had increased steadily, but the staff of lawyers had not. Allan Kornblum and the five lawyers in the Office of Intelligence Policy and Review wrote hundreds of FISA surveillance applications a year. The Office of Enforcement Operations in the Criminal Division of Main Justice, by contrast, had six lawyers who did nothing but review applications for Title III wiretaps. In 1995 the number of FISA surveillance applications exceeded six hundred; the number of Title III approvals was under four hundred.

In reading the FISA applications on file in Lawton's office, Scruggs began catching mistakes. So heavy was the volume of FISA cases moving through the office, the lawyers could spend only so much time on each one. "I found out that there were so many FISAs being conducted with so few attorneys," he said, "that the review process to prevent factual and legal errors was virtually nonexistent." Another thing he noticed was the primitive level of the office equipment. FISA applications were being logged in by hand in big books. There were security reasons for that, but in the age of computers it seemed ridiculous. Whenever Scruggs asked for an old case file the secretaries would often have trouble finding it. It was little wonder, he decided, that mistakes were being made.

The situation, Scruggs believed, was untenable. In his private conversations with Janet Reno, she repeatedly emphasized her determination to stay ahead of the terrorism curve. "She constantly stressed to me that terrorism—combating terrorism—was absolutely one of our main responsibilities," Scruggs said. "And she was constantly pushing me to do more and more on terrorism. She didn't want to work a criminal case after the bomb went off. She wanted to work FISA and counterintelligence methods to stop the bomb from going off in the first place."

Reno had to sign each FISA authorization, and did so based on the assurances of the lawyers in the Office of Intelligence Policy and Review. From his experience investigating the FBI's ill-fated raid on the Branch Davidian compound in Waco, Scruggs knew that Reno was a stickler for accuracy, particularly when it could reflect on her own judgment. She had been stung by the disclosure, which Scruggs had insisted be put into the Waco report, that she had not read the FBI's assessment of allegations of child abuse in the Branch Davidian compound.

The more he settled into the job, the more Scruggs decided that it was not just the Office of Intelligence Policy and Review that was overworked by the surge in international terrorism and counterintelligence surveillance. The big increase was putting stress on the FBI, too. Despite their numbers, the FBI agents assigned to counterintelligence investigations were having trouble keeping up with all the new cases. Such investigations could be far more labor intensive than criminal investigations, requiring round-the-clock physical surveillance, full-time monitoring of wiretaps, specialists in little-known languages, transcribers, secretaries and even accountants. The increasing demands were apparent to Scruggs. "I see that transcripts are coming slower," he said, "that persons are being lost on surveillances, people are moving and we don't know where they moved."

Few of the professional overseers outside Main Justice would have been likely to notice or even suspect that there was a problem. The FBI's work in the areas of domestic terrorism and counterespionage investigations had been a big success. Leaders of the terrorist groups that had been active in the early 1980s had largely been hunted down and locked up. There had been sixty-eight espionage prosecutions, with sixty-seven convictions. Through aggressive intelligence gathering—much of it under Mary Lawton's legal guidance—the FBI had prevented fifty-seven terrorist attacks, including plans to blow up a Boeing 747 jumbo jet and a scheme to set fire to a crowded movie theater.

For all the successes, however, there had been warning signs that things had begun to slip, particularly an episode that was disclosed in 1988. It was called the CISPES case, named for its target, the Committee in Support of the People of El Salvador. Not since the COINTELPRO investigation had the FBI seemed to go so far astray. Relying on an informant who proved unreliable, FBI agents conducted a massive nationwide investigation that put under surveillance 1,330 liberal groups, many of them religious or political organizations, yet no charges were ever filed. After two years Mary Lawton and the lawyers at the Office of Intelligence Policy and Review had sounded the alarm on the CISPES case, telling the FBI that it appeared to involve First Amendment–protected political activity.

The case highlighted the risks inherent in domestic intelligence operations and the need for tight management. It had not been Mary Lawton's proudest moment. The Senate Select Committee on Intelligence found that, while the CISPES case was an aberration, "the FBI does not appear to have received adequate guidance from the Justice Department on the extent to which FBI international terrorism investigations should collect information about peaceful political activities of domestic groups."

As Scruggs read more files and talked at length with Lawton's former aides, he came across an anomaly. While most of the intelligence community assumed Lawton had been vetting proposals for covert intelligence operations overseas, her other main area of responsibility, there was virtually no documentary proof that this had occurred. If the records existed, Scruggs could not find them. Eventually, he heard an amazing story from one of Lawton's aides. Shortly after the defeat of President Bush, two lawyers who had worked for his attorney general, William P. Barr, appeared at the door of Lawton's outer office at Main Justice carrying two boxes. These they left with Lawton's staff. When her lawyers looked inside, they saw several files on covert operations they had heard nothing about.

Scruggs eventually learned the meaning behind this incident. Under Barr, Lawton had been gradually cut out of the loop on legal reviews of covert operations by American intelligence agencies. During those years the reviews had been carried out by appointees in the Attorney General's Office. Barr was comfortable with this arrangement. He had previously worked in the CIA general counsel's office and felt he knew enough about intelligence law to make recommendations to the president. Lawton, Scruggs learned, had been philosophical about this turn of events. Her office still handled reviews of all FISA applications for electronic surveillance. On covert operations and matters of intelligence policy, the president—acting through the attorney general—could proceed as he wished. That's where the authority, through the Constitution, rested—in the White House.

Scruggs had stumbled upon a matter that had already been privately reported to President Clinton. "The intelligence-legal review process has been politicized," said the Justice Department transition team report. "It is not well coordinated and the OIPR experts are not consulted on covert-action findings and other important legal opinions." While department regulations said the Office of Intelligence Policy and Review represented Main Justice on interagency reviews of intelligence policy, Lawton had gradually been eased out of this role by the Bush appointees. Moreover, said the report, the intelligence agencies realized that Lawton's brief had been curtailed. The old practice of walking the halls of Main Justice for a favorable legal opinion had returned. "The Attorney General has permitted [the National Security Council staff] to determine which Justice Department attorneys participate in the legal review, thereby 'forum shopping,' " said the report. The intelligence policy office "has been excluded from certain inter-agency intelligence policy groups."

The Republicans had decided to bypass Mary Lawton and the intelligence policy office. In layman's terms, what had happened was simple. Part of the institutional safeguards that had been put in place after the Church committee hearings had been quietly rewired during the Bush administration.

With this discovery, history repeated itself. Nearly eighteen years after Edward Levi had his unsettling encounter with an FBI agent seeking immediate approval for a secret electronic surveillance operation, the newest civilian appointee at the top of the Department of Justice suddenly faced a similar question. When Reno had to make a recommendation on covert operations, where could she turn for answers to what the Justice Department had done before? The grand old lady of intelligence law was gone, and she had left behind a big hole. "The intelligence policy office," Deputy Attorney General Jamie Gorelick said later, "was a one-woman band, and when that woman died, there was a lot of expertise, and that died with her." John Lewis, the FBI's chief operations officer for national security investigations, put it a different way. After Mary Lawton died, Lewis said, everything "changed overnight."

In his conversations with the attorney general, Scruggs sounded a warning. The office was in dire need of expansion, he said. It needed more lawyers, more secretaries, more space. It needed computers and intelligence analysts. If it was going to do quality work, it was going to have to grow. The intelligence world would not wait. This concern, too, had already been reported to the president by the administration's transition team that had reviewed the operations of the Department of Justice.

Scruggs had no intention of making a career at the intelligence policy office. He had agreed to come to Main Justice only if he could retain his status as an assistant U.S. attorney. When Reno's tenure ended he wanted to go back to his old job as a prosecutor in Florida. But for now, he decided, there was a battle to be waged. Ominously, there was a proposal circulating to carve up Lawton's staff, putting the FISA review in the Criminal Division, the policy shop in the Office of Legal Counsel. Philip Heymann, Reno's first deputy attorney general, had first broached the idea, just as he had suggested folding Michael Shaheen's Office of Professional Responsibility into the Justice Department's Office of Inspector General. Shaheen was standing his ground, but with Lawton gone there was no one to do the same for the tiny intelligence policy office on the sixth floor. Scruggs decided to make it his business to save the place. In his view, it was not the time to cut back; on the contrary, it was time to expand the office and define its role more clearly.

It was in this context that the Ames case became a source of contention. Agents of the FBI's Nightmover squad arrested Ames on the morning of February 21, 1994, as he was driving to work at CIA headquarters in nearby Langley, Virginia. Soon after, Ames and his wife were summoned to a hearing before a federal magistrate. The morning after the bond hearing, Scruggs picked up a copy of The Washington Post and read an article about it. Plato Cacheris had been appointed as Ames's defense counsel; he was among the most adroit practitioners in the field of intelligence law. During the bond hearing the agent in charge of the case, Leslie G. Wiser Jr., deftly parried Cacheris's questions about when he and the Nightmover squad had initiated a "criminal" investigation of Aldrich Ames. "No, sir," Wiser told Cacheris when he asked if the FBI's investigation of Ames had become primarily criminal in nature early on. The Ames inquiry had been "a hybrid," Wiser explained, a counterintelligence inquiry in which evidence of criminal wrongdoing had also been uncovered, but whose primary purpose was intelligence gathering.

After reading the account of the bond hearing in the newspaper, Scruggs thought he saw where Cacheris was headed: The defense attorney was going to challenge the legality of the warrantless search of Ames's house in October 1993 by arguing that the "primary purpose" of the Nightmover case had shifted from intelligence gathering to criminal prosecution. If the judge accepted that argument, he might suppress all evidence gathered after the search. A second question also occurred to Scruggs. He could tell from the *Post* article that the prosecutors were using information gathered under the FISA act. Under that law, the attorney general must issue a formal authorization for the disclosure of evidence gathered under FISA. That is normally prepared by the intelligence policy office. Scruggs knew he had done no such thing.

The more he dug into the Ames case, the more he was concerned. Three issues came to the fore. One was the attorney general's authorization. The second was the question of Criminal Division contacts with FBI agents that might be construed as being in conflict with the FISA law. Last was the legal issue that had been addressed by the courts going back to Truong-Humphrey and earlier: Had the primary purpose of the FBI's investigation of Aldrich Ames shifted at some point from one of intelligence gathering to one that had as its primary purpose a criminal prosecution? The issues were thorny, but in the end—despite the hard work of the Nightmover squad in a long and highly delicate investigation—it appeared to Scruggs that part of the FISA law had not been scrupulously observed.

Scruggs decided to construct a detailed chronology of the Ames case to determine how it had been handled at Main Justice and define when and if it had shifted from primarily an intelligence-gathering operation to a criminal prosecution. In the command center on the sixth floor of Main Justice, just down the hall from the Office of Intelligence Policy and Review, Scruggs convened a meeting of Justice Department lawyers and FBI officials. "My focus," Scruggs said, "was to see who knew what when."

The more questions he asked, the fuzzier things appeared. Scruggs decided to brief the attorney general. Cacheris was bearing down on the warrantless search, he said. A full-blown hearing could lead to hard questions. At the moment, the answers weren't that good. Since Reno had authorized the warrentless search, it was possible she would be called as a witness. That had happened to Griffin Bell in the Truong-Humphrey case.

Reno's mood darkened. So soon after Waco, she did not welcome problems with another high-profile case. Even a remote possibility that so important a prosecution as the Ames case might be in jeopardy was intolerable. Grimly, she gave Scruggs an order: "Don't let this happen again."

Scruggs drafted a set of guidelines. Recalling how the Truong-Humphrey case had led to the suppression of evidence, Scruggs argued that the issue boiled down to who was directing the FBI agents: OIPR lawyers or Criminal Division prosecutors? He proposed a solution: When FBI agents wanted to talk to the Criminal Division, they should check in first with OIPR. That way, there would be a record of contacts for the FISA court and the attorney general.

Scruggs's memo dealt with the law, but he had more in mind. Having spent four years on the other side of the fence prosecuting espionage, he had the impression there were sometimes informal "backchannel" consultations between the FBI and the prosecutors that had circumvented Mary Lawton. If a backchannel existed, Scruggs decided, it should be closed.

Alerted by Scruggs's concerns, FBI Director Louis Freeh took his own precautionary measure. He moved the FBI's in-house legal review of FISA applications out of the National Security Division and into the General Counsel's Office. This grated on the operational personnel. "There was a difference of interpretation," said John Lewis, Bryant's deputy who supervised the Nightmover investigation. "Richard Scruggs was a pretty sharp cookie and he had a different viewpoint. And I hate to say it, but many people agreed with him."

John Martin is the Justice Department's most experienced spy chaser. Movie-star handsome, he began his career in government some three decades earlier as an FBI agent working civil-rights inves-tigations of members of the Ku Klux Klan. Outspoken, a man of little patience with whiners and makers of excuses, Martin eventually left the FBI, dusting off his law degree and hanging out his shingle for the first time as a lawyer in private practice. Government service eventually called him again, and Martin returned to the Department of Justice, where he was assigned as a prosecutor in the Internal Security Section. In the years afterward, Martin quarterbacked every important espionage case the FBI investigated. Before David Truong and Ronald Humphrey were arrested, it was Martin who urged Attorney General Griffin Bell to seek authority from President Jimmy Carter for the first-ever warrantless search in an espionage inquiry. Despite the challenge, affirmed by the Fourth Circuit Court of Appeal, on aspects of the electronic surveillance of Truong and Humphrey, the Court upheld the validity of the physical search, and Martin used evidence from the search to win convictions of, and long prison sentences for, both men.

In the 1980s, after the passage of the FISA law, the Internal Security Section became one of the busiest offices in the Criminal Division as John Martin moved up in seniority and the number of staff attorneys grew to thirty-five. During 1985, "the year of the spy," Internal Security lawyers were busier than ever, bringing a record thirteen espionage indictments in twelve months. Of those indicted, perhaps only John Walker exceeded Aldrich Ames in the amount of damage he did to American national security. The Walker case offered instructive parallels with that of Ames, Martin believed, particularly on the issue of contacts between the Criminal Division and the FBI on FISA surveillance.

The night Walker was arrested, a team of FBI agents was following him on a darkened road in suburban Maryland, less than an hour's drive from the White House. The agents believed Walker was going to leave a packet of classified documents for his Soviet handlers at a "drop site" in the area, and the money-hungry Navy spy did not disappoint. As agents moved in to examine the drop site after Walker left the documents, they maintained radio contact with supervisors in the FBI command center at the J. Edgar Hoover Building on Pennsylvania Avenue in Washington. John Dion, Martin's principal deputy, was in the command center at the time, on an open phone line to Martin, who was at home preparing to leave for Germany the following day for a spy swap. Such swaps involved an elaborate *pas de deux*, almost always at Berlin's historic Glienicke Bridge. They were among the most satisfying parts of Martin's job, and never more so than when he secured the release of Anatoly Shcharansky in 1985, after five years in a Soviet labor camp. In his Justice Department office, Martin has a photograph of himself escorting the diminutive Shcharansky, bundled into an oversize coat and big wool hat. It is one of his most prized possessions.

Dion is a fastidious, cerebral lawyer, and Martin trusted him implicitly. After agents flipped quickly through the documents Walker had left, they reported to Dion, who reported to Martin. The documents had come from the U.S.S. *Nimitz*, an aircraft carrier on which Walker's son, Michael, served. That was enough for Martin. The FBI agents trailing Walker that night had no plans to arrest him; they still needed to know much more about where he was getting his information. The *Nimitz* documents now answered that question. There was no reason to keep following Walker—or allowing him to do more damage.

"John," Martin told Dion, "we should go ahead with the arrest."

Dion relayed the order to his counterparts in the FBI command center, and they relayed it to the agents still tailing Walker as he made his way back toward suburban Maryland. Thus on his own responsibility did Martin, a career Justice Department lawyer with not so much as a nod from a superior, much less a political appointee from the Reagan administration, order the arrest of one of the most important spies in American history.

The reason the Walker case was instructive in the context of the questions being raised about the Ames case, Martin believed, was for the light it shed on the issue of primary purpose. Yes, the FBI agents had arrested Walker on the night in question. But did that mean the primary purpose of their investigation had shifted some time prior to the arrest from intelligence gathering to prosecution? "No—damn no," Martin said.

In the Ames case, Martin and Dion employed the same rationale as they had for Walker. Yes, they wanted to have an assistant U.S. attorney on call and fully prepared in case they had cause to arrest Ames suddenly. But they did not arrest Ames suddenly. Indeed, Martin and Dion supported the FBI brass in their decision to maintain the surveillance on the CIA spy for many weeks while they tried to learn more about his handlers. They arrested the man only when it became clear they could not further delay a long-planned overseas trip that Ames had scheduled on legitimate CIA business.

The questions about primary purpose rankled. But so did the others that were being raised. Scruggs worried that there might have been unauthorized contacts between Internal Security Section lawyers and the FBI. Howard Shapiro, the general counsel of the FBI, had provided his list of such contacts, as had Martin. Both men believed all contacts had been handled appropriately and legally. From November 19, 1993, until the date of Ames's arrest in February 1994, the Office of Intelligence Policy and Review had been apprised of or present at every meeting between Internal Security and the FBI, Shapiro and Martin said. John Dion had kept detailed notes of his meetings with Allan Kornblum, the operations deputy at the intelligence policy office, and Kornblum had been informed of the request to bring an assistant U.S. attorney into the Ames inquiry to prepare for a criminal case. Kornblum was similarly informed, on December 7, 1993, that a criminal case against Ames was proceeding; on that date, Kornblum received the first draft of Supervisory Special Agent Leslie Wiser's affidavit specifying the reasons for the arrest of Ames. Citing Dion's notes, Martin said, the issue of questionable contacts was one that simply had no foundation. "It just wasn't there," Martin said.

Last was the question of authorization of disclosure of information during Ames's bail hearing. Scruggs, as the acting head of the intelligence-policy office, did not go to Janet Reno to seek authorization for the disclosure of that information. But Dion's notes showed clearly that Allan Kornblum did—several days before Ames was arrested; in fact, before Agent Wiser's affidavit was even filed with the court. Kornblum had sought a verbal authorization from Reno for disclosure of the information obtained during the FISA surveillance. That was permissible under the law. If a mistake was made, in the judgment of others who later reviewed the matter, it was that Kornblum did not inform the attorney general of the latest status of the criminal investigation of Ames. That was not the fault of the Criminal Division or the FBI, John Martin and Howard Shapiro argued. They had done their jobs. In their view, Scruggs's proposal was an affront and implied that they had jeopardized the Ames case.

Harris called a meeting at Main Justice to discuss the proposed guidelines and plan the Criminal Division's response. The way bureaucracies work, she and her lawyers would have to reduce their objections to paper and send a memorandum up the chain of command. The fate of the Scruggs proposal would rest with Janet Reno and Jamie Gorelick, the deputy attorney general.

Jo Ann Harris believed the merits of the argument favored the Criminal Division. "There was an overreaching by process," she said, "to cut the Criminal Division out from ever knowing that certain investigations are going on. These were investigations that reasonable people believed could result in criminal prosecutions."

The issues raised by the Ames case were of such importance that they could be resolved only at the highest levels of Main Justice, and only after a wide range of legal opinions was solicited. Attorney General Janet Reno specifically wanted Walter Dellinger, the highly regarded Duke University law professor who heads the Office of Legal Counsel, to weigh in on the matter. In a seven-page memorandum dated February 14, 1995, Dellinger did just that. Quickly, he summarized the "primary purpose" test that had been established by the Fourth Circuit in the prosecution of David Truong and Ronald Humphrey. He then noted that trial courts had been "exceedingly deferential" to government lawyers arguing against defense counsel motions to suppress criminal evidence obtained during a FISA surveillance. While the law "unquestionably contemplates the use in criminal trials of evidence obtained in FISA searches," Dellinger wrote, the case law on the issue "offer[s] little guidance for identifying the precise line where the use of intelligence information by prosecutors might make law enforcement the 'primary purpose' of a FISA search."

Still, Dellinger concluded, some rules could be agreed on. "The greater the involvement of prosecutors in the planning and execution of FISA searches," Dellinger wrote, "the greater is the chance that the government could not assert in good faith that the primary purpose" of a FISA search was to prove the collection of U.S. intelligence for a foreign buyer. The involvement of prosecutors in the FISA process, in other words, was problematic by definition and had to be managed carefully.

This was the same point Scruggs had made, in arguing that the FISA process needed to be "regularized." The only way that could happen, Scruggs concluded, was to have specialists from the Office of Intelligence Policy and Review supervise contacts between FBI agents conducting surveillance operations under the FISA statute and attorneys from the Criminal Division who might one day seek to use evidence from such surveillance to build a criminal prosecution.

This was precisely the issue on which Janet Reno and her deputy, Jamie Gorelick, came down. On July 19, 1995, Reno issued a confidential four-page memorandum establishing new rules of conduct for FBI agents and Criminal Division lawyers working on counterintelligence investigations and employing electronic surveillance under the FISA statute. The FBI and the Criminal Division were forbidden, under the guidelines, from contacting each other independently, and the FBI was further prohibited from contacting a U.S. attorney's office without prior permission from both the Office of Intelligence Policy and Review and the Criminal Division of Main Justice. FBI agents working counterintelligence investigations would henceforth be required to "maintain a log of all contacts with the Criminal Division, noting the time and participants involved." Other requirements and prohibitions were outlined. A key provision, unsurprisingly, related to the FISA law. "The Criminal Division shall not . . . instruct the FBI on the operation, continuation or expansion of FISA electronic surveillance or physical searches," Reno ordered.

After Aldrich Ames and his wife Rosario agreed to plead guilty to the charges against them, Richard Scruggs's review of the investigation of the CIA traitor resulted in realizing precisely the objective he had sought. With Janet Reno's order, the process of conducting foreign-intelligence and foreign-counterintelligence investigations was now, in the word that was so dear to Reno's heart and so emblematic of her style of management, "regularized."

The issue was as thorny as any that had ever confronted Main Justice. "Given the persent uncertainty of the law," Scruggs said, "OIPR lawyers attempt to follow the more conservative course of requiring the applications to meet the 'primary purpose' test." Lawyers could argue endlessly about where the line was drawn, but "as attorneys for the government, it is OIPR's responsibility to ensure that the [FBI] Director's certification as to the purpose of the surveillance is correct and that the Attorney General is aware of all relevant information prior to signing the application."

What it boiled down to was oversight. To do the job, Scruggs said, OIPR had to be a more active overseer of the FBI. He proposed a rule that—except in emergencies where immediate action was required—the FBI should not contact the Criminal Division or a U.S. Attorney's Office on a case without consulting first with OIPR. "In order to maintain the foreign intelligence purpose of the electronic surveillance or physical search, it is imperative that contacts between FBI agents and prosecutors during an on-going foreign intelligence case be carefully proscribed and carefully monitored." Scruggs wasn't sure there were any problems with the Ames case; he certainly had no complaints about the prosecutors. But he was bound and determined that OIPR was not going to be shunted aside and that when Janet Reno signed an authorization for a warrantless search, the OIPR lawyer would be able to say for sure that it was a pure intelligence-gathering operation.

There was one more issue to deal with. After the Ames case, Reno said, she never again wanted to have to approve a warrantless search of any American citizen's property. At her urging, the Justice Department proposed to Congress that it place all such searches under the FISA law. This was one area on which all the disputants in the Ames case agreed. The Criminal Division, the Office of Intelligence Policy and Review and the FBI had all gone on the record several years earlier expressing their support for court authorization of physical searches in national security investigations. Mary Lawton and John Martin had been particularly vigorous advocates of the change.

Civil libertarians disagreed with it, offering the only formal dissent as the measure was debated on Capitol Hill. "We strongly oppose the present proposal to authorize black-bag jobs—warrantless secret searches of Americans' homes and papers for national security reasons," said Kate Martin, an attorney for the American Civil Liberties Union. "Black-bag jobs were one of the worst abuses of civil liberties during the Cold War era, and we urge the Congress, instead of authorizing them now, to outlaw them."

Members of Congress dismissed the objections with little discussion and agreed to amend the FISA law as requested. No one relished the idea of entering the home of an American citizen without a court-authorized warrant, under a little-understood exemption to the search warrant requirements of the Fourth Amendment. Now the exemption was removed. Any time a federal law-enforcement officer wanted to enter a private home to conduct an investigation of any type, he or she would have to secure the permission of a court first.

CHAPTER TWENTY-FOUR

TWO WORLDS MELD

T he Ames case crystallized for Janet Reno, Jamie Gorelick and others at Main Justice the need for a full review of the institution's relationship with the intelligence community.

The salient issues had been described for the attorney general in a thirty-eight-page document titled "Joint Task Force on Intelligence and Law Enforcement." It was the result of an effort by Main Justice and the CIA to identify ways that the two agencies could work together with greater effect and less friction than had sometimes been the case. It was the point of departure for a slow and mostly secret journey that would turn the Justice Department into a full-fledged member of the intelligence community.

The report was prepared in early 1993 by Mark Richard of the Criminal Division and Elizabeth Rindskopf, then the CIA's general counsel. An opening narrative traces the history of the relationship between federal law enforcement and the intelligence community. The two lawyers went all the way back to 1947, when the law creating the CIA also prohibited the agency from engaging in domestic law enforcement. The attorney general's guidelines for intelligence gathering drafted by Mary Lawton are enshrined in an executive order (No. 11905) signed by President Gerald Ford. Another executive order (No. 12333) signed by President Ronald Reagan broadened the scope of potential interaction. It declares that terrorism and international narcotics are legitimate threats to national security and ought to be part of the CIA's job.

The collapse of the Soviet Union had changed the landscape of challenges for the nation's intelligence agencies. Notwithstanding the abuses documented by the Church committee, the nation's spy agencies generally wanted nothing to do with domestic law enforcement, but that attitude was old thinking. With the Cold War ended, the intelligence community, in the words of a senior political appointee, was "looking for things to do" and crime fighting was an area with real potential for growth. While government was being cut back in many areas, the budgets for law enforcement continued to swell.

Yet, there had been little evolution in the relationship between the intelligence community and law enforcement. They had ad hoc ways of communicating on matters such as terrorism or drug enforcement. As institutions, however, the Justice Department and the CIA were mammoth icebergs adrift in the same sea. Occasionally they collided and the effect could be jarring. "Since the late 1980s," states the Richard-Rindskopf report, "a number of high-profile cases . . . in which intelligence information and equities have either played a key role or were the subject of controversy have caused a re-examination of the relationship between the two communities. In varying degrees, these cases have been characterized by conflict, miscommunication, and a perception on the part of some in the Congress, the press, and the public at large that the intelligence and law enforcement communities remain either unwilling or unable to work together effectively."

This was putting it mildly. The congressional inquiry inaugurated by Frank Church two decades earlier, and the reforms that followed on its heels, had so rattled the nation's spy agencies and the Department of Justice that there had been a mutual withdrawal—a refusal of the espionage agencies to share substantive information with federal prosecutors, and vice versa. "The relationship between law enforcement and intelligence was until relatively recently an oxymoron," the Richard-Rindskopf report continues, "largely because, during the last half century, the two communities have existed in largely separate spheres. They were two communities separated by law, mission, culture, scope of activity, and language."

Mark Richard and Elizabeth Rindskopf had laid out a series of twenty-three issues that needed to be resolved by prosecutors and intelligence operatives. To most people, these issues were hardly the stuff of high drama. Yet the questions were potentially volatile. America prided itself on having built a strong federal police force without becoming a police state. The Richard-Rindskopf report walked up to issues that could disturb this delicate balance. How closely should the nation's spies work with its federal agents? Should federal prosecutors share grand jury evidence with the intelligence agencies? If the National Security Agency intercepted a conversation about a drug deal, should it give the Drug Enforcement Administration a transcript?

Perhaps the most difficult issue involved a seemingly mundane concept called tasking. This is the highly classified process in which officials decide where to aim spy satellites and listening posts. Could the priorities of law enforcement be factored in to the selection of targets of surveillance?

A parallel issue was when law-enforcement agencies could and should provide to an intelligence agency information that had been collected during the course of a criminal inquiry; confidential sources, even the viability of a criminal investigation, could be jeopardized. The Richard-Rindskopf report was thorough and scholarly. It parsed the responsibilities of the intelligence and law-enforcement communities, but concluded that there was no real need for structural change. It offered no specific recommendations.

Other analysts were not so sanguine. Frederick Hitz, the CIA's inspector general, who provided some of the most trenchant criticism of CIA managers in the aftermath of the Aldrich Ames case, suggested that a de facto merger of the worlds of law enforcement and intelligence gathering was virtually inevitable:

"[T]he two communities, driven by the increasing intertwining of domestic and international interests, are moving inexorably toward one another," Hitz said. "Some accommodations have been made on each side, yet the two have failed to address adequately the fundamental distinctions in their practices, procedures and cultures."

For many months after Janet Reno took office, these two reports rattled around the bureaucracy at Main Justice. The death of Mary Lawton, who would have been integral to any change, put the issue off further. But it would not stay buried.

The lawyer who finally got the job of plotting the way forward for the nation's spy agencies and prosecutors was James McAdams. One day in October 1994, Richard Scruggs, the chief lawyer in the Office of Intelligence Policy and Review, walked into the Justice Department command center on the sixth floor where Jamie Gorelick was concluding a meeting. With Scruggs was McAdams, a handsome federal prosecutor from Florida who could have passed for a television anchorman. Scruggs wanted to introduce him to Gorelick. At the appropriate moment they stepped forward. "This is Jim McAdams," Scruggs said. In that instance he realized that Gorelick was drawing a complete blank. She had completely forgotten who McAdams was or why he happened to be with Scruggs. Eventually she would come to know him well enough. Within a year he would replace Scruggs in the job once held by Mary Lawton. By that time, Gorelick was pointing to McAdams as the kind of career prosecutor who would help the department navigate its way around the intelligence-related issues that had so confounded the Bush administration.

McAdams had spent most of his professional life in federal law enforcement. In the mid-1970s he had worked as a federal probation officer in Miami while living on a sailboat in Biscayne Bay. His job required him to supervise several notorious convicts, including two Watergate burglars and another man who put a $5,000 contract on the street for anyone willing to murder the earnest young probation officer. After several years McAdams decided to become a federal prosecutor and went to law school.

Upon graduation he joined the U.S. Attorney's Office in Miami, working first on appeals, then moving to the trial section where he took up his duties the same day as Richard Scruggs.

McAdams was fairly typical of the midcareer prosecutors who made up the rising generation of senior managers at Main Justice. Like Theresa Van Vliet in the field of narcotics, many had spent the 1980s in the trenches out in the major U.S. Attorneys' Offices. There, they had used the Justice Department's biggest weapons in sophisticated cases. The career paths of these assistant U.S. attorneys had given them a range and depth of experience that was not available to most lawyers who worked in the Criminal Division of Main Justice.

This was certainly true of McAdams. In 1989, shortly before the U.S. invasion of Panama set the stage for the trial in Miami of deposed dictator Manuel Antonio Noriega, McAdams was assigned to the prosecution team. There had never been a narcotics case quite like *United States v. Noriega*. The Panamanian was a former head of state who had been a vital asset of American intelligence, having worked closely with the CIA and the Defense Intelligence Agency. The prosecution set the stage for a head-on collision between the Department of Justice and the intelligence community.

Before the invasion McAdams was asked to accompany the U.S. attorney in Miami to a conference on the Noriega case at Main Justice. It was the first time McAdams had seen Deputy Assistant Attorney General Mark Richard conduct a meeting, and he was impressed.

In his office next door to Jack Keeney, Richard was the Justice Department lawyer most at home in the arcane area of the law where intelligence issues intersect with criminal prosecutions. His closest friends at Main Justice marveled at the apparent ease with which Richard had adapted himself to the requirements of dealing with both the twilight world of the intelligence services and the complexities of law-enforcement agencies abroad. David Margolis, for instance, did not possess a passport. He boasted that he had been abroad only twice, both times for quick dinners in Canada before he returned home to sleep in the security of the United

States. Richard, a soft-spoken lawyer from Brooklyn, seemed strangely at home abroad, and in dealing with the nation's foremost intelligence experts.

Richard's had been a peculiar career. He had arrived at the Justice Department in 1967, straight out of Brooklyn Law School, his abiding passion the prosecution of white-collar crime cases. Within a few short years Richard was pursuing Robert Vesco, the notorious fugitive financier, around the globe. The pursuit had led Richard through a dense welter of crooked offshore corporations. Vesco eluded arrest, but out of the chase had emerged a fraud prosecution so vast that Richard literally had to set up his own prison at Fort Holabird, Maryland, to house all the witnesses and informants who decided to provide information to the government. Richard had finally been dispossessed of the place by the Watergate prosecution team, whose members claimed they needed the lockup for their own growing stable of witnesses.

Despite the failure to apprehend and prosecute Vesco, the investigation had made Richard one of the few lawyers at Main Justice who had any direct experience in international law-enforcement matters. That fact had set Richard on a course that had expanded not just the ambit of his own career but also that of the entire Criminal Division. Because of the range of issues that came across Richard's desk, his authority sometimes led him into areas far removed from the usual cases prosecuted by the lawyers of the Criminal Division. Richard's were what insiders in the building called "cross-cutting" responsibilities. They allowed him to reach out, where the Criminal Division's other deputies could not, and take direct control of the Noriega case and other cases that had broad or tricky international implications.

Prosecutors in the Criminal Division handled difficult criminal cases. Many involved issues of great legal and ethical complexity. Within the division, the consensus was that Richard had had more than his share of legal exotica—much more. Where other lawyers had the U.S. Attorney's Manual and other legal road maps to guide them, Richard, when he went off to some distant and dirty capital to attempt to resolve an espionage issue or to bring a criminal suspect into American custody, often had little more than his wits, the native cunning of a smart boy from Brooklyn, and the confidence of his superiors that he would play fair and honorably—that he would do the right thing.

During the meeting on the Noriega case Jim McAdams had watched Richard tee up the legal and factual issues for discussion, then go around the room with a series of precise questions. Richard had given no hint of his own views. That he would save for his boss, the assistant attorney general of the Criminal Division. "I'm no hero," Richard said. "The process is set out by law. We follow cases wherever they take us. There is a process for not indicting where national security concerns intrude, but someone higher up the line makes that call. My job is to say, 'We have the evidence.' "

The Achilles' heel of the Noriega prosecution was the many years that the former head of the Panamanian Defense Forces had dealt with U.S. intelligence agencies. McAdams's job was to review the classified documents compiled on Noriega and determine what should be turned over to Noriega's lawyers as pretrial discovery material. If there was exculpatory evidence in the CIA's files, it had to be released under the Brady rule, which requires prosecutors to disclose such evidence to defendants in federal criminal proceedings. Complying with the Brady rule was especially important because Noriega's lawyers had served notice that one of their defenses at trial would be the "public authority" defense—that Noriega's alleged criminal conduct had been undertaken with the approval of U.S. intelligence agencies.

McAdams ventured out to the leafy, campuslike headquarters of the Central Intelligence Agency in suburban Virginia. He journeyed to the headquarters of the National Security Agency in Fort Meade, Maryland. At both places he got a cold reception. The spy agencies were not thrilled about having a prosecutor root around in their files.

After much frustration McAdams went to see Mark Richard. "I have to have help," he pleaded. Richard said he would see what he could do.

The soft-spoken Criminal Division lawyer was as good as his

word. The first thing Richard did was arrange for a lawyer who had experience in the ins and outs of the Classified Information Procedures Act (CIPA) to be assigned to assist McAdams. Next he wrote a cover memo for a series of "tasking" letters from McAdams to the CIA, Department of Defense and National Security Agency, asking them to produce all their files relating to Noriega or the Panamanian Defense Forces. Richard's signature unlocked the doors. After that memo, McAdams said, "Whatever I asked for to do with the Noriega case I got." More than 120,000 documents eventually were produced. McAdams was given six more lawyers to help with the review of the materials, including Theresa Van Vliet, who commuted from Florida. When he asked to interview an intelligence officer, the spy was summoned to Washington and produced for questioning, almost always without delay. "It was clear to the intelligence community," McAdams said, "that the very top of the Justice Department was behind us in this case."

Ultimately, the CIPA filings were an important part of the Miami prosecution: Noriega got his Brady material; the CIA's sources and methods were protected. By the end of the trial, the judge who presided over the Noriega prosecution was satisfied with the government's production of Brady evidence, even when it involved highly classified information. Without the assistance of Main Justice, McAdams said, "the Noriega prosecution would have been a disaster, because so much that had to be accomplished had to be accomplished out of the Justice Department."

When the U.S. attorney in Miami resigned in 1992, McAdams was named the acting U.S. attorney. When that job ended, he made another foray into the twilight world of intelligence after Attorney General William Barr asked him to help sort out the problems in the huge and troubled prosecution of the Banca Nazionale del Lavoro, the big Italian bank at the heart of the so-called Iraqgate scandal. It was already a major public embarrassment. McAdams's job was to review allegations that the prosecutors had withheld Brady material and to make sure all exculpatory documents were turned over. Since the intelligence agencies had records relating to BNL, he again ended up dealing with agencies like the CIA. As he developed more trust in them, they began to place more trust in him.

McAdams thought the BNL case had been mismanaged. In his view Main Justice should have stepped in sooner and taken firm control of the case. But he saw no evidence of corruption or political tampering. Ultimately, an exhaustive reinvestigation of the case by longtime Reno aide John Hogan cleared the Bush Justice Department of any wrongdoing. Reno and her top aides drew two lessons from the BNL case. First, even a spurious allegation of wrongdoing against Main Justice, when amplified by a hostile Congress and an aroused national news media, could do grievous damage to an administration. Second, the Justice Department's relationship with the nation's intelligence community required a major overhaul.

McAdams took up the task, working from a small room with a walk-in vault just down the hall from Mary Lawton's old office. He had assumed a unique challenge. In a nutshell, his job was to come up with a plan that solved the problems identified in the Richard-Rindskopf report. McAdams would share that responsibility with an opposite number from the intelligence community, Michael Smith, a lawyer from the National Security Agency and a veteran intelligence professional. Together, McAdams and Smith became co-chairs of a panel called the Joint Intelligence Community Law Enforcement Working Group. By law, the intelligence agencies had responsibilities that were very different from those of federal police agencies and Main Justice. But the working group concluded there were ways for the two communities to work together.

McAdams and Smith attempted to chart the way, drafting a new section for inclusion in the U.S. Attorney's Manual, the bible on criminal procedure for federal prosecutors. It didn't skirt the difficulties of blending the two worlds. "Although both are arms of the Executive Branch, the federal law enforcement and intelligence communities have very distinct identities, mandates and methods." The Justice Department had to comply with the

"United States Constitution, case law, statutes and rules of procedure and evidence," said one of their planning documents.

When it came to criminal prosecutions, the manual made clear
that Main Justice would assume the dominant role in sorting out
these issues. "The attorney general has determined that all criminal cases relating to activities against the national security . . . are
to be supervised by the Assistant Attorney General, Criminal Division." Along with the new rules, however, were new appointments that would begin to knit together the two separate worlds.
All ninety-four U.S. attorneys were to designate a local prosecutor as a "national security coordinator" who would be schooled in
working with the intelligence community and in dealing with
such cases in their districts. Their mission would be to help prosecutors and federal agents in the field avoid embarrassments like
the Iraqgate prosecution that had resulted in so much controversy
about the use of intelligence information. That would be easier
said than done.

Working out the new relationship between the law-enforcement
and intelligence communities was a challenge that was rife with
dramatic real-world implications. It was one thing to sit in a secret
office somewhere inside Main Justice and draft a plan. It was another to deal with the steady stream of close calls and secret operations that passed within the domain of the Office of Intelligence
Policy and Review.

Just before the height of the Tokyo rush hour, on March 20,
1995, invisible clouds of deadly sarin gas drifted through five high-
speed subway trains. Within hours twelve people were dead and
more than five thousand were injured. The attack was the worst
act of domestic terrorism Japan had ever witnessed.

More than two thousand miles away in Washington, D.C., special agents in the FBI's Counterterrorism Section viewed the images of the subway attack courtesy of the Cable News Network. By
dawn in Washington, the FBI and CIA were on full alert. Within
hours, intelligence analysts were feeding regular reports to the
command center on the sixth floor at Main Justice.

At FBI headquarters in Washington, James Kallstrom and Thomas Picard happened to be visiting from New York. Kallstrom is a former marine who had served with distinction in Vietnam, then gone on to become the FBI's ranking expert on electronic surveillance measures before he was promoted to head its flagship field office in New York. Picard is Kallstrom's top deputy for intelligence matters, a slender, soft-spoken man who served as the special agent–in–charge for all FBI counterintelligence investigations. In his seventh-floor office at the J. Edgar Hoover Building, FBI Director Louis Freeh was informed that the Tokyo gas attack was the work of an obscure religious cult known as Aum Shinrikyo, which translates as "teaching of the truth." Adherents of the cult practiced a form of Buddhism, worshiping Lord Shiva, the Hindu god of destruction and reproduction. In Japan, Aum Shinrikyo was not widely known. In the United States, it was unheard of—a total mystery.

Several floors below Director Freeh's office, agents and analysts assigned to the FBI's Counterterrorism Section checked files and computer databases but found no indication that cult members had ever been active inside the United States. In Tokyo, case officers assigned to the CIA station there heard otherwise. Several hours after the subway attack, CIA officers relayed information that a group of Aum Shinrikyo members were living in a four-story apartment house on East Forty-eighth Street in Manhattan, just off Fifth Avenue. The building was located just a few blocks from the subway station at Times Square.

The information was relayed to FBI Director Freeh. He summoned Jim Kallstrom, an old friend and valued colleague, to his office to tell him about the report.

Kallstrom listened carefully, then told Freeh he was heading back to New York immediately. On the shuttle from Washington's National Airport, Kallstrom and Tom Picard decided, before the plane even began its final approach to New York's La Guardia Airport, to request a FISA warrant to conduct both a physical search and electronic surveillance of the Aum Shinrikyo building on Forty-eighth Street.

First, though, they had more pressing business. In his conference room on the twenty-eighth floor of the Jacob K. Javits Federal Building on Lower Broadway, Kallstrom summoned all his special agents–in–charge and ordered an intensive but quiet investigation of the cult's members, of its building on Forty-eighth Street and of any vehicles seen entering or leaving the place. Separately, Picard ordered his intelligence people to plumb all their computer databases to see what they had on the strange Japanese cult. Other agents were assigned to get a full description of the building on Forty-eighth Street. This was easier than it might have seemed. In its command center on the twenty-fourth floor of the Javits Building, the FBI had a database that could produce architectural drawings and Building and Zoning Department records on virtually every building in New York City. Kallstrom's agents soon had a thorough fix on the building on Forty-eighth Street, and on which floors the cult members had shrines and which rooms they used as offices.

Other FBI agents soon reported a chilling piece of information. About two months earlier the New York City Transit Authority, which is responsible for operating the city's hundreds of miles of subway track, reported that the station at Times Square had had to be evacuated because of noxious odors. No one had died in the incident, and there was no evidence linking it to the cult. The Transit Authority had marked it down as an unexplained occurrence. In light of the tragedy in Japan, however, authorities could hardly dismiss the possibility that the episode was somehow linked to the group. The leaders of the doomsday cult, after all, had preached about the inevitability of war between the United States and Japan.

Kallstrom paid an emergency visit on Mayor Rudolph Giuliani and on New York Police Chief William Bratton. Transit Authority brass were also consulted. Kallstrom's agents had been doing some crash research on sarin gas. The poison was most effective in enclosed areas, the agents learned.

What happened when there were smoky conditions in the subway, the agents asked, when there was a trash fire or the like?

Transit Authority personnel turned on huge fans.

No! Kallstrom said. That would spread the poison.

After Kallstrom's conference with Giuliani, Bratton and Transit Authority executives, the word went out: In the event of a suspected gas attack, the big fans were not to be used.

With a heavy surveillance laid over the neighborhood and the semblance of an emergency response plan in place, Kallstrom and Picard turned to the business of getting a FISA warrant. After vetting all the information Kallstrom and Picard sent a secure fax to the Office of Intelligence Policy and Review on the sixth floor of Main Justice. And then they waited.

Behind the double doors that led to the OIPR, the lawyers contemplated what steps the FBI could take against the Japanese cult members in New York. Requesting and obtaining permission for a FISA wiretap—and for one of the new FISA search warrants that had become the norm in the wake of the Aldrich Ames investigation—involved a calculation based on the thinnest circumstantial evidence. As far as anyone knew, the Aum Shinrikyo members in New York had done nothing illegal. There was no "probable cause" to obtain a criminal search warrant. If, on the other hand, it was determined that the New York followers were, in effect, representatives of an international terrorist group, then they could become the subjects of FISA surveillance. Normally, that's all it took. Once the designation was made, the FISA warrant court would authorize the FBI to install the national security wiretaps and execute a search. The events in Japan were murky, the case against the group unproven. The issues were tricky, but somebody had to make the call. Judging whether the available facts met the legal test was up to the OIPR.

In New York, as the hours passed, Kallstrom was frustrated with the delay. He wanted to know what was taking so long. The answer, it seemed, was that the information available to Main Justice was sketchy. The best sources appeared to be newspaper clippings and television reports. In calls to the FBI and the CIA, Scruggs pressed for more investigation. At the J. Edgar Hoover Building, FBI Director Freeh telephoned the director of the Japanese National Police in Tokyo to see what more he could learn about the doomsday cult. He got nowhere.

Everyone was frustrated. When the FBI approached him about FISA warrants for the Aum Shinrikyo building on Forty-eighth Street, Scruggs told Bryant that he would be willing to recommend an emergency authorization bypassing the secret FISA court and saving time. This was an extremely rare step, requiring the approval of the FBI director, and in this case Director Freeh believed it was impossible to justify. The sarin gas attack in Tokyo was terrible, but the FBI had virtually no derogatory information about the religion's members in New York to warrant bugging their phones and entering their place of worship. Freeh decided instead to press for more information in Tokyo.

In New York, Kallstrom, Picard and the other FBI executives had done as much as they could. Their secure fax to Scruggs was a simple Teletype. Ordinarily, such communications were more formal, known in the trade as a "letterhead memo," or LHM. The Teletype included as much information as Kallstrom's agents could dig up in a short time, but legally it was not enough.

The breakthrough came when Director Freeh finally extracted some information of value from investigators in Tokyo about the cult members in New York. The information was enough for Scruggs and his lawyers in the intelligence policy office. They rushed the FISA application to Attorney General Reno, who signed it immediately. Next came the trip to the FISA court.

More than forty-eight hours after Tom Picard sent the FBI information to Main Justice, the FISA approvals were finally granted. "We went up on the wires immediately," a senior FBI official said. With the possibility that sarin gas or other lethal chemicals might be present in the building on Forty-eighth Street, Kallstrom and FBI Director Freeh didn't want to risk exposing their agents unnecessarily; listening in on phone conversations was something that could be accomplished remotely, however. After listening to several hours of conversations, FBI managers were relieved. There had been no discussion of chemicals or any talk about an impending attack.

The next step was to get inside the building housing the cult members and recover any dangerous chemicals FBI agents might find there. The entry plan involved arranging a disturbance so that agents could slip into the place more easily. The plan went off without a hitch.

FBI agents in disguise charged into the building. They headed immediately for two of the four floors used by the Aum Shinrikyo cult members. All the agents were armed; some carried tiny electronic bugging devices. Waiting nearby was a team of trained specialists in chemical warfare from the U.S. Army base at nearby Fort Monmouth, New Jersey.

Inside the cult's offices the agents found no chemicals or explosives, but they did locate several good places to hide their electronic listening devices. Within minutes the operation was over. It had taken longer than FBI executives wanted—much longer— but within days after the sarin gas attack on the Tokyo subway the New York outpost of the Aum Shinrikyo cult was thoroughly wired for sound. At Main Justice, the operation was viewed as a success. At the FBI, it was recalled as a source of acute frustration and aggravation.

It was a telling example of why the work of Jim McAdams and Mike Smith was important—and probably endless. It was an article of faith among the older officials that the congressional investigations led by Senator Church were counterproductive. They had focused on the dangers of mixing intelligence gathering with law enforcement. McAdams, a chief architect of the plan to interweave the intelligence community with federal law enforcement, doesn't see it that way. "There is a little ghost of the Church committee that sits on the shoulder of every intelligence agency," he said in an interview. "And it should. The Church investigation had to happen. But it shouldn't cause unnecessary paralysis." There were ways, he said, in which Main Justice could bring the two worlds legally together.

The goal of all the parties reviewing the conflicting needs and requirements of the law-enforcement and intelligence communities was "integration." Participants in the process like Richard Scruggs, who had decided to leave Main Justice and return to courtroom prosecutions in Miami, described the goal as "knitting the two communities together, from top to bottom." Jamie Gorelick, the deputy attorney general, agreed—to a point. "We are going to knit the systems together," she said, "where appropriate." Gorelick explained that "the intelligence community is saying, 'Let us help, let us help.' I am saying that there are certain places [where] that's appropriate and some places where it might be better for us to do what needs to be done ourselves."

Building a closer working relationship among police officers, prosecutors and intelligence operatives was, although not an unreachable goal, at the very least an elusive one. That did not prevent the attorney general from approving a host of changes proposed by Jim McAdams and Mike Smith. By the time the approval came the 1996 presidential campaign had already begun in earnest. It was impossible to say whether the efforts made in the area of intelligence and law enforcement during Janet Reno's stewardship at Main Justice would do much to guarantee that her successor would not face similar travails. What was clear was that the worlds of intelligence gathering and law enforcement were moving closer together—closer than they had ever been before.

McAdams and Smith had crafted a new working relationship. When major cases arose, they would be managed by small working groups of lawyers from both law enforcement and intelligence agencies. On an operational level, spies and federal agents would receive extensive cross-training, each learning about the other's job. The Central Intelligence Agency and National Security Agency were going to prepare classified intelligence reports that could be routinely shared with law enforcement. The CIA already operated two special units, the Counterterrorism Center and the Crime and Narcotics Center, with FBI agents. The Drug Enforcement Administration was already receiving information intercepted by the National Security Agency. Now that trend would be accelerated. DEA agents would be stationed at NSA headquarters in Fort Meade, Maryland. The NSA would detail its own cryptographic specialists to the DEA. There would be regular "tasking" of spy satellites and listening posts for information that could help drug investigations and counterterrorism efforts. Hundreds of federal agents would be cross-trained in some of the most arcane areas of intelligence work that the CIA and NSA performed; spies and intelligence analysts would spend time learning about the needs of criminal investigators.

At the nexus—standing at the crossroad as both monitor and facilitator of these new relationships—was a greatly enlarged Office of Intelligence Policy and Review. By 1995, Reno had doubled the staff, increasing it from six to twelve lawyers. The new responsibilities were daunting. By 1996, classified messages and documents from intelligence agencies were flooding into the sixth-floor office at Main Justice at the rate of 10,500 per month. Twenty years after Michael Shaheen recommended that Main Justice have a counsel for intelligence who would serve as a watchdog on behalf of the attorney general, the world had changed dramatically. Construction workers began knocking out walls on the sixth floor and expanding the grim offices that had been home for so long to Mary Lawton and the small team of lawyers in the OIPR. On a broad range of issues, from oversight of espionage cases to linking up with the nation's intelligence agencies, the tiny intelligence policy office had grown into something much larger. No longer would Main Justice rely only on a Mark Richard to work the back channels to the nation's spy agencies. Gone were the days when Mary Lawton carried the building's secrets around in her head. Now there was a formal process, and the rough beginnings, at least, of a better partnership with the intelligence agencies.

On May 3, 1994, President Clinton signed Presidential Decision Directive 24. The directive established the new partnership as a matter of policy. "Recent events at home and abroad make clear that numerous threats to our national interests—terrorism, proliferation of weapons of mass destruction, ethnic conflicts, sluggish economic growth—continue to exist and must be effectively addressed," Clinton said. The effect of the presidential order was to enlarge the power of the FBI even as it entwined the CIA and the FBI more closely than they had ever been before in the area of domestic intelligence investigations. Structurally, Clinton created the National Counterintelligence Center, to be headed by a senior FBI official. Another FBI executive was assigned to run the CIA's counterespionage group at the spy agency's headquarters in suburban Virginia.

This was only the beginning. After the bombing of the Alfred P. Murrah Federal Building in Oklahoma City, in April 1995, Clinton asked Congress for a $300 million special appropriation over two years to bolster the FBI's counterterrorism program, adding 1,040 more special agents, intelligence analysts, linguists and surveillance experts. The money and manpower would be used primarily to investigate individuals and organizations in the United States suspected of operating on behalf of international terrorist groups. To handle the anticipated flood of new cases, Janet Reno asked for funding for one hundred fifty-five new assistant U.S. attorneys nationwide and ten additional career lawyers for the Criminal Division's Office of International Affairs. Implicit in the funding requests were significant increases in the number of FISA wiretaps and domestic intelligence investigations by the FBI. It was for precisely this reason that Reno asked for three additional attorneys for the Office of Intelligence Policy and Review.

Part of the impetus behind the requests came from scrutiny that the intelligence committees of the House and Senate had given the Ames case. The two committees had taken testimony from FBI officials, and the House committee in particular had criticized the FBI for its confusion about use of the FISA surveillance in the investigation of the CIA traitor. "The committee is troubled," the House report said, "that various FBI officials gave different interpretations of what facts and circumstances would form the basis for a full investigation and a Foreign Intelligence Surveillance Act order."

It fell to Jim McAdams to put the new regime of domestic intelligence investigations into place. In February 1996, McAdams boarded a jet at Washington's National Airport for a flight to Florida, where he spent the weekend selling a cherished sailboat. On his return to Washington, he had a much bigger craft to navigate. When McAdams had moved up to Main Justice, he had promised his wife it would be a temporary duty assignment. Now things had changed. As Richard Scruggs's replacement as the head of the Office of Intelligence Policy and Review, McAdams brought a different style to the job. Mary Lawton had been the *éminence grise* of intelligence law, Scruggs the brash defender of an embattled outpost. McAdams, in contrast, served as a collegial administrator intent on regularizing the work of the office and smoothing out its relationship with the Criminal Division of Main Justice. From his days working on the blueprint to blend law enforcement and the intelligence agencies, McAdams knew the small intelligence policy office would soon be facing much larger demands.

Janet Reno had embraced a larger vision of the Justice Department's role in a world in which international crime had become a clear and present danger to the nation's security. Combatting international crime had first been made a priority during the Reagan administration by former Attorney General William French Smith, and shaped thereafter by precedents as diverse as the prosecution of former Panamanian dictator Manuel Noriega in Miami, the terrorist bombing of Pan Am Flight 103 over Lockerbie, Scotland, and prosecution of members of the Cali cocaine cartel. It was driven, as well, by FBI Director Louis Freeh's determination to expand the Bureau's overseas work against Russian organized crime, Middle Eastern terrorists, and economic espionage. Jamie Gorelick encouraged this trend, creating the Executive Office of National Security to look out over the horizon for the next big international crisis.

Reno and Gorelick were both voracious consumers of intelligence information, determined to be players on national security decisions and adamant about being fully briefed and prepared. One thing that had astonished McAdams during his first few months at Main Justice was the discovery that there was no unit in the building assigned to analyze intelligence data on a timely basis and prepare reports for senior executives. McAdams had come to see the intelligence community as a confluence of rivers of classified data that flowed out of the Pentagon, the CIA, the NSA, and the FBI. As the new head of the Office of Intelligence Policy and Review, he wanted his staff to be able to dip into each of those rivers quickly and pull out material that would arm the attorney general for the policy judgments she had to make.

Before too long, that is what happened. McAdams persuaded managers at the CIA and the NSA to assign analysts to his office on a permanent basis. Computer terminals with special encrypted channels were installed in his office. Each morning his staff prepared a short classified summary of the previous twenty-four hours of intelligence for the attorney general. Once a week, McAdams or one of his lawyers presented a more detailed briefing on hot-button issues that he thought Reno or Gorelick needed to know about.

The disagreements over the Ames case might never be settled, but to Janet Reno and Jamie Gorelick the issue was clear. The new rules they had authorized embodied their hope that never again would doubts about the "primary purpose" of a foreign counterintelligence investigation cloud a criminal case as important as the prosecution of Aldrich Ames. McAdams was acutely conscious of grumbling that the new rules would have a "chilling effect" on foreign counterintelligence inquiries, but he was determined to see that that not occur. He added two lawyers to his staff of attorneys reviewing FISA applications; three secretaries were also brought on board to process the paperwork more quickly. FISA applications were tracked by computer and the office was warned automatically when an authorization had to be renewed. McAdams wanted no down-time on his wiretaps. On a quarterly basis, he sent an OIPR lawyer out to at least one FBI office handling FISA wires to audit the process and spend time with the field agents, putting faces to names. When a surge of new cases came in, he borrowed lawyers from the Criminal Division.

McAdams had watched the conflicts that had developed in the aftermath of the Ames case and had sided with Richard Scruggs on the legal issues. But he was also a career prosecutor who knew how important it was for agents to consult with lawyers. Over time, McAdams steered a course that lay somewhere between Lawton's leniency and the harder line of Scruggs. McAdams insisted that his lawyers sign each FISA application as their own, attesting to its accuracy. In a December 1995 memorandum, McAdams made it clear how he and his lawyers intended to proceed. At the core of every intelligence operation launched by a foreign power against the United States, he explained, there lurked the potential for a criminal case of espionage or international terrorism. That meant that counterintelligence and law enforcement issues would often be intertwined. Still, as Walter Dellinger's opinion in the Ames case had explained, the legal requirement of "primary purpose" in FISA surveillances was a fact of life. Ames's guilty plea had spared Main Justice a challenge to the warrantless search of his home, but another court in another case might well suppress important evidence, McAdams cautioned, if a defendant could establish "bad faith" on the part of government investigators. So far, the federal courts had taken the secret FISA court seriously. They had been willing to accept the "veracity and regularity" of the FISA authorization, a step that was based on the secret, ex parte assurances from lawyers assigned to the Office of Intelligence Policy and Review that the purpose of the surveillance was intelligence gathering. To McAdams, the issue boiled down to the nub raised by John Martin's memos in prosecutions of David Truong and Ronald Humphrey. It was when the Criminal Division "circulated a proposed prosecution memorandum," McAdams explained, "that it became apparent that the government was assembling a prosecution." When courts had to decide if the "primary purpose" had shifted, he said, they would look back to the Truong case and try to see whether the FBI agents "can be described as assembling a criminal prosecution."

Resolving this dilemma, McAdams said, did not mean giving up criminal investigations; the answer was candor and documentation. Each FISA application should clearly explain the larger intelligence-gathering purpose of the wiretap or search. If a criminal investigation was part of the FISA case, that was fine; the application should simply let the FISA court know this was true. Appearances were important, McAdams concluded. "Ensure that the right people are controlling the investigation." Touching directly on the legal issue in the Ames case, he warned against action that would suggest that "the decision to continue a (FISA counterintelligence) investigation was influenced by the criminal investigation."

If there was now tighter oversight of the FBI, and a more formal relationship with the Internal Security Section, there was no evidence in the numbers that the new rules—put in place to avoid the dangers Scruggs had seen in the Ames case—had had a chilling effect on the FBI's foreign counterintelligence program or its efforts to combat international terrorism.

On the contrary, Janet Reno was presiding over a dramatic surge in national security wiretaps that matched the expansion of Title III wiretaps being overseen by the Criminal Division's Office of Enforcement Operations. Under the Clinton administration, the nation's two systems for wiretapping—one for criminal cases, the other for intelligence gathering—had become freight trains running at full throttle down parallel tracks.

In the last full year of the Bush administration, there were 484 FISA authorizations. In 1993, the tumultuous year of Mary Lawton's death, there were 509. In 1994, the year of the Ames case, there were 576. In 1995, the first full year in which the new guidelines were enforced, FISA authorizations rocketed to 697. By then, the secret little office at Main Justice was working at a brisk tempo. Its career lawyers—and the busy judges in the secret FISA court—were churning out FISA wiretaps at a prodigious rate. During the first quarter of 1996, the FISA authorizations were running more than 20 percent ahead of the first quarter of 1995. At that pace, Jim McAdams looked forward to processing more than 800 FISA applications (which now included FISA searches) by the end of the year. "We are projecting another substantial increase," he said, "in 1996."

Nearly two decades after FISA became a pillar of Mary's Law, intelligence wiretapping was big business at Main Justice.

EPILOGUE

Several days after his heart attack, as he lay resting in his hospital room a few blocks from Main Justice, David Margolis received a group of visitors. Attorney General Janet Reno led the delegation. She was accompanied by Jamie Gorelick, the deputy attorney general, and Jo Ann Harris, the head of the Criminal Division. Among the others in the group were Paul Coffey, the head of the Organized Crime and Racketeering Section, and Jack Keeney, the senior deputy in the Criminal Division. The visit was more than just a get-well call. Margolis had served in the Department of Justice for just over three decades. Reno had come to present him with his thirty-year pin. Only Jack Keeney and a handful of others had served longer.

Typically, Margolis punctured all attempts at solemnity with a few well-chosen barbs, but it wasn't hard to do. The fact that the former Mafia prosecutor was well on the road to recovery was one reason. The other was a basketball game scheduled for that evening between the Criminal Division and the Organized Crime and Racketeering Section. Coffey, the inveterate jock who had inherited the leadership of the section from Margolis several years earlier, had challenged Jo Ann Harris, the former Manhattan prosecutor who had led the women's basketball team from the U.S. Attorney's Office to a series of successful seasons many years before. Harris had accepted the challenge eagerly, scouring the Justice Department for former college players and other ringers. She had even enlisted Reno as a player. At six foot two, the attorney general promised to complement Harris, at six feet, in the forecourt. Coffey, at perhaps five ten, countered that the Harris-Reno team looked good only on paper. Across Margolis's sickbed, the challenges went back and forth, with Reno practicing imaginary hook shots while Harris laughed and Coffey made a show of looking unimpressed.

It was, if not a rare moment, a telling one. During the history of the Justice Department, relations between its political leadership and the career lawyers who made the place function had run the gamut. That was especially true for the lawyers who worked in the Criminal Division. During the administration of George Bush particularly, the Criminal Division had been beaten down, and the reputation of the Justice Department had been tarnished by persistent allegations of political meddling in criminal cases. Janet Reno set as her first priority the restoration of esteem at Main Justice. To the extent she succeeded, she did so with the help of the career officials. After the chill of the Bush years, the Criminal Division was brought back to the center of power at the department. In sensitive matters, she had chosen to rely on strangers who rapidly became confidants and trusted allies.

This dynamic was important not so much for assessing the legacy of a single attorney general but for taking the measure of the Department of Justice as it approached the twenty-first century—for assessing its strengths and weaknesses.

Main Justice will always attract strong lawyers with strong wills. It is one of the few major institutions in society where individuals can make a profound difference in the problems facing the nation. That was true of Brent Ward, the anti-pornography crusader; of Theresa Van Vliet, the drug warrior, and Jo Ann Harris, the architect of the anti-violence initiative.

After several years of reporting, we are left with the overriding impression that the institution will rise and fall on the work of its career professionals. The political leaders who rotate through the upper ranks often infuse Main Justice with new energy and new ideas. They see things fresh and craft new answers to old questions. Those appointees, be they Democrat or Republican, rightfully represent civilian control of a powerful government institution. They do their part to keep Main Justice honest and strong.

But the Justice Department is a vessel that can be quickly commandeered, for good or for evil. We made the claim at the outset that the Department of Justice is a major prize of each presidential election. We believe that claim has abundant support. Main Justice controls the powers of law and of coercion. It is a most effective tool for enforcing a social and political vision. If tyranny someday arrives in the United States, it will be accompanied by federal prosecutors and agents. If it is turned away, federal prosecutors and agents will be owed the nation's thanks.

Thankfully, the ranks of the career professionals are always renewed. The Jack Keeneys and David Margolises will be followed by the likes of Mary Lee Warren and Jim Reynolds. The Justice Department has a deep bench. When it has a loss—such as the death of Mary Lawton—it can turn to a Jim McAdams.

An examination of four principal areas of Justice Department activity yields several conclusions. In the area of narcotics, the sphere of criminal activity of greatest concern to most Americans, the Department of Justice operates at far from peak efficiency; it is too big and tangled a bureaucracy for that. But as the Cornerstone investigation of the Cali cartel demonstrated, Main Justice can be an implacable adversary. Indeed, after a national investment of billions of dollars and after thousands of federal drug investigations, it is now reasonable to assert that no trafficking organization anywhere in the world is so large or so powerful that it cannot be challenged by federal law enforcement.

It is customary, usually during congressional hearings on appropriations, for senior law-enforcement officials to lament the scope of their jobs and cite a need for more resources or more legal powers. The Cali cartel case demonstrates that the Justice Department has all the tools it needs. This is the result of years of evolution, of trial and error and refinement in investigative and prosecutive strategy. In Cornerstone, the critical tools were the laws that enabled Customs Service agent Edward Kacerosky and his colleagues to obtain court authorization for aggressive wiretap operations and for prosecutors William Pearson and Edward Ryan to use the powerful federal anti-racketeering laws against the cartel's top leadership. There were other tools, of course, such as the witness protection program that provided shelter for family members of cartel employees who agreed to cooperate with the government. But it was the collective focus of the agents and prosecutors, men and women with long experience and training, that made the difference. Their understanding of the Cali cartel, and of the business of going after large criminal organizations, drew on an institutional memory enriched by hundreds of earlier investigations.

The success of the Cornerstone case was a triumph for which Janet Reno and the Clinton administration's other political appointees could take only partial credit. The tools and tactics were in place and being used actively long before they arrived in Washington. In this regard, they were much like the Bush appointees before them. Reno and her lieutenants found themselves in command of a huge vessel that was already churning hard toward the kingpins of the Cali cartel. That said, Reno's choice of navigators made a difference. She put federal drug enforcement in the hands of Mary Lee Warren and Theresa Van Vliet, two case-hardened career prosecutors who had risen through the ranks.

Where Reno and her team made a more immediate difference was in a second area of concern to Americans, that involving violent crime. Her long experience as a local prosecutor in South Florida had shown Reno two things. The first was how powerful criminal syndicates, whether street gangs or drug-smuggling organizations, could so disrupt lives and communities. The second was how the vast power of federal law enforcement had almost no real effect in curbing the violence such criminal organizations were responsible for. Here, too, Reno came to an issue that had already been seized by her predecessor in the Bush administration. William

P. Barr had thrown resources at the problem. Yet Reno brought a clarity of vision and intensity of focus to the task that made the violent-crime initiative her lasting contribution. The Clinton administration turned the federal justice system decisively toward the task of combating violence in the major cities. In doing so, Reno relied on anonymous career officials like Jim Reynolds to get her where she wanted to go. He and others showed how to harness the brute force of federal law enforcement with the enterprise of state and local agencies. The result has been the widespread use of many of the same legal tools and tactics employed in the Cornerstone case to reduce violent crime in community after community across the United States. No one could seriously claim that the recent drop in homicides and other violent crimes is due solely or even mostly to the Justice Department's effort. But it would be foolish to think that the thousands of federal prosecutions that have been brought against the street gangs and armed career criminals made no contribution to the decline in the number of such crimes.

Our examination of a third area of Justice Department activity yields more troubling conclusions. The powerful legal tools and the growth in size of the Justice Department are partly responsible for the increase in incidents of prosecutorial misconduct since the early 1980s. There are other reasons as well. Supreme Court rulings that have denied trial judges recourse for punishing such misconduct and undoing its consequences have disturbed the adversarial balance in the federal justice system. In the Supreme Court's haste to join the War on Crime, it moved the nation toward an accusatorial system of law. The increasingly contentious nature of criminal proceedings in the federal courts, particularly in prosecutions of narcotics cases, is one symptom of this trend. When individual judges make findings of prosecutorial misconduct, they are warning the Justice Department to give attention and force to its professed commitment to fundamental fairness.

Reno set out to reform and toughen the department's internal discipline. Again, she ended up relying on career professionals, such as Michael Shaheen and David Margolis. Yet the federal privacy law virtually guarantees that the effectiveness of professional discipline at Main Justice will always turn on the willingness of the attorney general to take it seriously. The instinct to paper over the few rogue prosecutors who will always lurk within the federal system is resilient, not for reasons of corruption, but simply to save the institution from embarrassment and legal strife.

As more and more powers are conveyed to the federal prosecutors—while judicial supervisory power remains in decline—the burden of ensuring fairness in federal court will stay with Main Justice. Professional discipline will continue to be a challenge, and it may periodically require a Judge Ideman or a Judge Hoeveler to take up the unpleasant task of censuring a federal prosecutor in public. If there is a troubling aspect to the run of cases presented to the Office of Professional Responsibility, it lies in their source. The best-documented allegations are generally presented in cases where the defendant is represented by strong, aggressive, well-funded defense attorneys. It is hard not to suspect that most citizens caught up in federal criminal cases don't have the resources to mount a successful challenge to an overbearing prosecutor. The mix of more prosecutors, more powerful criminal laws, fewer judicial constraints and a more adversarial defense bar is a potentially volatile one. The Office of Professional Responsibility has seen its workload increase sharply in recent years. A larger staff and an emphasis on more open proceedings concluded in a more timely manner are among the more significant improvements instituted in the professional discipline process during Janet Reno's tenure at Main Justice. Whether those steps are enough remains to be seen. What is certain is that as more prosecutive authority moves away from Main Justice and into the hands of increasingly powerful U.S. Attorneys' Offices, the need for an impartial and aggressive professional discipline process will be more pressing and more essential. If federal prosecutions become known for their fundamental fairness, the country will owe Main Justice a large debt.

The fourth and last area of activity examined is the relationship between federal criminal prosecutions and the nation's intelligence community. Two issues are paramount. The first is Justice Department oversight of domestic counterintelligence operations conducted by the FBI. The second is the relationship between federal prosecutors within the United States and intelligence agencies that gather information overseas. Both issues bristle with potential problems because they take the department to the outer edges of constitutional conduct.

Domestic counterintelligence and counterterrorism are particularly difficult areas. The changes made in the aftermath of the Aldrich Ames investigation have created a more regularized process for conducting electronic and physical surveillances of suspects in espionage and terrorism investigations in the United States. Domestic terrorism of the type witnessed in the World Trade Center bombing is a relatively new phenomenon, and the number of investigations of such cases has increased significantly in just the past few years. Indeed, within the FBI there are two diverging groups of agents: those who work on traditional criminal investigations and those who spend their careers casting their gaze on very different targets. The oversight of the latter activity is tenuous and always in need of careful attention. Reno opted for making the Office of Intelligence Policy and Review more robust, doubling the number of lawyers, more clearly defining its mandate and relying for guidance on career prosecutors.

Coordinating Justice Department activity with the nation's intelligence community is a similarly daunting problem. Because more criminal activity that affects Americans originates overseas, it is important that there be cooperation between prosecutors and intelligence officers, and that information be shared whenever possible so that foreign criminals involved in terrorism, drug trafficking and economic and other crimes be thwarted before they commit crimes or punished after they do. That sounds simple in concept. In reality, it is likely to prove very difficult, challenging constitutional limits on domestic law-enforcement activity while drawing intelligence officers ever closer to proceedings that could compromise sources and methods of intelligence collection. The momentum is clearly headed toward something like a merger between the two worlds. The documents we obtained show that the plans for this outcome are made and are being pursued. The cautionary protests from senior political appointees that care will be taken is a promise that most of them will not be around to keep. It is dismaying that this move to reinvent the relationship between spies and federal agents took place with virtually no meaningful public debate and little journalistic scrutiny.

A NOTE ON SOURCES AND METHODS

BACKGROUND

Our work on this book has its roots in the reporting we both did in the 1980s as staff writers for the *Miami Herald*, the best of all possible homes for a young reporter. Brian covered the Miami U.S. Attorney's Office at a time when it was the centerpiece of the Reagan administration's efforts to transform federal law enforcement. In those years the office became a powerhouse, filing huge cases against the likes of Medellín cartel kingpin Carlos Lehder and Panamanian dictator Manuel Noriega. On a daily basis Brian saw the impact of the Justice Department growth as manifested on the street level in Miami.

Meanwhile, Jim was assigned to investigative projects that steeped him in the chief concerns of the modern Justice Department—drug enforcement, terrorism and international crime. In 1981, at the very outset of the Reagan buildup, he was part of a *Herald* team that produced a series titled "The Billion Dollar Bust," which described the failures of federal law enforcement in South Florida. This was followed by a seven-part series on anti-Castro terrorism and the efforts of the FBI to stop attacks by a shadowy group called Omega 7. Thereafter, he co-authored a series on drug-related corruption in the Bahamas called "A Nation for Sale."

Upon moving to Washington in 1987, Brian became an assistant managing editor for *U.S. News & World Report* and began writing cover stories on espionage and intelligence-related issues. In 1990 he was the co-author of *The Fall of Pan Am 103*, an account of the bombing of a passenger jet in the skies over Lockerbie, Scotland, and how the FBI and authorities in Scotland solved one of history's worst acts of terrorism.

After joining the investigative staff at *The Washington Post*, Jim did the newspaper's early reporting on the relationship between Clark Clifford's First American Bank and the Bank of Credit and Commerce International, a matter that sorely embarrassed Main Justice. Following that work he wrote a series for the *Post* titled "The Appearance of Justice" that examined judicial allegations of prosecutorial misconduct and the work of a small, obscure unit at Main Justice called the Office of Professional Responsibility (OPR). During the course of reporting for this book, he also wrote a series for the *Post* on the Cali cocaine cartel, gaining his first exposure to Operation Cornerstone.

BOOKS AND PUBLICATIONS

Every business day a publication unmatched anywhere in the United States is circulated within Main Justice. Called the "AM News Summary for the Attorney General," it is a digest of the full text of articles published in the previous twenty-four hours relating to crime, law enforcement and the Justice Department. Not uncommonly, it runs to more than fifty pages and is usually the one document that always lands on the desks of senior officials. It reflects the extent to which Main Justice is saturated with scrutiny. Many of the reporters who cover the institution have offices in the building and have relatively easy access to senior officials. During the Clinton administration Attorney General Janet Reno held weekly press briefings. She very often parried questions and declined to comment, but the questions would generally get answered eventually, often by the staff member assigned to find out the facts.

As a consequence, we were blessed with an extraordinary amount of daily journalism on the institution. All of it was valuable in different ways, but there were a few reporters whose work was essential. Ronald Ostrow of the *Los Angeles Times* is the dean of the Justice Department press corps and a great reporter. Of all the major dailies, the *Los Angeles Times* stands the furthest from Main Justice, yet he makes their coverage the most relevant and has done his part to keep the institution honest. For penetrating insight about the Justice Department's affairs, the *Legal Times* newspaper was indispensable, especially the work of Daniel Klaidman, Greg Rushford, Ben Wittes and Stuart Taylor. Just when we thought we'd found a rare, unnoticed truth, it would become a front-page story in the

Legal Times. Close behind was the reporting of reporters from *The New York Times*, especially David Johnston, and that of *The Washington Post's* Pierre Thomas. An excellent library reference was a newsletter, now sadly defunct, called *DOJ Alert*. Outside Washington, the coverage of the Justice Department was spotty and driven by press releases. Yet the nation is well served by a vigorous and smart network of legal publications that watch the federal courts and are the early warning system for major stories and trends. The same could be said for the *National Law Journal* and *American Lawyer;* both are astute analysts of the legal process. So much of the book has one foot in Miami that two reporters deserve special mention. The first is Jeff Leen, whose fiercely intelligent investigative stories about crime and government for the *Miami Herald* are unrivaled. Alongside Jeff's work was the careful and thorough reporting of the *Herald's* David Lyons, who covers the country's busiest federal court for the paper. He is the Ron Ostrow of the South.

Very often good lawyers are also good writers. We benefited from a large body of writing by current and former members of the Justice Department and by longtime observers of the department. A lot of the best was layered into many volumes of the *U.S. Attorney's Manual*. Dry as a bone in some places, it still offers up such gems as a long essay by Paul Coffey on the racketeering statute and an introduction by Daniel Meador, a law professor at the University of Virginia, who seems to know the Justice Department's history and culture as if it were his own.

There are many books we could cite, but a few loom large. A touchstone is *Federal Justice* by Homer Cummings and Carl McFarland. Victor Navasky's *Kennedy Justice* is the benchmark text for any reporter writing on the institution. Books by former Attorneys General Griffin Bell (with Ronald Ostrow) and William French Smith offer their view of events that shaped the modern Justice Department. Their predecessor Edward Levi did not write a book after leaving the department. He didn't have to. He left behind a large body of learned and literate statements that he gave as speeches or congressional testimony. They form an eloquent account of his struggle to resurrect Main Justice out of the wreckage of Watergate. On the FBI, two books tower above all others. Both are titled *The FBI*. The first, by Sanford Ungar, covers the years of Director J. Edgar Hoover and the arrival of Director Clarence Kelley. The second, by Ronald Kessler, examines the modern FBI under former Directors William Webster and William Sessions. Both Ungar and Kessler are careful reporters who were granted special access to senior FBI officials who very often answered their questions on the record. Finally, as we were completing our work, *Above the Law* by former *New York Times* reporter David Burnham appeared. A careful researcher and indefatigable investigator, Burnham raises important questions about the Justice Department and puts them in a historical context that has its dark moments.

DOCUMENTS

When it came to the Clinton administration's stewardship of the Justice Department, we were fortunate to obtain a copy of the transition team's four-hundred-page report to the president, the vice president and the attorney general. It is a work of investigative reporting that no newspaper could match. The transition team report reveals what the new president was told about Main Justice. Although the authors were Clinton Democrats analyzing an institution shaped by Bush Republicans, they nevertheless got most of the story right and accurately forecast the problems and issues that would confront Janet Reno in 1993. More than that, the report sounds the themes she would make her own. After correcting for its political bias, we used this document throughout our work much as Reno did—as a point of departure and an accurate take on what the Clinton people thought they found at Main Justice. More generally, we also relied on official documents, including many that were publicly available.

SOURCES

We ended up with remarkable access in the Criminal Division, but it took a long time to gain. Career deputies are trained to be anonymous technicians of fact and law. While their work is very often the subject of great controversy in the press and Congress, as a rule they stand silent. This condition is their refuge and their special burden. They are in the business of making hard decisions, not explaining themselves to reporters. Like David Margolis in the Cornerstore case, they make the call

and then move on to the next case. It took months of repeated interviews to get past this instinct, but we succeeded with many, though not
all, of the main characters in our narrative.

We don't imagine for a minute that they told us everything. We believe they let us far enough inside the tent so that we could accurately
convey to readers a sense of their world. If we end up with a bias—and
we almost certainly do—it is the overriding impression that the career
deputies are honorable men and women doing difficult jobs in uncertain
times. If that colors our vision, so be it. The great bulk of our narrative,
as any reader can see, rests on documents and on-the-record statements.
For that reason, we think it unnecessary to provide a more detailed list of
sources. This is not a book for specialists or researchers, but for the general reader. Moreover, despite our success at getting statements on the
record, the great bulk of our interviews were done on background and
not for attribution. Listing some of our sources but not others seems
counterproductive, and so we have not done so.

DRUGS AND VIOLENT CRIMES

In addition to interviews on the violent-crime initiative, we obtained the
underlying documents that chronicle the development of this effort. The
court record in Operation Cornerstone is massive. In the end, almost
every relevant fact was put into the public record, through affidavits written by the case agent or the indictment drafted by the prosecutors. Sup-
plementing this material was testimony during the initial trial of Harold
Ackerman. A strong caution is in order. The criminal case arising from
Operation Cornerstone is still pending. It is therefore important to note
that Michael Abbell and William Moran have entered pleas of not guilty
and are vigorously contesting the charges against them. It is also worth
noting that the alleged kingpins of the Cali cartel have never faced the
U.S. government charges in court, so their guilt remains a matter of dispute as well. In our account, we are trying to reflect how a large, state-of-
the-art federal drug case is assembled. In the course of such work, it is
tempting to adopt the government's view of the evidence. We've done
our best to resist that lure. We have seen the available evidence and, like
the grand jury, find it credible. But the defendants are entitled to the pre-
sumption of innocence. That said, we believe we have captured a sense of

how the drug-enforcement system works against the biggest targets. In addition to other assistance, we were granted a tour of the Miami facility that launched the Cali cartel prosecution. Known as the High Intensity Drug Trafficking Area facility in Miami, it functions under the adroit guidance of its director, Douglas Hughes.

PROFESSIONAL DISCIPLINE

The reporting on the issue of prosecutorial misconduct begins and ends with legal opinions written by federal judges who witnessed this conduct in their courtrooms. One of the surprises of our reporting was the extent to which conventional wisdom about Reagan appointees was wrong. While these judges certainly have a conservative view of criminal law, they also possess a sense of fundamental fairness. We were struck by the eloquence that many of these judges brought to their legal opinions as they wrestled with agonizing questions. That said, it is worth mentioning that trial judges are dealing with a limited record—that which is presented to them in court—and can therefore misapprehend complex matters. We based our work on eight hours of interviews Jim conducted with OPR counsel Michael Shaheen and his staff in 1992 during reporting for *The Washington Post*. Later research for this book consisted of additional interviews supplemented by documents that the OPR has produced over the years. It was buttressed further by the public OPR reports that were issued under the new disclosure policy. We have worked to be fair to the prosecutors of whom we wrote at length. It was disappointing, but understandable, that William Lynch declined to be interviewed. Assistant U.S. Attorney Lothar Genge was constrained from commenting on the case of *U.S. v. Treadwell*, but his views were described at length in government motions and his own statements in court. It is important to note that the measure of Genge's actions in the Treadwell case is presently being taken by the OPR. They may well develop information that is not available to us that exonerates Genge. We have tried to make clear in the text that, from the prosecutor's point of view, he had what prosecutors refer to as a "righteous case" and a daunting opponent. In preparing the chapters on the Meese obscenity crusade, we relied almost exclusively on the court record in *PHE v. the United States Department of Justice*, wherein the subjects of the article, Brent

Ward, Robert Showers and Paul McCommon, testified at length about their actions at a time when their memories were fresh. In addition, Jim had previously interviewed Ward and Showers for an article in the *Post*.

INTELLIGENCE

If Michael Shaheen's OPR was a place of secret power within Main Justice, hidden even deeper inside the cocoon was the domain of Mary Lawton and the Office of Intelligence Policy and Review. We found virtually no significant interviews with Lawton, and little reporting on her work. Her aides said that Lawton believed strongly that it was wrong for her to discuss her work publicly. Following her death, however, it was possible to build a reasonably complete portrait of this extraordinary woman and her deep impact on Main Justice and on intelligence law. For this we are grateful to many sources. For background, the indispensable documents are the writings of Edward Levi and the masterful work of the Church Senate investigating committee. These were supplemented in later years by the many reports from the intelligence committees in the House and Senate and other material provided by the Justice Department.

On more current matters, we conducted multiple interviews with senior officials who stood at the center of domestic counterintelligence operations and policy at Main Justice. We had similar access to senior officials in the National Security Division of the FBI, OIPR's biggest client. As reporters, we believe it is valuable to record in 1996 what they say about their work and where they think it is headed. The destination looks very much like uncharted waters. We've presented what is, at best, an early inside report on the work of the chief navigators. They operate in a secret world and there is almost certainly a great deal we did not discover about the OIPR and the expansive impact that the Clinton administration had on domestic intelligence gathering. But the careful reader will note that our account is based on documents and on-the-record interviews.

ACKNOWLEDGMENTS

For years it has seemed that the best nonfiction books of our time bore acknowledgments that lavished praise on the skill, intellect, drive, and faith of Alice Mayhew, our editor at Simon & Schuster. We are happy to report that it's all true. She is a strong wind that carries authors a lot further than they ever imagined they'd be going. She has an eye, too, for picking talented assistants. In our case, it was Roger Labrie, whose careful work on the manuscript was tough, patient and smart. Another perennial mark of books we have admired over the years is a note of thanks to Esther Newberg, our agent at ICM Artists. In an instant she grasped our idea and knew exactly who to call.

It is a small miracle of modern times that a Fortune 500 company such as *The Washington Post* continues to support so unprofitable an enterprise as investigative reporting. The commitment of the Graham family to aggressive journalism on public institutions is so solid and deep that it tends to be taken for granted. In fact, it is a rare commitment among American publishers. Part of their commitment is providing great editors at the *Post* who help reporters convey what they think they have discovered. Jim's early work on the subject of professional misconduct by federal prosecutors was directed by Fred Barbash, then the *Post*'s National Editor. Having formerly covered the Supreme Court, Fred brought to the subject a broad field of vision. Executive Editor Leonard Downie Jr. did not hesitate to publish the original series and later granted Jim a leave of absence to complete this book.

Michael Ruby and Merrill McLoughlin, the co-editors of *U.S. News*, have for years supported reporting that takes readers inside their government. Their sense of purpose enlarged our own and their kindness in freeing Brian from his duties at the magazine was invaluable.

The *Post* library staff was a rock, particularly Margot Williams, Jennifer Belcher, Kathy Foley and Melinda Blake. Thereafter we were assisted by Barbara Saffir, the National Desk's adroit researcher, and Sean Savage, a young reporter of promise. At *U.S. News*, chief librarian Kathleen N. Trimble and her gifted staff were miracle workers; Kathleen Phillips, the news magazine's chief of research, saved us a hundred times. Copy editor Charlotte Gross and copy supervisor Lydia Buechler at Simon & Schuster brought great care to the manuscript, as did Michele Braithwaite, Jim's wife, who made herself indispensable, and *Post* copy editor Peter Masley. Thanks to attorney Nira Wiesel for her careful vetting of our work.

By coincidence we both grew up as reporters at the *Miami Herald* during a time when the Justice Department was becoming a large presence in South Florida. Our reporting from those days informs this book and much of it was guided by James Savage, the *Herald*'s investigations editor. A brilliant coach of young reporters, Jim saw first that an important story was unfolding in our midst and forever urged his reporters to go deep. Readers in South Florida are blessed by his strong presence and we owe him an old debt.

INDEX